DIGITAL LABOUR MARKETS IN CENTRAL AND EASTERN EUROPEAN COUNTRIES

This book examines the impact of the COVID-19 pandemic on changing labour markets and accelerating digitalisation of the workplace in Central and Eastern Europe (CEE). It provides an innovative and enriching take on the work experience from the pandemic times and discusses the challenges of ongoing changes in labour markets and workplaces in a way that is not covered by the extant literature.

The impact of the COVID-19 pandemic and digitalisation on labour market outcomes is analysed throughout 12 chapters, by 34 labour market experts from various CEE countries. Most chapters are based on empirical methods yet are presented in an easy-to-follow way to make the book also accessible for a non-scientific audience. The volume addresses the following three key goals:

- to better understand the impact of the COVID-19 pandemic on the adoption of workplace digitalisation in the selected labour markets in CEE countries and the potential trade-offs facing those who do and do not have access to this benefit;
- to complement the labour market research by incorporating the outputs of changing demand for skills;
- to contribute new insight into policies and regulations that govern the future of work.

The book argues that the recent COVID-19 pandemic was a sombre reminder of the relevance and necessity of digital technology for a variety of sectors and market activities. It concludes that to downside the risks of vanishing jobs, as well as to minimise the threats and maximise the opportunities of digitalisation in CEE countries, labour market partners need to consider an effective governance tool in terms of inclusive access to the digital environment, re-skilling, and balanced regulations of the more problematic facets of digital work.

The book will be of interest to postgraduate researchers and academics in the fields of labour economics, regional economics, and macroeconomics. Additionally, due to the broader policy implications of the topic, the book will appeal to policymakers and experts interested in labour economics.

Beata Woźniak-Jęchorek is an associate professor in the Department of Macroeconomics and Development Research at the Institute of Economics at the Poznań University of Economics and Business (PUEB) in Poland.

Kamilla Marchewka-Bartkowiak is an associate professor in the Department of Investments and Financial Markets at the Institute of Finance Poznań University of Economics and Business (PUEB) in Poland.

Routledge Studies in Labour Economics

Economic and Social Perspectives on European Migration
Edited by Francesca Fauri, Debora Mantovani, and Donatella Strangio

Foundations of Modern Slavery
Profiles of Unfree and Coerced Labor Through the Ages
Caf Dowlah

Universities and the Labour Market
Graduate Transitions from Education to Employment
Magdalena Jelonek

The Dynamics of Marginalized Youth
Not in Education, Employment, or Training Around the World
Edited by Mark Levels, Christian Brzinsky-Fay, Craig Holmes, Janine Jongbloed and Hirofumi Taki

The Digital Economy and the European Labour Market
Edited by Maria Urbaniec

Digital Labour Markets in Central and Eastern European Countries
COVID-19 and the Future of Work
Edited by Beata Woźniak-Jęchorek and Kamilla Marchewka-Bartkowiak

For a full list of titles in this series, please visit: www.routledge.com/Routledge-Studies-in-Labour-Economics/book-series/RSLE

DIGITAL LABOUR MARKETS IN CENTRAL AND EASTERN EUROPEAN COUNTRIES

COVID-19 and the Future of Work

Edited by Beata Woźniak-Jęchorek and Kamilla Marchewka-Bartkowiak

Routledge
Taylor & Francis Group
LONDON AND NEW YORK

Designed cover image: piranka/Getty Images

First published 2023
by Routledge
4 Park Square, Milton Park, Abingdon, Oxon OX14 4RN

and by Routledge
605 Third Avenue, New York, NY 10158

Routledge is an imprint of the Taylor & Francis Group, an informa business

The funder for these chapters is the University of Primorska Poznan University of Economics and Business

British Library Cataloguing-in-Publication Data
A catalogue record for this book is available from the British Library

Library of Congress Cataloging-in-Publication Data
Names: Woźniak-Jęchorek, Beata, editor. | Marchewka-Bartkowiak, Kamilla, 1973- editor.
Title: Digital labour markets in Central and Eastern European countries : COVID-19 and the future of work / edited by Beata Woźniak-Jęchorek and Kamilla Marchewka-Bartkowiak.
Description: Milton Park, Abingdon, Oxon ; New York, NY : Routledge, 2023. | Includes bibliographical references and index.
Identifiers: LCCN 2022037652 | ISBN 9781032354118 (hardback) | ISBN 9781032354125 (paperback) | ISBN 9781003326779 (ebook)
Subjects: LCSH: Labor market—Europe, Central. | Labor market—Europe, Eastern. | Telecommuting—Europe, Central. | Telecommuting—Europe, Eastern. | COVID-19 Pandemic, 2020—Europe, Central—Influence. | COVID-19 Pandemic, 2020—Europe, Eastern—Influence.
Classification: LCC HD5764.7.A6 D54 2023 | DDC 331.1/0943—dc23/eng/20220823
LC record available at https://lccn.loc.gov/2022037652

ISBN: 978-1-032-35411-8 (hbk)
ISBN: 978-1-032-35412-5 (pbk)
ISBN: 978-1-003-32677-9 (ebk)

DOI: 10.4324/9781003326779

Typeset in Bembo
by Apex CoVantage, LLC

We would like to thank all contributors for their commitment and cooperation.
The book was financed within the Regional Excellence Initiative programme of the Minister of Science and Higher Education of Poland,
years 2019–2023, grant no. 004/RID/2018/19, financing 3,000,000 PLN.

CONTENTS

FIGURES

TABLES

CONTRIBUTORS

Editors

Kamilla Marchewka-Bartkowiak is an associate professor in the Department of Investments and Financial Markets at the Poznań University of Economics and Business (PUEB) in Poland, director of the Institute of Finance, and head of the PUEB project entitled 'Economics in the face of the New Economy' implemented as a part of Poland's Regional Initiative of Excellence for 2019–2022 and financed by the Minister of Science and Higher Education of Poland. Her research fields include finance, regional and state finance, public economics, regulatory economics, and new financial and regulatory technologies. She is also an expert at the Bureau of Research of the Chancellery of the Sejm (the lower house of the Polish Parliament), the chair of the editorial board in the BAS Studia (the scientific parliamentary journal), and guest editor of special issues in Eastern European Economics.

Beata Woźniak-Jęchorek is an associate professor in the Department of Macroeconomics and Development Research at the Institute of Economics at the Poznań University of Economics and Business (PUEB) in Poland. Her theoretical and empirical works cover institutional problems of labour markets, technological change, and the future of work. In 2021, she was granted a scholarship by the Polish National Agency for Academic Exchange for a one-year stay at Northwestern University in the United States. Her current project aims to identify the future of remote working. In 2021, she co-edited the book *Labour Market Institutions and Productivity. Labour Utilisation in Central and Eastern Europe*, published by Routledge.

Contributors

Dragoş Adăscăliţei is a research officer at the European Foundation for the Improvement of Living and Working Conditions (Eurofound) in Ireland. His current research focuses on topics related to labour markets and the future of work, including the impact of artificial intelligence on jobs, the consequences of automation for employment, and regulatory issues surrounding the platform economy.

Branka Andjelkovic is the co-founder and Programme Director of the Public Policy Research Center in Belgrade, Serbia. She has been a researcher in various international projects and has worked as a senior expert for think tanks, research centres, and international organisations (European Union Delegations, International Labour Organisation, United Nations Development Programme) in Serbia, Turkey, the United States, and Southeast European countries. She pursued her PhD in international relations at the Bilkent University (Turkey), holds an MA in public administration from Harvard University (USA), and a BA in the theory of literature from the University of Belgrade (Serbia). Her research interests are related to labour market institutions, employment relations, digitalisation and automation, and ethics in innovation. Her current research focus is on non-standard forms of employment and platform work in the context of the knowledge-based economy, digital transformation, privacy data protection, and Web3. Branka is the lead author and editor of several pioneering studies about the platform economy and digital work in Serbia.

Łukasz Arendt is an associate professor in the Department of Economic Policy in the Faculty of Economics and Sociology at the University of Łódź in Poland. He was a director of the Educational Research Institute in Warsaw (April 2020–July 2021), director of the Institute of Labour and Social Studies (July 2016–October 2019), and currently, he is a member of the Committee of Labour and Social Policy of the Polish Academy of Sciences for the term 2020–2023. His research interests focus on labour market – with special emphasis on technical change and labour market polarisation, employment forecasting, development of information society, and labour market-driven changes in educational systems. He is an expert in many international and national research projects commissioned by, among others, DG Education and Culture, European Parliament, CEDEFOP, EUROSTAT, European Bank for Reconstruction and Development, and Polish Ministry of Family, Labour, and Social Policy.

Olga Chesalina is a senior researcher in the Department of Foreign and International Law at the Max Planck Institute for Social Law and Social Policy in Munich in Germany. She received her PhD in Law in Minsk in 2002 and her LLM from the Ludwig Maximilian University in Munich in 2009. Her main research interests comprise social and labour law, European Union law, and the law of Eastern European countries as well as legal comparison. She has authored over 80 articles and given presentations at numerous international conferences on labour and social law. She is a co-editor and co-author of the book *Social Law 4.0: New Approaches for Ensuring and Financing Social Security in the Digital Age* published by Nomos in 2021.

Jan Czarzasty is an assistant professor at the Institute of Philosophy, Sociology and Economic Sociology, in Warsaw School of Economics (SGH) in Poland. He is the head of the Economic Sociology Unit; chief expert in the field of industrial relations and social dialogue at the Institute of Public Affairs (ISP) in Warsaw; assistant-chief editor of the Warsaw Forum of Economic Sociology; research fellow at the Central European Labour Studies Institute (CELSI) in Bratislava; and independent expert working for social partners both at the national and cross-national level.

Brian Fabo is a lecturer in Economics at the Institute of Public Policy, a faculty of Social and Economic Sciences Department of Public Policy at Comenius University in Bratislava in Slovakia, and a senior economist at the National Bank of Slovakia. His research focuses on the application of novel data sources in social science research, digitalisation, and bias in research.

Ewa Gałecka-Burdziak is an associate professor in the Department of Economics I at the Warsaw School of Economics in Poland. Her research interests focus on labour economics and social policy. She is also a principal investigator of the projects financed by National Science Centre, Poland, and CERGE-EI Foundation. She has received the START scholarship founded by the Foundation for Polish Science and the Minister of Science and Higher Education scholarship for young scientists (2020–2022).

Sven M. Gruner is a PhD candidate at Poznań University of Economics and Business in Poland. He completed Bachelor's degree in business administration at the University of Duisburg-Essen in Germany and a Master of Business Administration at the FOM University of Applied Sciences in Essen in Germany. In his PhD dissertation, he focuses on the economic context of unconditional basic income and its potential introduction in Germany. Besides his academic activities, he works in the financial area in the renewable energy sector.

Martin Guzi is an assistant professor at Masaryk University in Brno and a researcher at Central European Labour Studies Institute (CELSI) in Bratislava in Slovakia. He has an educational background in mathematics and economics and research experience in labour economics with a focus on income inequality, migration, living wages, subjective well-being, social welfare schemes, and integration policies. He participated as a senior researcher in several EU-funded collaborative research projects and has led projects funded by the Czech Science Foundation.

Tanja Jakobi is the executive director of the Public Policy Research Centre in Belgrade, Serbia. She holds MA in business journalism from Baruch College (US) and a BA in philosophy from the University of Belgrade (Serbia). Her research interests are focused on labour markets, discrimination at work, and precarisation. She has been writing about living standards in transitional economies, precarisation and collective organising in the media, poverty alleviation, education, and access to labour markets of vulnerable groups. As a researcher, she is currently focused on the impact of new technologies on the labour market, labour contracts, and unionisation. Tanja writes about the digital economy and new forms of work such as online and on-location platform work, and remote work and related questions of privacy of data in the era of rising the artificial intelligence, intrusive applications for efficiency tracking at work, and application of wearables.

Martin Kahanec is a founder and Scientific Director of the Central European Labour Studies Institute in Bratislava IN Slovakia. He is a professor and head of the Department of Public Policy at the Central European University (CEU) in Vienna, where he acted as the Dean of its School of Public Policy in 2017–2019 and 2020–2021. He is a member of the Advisory Board at the Global Labour Organisation and an affiliated researcher at the University of Economics in Bratislava. Since 2021, he chairs the section committee 'Economics, Business and Management Sciences' of Academia Europaea. Kahanec has published extensively in the areas of labour and population economics, migration, EU mobility, ethnicity, and policy reforms in European labour markets; served as an editor in several journals; and acted in a range of international and national policy advisory roles.

Vassil Kirov is an associate professor at the Institute of Philosophy and Sociology of the Bulgarian Academy of Sciences in Bulgaria and visiting professor at Sciences Po in France. His research interests are in the sociology of work and organisations, employment relations, and digitalisation. He has been a researcher in large EU-funded research projects and has worked as an external expert for the European Commission, the ILO, and EUROFOUND. He was a member of the European Commission High-Level Expert Group on the Impact of the Digital Transformation on EU Labour Markets (2018–2019).

Maja Kovac is a senior research fellow within the Public Policy Research Centre in Belgrade, Serbia. She received her PhD in sociology from the University of Central Lancashire, UK. Her research focus has broadened from re-examining the concepts of social and human capital in a variety of contextual environments, and their linkages with labour, education, and future skills into issues of decent work and labour rights in the new forms of work such as platform work. She led and participated in a vast array of research projects in the fields of social and human capital, platform economy and decent work, social inclusion and anti-discrimination, access to education and labour markets, and poverty reduction.

Lucia Kováčová works as a researcher and data manager for the research institute Central European Labour Studies Institute (CELSI) based in Bratislava in Slovakia.

With a background in public policy, she has been involved in multiple research projects (both international and domestic) on different topics, mainly social dialogue, working conditions, employment policies, and labour integration of vulnerable groups such as people with disabilities or ethnic minorities.

Ladislava Kuchynková works as a lecturer in the Department of Corporate economy at the Masaryk University Faculty of Economics and Administration in the Czech Republic. She has been focusing on current issues in business and management. She is the author of several articles dealing with gender in management, franchising, or the influence of globalisation on small- and medium-sized enterprises.

Sławomir Kuźmar is an assistant professor in the Department of Macroeconomics and Development Studies at the Institute of Economics at the Poznań University of Economics and Business in Poland. His research interests include institutional analysis of labour market, political analysis, and regional development studies. He is the author of several scientific papers and participated in several national research programmes and projects.

Suzana Laporšek is an associate professor in the Faculty of Management at the University of Primorska in Slovenia. In 2014, she received a PhD in Economics from the Faculty of Economics, the University of Ljubljana with a doctoral thesis 'Minimum Wage Effects in Slovenia: Empirical Analysis with Microdata'. Her research interests include finance and labour market analyses, with a special interest in the evaluation of the labour market policy effects.

Michał Litwiński is an assistant professor in the Department of Sociology and Business Ethics at the Institute of Socio-Economics at Poznań University of Economics and Business in Poland, and a post-doc in the Department of Studies on Social Dynamics at Adam Mickiewicz University in Poznań, Poland. He works on income inequality and socio-economic development, as well as the application of econometric methods in economic research.

Pavla Marciánová works in the Department of Corporate Economy at Masaryk University Faculty of Economics and Administration in the Czech Republic. Her research interests are related to family business and small and medium businesses. She participates in the international research of Masaryk University and Johannes Kepler University, and FH Wien.

Piotr Matuszak works as a researcher at the Institute of Economics of the Polish Academy of Sciences. He obtained Ph.D. in Economics from the Poznań University of Economics and Business. His research focuses primarily on the empirical analysis of the role of the state as an owner of enterprises, both at the microeconomic and macroeconomic levels.

Peter Mikuš is a PhD candidate in corporate economics in the Department of Corporate economy at Masaryk University Faculty of Economics and Administration in the Czech Republic. His research is focused on customer satisfaction and business performance specifically in the gaming industry.

Karolina Nowak is an assistant professor in the Department of Sociology and Business Ethics at the Institute of Socio-Economics at Poznań University of Economics and Business in Poland. She is a philosopher and ethicist. Her research focuses on the axiological (ethical) contexts of human activities undertaken in various sectors of social practice, including economic practice; she is the author of the monographs *Laugh(ter) as a form of social communication. Cultural perspective* (2012), *Axiology of irony* (2020), and several journal papers.

Tomáš Ondráček is an assistant professor in the Department of Corporate Economy at the Masaryk University Faculty of Economics and Administration in the Czech Republic. He studied psychology and philosophy and wrote his PhD thesis on the philosophy of pseudo-science. His long-term research topics are crisis communication, business and research ethics, scientific and pseudo-scientific argumentation, and defeasible reasoning.

Robert Pater is an associate professor of economics in the Department of Economics and Finance at the University of Information Technology and Management (UITM) in Rzeszów, Poland. He holds the position of the Head of the Department of Economics and Finance at UITM. He is an expert of the Educational Research Institute in Warsaw in the National Qualifications Framework and a specialist in the field of macroeconomics and applied econometrics with particular application to the job vacancy market and labour demand. Since 2004, he has been conducting regular research on estimating the job offers in a market in Poland, named the Help-Wanted Index for Poland. He cooperates with the Bureau for Investments and Economic Cycles in Warsaw in forecasting the situation in the labour market. Since 2020, he has been supervising a research team whose goal is to provide information for the preparation by the Ministry of Education and Science in Poland of the annual Forecast of the demand for employees in vocational education occupations in the national and regional labour markets. Author of 60 scientific publications on the labour market and many other publications, including research reports and press articles, he has published in the national economic magazines and main Internet media in the country.

Petr Pirožek works in the Department of Corporate Economy at Masaryk University Faculty of Economics and Administration in the Czech Republic. His specialisation is management, especially managerial components in organisations, health care management, and managerial economics. He has participated in many research projects and is the author or co-author of several scientific papers, mainly from the area of organisational strategy, corporate governance, family business, and international management.

Suzana Sedmak is a lecturer and researcher at the University of Primorska in Slovenia. She studied at the University of Ljubljana, Slovenia, where she graduated from the Faculty of Social Sciences and obtained her Master's degree at the Faculty of Arts. At the Faculty of Management, she lectures subjects in the field of business communication, intercultural communication, and sociology of work. She took part in various national and transnational projects either as a coordinator and/or researcher. Recently she took part in a transnational project POW-Bridge as a national researcher; the project addressed the issue of posting of workers.

Olena Shelest-Szumilas is an assistant professor in the Department of Education and Personnel Development at the Institute of Socio-Economics at Poznań University of Economics and Business in Poland. Her main research interests include education economics, labour economics, and human resource management.

Klemen Širok is an associate professor at the Faculty of Health Sciences and the Faculty of Management at the University of Primorska in Slovenia. He teaches human resource management, sociology of work, organisational behaviour, and project management. He also taught courses on quality management in education, labour market, employee resourcing and career management, business communication, and management of cross-cultural differences. In the past eight years, Klemen also accumulated more than 300 hours teaching in Finland, Poland, and Austria. His research interests include evaluation studies within the area of labour market, quality assurance in education, and innovation management.

Petr Suchánek is an associate professor in the Department of Corporate Economy at Masaryk University Faculty of Economics and Administration in the Czech Republic. He is an expert in corporate economics. He mainly examines the performance of a company in various contexts: product quality, customer satisfaction, customer loyalty, and knowledge, especially in the food industry or in commerce (in e-shops focused on electronics).

Bartosz Totleben is an assistant professor in the Department of Macroeconomics and Development Studies at the Institute of Economics at the Poznań University of Economics and Business in Poland. His research interests include political analysis, determinants of state failure, rent-seeking activities, and development in fragile states.

Marcin Woźniak is an assistant professor at the Faculty of Human Geography and Planning at the Adam Mickiewicz University in Poland. His primary research interests concern labour economics and spatial econometrics.

Elizabeta Zirnstein is an associate professor at the Faculty of Management at the University of Primorska in Slovenia. Her research interests are mainly labour law and intellectual property law. Much of her work has been on understanding the effects of labour regulation and intellectual property legislation on improving the innovative performance of employees. She has also investigated other labour law issues, such as workers' representation, deregulation of professions, effects of digitalisation on labour law, and employees' copyright. She is also the Chair of the Legal Department at the Faculty of Management and a member of the faculty senate. She participated in several national and international research projects and authored a number of scientific papers, articles, book chapters, and research reports.

INTRODUCTION

Beata Woźniak-Jęchorek and
Kamilla Marchewka-Bartkowiak

This book focuses on the impact of the COVID-19 pandemic on changing labour markets and accelerating digitalisation of the workplace in Central and Eastern Europe. The COVID-19 pandemic disrupted workplaces substantially. As the lockdowns or stay-at-home measures entered into force, a large proportion of the workforce was instructed to stay home and continue to work remotely if their functions made it possible. This policy accelerated the introduction of many digital solutions, requiring the establishment of new patterns of work, and new institutional logic guiding daily activity for both organisations and individuals. In a relatively short time, remote working has become a kind of commonly accepted new institution with its own new logic, structures, rules, and behaviours (Jacks, 2021).

The trends contributing to a shift towards more flexible, digital working patterns were emerging before the pandemic (over the last decade) in response to societal developments, the increasing participation of women, and greater global competition. In 2020, the combined health and economic shocks have only deepened the concerns about technology-driven displacement of jobs, growing income inequality, and rising societal discord towards globalisation.

Yet with the global innovation and technology landscape changing rapidly and with the winner-takes-all tendencies of digital technologies, Europe and especially Central and Eastern European (CEE) countries risk becoming entrenched in their position as a follower of digitalisation. During the pandemic time, the adoption of digital technologies by firms in the European Union was improving, but only some EU countries are at the global forefront of digital transformation, while others risk being left behind (EIB, 2021).

Many research states that digitalisation is mainly an opportunity, now more than ever. The digital firms are more productive, employ more skilled workers, and foresee more employment growth opportunities ahead. Recently rising remote working patterns offer autonomy, which can lead to increased motivation and

DOI: 10.4324/9781003326779-1

commitment of employees (Rupietta & Beckmann, 2018; Chen & Fulmer, 2018; Clancy, 2020; Gorlick, 2020). Work from home (WFH) in its initial incarnation or in the emerging form of work from anywhere (WFA) allows the employee increased flexibility over their time and geographic location. This may expand the labour market, allowing employees to compete for a wider set of jobs, potentially contributing to both job satisfaction (Ipsen et al., 2021) and productivity (Ahrendt et al., 2020).

Although the COVID-19 pandemic highlighted the feasibility of remote working in many occupations, the ability to go digital is not universal to all types of jobs. Analyses of COVID-19 job losses in the wake of the introduction of remote work revealed the vulnerability of the young, women, the digitally less literate, and self-employed as well as those with jobs that cannot be done remotely and disenfranchised such as labour migrants and others engaged in physical labour (ILO, 2020). Moreover, more generally, accelerating digital substitution of routinised tasks may culminate in the loss of middle-skilled jobs and subsequent crowding around jobs with non-routinised but low-skilled tasks (e.g., requiring physical dexterity or social skills) and – to a lesser extent – around jobs requiring cognitive skills and creativity of human workers (Acemoglu & Autor, 2011; Goos et al., 2014; Vermeulen & Psenner, 2022). Therefore, while the digital revolution has the potential to mitigate persistent individual, sectoral, and regional labour disparities, which are partly attributed to historical or compositional differences (e.g., natural advantages, and productive amenities) and institutional settings, the speed and diversity of these changes can exacerbate the new discrepancies.

Remote working also presents challenges related to new organisational culture, managerial capability, and technological infrastructure. Yet, research also finds that remote work can lead to increased feelings of isolation, loneliness, overworking, prioritising work over personal or family life, inability to switch off, and technostress (Henke et al., 2015; Shepherd-Banigan et al., 2016; Wang et al., 2020). The higher flexibility and autonomy associated with remote working are often accompanied by greater work intensity and longer working hours. Zoom fatigue is now real (Fauville et al., 2021). Long working hours and the sense of isolation associated with remote work, together with the increased use of online monitoring and surveillance methods, may, however, negatively affect the mental health of teleworkers, besides raising privacy issues. Thus, there are the well-being costs of digital technology (Messenger et al., 2017).

Therefore, exploiting the full potential of remote working arrangements requires skills and managerial capabilities. Pre-pandemic literature has identified the factors managers consider when deciding who should be able to telework (Lautsch & Kossek, 2011; Williamson et al., 2021). These are work-related considerations (such as suitability of the job for teleworking), personal and household characteristics, and technological limitations. Work-related factors are the most important.

Moreover, the level of access to digital infrastructure is converging across Europe, but more needs to be done to accelerate the spread of fast connections. Effective technology, a well-equipped and dedicated workspace at home, regular communications with colleagues, job characteristics and managers' understanding of the permeability of boundaries (work-life balance) are all factors enabling successful working from home (Greer & Payne, 2014; Basile & Beauregard, 2016; Morikawa, 2020).

Shaping opportunities and understanding the challenges of the new digital world require a human-centred approach to ensure decent digiwork. Decent digiwork is about creating opportunities for all to participate fully in a future of digital work that affords self-respect and dignity, security and equal opportunity, representation, and voice. It is also about fostering inclusive innovation policy while meeting the changing needs facing businesses and securing sustainable economic growth (ILO, 2019). Through its attention to democratic participation, fairness, and legitimacy (Papadakis, 2006; ILO, 2013; Hermans & Ramiou, 2016), social dialogue can play a central role in addressing both the innovation potential of new working patterns and the problems associated with digital work.

All these trends of the future are present in Europe. In this context, the following questions arise: how have labour markets in Eastern Europe dealt with the coronavirus crises, has the rapidly introduced digitalisation brought about more advantages or disadvantages for employees and employers, what kind of advantages and disadvantages prevail in the digitalisation of the European labour market after the pandemic, and finally – to what extent does the digitalisation of the labour market require changes to existing regulations?

Thus, this book aims to assess the impact of digitalisation on the future of work in the CEE by exploiting the unique experience of the COVID-19 pandemic. More specifically, we will investigate the ongoing changes in the world of work during the COVID-19 pandemic and identify the challenges for the post-pandemic digital labour markets in CEE countries. The geographical scope of the study concerns Bulgaria, the Czech Republic, Poland, Serbia, Slovakia, Slovenia, and Romania, but some chapters present the largest context analysing EU-27 countries. The book concentrates predominantly on the current data from the pandemic period, however, to understand better the determinants of the ongoing changes, and particular chapters will also describe the theoretical aspects of these shifts and present the earlier trends.

The presented research will be important in formulating policy that will ensure that the benefits of this digital revolution are shared by all. Exploiting the full potential of digital transformation requires skills and managerial capabilities, better access to digital infrastructure, regional development policy, strengthening of cohesion, and new regulations of flexible working patterns. Moreover, in this book, we argue that the adoption of digital technologies in CEE countries has improved during the COVID-19 pandemic, but the region has not yet closed the gap with Western Europe or among different groups of employees. Thus, to achieve sustainable growth and lasting competitiveness, Europe must support the shifts that are only just started in many industries, as well as in the lives of many Europeans.

The expected contributions of this research are to address the three key goals. First, a better understanding of the impact of the COVID-19 pandemic on the adoption of workplace digitalisation in the selected labour markets in CEE countries and the potential trade-offs facing those who do and do not have access to this benefit. Further, the book is to complement the labour market research by incorporating the outputs of changing demand for skills. Finally, this book will contribute new insight into policies and regulations that govern the future of work.

The structure of the book

The book comprises 12 chapters and is divided into two parts. The first concerns the new work experience from the pandemic time and the second, new challenges and policy needs for the post-pandemic digital work. The first part (consisting of the first seven chapters) discusses how the COVID-19 pandemic has impacted the labour markets in selected CEE countries. In this part, the authors will identify the factors deepening the digital divide at the EU regional level, the scale of changing digital skills demand and deepening jobs polarisation, labour mobility of posting workers and demand for migrant workers during the corona crisis, changes of labour productivity, and the role of social partners in job prevention in times of COVID-19 crisis. The second part of the book (comprising five chapters) tries to identify the challenges for the future of work in terms of new labour law (the right to disconnect or appropriate monitoring and surveillance of remote work), the potential application of an unconditional basic income (UBI), the potential of Google's Trends Data (GTD) in the assessment of the current labour market situation, and the problem of NFT gig tokens.

In both parts, the authors focus their attention on particular case studies or, more broadly, analyse and compare the dataset for CEE or EU27. The authors apply various methods (quantitative and qualitative) in their research, considering the investigated problems on different levels of analysis – micro, mezzo, and macro. Such diversity provides us with a broad perspective on the problem of the COVID crisis and its impact on labour markets and workplaces, and at the same time gives us a wider audience for our research results.

The first three chapters focus on how the pandemic impacts the digital divide and polarisation of labour markets. In Chapter 1, Beata Woźniak-Jęchorek and Piotr Matuszak investigate the changes in the scale of work from home (WFH) during the COVID-19 pandemic concerning the pre-existing inequalities in the EU regions, including differences in the income level, economic structure, demographics, and education. More specifically, this explanatory study investigates the factors related to the scale of WFH in the EU regions and aims at indicating which of them were the drivers of the deepening digital divide during the COVID-19 pandemic. To econometrically analyse the potential determinants of the observed discrepancies at regional levels, they use the dataset including 218 regions (NUTS 2 level) in the 27 European countries for which data on WFH is available in both 2019 and 2020. This explanatory study reveals that the scale of WFH increased more in 2020 in the regions with relatively larger WFH indicators already in 2019 and had larger income levels and employment share of the finance and insurance sector, and in countries that introduced stricter COVID-19-related restrictions.

In Chapter 2, Brian Fabo studies the impact of the pandemic on labour market matching and skills demand in Slovakia during the pandemic period. To show the changes to digital skills demand caused by the COVID-19 pandemic, he examines a large database of nearly 500,000 job vacancies posted on the website *Profesia.sk* in 2020 and 2021. His findings confirm a major increase in demand for office and teleworking (Zoom, MS Teams, and Cisco Webex) software, but mainly limited to clerical support workers and managers. He identifies that the increase was particularly pronounced in small firms, which are likely more nimble and thus more likely to modify their job postings. The increase appears to remain sustained even after the end of lockdowns, suggesting a possibly permanent shift to working from home. If the shift to working from home remains permanent, it might lead to a deepening digital divide between workers whose work is possible to be performed from home and service or blue-collar workers, who are by the nature of their jobs unable to take advantage of this shift.

In Chapter 3, Łukasz Arendt, Ewa Gałecka-Burdziak, and Robert Pater explore how the dynamic implementation of digital technologies, being a result of the COVID-19 pandemic outburst, cause deepening polarisation of the labour market in Poland. More specifically, they analyse online job offers from selected Polish job portals before and after the COVID-19 outbreak and verify indirectly the extent to which potential COVID-driven enhanced automation and robotisation processes lead to changes in the routine and non-routine mix of jobs available in the Polish labour market. The empirical part of this study is based on data on job vacancies posted online, retrieved from the System of Online Job Offers (SOJO) developed by the Institute of Labour and Social Studies in Warsaw. Changes in the demand for task content of jobs and skill mix are estimated with the use of difference-in-difference methodology and multinomial logistic models. Their findings reveal a structural shift in demand which favours non-routine jobs and shall translate into more dynamic labour polarisation. Moreover, with the use of logistic regression, they match skill requirements specified in job offers with task-content groups, showing a COVID-19-driven increase in demand for computer, mathematical, and cognitive skills, and lower requirements for self-organisation, communication, managerial, and office skills.

During the COVID pandemic, workers have experienced a tremendous amount of upheaval, and the changes are both seismic and persistent. In some occupations, the possibility to work remotely is limited or impossible, potentially excluding some workers from enjoying a valuable non-pecuniary benefit (Garrote Sanchez et al., 2020). This is potentially the case of posted workers. Therefore, in Chapter 4, Elizabeta Zirnstein, Klemen Širok, Suzana Sedmak, and Suzana Laporšek attempt to reveal how the pandemic affected the posting of workers within the EU, with a special focus on the posting of workers from Slovenia – one of the European leaders with the highest number of posted workers. Although according to official data, the posting of workers seems a marginal topic; it is a topical issue, as labour mobility is crucial for the future of Europe, due to huge work shortages in the EU with big structural disparities in the labour markets. The chapter presents the regulatory framework for posting workers in the EU and Slovenia and discusses the characteristics and specifics of posting over the pandemic. The findings are based on primary data collected through semi-structured interviews with key stakeholders and on secondary data on the numbers of posted workers in Slovenia. The authors argue that the number of posted workers in Slovenia has been increasing steadily since 2004 and kept rising throughout the pandemic period. However, during the pandemic, the biggest obstacles to posting were constant changes in containment measures, uncoordinated measures between EU countries, and obligatory quarantines. For posted workers, the pandemic resulted in numerous lay-offs, high risk of infection, limited access to medical treatment, undeclared work, and no wage compensation in case of illness. Consequently, the pandemic deepened the vulnerability of posted workers.

Similarly, adopting the disadvantaged labour market participants groups' perspective in Chapter 5, Olena Shelest-Szumilas and Marcin Woźniak investigate how the demand for migrant workers in the local market in Poland was affected by the COVID-19 pandemic shock. Based on their own survey conducted in the Poznań region, they present quantitative data on the employment changes and employers' plans in terms of hiring migrants in the short term. To identify the factors that may increase or decrease the probability of hiring migrant workers by local Polish enterprises in 12 months following the survey, they develop three ordinal logistic regression models. As was expected, the results indicate that the situation of foreign workers became much more uncertain in the local labour market. The factors of particular risk are mainly connected with firm characteristics (e.g., firm size and economic sector) and working conditions (e.g., type of job contract).

The COVID-19 pandemic has also caused a profound disruption in the business activity, forcing firms to introduce new solutions, replacing standard work with teleworking, breaking the supply chains, and decreasing production and sales. Therefore, in Chapter 6, Petr Suchánek, Tomáš Ondráček, Ladislava Kuchynková, Pavla Marciánová, Petr Pirožek, and Peter Mikuš aim to assess how Czech companies dealt with the COVID-19 crisis at the beginning of the pandemic and how this crisis impacted labour productivity in selected sectors of the Czech economy. Their study is based on two data sources – a secondary statistical database and a survey conducted in the firms in the Czech Republic under the declared state of emergency in autumn of 2020. Their findings show that labour productivity measured in hours worked has increased, but labour productivity measured as the ratio of the total sales to the number of employees has decreased. Supplementary data from online surveys showed that manager and government policies during the COVID shock were generally targeted to achieve the interests of the business or the interests of customers but did not stop the decline in sales.

The emerging new digital reality of the labour markets with the ambiguous effects of the remote working poses a challenge for the public policy analogous to the regulation of temporary contracts which despite their capability to increase overall productivity and labour utilisation often resulted in labour market segmentation and increased precarity. The policy and social partners' response to the pandemic crises are the subject of research conducted in Chapter 7. Here Vassil Kirov, Lucia Kováčová, Martin Guzi, Jan Czarzasty, Dragoş Adăscăliţei, and Martin Kahanec provide early evidence on the role of social partners in shaping job preservation policies and measures, focusing on three main types: short-time working arrangements (e.g., *Kurzarbeit*); wage subsidies; and flexible work arrangements (e.g., teleworking) in five CEE countries: Bulgaria, the Czech Republic, Poland, Romania, and Slovakia. More specifically, they critically explore how social partners have been involved in designing and adopting job preservation policies responding to the recent COVID-19 economic crisis and increasing unemployment rates. They also focus on teleworking; however, the social dialogue in the implementation of this new work arrangement has been done rather at the company level. Their findings indicate strong involvement of social partners in the design of short-term working schemes but less engagement in the introduction of teleworking as a novel form of work organisation in CEE countries.

The next two chapters concentrate on the challenges of the new working solutions and workers' rights. Blurring the boundary between working time and leisure may introduce difficulties in separating work-familly life (work-life balance) and increase the risk of working overtime without proper remuneration (Yarmolyuk-Krock, 2022; Vargas Llave et al., 2020). In Chapter 8, Branka Andjelkovic, Tanja Jakobi, and Maja Kovac discuss the effects of monitoring and surveillance practices that emerged with remote work in Serbia. Conceptually, their research seeks to explore the practices and ramifications of monitoring remote workers via constructs of power asymmetry in the (remote) workplace in the context of employee privacy and labour rights. They argue that a lack of institutional response, primarily in the fields of labour law and data protection, increases the grey zone of remote work and exposes workers to several unforeseen vulnerabilities. Their findings relied on a mixed-method approach with two separate surveys, one of the workers and one of the employers, who worked remotely during the pandemic. In addition, semi-structured interviews were conducted with labour and personal data protection experts, representatives of trade unions, policymakers, and regulators. The main findings of the research show that power asymmetry has increased in all fundamental privacy and data protection domains. However, this shift in power has provoked neither collective action nor individual resistance by Serbian remote workers. Instead, they continued to comply with the new practices primarily due to ignorance.

In Chapter 9, Olga Chesalina explores the legal nature and the regulation of the right to disconnect in the EU member states and the EU Draft Directive, which become a crucial problem for hyper-connected teleworkers. Special attention is paid here to the character of the right to disconnect, the personal and material scope of this right, the relationship to other labour rights, and the role of this right in the prevention of psychosocial risks. The chapter also investigates different factors that influence the effective implementation of the right to disconnect.

It concludes that the right to disconnect is not a new labour right but rather a remedy to prevent hyper-connection from the employer's side and the constant over-accessibility of employees.

In turn, in Chapter 10, Sven M. Gruner takes a more general view, assessing the role of an Unconditional Basic Income (UBI) in the post-COVID time. The emerging form of Work from anywhere (WFA) could expand the pool of potential employees, allowing the companies to search for workers outside their local labour markets. As a result, the firms may hire more productive employees for similar or lower wages (Clancy, 2020). Therefore, Sven M. Gruner addresses the question of how UBI can become a policy tool in reducing the negative aspects of labour market technological changes. More specifically, the chapter will focus on UBI in the context of growing flexibility of working relationships, decreasing social security, the need for quick skill adaptation to the new digital environment, and work-life balance challenges in the case of remote working. The chapter reveals findings that COVID-caused elements might be a nutrient medium for UBI. On the one hand, the pandemic exacerbated existing problems; and on the other hand, the crisis drew attention to the problems already known but so far discussed on the border of the mainstream economics.

Technology brings many benefits such as easy access to information, time savings, better mobility, better communication, cost efficiency, less wastage, and more optimal usage of resources. Because of technology, companies can act faster, make quicker decisions, and remain adaptable. To do that, new digital data are used. The generation of this data significantly accelerated during the COVID time. Therefore, in Chapter 11, Sławomir Kuźmar and Bartosz Totleben put forward an interesting explanation of the potential of Google Trends Data (GTD) in the assessment of the current labour market situation, paying special attention not only to the research potential but also to the limitations and possible drawbacks of studies based on this data. The authors trace the general trends in scientific research based on GTD and present some empirical examples of these studies related to the labour market. Discussing the potential limitations of Internet search data, they focus on some external or general factors that may impact the representatives of search queries such as the demographic dimensions of Internet users, differences in behaviour, and sources used in web searching. They also concentrate on factors related directly to the methodology of collecting and sharing data by Google, including sampling, time range sensitivity, and categories. The chapter concludes that the authors and reviewers of studies based on Internet search data should adopt an enthusiastic but critical approach, particularly regarding key assumptions and methodological aspects of their studies.

Finally, in Chapter 12, Kamilla Marchewka-Bartkowiak, Michał Litwiński, and Karolina Nowak address the problem of labour valuation in the gig economy which has increased significantly in the last couple of years and could offer flexibility that was much appreciated during the pandemic time and in the new digital world. Specifically, they explore the question of whether NFT gig tokens constitute a tool for valuing one's work that will consider both the financial and network dimensions of the individual. Authors assume here that NFT gig tokens have the potential to become a new means of labour valuation for and by gig workers. In this chapter, we can find the newly developed classification of work offered by digital token issuers, axiological reasoning of network factor of valuation, and identification of factors influencing the valuation of work using personal tokens. The financial benefits seem to be of lower relevance here. The main criteria of work valuation are the appearance in the virtual world and the development of a network of contacts, which will enable them to achieve a network effect in the long term.

The chapters presented in the book discuss how new digital technologies affected the labour markets and workplaces during the specific and extraordinary time of the COVID pandemic. These experiences might develop scenarios on how digitalisation is likely to affect the CEE labour markets in the next years and derives implications for policymakers on how to shape the future of work. The main challenge will be the structure of jobs and the corresponding need for supply-side adjustments to meet the shift in demand both within and between occupations and sectors; also appropriately capturing the benefits of digital work while mitigating its social costs will largely depend on public policy design and regulation of this new paradigm.

The COVID-19 crisis has clearly shown that being able to get online was a crucial determinant of people's ability to continue engaging in the workplace. Investing in digital infrastructure and closing the digital divide will allow disadvantaged groups to participate meaningfully in the future economy. To reduce inequality and give people better prospects, governments need to strengthen education and training to better prepare workers for the jobs of the future. Lifelong learning also means bolstering access to schooling and skills training to help workers displaced by economic shocks like COVID-19. Wage subsidies and public-works programmes can help people regain their livelihoods during the recovery, but the pandemic was likely to change how work is done. For shaping a decent digital work environment, the will of social dialogue actors to engage in intensified and better organised dialogue and to adapt more quickly to the new realities must also play a central role. It is also about fostering development-driven innovations while reshaping the business models, meeting the changing needs facing companies, and securing inclusive and sustainable economic growth. Ensuring decent digitally enabled work is still a challenge in current times.

Looking to the future, we do hope that this book has captured at least a small part of contemporary digitalisation process and its impact on labour markets and workplaces, and that it will help us to have a better understanding of this extraordinary phenomenon shaping our working life.

Acknowledgements

The study has been financed within the Regional Initiative for Excellence programme of the Minister of Science and Higher Education of Poland, years 2019–2023, grant no. 004/RID/2018/19, financing 3,000,000 PLN.

The book authors are also very grateful to Piotr Michoń and Michał Pilc from Poznań University of Economics and Business, for their helpful advice, suggestions, and insightful comments on their texts.

References

Acemoglu, D., & Autor, D. (2011). Skills, tasks and technologies: Implications for employment and earnings. In D. Card & O. Ashenfelter (Eds.), *Handbook of labor economics* (Vol. 4, pp. 1043–1171). Elsevier. www.sciencedirect.com/science/article/pii/S0169721811024105

Ahrendt, D., Cabrita, J., Clerici, E., Hurley, J., Leoncikas, T., Mascherini, M., Riso, S., & Sandor, E. (2020). Living, working and COVID-19. *Eurofound*. https://www.eurofound.europa.eu/publications/report/2020/living-working-and-covid-19

Basile, K. A., & Beauregard, T. A. (2016). Strategies for successful telework: How effective employees manage work/home boundaries. *Strategic HR Review, 15*(3).

Chen, Y., & Fulmer, I. S. (2018). Fine-tuning what we know about employees' experience with flexible work arrangements and their job attitudes. *Human Resource Management, 57*, 381–395.

Clancy, M. (2020). The case for remote work. (*Economics Working Papers* 20007). Iowa State University, Department of Economics. https://lib.dr.iastate.edu/econ_workingpapers/102

EIB (European Investment Bank). (2021). *Digitalisation in Europe 2020–2021: Evidence from the EIB investment survey*. www.eib.org/en/publications-research/economics/surveys-data/eibis/about/index.htm

Fauville, G., Luo, M., Queiroz, A. C. M., Bailenson, J. N., & Hancock, J. (2021). *Zoom exhaustion & fatigue scale*. SSRN: https://ssrn.com/abstract=3786329 or http://dx.doi.org/10.2139/ssrn.3786329

Garrote Sanchez, D., Gomez Parra, N., Ozden, C., & Rijkers, B. (2020). Which jobs are most vulnerable to COVID-19? What an analysis of the European union reveals. *World Bank Group, Research & Policy Briefs from the World Bank Malaysia Hub*. https://documents1.worldbank.org/curated/en/820351589209840894/pdf/Which-Jobs-Are-Most-Vulnerable-to-COVID-19-What-an-Analysis-of-the-European-Union-Reveals.pdf

Goos, M., Manning, A., & Salomons, A. (2009). Job polarization in Europe. *The American Economic Review: Papers and Proceedings, 99*(2), 58–63. https://doi.org/10.1257/aer.99.2.58

Goos, M., Manning, A., & Salomons, A. (2014). Explaining job polarization: Routine-biased technological change and offshoring. *American Economic Review, 104*(8). https://www.aeaweb.org/articles?id=10.1257/aer.104.8.2509

Gorlick, A. (2020). *The productivity pitfalls of working from home in the age of COVID-19*. Stanford News. https://news.stanford.edu/2020/03/30/productivity-pitfalls-working-home-age-covid-19/

Greer, S., & Payne, S. (2014). Overcoming telework challenges: Outcomes of successful telework strategies. *The Psychologist-Manager Journal, 17*(2).

Henke, R. M., Benevent, R., Schulte, P., Rinehart, C., Crighton, K. A., & Corcoran, M. (2015). The effects of telecommuting intensity on employee health. *American Journal of Health Promotion*, 30(8).

Hermans, M., & Ramiou, M. (2016). *Representative employee participation in industrial innovation processes: EUROWIN country case report*. HIVA-KU Leuven.

ILO. (2013). *Social dialogue interventions: What works and why? A synthesis review 2002–2012*. ILO.

ILO. (2019). *Social dialogue and the governance of the digital platform economy: Understanding challenges, shaping opportunities*. ILO. www.ilo.org/wcmsp5/groups/public/ – ed_dialogue/ – dialogue/documents/meetingdocument/wcms_723431.pdf

ILO. (2020). *Teleworking during the COVID-19 pandemc and beyond. A practical guide*. https://www.ilo.org/wcmsp5/groups/public/---ed_protect/---protrav/---travail/documents/instructionalmaterial/wcms_751232.pdf

Ipsen, C., van Veldhoven, M., Kirchner, K., & Hansen, J. P. (2021). Six key advantages and disadvantages of working from home in Europe during COVID-19. *International Journal of Environmental Research and Public Health, 18*(4), 1826. https://doi.org/10.3390/ijerph18041826.

Jacks, T. (2021). Research on remote work in the era of COVID-19. *Journal of Global Information Technology Management, 24*(2), 93–97.

Lautsch, B., & Kossek, E. E. (2011). Managing a blended workforce: Telecommuters and non-telecommuters. *Organisational Dynamics, 40*.

Messenger, J., Llave, O. V., Gschwind, L., Boehmer, S., Vermeylen, G., & Wilkens, M. (2017). *Working anytime, anywhere: The effects on the world of work*. Publications Office of the European Union, Luxembourg, and the International Labour Office.

Morikawa, M. (2020). *COVID-19, teleworking, and productivity*. VoxEU.org. https://voxeu.org/article/covid-19-teleworking-and-productivity

Papadakis, K. (2006). *Civil society, participatory governance and decent work objectives: The case of South Africa*. ILO/IILS.

Rupietta, K., & Beckmann, K. (2018). Employees working from home: What is the effect on employees' effort? *Schmalenbach Business Review, 70*.

Shepherd-Banigan, M., Bell, J. F., Basu, A., Booth-LaForce, C., & Harris, J. R. (2016). Workplace stress and working from home influence depressive symptoms among employed women with young children. *International Journal of Behavioural Medicine, 23*.

Vargas Llave, O., Mandl, I., Weber, T., & Wilkens, M. (2020). Telework and ICT-based mobile work: Flexible working in the digital age. *Eurofound*. https://www.eurofound.europa.eu/publications/report/2020/telework-and-ict-based-mobile-work-flexible-working-in-the-digital-age

Vermeulen, B., & Psenner, E. (2022). Exploiting the technology-driven structural shift to creative work in regional catching-up: Toward an institutional framework. *European Planning Studies*. https://doi.org/10.1080/09654313.2022.2028737

Wang, W., Albert, L., & Sun, Q. (2020). Employee isolation and telecommuter organizational commitment. *Employee Relations, 42*(3).

Williamson, S., Pearce, A., Dickinson, H., Weeratunga, V., & Bucknall, F. (2021). *Future of work literature review: Emerging trends and issues*. UNSW Canberra. www.unsw.adfa.edu.au/sites/default/files/documents/Future_of_Work_Literature_Review.pdf

Yarmolyuk-Krock, K. (2022). A case for an EU directive addressing work-related psychological risks: An eastern European perspective. *ETUI Policy Brief, European Economic, Employment and Social Policy*. https://www.etui.org/sites/default/files/2022-03/A%20case%20for%20an%20EU%20directive%20addressing%20work-related%20psychological%20risks-an%20eastern%20European%20perspective-2022.pdf

PART 1

New Work Experience from the COVID-19 Pandemic Time

1

WORK FROM HOME

Regional Digital Divide in EU Countries

Beata Woźniak-Jęchorek and Piotr Matuszak

Introduction

The COVID-19 pandemic has changed the face of global IT forever. The use of technology has increased dramatically due to business demands for higher agility and flexibility (Elragal et al., 2020). The organisations that had previously resisted the idea of telecommuting were forced to change to adapt quickly to the new reality. Setting up the infrastructure and equipment to enable distance working such as cloud computing, video conferencing, collaboration platforms, and broadband Internet, has sparked large-scale innovation and experimentation for organisations (Rai, 2020) and seems to become a transformative force over the long term (Hadidi & Power, 2020). It is a cultural norm around the world that 'work from home' (also known as work-at-home, remote work, telework, virtual work, and telecommuting) is now simply 'work' (Jacks, 2021).

While white-collar knowledge workers were able to shift to remote work with relative ease during the pandemic, the impact on blue-collar workers has been more severe, frequently leading to unemployment (Rai, 2020). Consequently, the new social inequalities, between those who can telework and those who cannot, because they are employed in non-teleworkable sectors/occupations, lack of the required digital skills or equipment, or have no access to a broadband connection, have emerged. The labour market polarisation manifests itself as a digital divide between groups and regions with low-skilled, low-wage labour and higher risk of unemployment, and groups and regions with high-skilled, high-wage labour and low risk of unemployment. In this sense, the digital divide is a restriction to access to not only the technical infrastructure but also the social infrastructure that supports information and communication technologies (ICTs) (Rooksby et al., 2002). This includes socio-demographic factors such as income, gender, race, ethnicity, education, age, location, and institutions (Choudrie et al., 2005).

DOI: 10.4324/9781003326779-3

The digital divide raises several questions about the technology and institutional issues with a strong social justice which is even more important in the wake of the pandemic and the accelerating unequal technology-driven structural shift. A tendentious narrative of regional development is that, on the one hand, there are 'making regions' that experience a virtuous cycle of increasing employment for and in-migration of high-skilled, high-wage creative workers that research, develop, and make the focal technologies, and, on the other hand, there is a wide range of 'applying regions' that befall a vicious cycle of decreasing competitiveness, increasing unemployment of low-skilled workers, and out-migration (Vermeulen & Psenner, 2022).

Therefore, the aim of this chapter is to analyse changes in the scale of work from home during the COVID-19 pandemic with respect to the pre-existing inequalities in access to ICTs, differences in the economic structure, demographics, and education in the regions of the EU. More specifically, our explanatory study investigates the factors related to the scale of work from home in the EU regions and aims at indicating which of them were the drivers of the deepening digital divide during the COVID-19 pandemic.

In this research, we focus on work from home (WFH) referring to a working arrangement in which a worker fulfils the essential responsibilities of his/her job while remaining at home.[1] The term 'digital divide' refers to the gap between individuals, households, businesses, and geographic areas at different socio-economic levels with regard to both their opportunities to access ICTs and their use of the Internet for a wide variety of activities (OECD, 2001). We employ data from Eurostat over the period 2019 and 2020 at the NUTS 2 level to analyse the potential determinants of the observed discrepancies at regional levels.

We contribute to the literature on the digital divide by investigating determinants of work from home in the extraordinary period of the pandemic. Based on the obtained results, we also discuss the potential consequences of (possibly) deepening inequalities in the scale of work from home for future regional development.

The emerging literature on remote work (e.g., Messenger, 2019; Dingel & Neiman, 2020; Garrote Sanchez et al., 2020; Hensvik et al., 2020; Pennington & Stanford, 2020; Samek Lodovici, 2021; Ramani & Bloom, 2021; Barrero et al., 2022; Woźniak-Jęchorek et al., 2022) examines a range of issues including staff and managerial experience with working remotely, workplace productivity, emerging trends in accommodation and digital infrastructure, work health and safety, employees preferences for working remotely, and reallocation of the remote workforce. There is still a lack of research on digital disparity issues related to the ability to work from home and highlighting the relationship between technology and social concerns. To the best of our knowledge, only the paper of Sostero et al. (2020) discusses the extent of teleworking in the EU before and during the COVID-19 outbreak and develops a conceptual analysis to identify the jobs that can be done from home by occupations across EU countries, sectors, and socio-economic profiles. Our study is the first to examine explicitly the scale of work from home in the EU countries in 2019–2020, from the regional digital divide perspective.

The basic results of this research show that the scale of work from home increased more in 2020 in the regions with relatively larger WFH indicators in 2019 and in the regions that had larger income levels and employment share of the finance and insurance sector. Moreover, the introduction of the stricter COVID-19-related restrictions was related to the larger increases in work from home in 2020.

The remainder of this chapter is organised as follows. We begin with a literature review on the digital divide. Then, next section presents the scale of working from home during the COVID-19 pandemic. In the following section, we describe the data collected and used in the empirical analysis. Then we present the econometric approach and the results of our research. Last section provides conclusions and directions for further research.

Determinants of the digital divide

According to the related literature, the term digital divide entered public discourse and became very popular in the last year of the 1990s (van Dijk, 2000). NTIA (1999) defines the digital divide as the divide between those with access to ICTs and those without. The gap in access could also be understood as a phenomenon with three distinct aspects, including a global divide (referring to ICTs disparities between countries), a social divide (referring to the gap in access to ICTs between different sections of a nation's society), and a democratic divide (referring to the difference between those who do and those who do not use the variety of digital means to engage in public life) (Norris, 2001). The digital divide can also exist between those living in rural areas and those living in urban areas, between the educated and uneducated, between economic classes, and on a global scale between more and less industrially developed nations (van Dijk & Hacker, 2003). More specifically, it affects certain population segments, for instance, low-income and rural communities, due to the lack of digital infrastructure, affordability, and skills (Shenglin et al., 2017).

Many empirical studies focus on the equalisation of access to ICTs in terms of physical access, using technological determinism theory in their hypotheses and conclusions. Based on this assumption, the important factors at this level should be the availability of the infrastructure (including the availability of related technologies, for example, Wi-Fi, electronic devices, software, and applications) (Middleton & Chambers, 2010) and infrastructure investment leading to a greater diffusion rate (Struzak, 2010). Some research argues, however, that the challenge is not about the availability, instead, it is about the affordability, due to the higher costs of acquiring necessary devices and services (Facebook, 2016).

Other research focuses on the multidimensional approach pointing out the factors influencing the digital divide (van Dijk, 2002, 2006; Helbig et al., 2009; Srinuan & Bohlin, 2011). Among these factors, research focuses on income/socio-economic status (SES)/GDP per capita assuming that an individual or country in a more privileged socio-economic situation is expected to have a smaller digital gap (Yoon et al., 2020). There is also evidence that the digital divide is higher in ethnic and racial minorities (Adkins & Sandy, 2020). Other research focuses on skills and experience confirming that a lack of ICTs skills and experience will widen the digital divide. In terms of rural-urban location and population density, the literature argues that urban populations may benefit from easier and cheaper access to ICTs infrastructure because adoption costs will decrease with population size and density increase (Philip et al., 2017). Lai and Widmar (2020) argued that during the COVID-19 pandemic, the digital divide between rurality and cities has limited opportunities for those without ready access to the Internet. As a result, schools tackled challenges of providing equitable educational access by attempting to provide access for students, while even households with service available struggled to maintain sufficient speeds and/or to afford it. Another study shows that people with higher education will be more prone to use and adopt ICTs than less educated people (Hassler & Jackson, 2010).

The family structure is also important. Children's current use of ICTs in the home will increase the probability of ICTs use among other family members (e.g., Hohlfied et al., 2010) and elderly people show greater reluctance to adopt new technologies than teenagers (Hargittai et al., 2019; Hunsaker & Hargittai, 2018; Lissitsa et al., 2022). The digital technologies, tools, and services can also make a difference in single mothers' social inclusion and welfare; however, digital inequalities among single and married mothers are better explained by SES, than by family status (Lissitsa & Chachashvili-Bolotin, 2022). Finally, occupation matters, because professional, scientific, and/or creative workers are more likely to access and use ICT tools than are other workers (Adams-Prassl et al., 2020; Sostero et al., 2020).

So far, many studies have tried to clarify whether the Internet utilised by disadvantaged groups enhances their social mobility (Arie & Mesch, 2016; Mesch et al., 2012; Milioni et al., 2014; Rosenberg et al., 2021) or extend existing social inequalities (Helsper, 2012; Helsper & Reisdorf, 2017), and whether digital inequalities are disappearing, persisting, or (re)emerging over time (Dobransky & Hargittai, 2016; Lissitsa & Chachashvili-Bolotin, 2015). Research from the COVID-19 outbreak suggests that the large expansion of telework has been strongly skewed towards high-paid white-collar employment. Enforced closures have, however, likely resulted in many new teleworkers among low- and mid-level clerical and administrative workers who previously had limited access to this working arrangement (Sostero et al., 2020).

Work from home during the COVID-19 pandemic

The scale of work from home increased in an aftermath of the COVID-19 pandemic from 5.49% in 2019 to 12.38% in the European Union in 2020 (for details on data, see the next section). The shares of WFH in 2019 and 2020, as well as the year-by-year change, are presented in Figure 1.1. In 2019, the share of people usually working from home ranged from 0.50% (Southwestern Region, Bulgaria) to 18.87% (Utrecht, the Netherlands), while in 2020 from 1.1% (Southern Central Region, Bulgaria) to 37.0% (Helsinki-Uusimaa, Finland). The largest increase

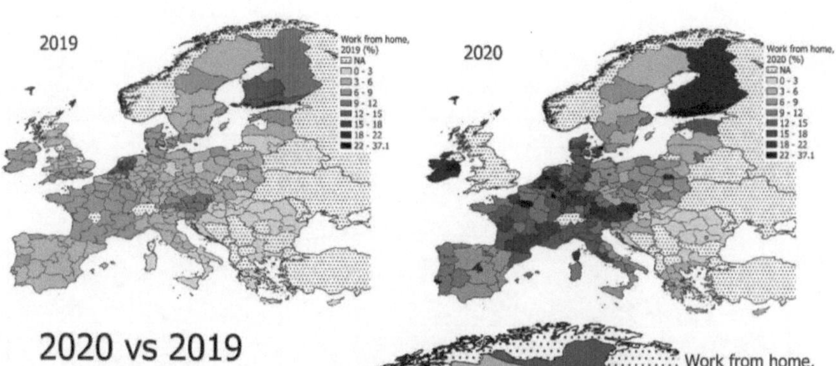

FIGURE 1.1 Work from home in the EU regions, 2019, 2020, and 2019–2020 change

Source: Own elaboration based on data from Eurostat (2021).

Note: Share of people usually working from home in employment aged 20–64 years. 'Usually working from home' is defined as 'doing at home any productive work related to the current job for at least half of the days worked in a reference period of four weeks.

in the share of the employed working usually from home was noticed in Brussels in Belgium (19.3pp), while it decreased the most in Zeeland in the Netherlands (−1.9pp).

Figure 1.2 presents the correlation between the share of work from home in 2019 and its change in 2020 (in pp). Two patterns can be observed. First, the share of work from home increased in a vast majority of the EU regions (216 out of 218 in the sample) in 2020. Second, the relationship between the 2019 share and the 2020 increase seems to be not monotonic – the 2020 change in WFH is increasing up to around the 10% level of WFH in 2019, while further increases were associated with smaller – though still positive – changes in 2020. Nevertheless, as most

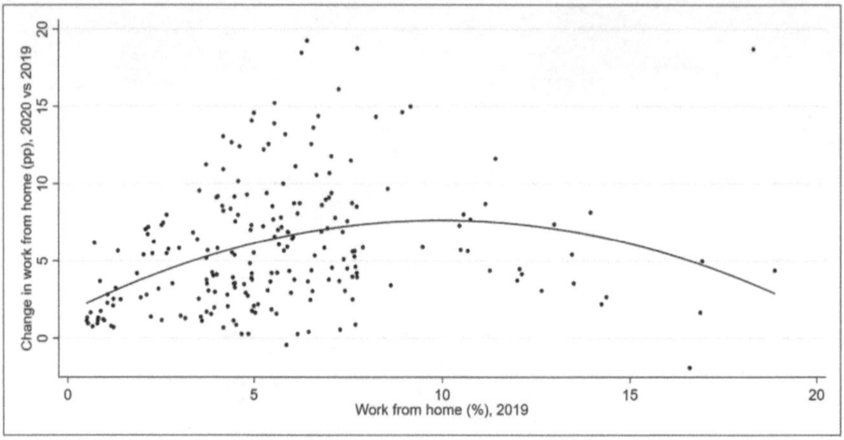

FIGURE 1.2 Work from home in the EU regions – correlation between the 2019 level and 2020 change

Source: Own elaboration based on Eurostat data.

EU regions (195 out of 218 in the sample) had the WFH indicator below 10% in 2019, the linear correlation between the 2019 level and 2020 change is significantly (at the 1% level) positive, with the correlation coefficient equal to 0.22 (0.40 when only regions with WFH <10% in 2019 are considered). This emphasises that the digital divide – as measured by the scale of work from home – deepened during the COVID-19 pandemic.

Data

In the next steps of our study, we investigate the factors explaining the scale of work from home in both 2019 and 2020, with a particular focus on the drivers of changes in the WFH indicator during the COVID-19 pandemic. Following the literature review on the digital divide, we will concentrate on a broad set of economic, infrastructure, demographic, educational, and COVID-19-related variables as potential determinants of the observed discrepancies.

The dataset includes 218 regions (NUTS 2 level) in the 27 European countries for which data on work from home is available in both 2019 and 2020. Work from home is calculated as a share of people usually working from home in employment aged 20–64 years. 'Usually working from home' is defined as 'doing at home any productive work related to the current job for at least half of the days worked in a reference period of four weeks' (Eurostat, 2021).

In the set of independent variables, we include the income level (measured as GDP per capita in PPP), the economic structure (based on the sectoral shares in total employment), infrastructure (share of the population with access to the Internet), demographic (population density, the share of the population aged 60+)

and educational factors (share of the population aged 25+ with tertiary education). All data at the NUTS 2 level were collected from Eurostat (2021). Due to the widespread effects of the COVID-19 pandemic, the independent variables are based on values from 2019 to avoid the problem of reverse causality. Additionally, the stringency index by Hale et al. (2021) was included in the analysis for 2020 to control for policies such as workplace closures and travel bans which could influence the scale of work from home during the pandemic. The dataset is summarised in Table 1.1.

TABLE 1.1 List of variables

Variable	*Description*	*N*	*Mean*	*SD*	*Min*	*Max*
WFH (2019)	Share (in %) of people usually working from home in employment aged 20–64 years.	218	5.68	3.41	0.50	18.87
WFH (2020)	'Usually working from home' is defined as 'doing at home any productive work related to the current job for at least half of the days worked in a reference period of four weeks'	218	11.51	5.86	1.41	37.01
WFH change (2020 vs 2019)	Change (in percentage point) in WFH calculated as a difference between WFH in 2020 and WFH in 2019	218	5.83	4.09	-1.91	19.26
GDP pc	Log of GDP per capita in EUR in PPP in 2019	218	10.22	0.52	8.88	11.53
	Share of NACE Rev. 2 main sections # in total employment aged 25–64 in 2019:					
Agriculture	A (agriculture, forestry, and fishing)	218	4.38	5.18	0.00	39.27
Manufacturing	B (mining and quarrying), C (manufacturing), D (electricity, gas, steam, and air-conditioning supply), E (water supply, sewerage, and waste management and remediation)	218	18.40	7.56	3.63	42.53
Construction	F (construction)	218	7.04	1.51	1.95	11.16
Trade, Transport & Accom.	G (wholesale and retail trade and repair of motor vehicles and motorcycles), H (transportation and storage), I (accommodation and food service activities)	218	23.35	5.05	15.10	54.70
Information & Commun.	J (information and communication)	218	2.79	1.87	0.00	10.55

(Continued)

TABLE 1.1 (Continued)

Variable	*Description*	*N*	*Mean*	*SD*	*Min*	*Max*
Finance & Insurance	K (financial and insurance activities)	218	2.50	1.43	0.00	12.11
Real Estate	L (real estate activities [excluding construction])	218	0.59	0.56	0.00	2.90
Profess., Scientific & Techn.	M (professional, scientific, and technical activities) and N (administrative and support service activities)	218	9.21	3.16	2.45	18.57
Administration	O (public administration and defence, compulsory social security), P (education), Q (human health and social work activities)	218	26.82	5.94	11.68	42.11
Arts, Entert. & Recr.	R (arts, entertainment, and recreation), S (other service activities), T (activities of households as employers; undifferentiated goods- and services-producing activities of households for own use), U (activities of extra-territorial organisations and bodies)	218	4.92	1.80	1.87	12.63
Internet Access below 80%	Dummy variable indicating that less than 80% of households have access to the Internet in 2019	218	0.08	0.28	0.00	1.00
Pop. density	Log of the population density in 2019	218	5.00	1.10	1.48	8.93
Tertiary education	Share of the population with tertiary education aged 25–64 in 2019	218	31.32	9.64	11.70	55.90
Aged 60+	Share of the population aged 60+ in the total population in 2019	218	26.92	3.27	17.40	36.70
Stringency index	The stringency index is a measure of the stringency of governmental responses to the COVID-19 pandemic, including school closures, workplace closures, and travel bans (values 0–100, when 100 is the strictest), average values in 2020	27	54.76	6.07	38.49	68.41

Source: Own elaboration.

Note: All data, except the *Stringency index* (Hale et al., 2021), were collected from Eurostat (2021). Aggregation of employment by NACE Rev. 2 main section is due to the availability of data at the NUTS 2 level from Eurostat. For details on the NACE Rev. 2 classification, see: https://ec.europa.eu/eurostat/documents/3859598/5902521/KS-RA-07-015-EN.PDF

TABLE 1.2 Correlation matrix

	WFH (2020)	*WFH (2019)*	*WFH change (2020 vs 2019)*
WFH (2020)	1		
WFH (2019)	0.7509*	1	
WFH change (2020 vs 2019)	0.8230*	0.2157*	1
GDP pc	0.7248*	0.4880*	0.6134*
Agriculture	−0.5053*	−0.3564*	−0.3728*
Manufacturing	−0.3287*	−0.2842*	−0.2713*
Construction	−0.2035*	−0.0959	−0.3260*
Trade, Transport & Accom.	−0.2598*	−0.3358*	−0.1109
Information and Commun.	0.5227*	0.2985*	0.4916*
Finance & Insurance	0.5935*	0.3659*	0.5585*
Real Estate	0.2665*	0.2984*	0.0919
Profess., Scientific & Techn.	0.6589*	0.4234*	0.5739*
Administration	0.3557*	0.5246*	0.1237
Arts, Entert. & Recr.	0.3481*	0.0754	0.3998*
Internet Access Below 80%	−0.3228*	−0.2899*	−0.1682
Pop. Density	0.4395*	0.1909*	0.5042*
Tertiary Education	0.5328*	0.4852*	0.3620*
Aged 60+	−0.1599	−0.1068	−0.1508
Stringency Index	−0.0072	−0.2706*	0.1892*

Source: Own elaboration.

Note: Asterisk denotes the 1% significance level.

Table 1.2 presents the correlations between the analysed variables. The largest positive correlations with the change in work from home in 2019–2020 were recorded for the income level (0.61), employment shares in finance and insurance (0.56), professional, scientific, and technical activities (0.57), and population density (0.50). *WFH change* was in turn negatively associated with the shares of agriculture (−0.37), manufacturing (−0.27), and construction (−0.33) in employment. The next section checks which of the analysed factors remain robust predictors of work from home when econometric tools considering the spatial nature of the data are employed.

Empirical strategy and results

Our study aims at identifying factors related to the scale of work from home in the EU regions and at investigating how the role of potential determinants of this phenomenon changed during the COVID-19 pandemic. Therefore, we estimate three sets of models – we focus on the years 2019 and 2020 separately, and on the 2019–2020 change in work from home. For the first two models, the levels of WFH in respective years are the dependent variables. For the latter, the change in WFH in 2019–2020 in percentage points is the dependent variable. The set of independent variables is as introduced in the previous section. In the models with the 2019–2020 change as a dependent variable, we also control for the level of WFH in 2019 and its quadratic term to capture a non-monotonic relationship as suggested in the correlation presented in Figure 1.2.

The spatial nature of our data and the fact that the EU regions are clustered within countries pose some methodological challenges. First, the EU countries might substantially differ in terms of their policies towards work from home or their steps to counteract the COVID-19 pandemic. This in turn might be a relevant factor shaping the scale of WFH and the omission of country fixed effects could lead to omitted variable bias. However, by including country FEs, a large part of the variation between the EU regions might be ruled out from the analysis, leading to less insightful findings on the independent variables of interest. Given the exploratory character of our study, we decided not to include country FEs in the basic specification and consider them in the robustness check only. Second, in the spatial analysis, unobserved heterogeneity might be correlated across adjacent units and by not considering this spatial correlation, one can obtain standard errors rejecting the null hypothesis too often (Colella et al., 2019). Therefore, standard errors in our analysis are calculated based on an estimator for the variance-covariance matrix and statistical package proposed by Colella et al. (2019). We also include latitude and longitude to control for linear spatial trends in our sample.

Table 1.3 presents the results of the econometric analysis. In Model 1, the WFH level in 2019 is considered and the scale of work from home was positively and significantly (at least at the 10% level) associated with the income level, employment shares of agriculture, finance and insurance, real estate, and administration (as compared to manufacturing) and share of people with tertiary education. In turn, employment in the information and communication sector was negatively correlated with the *WFH* variable in 2019. WFH in 2020 is included in Model 2 and it can be observed that – apart from the changes in the magnitudes of coefficients which we discuss below – the coefficient by the information and communication sector is no longer significant, while the population density turned out to be significantly (at the 10% level) and positively linked to the scale of work from home in 2020. Finally, the change in WFH in 2019–2020 is analysed in Model 3. The results show that the relationship between the increase in work from home and the level in 2019 is non-monotonic even when controlling for a broad set of factors potentially influencing the scale of WFH, with the increasing function in the range of 0–8% of WFH in 2019 (i.e., the level of 8% of WFH in 2019 was associated with the largest [2.56 pp] increases in WFH in 2020). The income level, population density, and more strict policies against COVID-19 were significantly (at least at the 5% level) and positively related to the change in WFH. Concerning the economic structure, larger employment shares in agriculture, finance and insurance, arts, entertainment, and recreation were significantly associated with the larger increases in WFH in 2020, while for real estate this relationship was negative.[2]

TABLE 1.3 Regression results

Specification	*Basic*			*Country FE*		
Model #	(1)	(2)	(3)	(4)	(5)	(6)
Dep. variable	*WFH (2019)*	*WFH (2020)*	*WFH change (2020 vs 2019)*	*WFH (2019)*	*WFH (2020)*	*WFH change (2020 vs 2019)*
GDP pc	2.537**	6.073***	2.743***	0.306	2.728***	2.544***
	(1.270)	(1.433)	(0.931)	(0.510)	(1.01)	(0.913)
Manufacturing	ref.	ref.	ref.	ref.	ref.	ref.
Agriculture	0.094*	0.187***	0.092**	0.029	0.017	−0.003
	(0.049)	(0.061)	(0.045)	(0.024)	(0.039)	(0.037)
Construction	0.060	−0.085	−0.110	0.106	−0.104	−0.174
	(0.198)	(0.252)	(0.160)	(0.070)	(0.186)	(0.194)
Trade, Transport &Accom.	−0.006	−0.003	0.024	0.043*	−0.097	−0.126**
	(0.048)	(0.068)	(0.053)	(0.023)	(0.061)	(0.053)
Information & Commun.	−0.371*	−0.122	0.293	0.249**	0.674**	0.508**
	(0.224)	(0.405)	(0.319)	(0.126)	(0.273)	(0.226)
Finance & Insurance	0.337*	0.955**	0.612**	0.221**	0.803***	0.656***
	(0.179)	(0.371)	(0.245)	(0.090)	(0.163)	(0.145)
Real Estate	0.685**	−0.271	−1.018**	0.238	0.192	0.029
	(0.345)	(0.483)	(0.430)	(0.200)	(0.431)	(0.450)
Profess., Scientific & Techn.	0.117	0.224	0.029	−0.224***	0.040	0.190
	(0.202)	(0.187)	(0.183)	(0.059)	(0.163)	(0.156)
Administration	0.149***	0.156***	0.010	−0.018	−0.023	−0.011
	(0.045)	(0.059)	(0.049)	(0.026)	(0.070)	(0.066)
Arts, Entert. & Recr.	−0.189	0.321	0.405*	0.039	0.410**	0.384**
	(0.246)	(0.309)	(0.246)	(0.041)	(0.168)	(0.170)

(*Continued*)

TABLE 1.3 (Continued)

Specification	*Basic*			*Country FE*		
Model #	(1)	(2)	(3)	(4)	(5)	(6)
Dep. variable	*WFH (2019)*	*WFH (2020)*	*WFH change (2020 vs 2019)*	*WFH (2019)*	*WFH (2020)*	*WFH change (2020 vs 2019)*
Internet Access Below 80%	−0.139	0.369	1.008	−0.298	−0.014	0.177
	(0.529)	(0.956)	(0.622)	(0.268)	(0.612)	(0.549)
Pop. Density	0.210	0.862*	0.824**	−0.042	0.162	0.192
	(0.240)	(0.493)	(0.345)	(0.117)	(0.335)	(0.336)
Tertiary Education	0.056*	0.011	−0.000	0.062*	−0.048	−0.090
	(0.032)	(0.062)	(0.051)	(0.036)	(0.070)	(0.075)
Aged 60+	−0.005	0.042	−0.011	0.018	−0.123	−0.134
	(0.072)	(0.125)	(0.090)	(0.034)	(0.094)	(0.087)
WFH			0.656**			−0.362
			(0.286)			(0.324)
WFH2			−0.042*			0.002
			(0.025)			(0.019)
Stringency index		−0.040	0.128**			
		(0.100)	(0.057)			
Country FE						
Latitude, Longitude, Intercept						
Observations	218	218	218	218	218	218
R-squared	0.494	0.655	0.571	0.924	0.899	0.815

Source: Own elaboration.

Note: Conley (1999) standard errors are reported in parentheses (calculated with *acreg* package by Colella et al., 2019). Asterisks denote significance levels: *** – 1%, ** – 5%, * – 10%. A list of variables is described in Table 1.1.

To assess the economic importance of independent variables included in the analysis, we recalculated our models with the variables after standardisation. Figure 1.3 presents the standardised coefficients from Models 1–3 along with their 95% confidence bands, which allows checking how much the dependent variable changes due to a one-standard deviation change in the independent variable. Our focus is now primarily on factors explaining the change in 2020 (coefficients presented by black triangles in Figure 1.3). It turned out that the income level (standardised coefficient = 0.28), the employment share of finance and insurance (0.25), and population density (0.23) were the best predictors of the change in the scale of work from home in 2020 among the EU regions, with the higher levels of these variables associated with larger increases in WFH. These variables were followed by the stringency index (0.19) and employment share of agriculture (0.18).

In the next step, we check if the obtained results are robust to the inclusion of country fixed effects (Models 4–6 in Table 1.3). The income level, employment shares in information and communication, finance and insurance, and arts,

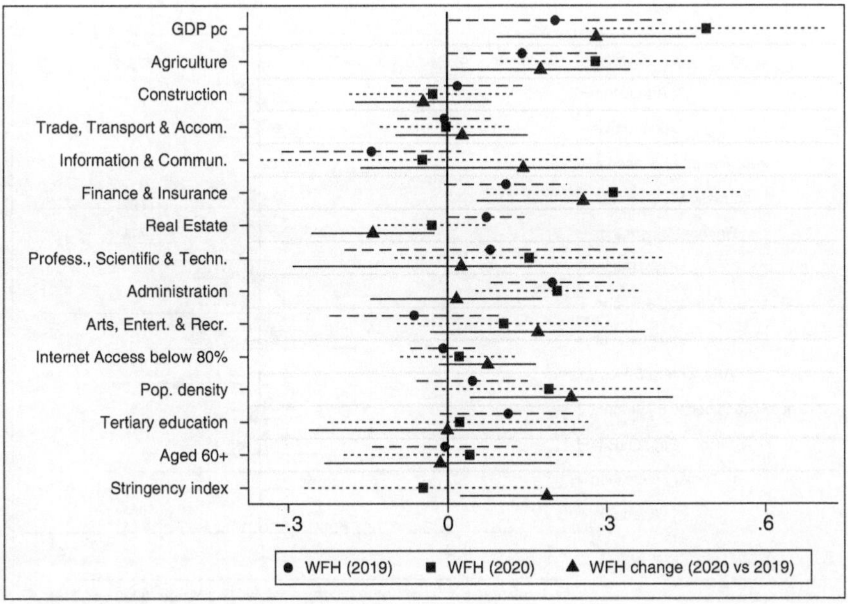

FIGURE 1.3 Regression results, standardised coefficients – basic specification, no country fixed effects

Source: Own elaboration.

Note: The figure presents the standardised coefficients from Models 1–3 in Table 10.3. The legend presents the dependent variables. Lines show 95% confidence intervals. Both dependent and independent variables were standardised. Models control for latitude and longitude (all models), and for the level of WFH and its quadratic term in 2019 in the analysis with *WFH change (2020 vs 2019)* as a dependent variable. Confidence intervals are based on Conley (1999) standard errors (calculated with the acreg package by Colella et al., 2019). A list of variables is described in Table 1.1.

entertainment, and recreation were positively and significantly associated with the WFH increase in 2020 when only the within-country variation was employed. Trade, transport, and accommodation employment were in turn negatively linked with the change in WFH in 2019–2020. Standardised coefficients for regression with country FEs are shown in Figure 1.4. Employment shares in finance and insurance (standardised coef. = 0.28) and information and communication (0.25) and income level (0.26) turned out to be the best predictors of the change in WFH when country fixed effects were considered.

Our results lead to three main indications. First, the relationship between the level of work from home in 2019 and the increase in 2020 was non-monotonic, though higher 2019 levels were associated with larger 2020 increases for a majority of the sample. Second, stricter COVID-19-related policies were associated with larger increases in WFH in 2020. Third, the income level and employment share of finance and insurance were the most relevant and robust predictors of the increase in the scale of work from home in 2020. The higher values of these variables in 2019 led to larger 2020 increases. What is important, these variables were positively

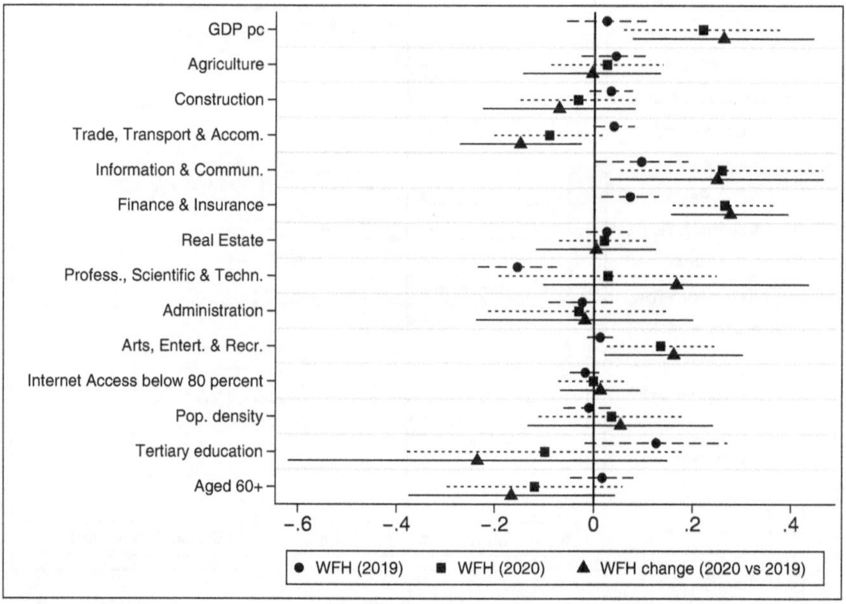

FIGURE 1.4 Regression results, standardised coefficients – country fixed effects included

Source: Own elaboration.

Note: The figure presents the standardised coefficients from Models 4–6. The legend presents the dependent variables. Lines show 95% confidence bands. Both dependent and independent variables were standardised. Models control for latitude, longitude, and country fixed effects (all models), and for the level of WFH and its quadratic term in 2019 in the analysis with *WFH change (2020 vs 2019)* as a dependent variable. Confidence intervals are based on Conley (1999) standard errors (calculated with the acreg package by Colella et al., 2019). A list of variables is described in Table 1.1.

correlated with the WFH indicator already in 2019 which shows that differences in the income level and the share of the finance and insurance sectors can be considered as the drivers of deepening the digital divide during the COVID-19 pandemic.

Our findings are in line with previous studies emphasising the importance of the economic structure in shaping the ability of people to work from home. Specifically, a positive relationship between employment in finance and insurance and WFH was also indicated for the US economy (US Census, 2021). The similar conclusions were presented in the report by the International Labour Organization (ILO), in which the role of manufacturing – which was a reference sector in our analysis – as a non-teleworkable sector was also underlined. The analysis in our paper showed that the income level was a robust predictor of the change in the scale of work from home. This is in line with micro-level studies pointing out that individuals with higher earnings are more capable to do a large proportion of their tasks from home (Adams-Prassl et al., 2020; Cetrulo et al., 2020; Sostero et al., 2020) and that regions with lower incomes were less likely to turn towards WFH (Dingel & Neiman, 2020; Garrote Sanchez et al., 2020; Hensvik et al., 2020).

Our study shows also that the infrastructure – namely, access to the Internet – is not a relevant factor in explaining the heterogeneity in the scale of work from home in the EU regions. This indication is likely to be driven by the fact that at least 80% of households had access to the Internet in 92% of the EU regions in 2019. Demographic (share of the population aged 60+) and educational (share of people with tertiary education) factors also turned out to be insignificantly related to the changes in the scale of WFH during the COVID-19 pandemic once the income level and economic structure are controlled for. These findings are not in line with the studies of Barrero et al. (2022), which shows in the periodically conducted survey that the shift to WFH brings large benefits but is disproportionately enjoyed by men and highly educated American employees.

Conclusion

Digitalisation is a double-edged sword: It can either exacerbate or stem the innovation divide, depending on the type of technologies deployed. Although the COVID-19 pandemic highlighted the feasibility of remote working in many occupations, the ability to go remote is not universal to all types of jobs and regions. This chapter addressed the changes in the scale of work from home during the COVID-19 pandemic concerning the pre-existing inequalities in access to ICTs, differences in the economic structure, demographics, and education in the regions of the EU. Our findings confirm the intuition that the well-developed regions benefit more from the development of remote work arrangements.

We presented strong evidence that regions with higher levels of WFH before the pandemic had larger increases in remote working arrangements in 2020. Remote working did not emerge during the pandemic. The prior decade saw modest adoption of remote working in a number of firms, particularly in tech and consulting, to provide more flexibility for their employees (Vargas-Llave et al., 2020; Eurofound & ILO, 2017; OECD, 2020). In the pre-COVID time, it was, however, common for firms to have no remote employees or restrict remote work altogether, with a relatively small percentage of the workforce working remotely full-time. The pandemic forced employers to adopt remote work more broadly, which was undoubtedly easier in sectors, industries, and regions with strong tech adoption.

Moreover, stricter COVID-19-related policies were associated with larger increases in WFH in 2020. With the severe, country-specific impact that the COVID-19 emergency, and the associated economic costs, had on areas in the southwest of the EU27, the regional disparities in terms of implementing remote work have deepened even more (Capello & Caragilu, 2021). This phenomenon is also related to the regions with higher population density, where the potential of jobs that can be done remotely is most significant. For example, it is estimated that in America's densest cities, around 45% of local jobs have the potential to be done remotely, corresponding to about 65% of the local payrolls (Althoff et al., 2022).

Finally, the higher income level associated with higher regional development and innovativeness was the most relevant and robust predictor of the increase in the scale of work from home in 2020. It means that well-developed regions were capable to exploit faster the new opportunities and focal technologies of remote work. While trends towards remote work may represent a promising avenue to reduce disparities of regional development by reducing the out-migration of workers from these areas, in the short run the regional technological disparities may deepen the income inequalities and result in compromising the sustainable long-run growth. For instance, Paas and Vahi (2012) showed that a large portion of GDP variability in EU regions is explained by the composite indicators of regional innovation performance. As such, some regions may benefit unequally from the increasing trend of using remote work.

A possible limitation of the analyses carried out with the pandemic still going on is that the economic impacts of further restrictions, in their turn due to the reprisal of pandemic waves, could have been underestimated, and may change the path of technological transformation between regions in the future. There is local multiplication of structural change in otherwise unaffected sectors with the further decrease in income. At this stage, we recognise that for regions falling behind, it is commendable to support firms to improve their existing product and service propositions. In the long run, however, there are three types of process technologies that are driven by the use of data and can be applied to a range of sectors increasing their capabilities for facing the challenges and changing their product propositions. It includes – the transactional technologies that better match supply and demand to facilitate market transactions by lowering information asymmetries (digital e-commerce platforms and blockchain); informational technologies that exploit the exponential growth of data and the reduced cost of computing (business management software, cloud computing, big data analytics, and machine learning); and operational technologies that combine data with physical automation to reduce production costs, including labour, materials and, in many cases, energy;

examples include smart robots, 3D printing, and the Internet of Things (IoT) (World Bank, 2020).

Therefore, there are several avenues for further research. So far, the findings presented in this chapter are short term. Further analysis is to reveal how the development of working from home is to be differentiated in the long term and to regional specificities such as the existing state of institutional arrangements (e.g., labour policy, social security, and development strategy), different varieties in the (inter)national institutions at higher special scales, and the changing sectoral composition (due to the pandemic). The potential variables of interest are countless: the appropriate infrastructure to support remote work, regulations, education, development of digital skills, implementation of the new digital technologies, etc.

The recovery from the COVID-19 pandemic presents a unique opportunity to drive deeper digitalisation for productivity and convergence in EU regions. Looking ahead, to bridge the innovation divide between regions, smaller firms and lagging regions must concentrate more on the absorption of new digital technologies. As the World Bank argues: the COVID-19 pandemic has highlighted the importance of the data economy. Companies that have embraced digital technologies are better able to cope with the disruptions posed by the pandemic.

> Europe has converged in digital infrastructure, but more needs to be done to accelerate the commercial use of digital technologies. Europe has done well in expanding access to broadband. At least 69 percent of households have access to broadband in every European region, and over 90 percent of households are fully connected in most regions. But convergence between regions in the use of digital services has been slow.
>
> *(World Bank, 2020)*

Transactional technologies have the maximum potential to promote market inclusion and geographic convergence. In these digital services, there is a lot of space for remote working arrangement development.

Acknowledgements

Beata Woźniak-Jęchorek acknowledges the support from the National Agency for Academic Exchange in Poland under the 1-year Bekker scholarship at Northwestern University in the United States.

Piotr Matuszak acknowledges the support from the National Science Center Poland under the ETIUDA 8 Programme (2020/36/T/HS4/00048).

Notes

1 The terms 'remote work', 'teleworking', and 'working from home' each relate to the spatial distribution of work. These concepts are interrelated and, inevitably, have some degree of overlap. According to Eurofound, telework and ICT-based mobile work

(TICTM) is a work arrangement characterised by working from more than one place (not necessarily from home) and is enabled by ICT. It can be performed by both dependent and independent workers (Eurofound, 2020). Teleworking may include various locations away from the primary worksite or the employer's premises (such as mobile working) (Messenger, 2019), and may not always be substitute for commuting.

2 A positive relationship between the scale of work from home and employment in agriculture might be perceived as surprising. Nevertheless, there might be at least two reasons for such an association. First, as indicated by Redmond and McGuinness (2020) for Ireland, a large part of employment in the agriculture sector in developed regions is in occupations that are not directly related to the field work, such as managers or sales. Second, in the less-developed regions, a substantial share of employment is in subsistence agriculture based on fields near home which might allow classifying this as work from home (Gottlieb et al., 2020; Garrote Sanchez et al., 2020).

However, this relationship is not robust to the inclusion of country fixed effects (see Table 1.3) and, therefore, might be driven by country-specific characteristics which are not controlled for in the basic specification.

References

Acemoglu, D., Johnson, S., & Robinson, J. (2006). Understanding prosperity and poverty: Geography, institutions, and the reversal of fortune. In A. V. Banerjee, R. Bénabou, & D. Mookherjee (Eds.), *Understanding poverty*. Oxford University Press.

Adams-Prassl, A., Boneva, T., Golin, M., & Rauh, Ch. (2020). *The large and unequal impact of COVID-19 on workers*. VOX EU, CEPR. https://voxeu.org/article/large-and-unequal-impact-covid-19-workers

Adkins, D., & Sandy, H. M. (2020). Information behavior and ICT use of Latina immigrants to the US Midwest. *Information Processing & Management, 57*(3).

Althoff, L., Eckert, F., Ganapati, S., & Walsh, C. (2022). The geography of remote work. (*NBER Working Paper* 29181). www.nber.org/system/files/working_papers/w29181/w29181.pdf

Arie, Y., & Mesch, G. S. (2016). The spatial and social network dimensions of mobile communication: A test of the social stratification and social diversification hypotheses. *Communication Research, 43*(5), 713–734.

Barrero, J. M., Bloom, N., & Davis, S. J. (2022). *The work-from-home outlook in 2022 and beyond*. https://wfhresearch.com/wp-content/uploads/2022/01/Barrero-AEA-NABE-Jan22.pdf

Capello, R., & Caragilu, A. (2021). Regional growth and disparities in a post-COVID Europe: A new normality scenario. *Journal of Regional Science*, Wiley, *61*, 710–727.

Cetrulo, A., Guarascio, D., & Virgillito, M. E. (2020). The privilege of working from home at the time of social distancing. *Interconomics, 55*, 142–147.

Choudrie, J., Weerakkody, V., & Jones, S. (2005). Realising e-government in the UK: Rural and urban challenges. *Journal of Enterprise Information Management, 18*(5), 568–585.

Colella, F., Lalive, R., Sakalli, S. O., & Thoenig, M. (2019). Inference with arbitrary clustering. (*IZA Discussion Paper* 12584). IZA Institute of Labor Economics. https://docs.iza.org/dp12584.pdf

Conley, T. G. (1999). GMM estimation with cross sectional dependence. *Journal of Econometrics, 99*(1), 1–45.

Dingel, J., & Neiman, B. (2020). How many jobs can be done at home? *Journal of Public Economics, 189*. https://doi.org/10.1016/j.jpubeco.2020.104235

Dobransky, K., & Hargittai, E. (2016). Unrealized potential: Exploring the digital disability divide. *Poetics, 58*, 18–28.

Elragal, A., Haddara, M., & Hustad, E. (2020). Rejuvenating enterprise systems. *Scandinavian Journal of Information Systems, 32*(2), 127–138.

Eurofound. (2020). *Telework and ICT-based mobile work: Flexible working in the digital age, New forms of employment series*. Publications Office of the European Union.

Eurofound and ILO. (2017). *Working anytime, anywhere: The effect on the world of work*. www.eurofound.europa.eu/publications/report/2017/working-anytime-anywhere-the-effects-on-the-world-of-work

Eurostat. (2021). *Eurostat database*. Retrieved March 15, 2022, from https://ec.europa.eu/eurostat/data/database

Facebook. (2016). *State of connectivity 2015: A report on global internet access*. https://about.fb.com/news/2016/02/state-of-connectivity-2015-a-report-on-global-internet-access/

Garrote Sanchez, D., Gomez Parra, N., Ozden, C., Rijkers, B., Viollaz, M., & Winkler, H. (2020). Who on earth can work from home? (*Policy Research Working Paper* 9347). World Bank. https://openknowledge.worldbank.org/handle/10986/34277

Gottlieb, Ch., Grobovsek, J., & Poschke, M. (2020). Working from home across countries. *CIREQ Cahier 07–2020*. https://cireqmontreal.com/wp-content/uploads/cahiers/07-2020-cah.pdf

Graham, M. (2011). Time machines and virtual portals: The spatialities of the digital divide. *Progress in Development Studies, 11*(3), 211–227. https://doi.org/10.1177/146499341001100303

Hadidi, R., & Power, D. (2020). Technology adaption and disruption – organizational implications for the future of work. *Journal of the Midwest Association for Information Systems, 1*, 1.

Hale, T., Angrist, N., Goldszmidt, R., Kira, B., Petherick, A., Phillips, T., Webster, S., Cameron-Blake, E., Hallas, L., Majumdar, S., & Tatlow, H. (2021). A global panel database of pandemic policies (Oxford COVID-19 Government Response Tracker). *Nature Human Behaviour*. https://doi.org/10.1038/s41562-021-01079-8

Hargittai, E., Piper, A. M., & Morris, M. R. (2019). From internet access to internet skills: Digital inequality among older adults. *Universal Access in the Information Society, 18*(4), 881–890.

Hassler, B., & Jackson, A. M. (2010). Bridging the bandwidth gap: Open educational resources and the digital divide. *IEEE Transactions on Learning Technologies, 3*(2), 110–115.

Helbig, N., Gil-Garcia, J. R., & Ferro, E. (2009). Understanding the complexity of electronic government. Implications from the digital divide literature. *Government Information Quarterly, 26*(1), 89–97.

Helsper, E. J. (2012). A corresponding fields model for the links between social and digital exclusion. *Communication Theory, 22*(4), 403–426.

Helsper, E. J., & Reisdorf, B. C. (2017). The emergence of a "digital underclass" in Great Britain and Sweden: Changing reasons for digital exclusion. *New Media & Society, 19*(8), 1253–1270.

Hensvik, L., Le Barbanchon, T., & Rathelot, R. (2020). Which jobs are done from home? Evidence from the American time use survey. (*IZA Discussion Paper* 13138). | IZA – Institute of Labor Economics. www.iza.org/publications/dp/13138

Hohlfied, T. N., Ritzhaupt, A. D., & Barron, A. E. (2010). Connecting schools, community, and family with ICT: Four-year trends related to school level and SES of public schools in Florida. *Computers & Education, 55*(1), 391–405.

Hunsaker, A., & Hargittai, E. (2018). A review of internet use among older adults. *New Media & Society, 20*(10), 3937–3954.

International Labour Organization (ILO). (2020a). *An employers' guide on working from home in response to the outbreak of COVID-19*. www.ilo.org/wcmsp5/groups/public/ – ed_dialogue/ – act_emp/documents/publication/wcms_745024.pdf

International Labour Organization (ILO). (2020b). *ILO monitor: COVID-19 and the world of work* (3rd ed.). www.ilo.org/wcmsp5/groups/public/@dgreports/@dcomm/documents/briefingnote/wcms_743146.pdf

Jacks, T. (2021). Research on remote work in the era of COVID-19. *Journal of Global Information Technology Management, 24*(2), 93–97.

Keane, J. (2000). Structural transformations of the public sphere. *The Communication Review, 1*(1), 1–22.

Lai, J., & Widmar, N. O. (2020). Revisiting the digital divide in the COVID-19 Era. *Applied Economic Perspectives and Policy*. https://doi.org/10.1002/aepp.13104

Lissitsa, S., & Chachashvili-Bolotin, S. (2015). Does the wind of change blow in late adulthood? Adoption of ICT by senior citizens during the past decade. *Poetics, 52*, 44–63.

Lissitsa, S., & Chachashvili-Bolotin, S. (2022). Socioeconomic or marital status? Factors driving digital inequality among single and married mothers – findings of a repeated cross-sectional study, 2014–2019. *Poetics*. https://doi.org/10.1016/j.poetic.2022.101666

Lissitsa, S., Zychlinski, E., & Kagan, M. (2022). The silent generation vs baby boomers: Socio-demographic and psychological predictors of the "gray" digital inequalities. *Computers in Human Behavior, 128*.

Mason, S. M., & Hacker, K. L. (2003). Applying communication theory to digital divide research. *IT&Society, 1*(5), 40–55.

McSorley, K. (2003). The secular salvation story of the digital divide. *Ethics and Information Technology, 5*(2), 75–87.

Mesch, G., Mano, R., & Tsamir, J. (2012). Minority status and health information search: A test of the social diversification hypothesis. *Social Science & Medicine, 75*(5), 854–858.

Messenger, J. C. (Ed.). (2019). *Telework in the 21st century: An evolutionary perspective*. The ILO Future of Work, Edward Elgar, ILO.

Middleton, K. L., & Chambers, V. (2010). Approaching digital equity: Is Wi-Fi the new leveler? *Information Technology & People, 23*(1), 4–22.

Milioni, D. L., Doudaki, V., & Demertzis, N. (2014). Youth, ethnicity, and a 'reverse digital divide' a study of internet use in a divided country. *Convergence, 20*(3), 316–336.

Norris, P. (2001). *Digital divide: Civic engagement, information poverty, and the Internet worldwide*. Cambridge University Press.

NTIA. (1999). *Falling through the NET III: Defining the digital divide*. U.S. Department of Commerce.

Ocasio, W., Mauskapf, M., & Steel, C. J. (2016). History, society, and institutions: The role of collective memory in the emergence and evolution of societal logics. *Academy of Management Review, 41*(4), 676–699.

Organisation for Economic Co-operation and Development (OECD). (2001). *Understanding the Digital Divide*. OECD.

Organisation for Economic Co-operation and Development (OECD). (2020). *Keeping the internet up and running in times of crisis, OECD Policy Responses to Coronavirus (COVID-19)*. www.oecd.org/coronavirus/policy-responses/keeping-the-internet-up-and-running-in-times-of-crisis-4017c4c9/.

Paas, T., & Vahi, T. (2012). *Regional disparities and innovations in Europe* [Paper presentation]. 52nd Congress of the European Regional Science Association: "Regions in Motion – Breaking the Path", 21–25 August 2012, Bratislava, Slovakia, European Regional Science

Association (ERSA), Louvain-la-Neuve. www.econstor.eu/bitstream/10419/120468/1/ERSA2012_0080.pdf

Pennington, A., & Stanford, J. (2020). *Briefing paper: Working from home: Opportunities and risks*. Centre for Future Work. www.futurework.org.au/working_from_home_in_a_pandemic_opportunities_and_risks

Philip, L., Cottrill, C., Farrington, J., Williams, E., & Ashmore, F. (2017). The digital divide: Patterns, policy and scenarios for connecting the 'final few' in rural communities across Great Britain. *Journal of Rural Studies*, *54*, 386–398.

Rai, A. (2020). The COVID-19 pandemic: Building resilience with IS research. *Management Information Systems Quarterly*, *44*(2).

Ramani, A., & Bloom, N. (2021). The donut effect of COVID-19 on cities. (*National Bureau of Economic Research Working Paper* 28876). NBER. www.nber.org/papers/w28876.

Redmond, P., & McGuinness, S. (2020). Who can work from home in Ireland? *ESRI Survey and Statistical Report Series*, No. 87. www.esri.ie/system/files/publications/SUSTAT87.pdf

Rodriguez-Pose, A. (2013). Do institutions matter for regional development. *Regional Studies*, *47*(7), 1034–1047.

Rogers, E. M. (2003). *Diffusion of innovations* (5th ed.). Free Press.

Rooksby, E., Weckert, J., & Lucas, R. (2002). The rural digital divide. *Rural Society*, *12*(3), 197–209.

Rosenberg, D., Mano, R., & Mesch, G. S. (2021). Ethnic origin and health participation on social media: A test and an extension of social diversification hypothesis. *Journal of Communication in Healthcare*, 1–10.

Samek Lodovici, M. (Ed.). (2021). *The impact of teleworking and digital work on workers and society. Special focus on surveillance and monitoring, as well as on mental health of workers*. European Parliament.

Shenglin, B., Simonelli, F., Ruidong, Z., Bosc, R., & Wenwei, L. (2017). *Digital infrastructure: Overcoming the digital divide in emerging economies*. G20 Germany 2017, Think 20 Dialogue.

Sostero, M., Milasi, S., Hurley, J., Fernandex-Macias, E., & Bisello, M. (2020). Teleworkability and the COVID-19 crisis: A new digital divide? (*JRC Working Papers Series on Labour, Education, and Technology*). Eurofound. https://joint-research-centre.ec.europa.eu/system/files/2020-07/jrc121193.pdf

Srinuan, Ch., & Bohlin, E. (2011). Understanding the digital divide: A literature survey and ways forward. (*Working Paper*). https://ideas.repec.org/p/zbw/itse11/52191.html

Struzak, R. (2010). Broadband Internet in EU countries – limits to growth. *IEEE Communication Magazine*, 52–57.

Thornton, P. H., Ocasio, W., & Lounsbury, M. (2012). *The institutional logics perspective: A new approach to culture, structure, and process*. Oxford University Press.

US Census. (2021). *Remote working, commuting time, life events all affect home Buyers' decisions*. www.census.gov/library/stories/2021/10/zillow-and-census-bureau-data-show-pandemics-impact-on-housing-market.html

Van Dijk, J. (2000). Widening information gaps and policies of prevention. In K. Hackers & J. van Dijk (Eds.), *Digital democracy: Issue of theory and practice* (pp. 166–183). Sage Publications.

Van Dijk, J. (2002). A framework for digital divide research. *The Electronic Journal of Communication*, *12*(1), 1–6.

Van Dijk, J. (2006). Digital divide research, achievements, and shortcomings. *Poetics*, *34*(4–5), 221–235.

Van Dijk, J., & Hacker, K. (2003). The digital divide as a complex and dynamic phenomenon. *The Information Society*, *19*(4), 315–326.

Vargas-Llave, O., Mandl, I., Weber, T., & Wilens, M. (2020). *Telework and ICT-based mobile work: Flexible working in the digital age*. Eurofound. www.eurofound.europa.eu/publications/report/2020/telework-and-ict-based-mobile-work-flexible-working-in-the-digital-age

Vermeulen, B., & Psenner, E. (2022). Exploiting the technology-driven structural shift to creative work in regional catching-up: Toward an institutional framework. *European Planning Studies*. https://doi.org/10.1080/09654313.2022.2028737

World Bank. (2020). *Europe 4.0: Addressing Europe's digital dilemma*. www.worldbank.org/en/region/eca/publication/addressing-europes-digital-dilemma

Woźniak-Jęchorek, B., Sahar d'Urso, A., & Thurston, Ch. N. (2022). Remote work preferences of American employees: evidence from conjoint survey experiment. (*Working Paper*).

Yoon, H., Jang, Y., Vaughan, P. W., & Garcia, M. (2020). Older adults' internet use for health information: Digital divide by race/ethnicity and socioeconomic status. *Journal of Applied Gerontology*, *39*(1), 105–110.

2

THE CORONA-INDUCTED SHIFT TOWARDS INTERMEDIATE DIGITAL SKILLS ACROSS OCCUPATIONS IN SLOVAKIA

Brian Fabo

Introduction

The COVID-19 pandemic represents a major shock for economies and societies. Several high-profile papers have been published discussing the applications for various economic and social dimensions (see Maital & Barzani, 2020 for an overview). Even though the impact of the pandemic was present everywhere, the scale of the disruption varied greatly. As a result, a large body of the COVID-impact literature has been focused on individual country studies, reflecting the local specificities (e.g., Singh & Misra, 2020 for India; or Lyu & Wehby, 2020 for the United States). Slovakia specifically was among the most affected countries (having lost 0.8% of the country's population to the disease according to the John Hopkins University of Medicine data) and went through a series of draconic lockdowns and even mass population testing exercises (Pavelka et al., 2021). A number of studies have been published on various aspects of the pandemic's impact on the Slovakian economy (Klimovský et al., 2021; Nemec, 2020; Nemec & Špaček, 2020).

The impact of the pandemic on skills demand has been a major topic for scholars around the world. According to some evidence, there has been a reallocation of labour from the most affected industries such as retail or hospitality to other sectors, such as healthcare or the information and communication technology (ICT) sector, where productivity is generally higher and workers are likely to pick up highly-valued, marketable skills (Bauer et al., 2021). Meanwhile, other evidence suggests that companies cut on hiring for high-skill jobs more than for low-skill jobs (Campello et al., 2020), perhaps as a result of moot growth prospects, which could be associated with stalled skill growth for workers. When it comes to specific skills, an OECD study identified a change in skills requirements, with the demand of skills relevant for working from home experiencing a sharp increase (OECD, 2021). As far as I am aware, no such study has been produced for Slovakia, which

DOI: 10.4324/9781003326779-4

leads to an important research gap that needs to be closed to fully evaluate the structural impact of the pandemic on the Slovak economy.

In this chapter, I attempt to contribute to bridging the gap in understanding of skills demand impact of the pandemic by examining the change in demand for digital skills using a complete database of nearly half a million job vacancies posted on the website *Profesia.sk* in 2020 and 2021. Specifically, I am exploring whether there has been a noticeable increase in the demand for digital skills, in particular the ones relevant to working from home.

Methodologically, I am building upon the already substantial and ever-expanding body of publications using online job vacancies to analyse skill demand in the labour market (Acemoglu et al., 2020; OECD, 2021; van Loo & Pouliakas, 2020; Winzenried, 2020) and specifically on changes of skills demand caused by the COVID-19 pandemic (Campos-Vazquez et al., 2021; Fang et al., 2020; Hensvik et al., 2021; Kahn et al., 2020). More precisely, my contribution is similar to papers examining the demand for specific skills (Beblavý, Kureková, et al., 2016; Drahokoupil & Fabo, 2022; Fabo et al., 2017; Fabo & Kahanec, 2020; Kureková et al., 2016).

The motivation behind my analysis is that the mobility restrictions associated with the pandemic have greatly accelerated the pre-existing trends of digitalisation of societies and economies around the world (Stiglitz et al., 2020). Yet, not everybody belongs to the educated strata that could easily switch to Zoom meetings and Virtual Private Network (VPN) connection as their workstations. In particular, the blue-collar workers had to keep on going to work despite the pandemic. In consequence, some speak of the new 'digital divide' between those who are able to work remotely and those who are not (Sostero et al., 2020). Countries with highly digital, innovative economies have a stronger potential to switch to working from home than more traditional, industrialised countries, like Slovakia, where the potential is more limited. (Kucserová Jurášeková, 2021). For this reason, I consider it beneficial to complement the existing body of research based on data from elsewhere with a look at the specific situation of Slovakia embedded within a book containing insights from other countries in the region.

The data scope allows me to slice the dataset among several dimensions beyond the standard occupation-industry matrix. Specifically, I am able to take a look specifically at the breakdown per education requirements, company size, and region or education requirement.

In general, I find a spike in demand for relevant digital skills that chronologically aligns with the outbreak of the pandemic in Europe and the introduction of mobility restrictions. This effect, however, cannot be seen everywhere across the entire labour market but varies based on factors such as industry or occupation.

The rest of the chapter is organised as follows. First, a short discussion of the generalisability and reliability issues of the data used is presented with references to the relevant literature. This is followed by a presentation of the dataset and the analytical strategy utilised in this chapter. The third part of the chapter contains the presentation and discussion of the results. The final section concludes.

Data and analytical strategy

The data set contains the full sample of job vacancies that were published on the website *Profesia.sk* between January 2020 and December 2021 (see Drahokoupil & Fabo, 2022 for the detailed description of the dataset and variables). *Profesia.sk* is the dominant actor in the Slovak employment portal market by a substantial margin, which is important for the generalisability of the analysis. Labour market analysis on the basis of data from the dominant job vacancies portal in the country is a widely adopted approach in the literature (Bilal et al., 2017; Marinescu, 2017; Nomura et al., 2017; Turrell et al., 2021).

A large body of literature is concerned with the representativeness of online job vacancies as a data source (see Kureková et al., 2015 for an overview of some of the relevant literature). A technique that is commonly applied to assess the representativeness of the dataset is benchmarking some data properties (inflows of vacancies or their structural and/or occupational structure) with an alternative data source, such as a vacancy survey or administrative data (Acemoglu et al., 2020; Burke et al., 2020; Fabo & Kahanec, 2020; Hershbein & Kahn, 2016). This has also been done specifically for *Profesia.sk* data with satisfactory results (Drahokoupil & Fabo, 2022; Kureková & Žilinčíková, 2018).

Following the methodology developed in previous work (Drahokoupil & Fabo, 2022), I do not infer skills requirements directly from the text of the vacancy, but rather follow the skill tags the company posting the vacancy associated with the job, following the approach developed in previous work (Beblavý, Akgüc, et al., 2016; Drahokoupil & Fabo, 2022; Fabo, 2017). These tags are assigned by the employer when posting the vacancy and thus are likely to signal their strong preference for a candidate to possess the associated skill. It is also possible that the practices differ between employers in terms of the extent to which these preferences are revealed in the vacancy as opposed to being assumed implicitly. For example, when hiring a computer programmer, companies might not consider it important to explicitly state the candidate should be able to use the computer or browse websites online.

The period this chapter is concerned with is remarkable for the extraordinary volatility of the hiring market. The number of vacancies advertised declined sharply in March 2020, when the first covid restrictions were introduced in Slovakia, and remained at a relatively low level throughout 2020 and the first quarter of 2021. The pace of vacancy posting picked up sharply afterwards and the remaining three quarters of 2021 all substantially overperformed the number of vacancies typically posted in the given period before the pandemic (see Figure 2.1). *Profesia.sk* allows job seekers to post their CVs to attract potential employers. The number of CVs posted increased in 2020, representative of job seekers having a hard time to find a suitable job but decreased considerably in 2021 (Profesia, 2022).

The fluctuations in the number of vacancies posted composition are likely to be related to the structure of occupations being advertised. To ensure the result is not influenced by this dynamic, I calculated the average share of requirements for each of the 739 occupations in the dataset for each month. I excluded all occupations

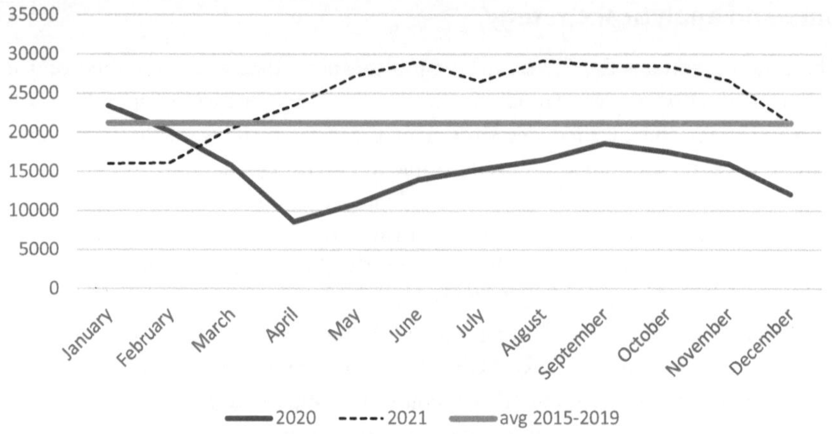

FIGURE 2.1 Number of vacancies in 2020 and 2021 compared to the 2015–2019 average

Source: Own calculation based on Profesia.sk dataset.

for which there are not at least 10 observations every month to eliminate statistical noise. The reported figures represent the average demand in the well-covered occupations that remain in the sample. Each occupation has been associated with a one-digit aggregated group as defined by the International Standard Classification of Occupations (ISCO). In the analysis, I excluded military and skilled agricultural occupations (categories 6 and 10) because the number of vacancies in these categories is very low.

In line with research design, the main response variable I use is the demand for digital skills. There are hundreds of digital skills contained in the *Profesia.sk* dataset, so I use aggregation as defined in Drahokoupil and Fabo (2022, see that paper for the full list of relevant skills). In that study, the digital skills are split into three categories: basic (such as the ability to use a computer or access the Internet), intermediate (such as MS Office packages and other common software), and advanced (programming language, data analysis software, and specialised ICT skills such as server management or SQL databases). With respect to the research question, I included some tools for remote work (Zoom, Microsoft Teams, and Cisco Webex) among the intermediate digital skills.

This chapter examines the evolution of demand for intermediate digital skills only. The focus on the intermediate skills is justified for two reasons. First, they are most widely in demand (see Table 2.1). Second and more importantly, the relation with mobility restrictions due to the pandemic is the clearest cut – a switch to working from home creates the need for workers to effectively communicate online as well as be able to use office software to produce outputs in the digital form which is why I focus only on this category in this chapter.

TABLE 2.1 Share of vacancies per occupation group requiring digital skills

	Basic	*Intermediate*	*Advanced*
1. Managers	3%	33%	4%
2. Professional	2%	16%	15%
3. Technicians and associate professionals	4%	31%	11%
4. Clerical support workers	4%	47%	3%
5. Service and sales workers	4%	25%	1%
6. Skilled agricultural, forestry, and fishery workers	1%	4%	0%
7. Craft and related trades workers	3%	13%	3%
8. Plant and machine operators, and assemblers	2%	7%	0%
9. Elementary occupations	1%	4%	0%

Source: Own calculation based on the *Profesia.sk* dataset.

The granularity of the dataset allows me to slice the data in several ways. First, I can look at the characteristic of the firms that posted the vacancy. Specifically, I look at the regional dimension to see whether there is anything supporting the notion in the literature that the capital region of Bratislava offers better infrastructure in terms of broadband Internet, and thus it is easier to switch to working from home there than in other regions (Kucserová Jurášeková, 2021). I further look at the size of the firm. While it is not possible to observe it directly as the necessary information is not present in the data, I use the number of vacancies posted by a firm to proxy the size of the firm. I do so by defining all vacancies posted by firms that posted less than 100 vacancies in total over the past two years as 'small firms' (this is about a third of the full sample), while all the other vacancies (after the exclusion of vacancies posted by HR companies, which can hire for both big firms and small firms) are defined as being posted by firms which are 'not small'. I do not have any prior belief regarding the firm size effect – it is possible that big firms can better utilise the economy of scale and find equipping their workers easier with the necessary hardware for remote work. At the same time, the risk of infection spreading is arguably higher in big companies where many people are often cramped in limited space. On the other hand, small companies, including start-ups, are likely to be more flexible and able to adjust to changes.

Furthermore, I can split the data by sectors. Following Drahokoupil and Fabo (2020), I look separately at manufacturing, which is still very important for the Slovak economy (in particular automotive), and white-collar occupations (finance, ICT, and administrative support). The actual impact of the pandemic on the individual sectors is likely to highly vary (Kahn et al., 2020), although some literature has found little variance beyond extremely affected sectors such as non-essential retail, which faced complete closure (Forsythe et al., 2020).

In the final analysis, I am looking at the education requirement, separating between jobs for which a high school degree is sufficient from jobs requiring a college degree. Jobs advertised specifically for college students are treated as a separate category.

Results

The evolution of demand for intermediate digital skills follows a pattern of increase since the outbreak of the pandemic. At the same time, it is important to mention that when the data are sliced among the key analytical dimensions discussed in this chapter, the development seems quite uneven.

Occupation-wise, as shown in Figure 2.2, there has been a sizable and sustained increase in demand for intermediate digital skills among clerical workers and managers. Timing-wise, this increase coincides with the introduction of mobility restrictions in March 2020. While the market's reaction for the administrative workers already had taken place in March, the vacancies for management positions started to change only in April that year. In other occupation groups, an increase can also be seen but is much less pronounced. This likely reflects the large-scale shift towards working from home.

A breakdown by firm characteristics shows several interesting patterns. Small firms seemed to react to the crisis faster than big firms (Figure 2.3a). Furthermore, contrary to prior expectations, there appears to be a more robust increase in demand for intermediate digital skills also among firms located outside of Bratislava

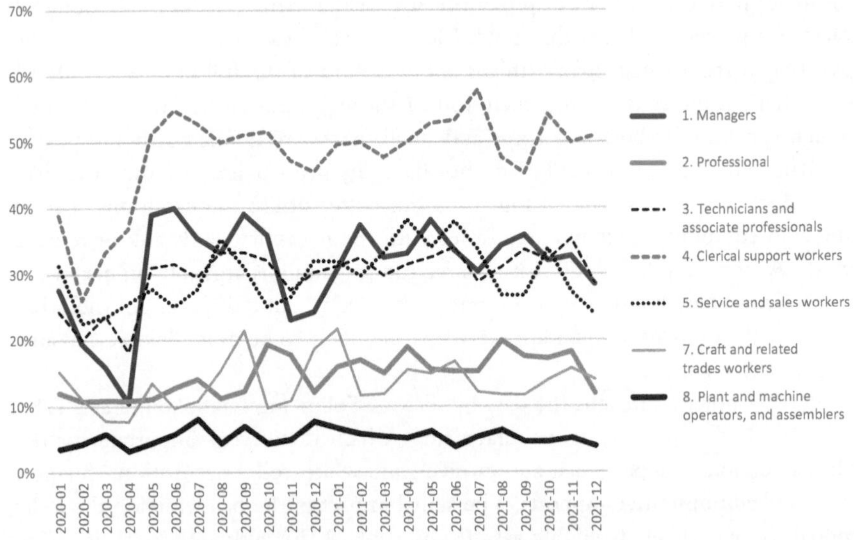

FIGURE 2.2 Evolution of demand for intermediate digital skills per occupational group

Source: Own calculation based on Profesia.sk dataset.

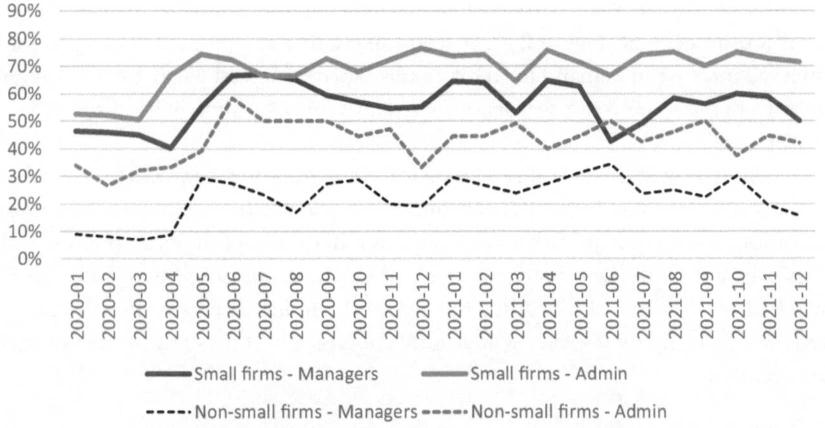

FIGURE 2.3A Evolution of demand for intermediate digital skills for managers and administrative workers in small and non-small firms

Source: Own calculation based on Profesia.sk.

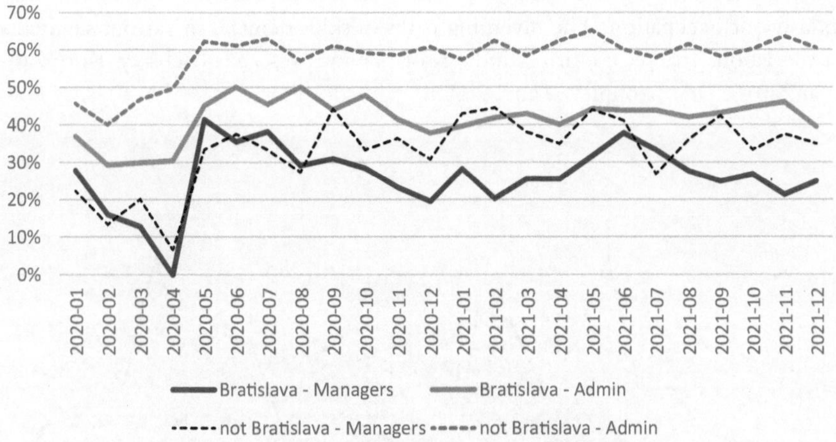

FIGURE 2.3B Evolution of demand for intermediate digital skills for managers and administrative workers advertised in Bratislava and other regions

Source: Own calculation based on Profesia.sk.

than companies located in the capital region (Figure 2.3b). One possible explanation is that companies outside of Bratislava are drawing from a less qualified workforce generally, which is why they do not take it for granted that candidates will possess intermediate digital skills.

Next, I sliced the data by the industry, where there appears to be a very strong reaction in management positions in manufacturing, which levels out with time.

There is no clear pattern for either manufacturing administrative jobs or white-collar jobs in general (Figure 2.4). It seems likely that at least part of the generally observed increase in demand for digital skills is driven at least partly by the realignment of demand between sectors, rather than purely by shifts within the sectors themselves.

Finally, a look at the data sliced by education requirements shows that the effect of the pandemic was likely more pronounced for positions requiring a college education and less for jobs that only require a high school diploma (Figure 2.5). This is in line with the expectations regarding the nature of jobs, which can be switched to a home office. Also, the demand for intermediate digital skills in student jobs is highly volatile, which suits the typically short-term nature of such arrangement.

Closing discussion

In this chapter, I present some evidence that the pandemic, or more precisely mobility restrictions enacted because of the pandemic, has resulted in the increase in demand for intermediate digital skills in the Slovak labour market. At the same time, the extent to which this took place varies depending on the factors such as industry or occupation. The diverging paths of skills demand in various segments of the labour market confirms findings of previous research (Beblavý, Kureková, et al., 2016; Drahokoupil & Fabo, 2022).

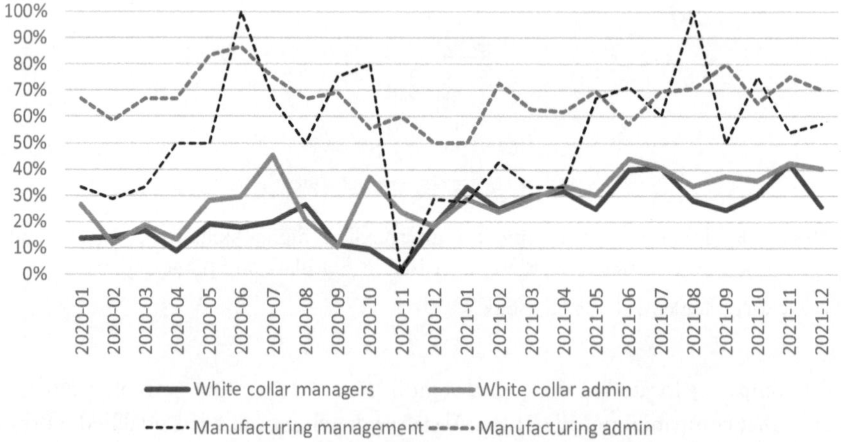

FIGURE 2.4 Evolution of demand for intermediate digital skills for managers and administrative workers in manufacturing and white-collar occupations

Source: Own calculation based on Profesia.sk.

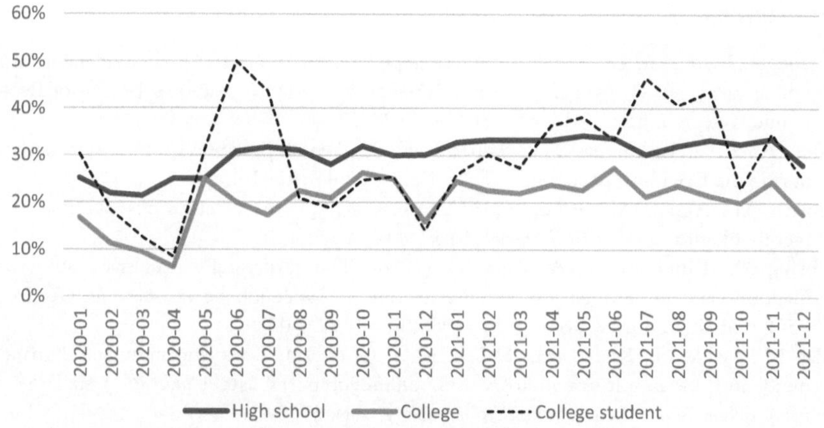

FIGURE 2.5 Evolution of demand for intermediate digital skills for high school educated workers, college-educated workers, and student workers

Source: Own calculation based on Profesia.sk.

While the evidence presented is far from conclusive and not causal, it leads to several policy implications. First, the nature of jobs will keep changing dramatically due to unforeseen events. In 2020 it was the pandemic; in the future, it might be climate change or something else. Flexibility and the ability to learn and embrace new forms of work organisation will be crucial to preparing for the world of tomorrow. Second, the rise of digital skill requirements seems to be quite pervasive in many cases. Work from home and assorted digitalisation gains are here to stay and should be treated as a new reality rather than temporary measures that can be attributed to the pandemic.

Finally, the effect of the digital divide deepening represents quite a relevant point of study in the future. Commuting to work used to be an experience felt across class lines but that might not be the case any longer as parts of the workforce learned to enjoy the newfound freedom to work from home and will not be willing to give it up. Others, particularly service and blue-collar workers will typically be forced to keep showing up at work every morning. Given the implications of commuting for happiness, work-life balance, as well as urbanism, and opening hours of shops and institutions, the implications of this growing divide, might be quite far-reaching.

Acknowledgements

This publication has received financial support from the project VEGA 1/0628/20 provided by the Ministry of Education, Science and Sports.

References

Acemoglu, D., Autor, D., Hazell, J., & Restrepo, P. (2020). AI and jobs: Evidence from online vacancies. (*Working Paper Series, Working Paper* 28257). National Bureau of Economic Research. https://doi.org/10.3386/w28257

Bauer, A., Hartl, T., Hutter, C., & Weber, E. (2021). Search processes on the labor market during the Covid-19 pandemic. *CESifo Forum*, *22*(04), 15–19.

Beblavý, M., Akgüc, M., Fabo, B., & Lenaerts, K. (2016). Occupations observatory-methodological note. *CEPS Special Report*, *144*.

Beblavý, M., Kureková, L., & Haita, C. (2016). The surprisingly exclusive nature of medium- and low-skilled jobs: Evidence from a Slovak job portal. *Personnel Review*, *45*(2), 255–273. https://doi.org/10.1108/PR-12-2014-0276

Bilal, M., Malik, N., Khalid, M., & Lali, M. I. U. (2017). Exploring industrial demand trend's in Pakistan software industry using online job portal data. *University of Sindh Journal of Information and Communication Technology*, *1*(1), 17–24.

Burke, M. A., Sasser, A., Sadighi, S., Sederberg, R. B., & Taska, B. (2020). No longer qualified? Changes in the supply and demand for skills within occupations. (*Working Papers* 20–3). https://doi.org/10.29412/res.wp.2020.03

Campello, M., Kankanhalli, G., & Muthukrishnan, P. (2020). Corporate Hiring under COVID-19: Labor Market Concentration, Downskilling, and Income Inequality. (*Working Paper Series, Working Paper* 27208). National Bureau of Economic Research. https://doi.org/10.3386/w27208

Campos-Vazquez, R. M., Esquivel, G., & Badillo, R. Y. (2021). How has labor demand been affected by the COVID-19 pandemic? Evidence from job ads in Mexico. *Latin American Economic Review*, *30*, 1–42.

Drahokoupil, J., & Fabo, B. (2022). The limits of foreign-led growth: Demand for skills by foreign and domestic firms. *Review of International Political Economy*, *29*(1), 152–174. https://doi.org/10.1080/09692290.2020.1802323

Fabo, B. (2017). *Towards an understanding of job matching using web data*. Tilburg University, School of Economics and Management. https://pure.uvt.nl/portal/files/18757037/Disertation_Draft_final_manuscript.pdf

Fabo, B., Beblavý, M., & Lenaerts, K. (2017). The importance of foreign language skills in the labour markets of Central and Eastern Europe: Assessment based on data from online job portals. *Empirica*, *44*(3), 487–508. https://doi.org/10.1007/s10663-017-9374-6

Fabo, B., & Kahanec, M. (2020). The role of computer skills on the occupation level. *European Journal of Business Science and Technology*, *6*(2), 87–99.

Fang, H., Ge, C., Huang, H., & Li, H. (2020). Pandemics, global supply chains, and local labor demand: Evidence from 100 million posted jobs in China. (*Working Paper Series, Working Paper* 28072). National Bureau of Economic Research. https://doi.org/10.3386/w28072

Forsythe, E., Kahn, L. B., Lange, F., & Wiczer, D. (2020). Labor demand in the time of COVID-19: Evidence from vacancy postings and UI claims. *Journal of Public Economics*, *189*, 104238. https://doi.org/10.1016/j.jpubeco.2020.104238

Hensvik, L., Le Barbanchon, T., & Rathelot, R. (2021). Job search during the COVID-19 crisis. *Journal of Public Economics*, *194*, 104349. https://doi.org/10.1016/j.jpubeco.2020.104349

Hershbein, B., & Kahn, L. B. (2016). Do recessions accelerate routine-biased technological change? Evidence from vacancy postings. (*Working Paper* 22762). National Bureau of Economic Research. https://doi.org/10.3386/w22762

Kahn, L. B., Lange, F., & Wiczer, D. (2020). Labor supply in the time of COVID19. *Cahiers de Recherche, Cahiers de recherche* 06–2020. Centre interuniversitaire de recherche en Ã©conomie quantitative, CIREQ. https://ideas.repec.org/p/mtl/montec/06-2020.html

Klimovský, D., Nemec, J., & Bouckaert, G. (2021). The COVID-19 pandemic in the Czech Republic and Slovakia. *Scientific Papers of the University of Pardubice, 29*(1).

Kucserová Jurášeková, J. (2021). *Kto pracuje z domu na Slovensku? [Who works from home in Slovakia.* National Bank of Slovakia. www.nbs.sk/_img/Documents/_komentare/AnalytickeKomentare/2021/AK99_Kto_pracuje_z_domu_na_Slovensku.pdf

Kureková, L., Beblavý, M., Haita, C., & Thum Thysen, A. E. (2016). Employers' skill preferences across Europe: Between cognitive and non-cognitive skills. *Journal of Education and Work, 29*(6), 662–687. https://doi.org/10.1080/13639080.2015.1024641

Kureková, L., Beblavý, M., & Thum Thysen, A. E. (2015). Using online vacancies and web surveys to analyse the labour market: A methodological inquiry. *IZA Journal of Labor Economics, 4*(1), 18. https://doi.org/10.1186/s40172-015-0034-4

Kureková, L., & Žilinčíková, Z. (2018). What is the value of foreign work experience for young return migrants? *International Journal of Manpower, 39*(1), 71–92. https://doi.org/10.1108/IJM-04-2016-0091

Lyu, W., & Wehby, G. L. (2020). Community use of face masks and COVID-19: Evidence from a natural experiment of state mandates in the US. *Health Affairs, 39*(8), 1419–1425. https://doi.org/10.1377/hlthaff.2020.00818

Maital, S., & Barzani, E. (2020). The global economic impact of COVID-19: A summary of research. *Samuel Neaman Institute for National Policy Research, 2020*, 1–12.

Marinescu, I. (2017). The general equilibrium impacts of unemployment insurance: Evidence from a large online job board. *Journal of Public Economics, 150*, 14–29. https://doi.org/10.1016/j.jpubeco.2017.02.012

Nemec, J. (2020). Government transition in the time of the COVID-19 crisis: Slovak case. *International Journal of Public Leadership, 17*(1), 7–12. https://doi.org/10.1108/IJPL-05-2020-0040

Nemec, J., & Špaček, D. (2020). The COVID-19 pandemic and local government finance: Czechia and Slovakia. *Journal of Public Budgeting, Accounting & Financial Management, 32*(5), 837–846. https://doi.org/10.1108/JPBAFM-07-2020-0109

Nomura, S., Imaizumi, S., Areias, A. C., & Yamauchi, F. (2017). Toward labor market policy 2.0: The potential for using online job-portal big data to inform labor market policies in India. (*Working Paper*). World Bank. https://doi.org/10.1596/1813-9450-7966

OECD. (2021). *OECD skills outlook 2021: Learning for life*. www.oecd.org/education/oecd-skills-outlook-e11c1c2d-en.htm

Pavelka, M., Van-Zandvoort, K., Abbott, S., Sherratt, K., Majdan, M., CMMID COVID-19 WORKING GROUP, INŠTITÚT ZDRAVOTNÝCH ANALÝZ, Jarčuška, P., Krajčí, M., Flasche, S., & Funk, S. (2021). The impact of population-wide rapid antigen testing on SARS-CoV-2 prevalence in Slovakia. *Science, 372*(6542), 635–641. https://doi.org/10.1126/science.abf9648

Profesia. (2022). *Covid19 recruitment report*. https://public.tableau.com/app/profile/profesia.analytics4840/viz/ProfesiaReport_V2/Covid?publish=yes

Singh, A. K., & Misra, A. (2020). Impact of COVID-19 and comorbidities on health and economics: Focus on developing countries and India. *Diabetes & Metabolic Syndrome: Clinical Research & Reviews, 14*(6), 1625–1630. https://doi.org/10.1016/j.dsx.2020.08.032

Sostero, M., Milasi, S., Hurley, J., Fernández-Macías, E., & Bisello, M. (2020). Teleworkability and the COVID-19 crisis: A new digital divide? (*JRC Working Papers Series on Labour, Education and Technology, Working Paper* 2020/05). www.econstor.eu/handle/10419/231337

Stiglitz, J. E., Shiller, R. J., Gopinath, G., Reinhart, C. M., Posen, A., Prasad, E., Tooze, A., Tyson, L. D., & Mahbubani, K. (2020). How the economy will look after the coronavirus pandemic. *Foreign Policy, 15.*

Turrell, A., Speigner, B., Copple, D., Djumalieva, J., & Thurgood, J. (2021). Is the UK's productivity puzzle mostly driven by occupational mismatch? An analysis using big data on job vacancies. *Labour Economics*, *71*, 102013. https://doi.org/10.1016/j.labeco.2021.102013

van Loo, J., & Pouliakas, K. (2020). Cedefop and the analysis of European online job vacancies. In *The feasibility of using big data in anticipating and matching skills needs*. ILO.

Winzenried, S. (2020). Cedefop and the analysis of European online job vacancies. In *The feasibility of using big data in anticipating and matching skills needs*. ILO.

3

HAS COVID-19 ENHANCED LABOUR POLARISATION IN POLAND? CHANGES IN UNMET LABOUR DEMAND BASED ON ONLINE JOB OFFERS

Łukasz Arendt, Ewa Gałecka-Burdziak, and Robert Pater

Introduction

Even before the outburst of the COVID-19 pandemic, discussion on the impact of technical change on the labour market and employment – this time embodied by automation and robotisation processes – had been vivid. In the previous decade, the fear of automation was fuelled by a Frey and Osborne (2017) study, that claimed 47% of the US labour force may face a high risk of being replaced by technology. Although there have been many critical arguments raised towards Frey and Osborne's methodology (Arntz et al., 2016), their results had a perceptible impact on individuals' concerns about losing their jobs and 'the end of work' in the coming years.

Contemporary theoretical models, which shift from occupations towards task content of jobs analysis, predict a substitution effect between robots/AI and labour in the short run, and potential growth of labour demand in the long run, depending on the scale of displacement and reinstatement effects. In the model based on task-content group taxonomy, developed by Acemoglu and Restrepo (2019, 2020), the final result of automation depends on the difference in dynamics between automation and creation of new tasks, with positive employment outcomes if the pace of tasks creation is similar to or faster than the pace of investments in automation. The creation of new tasks is endogenous and depends on the decisions of companies, workers, and institutions (governments and social planners). Since companies compare wage rates with opportunity cost of labour and cost of capital while making decisions regarding automation, but not accounting for the externalities of these decisions, this may lead to 'excessive automation'– automation being faster than socially desirable/acceptable (Acemoglu & Restrepo, 2020). COVID-19 creates the conditions in which the 'excessive automation' may take place. As Frey argued in an interview, '[the] Coronavirus is likely to accelerate automation'. Coombs (2020)

DOI: 10.4324/9781003326779-5

provides three broad arguments in favour of accelerating automation: changing consumer preferences towards automation (the need of social distancing translated into a higher acceptance of online solutions) combined with increased familiarity with ICT technologies (many people were 'forced' to learn and use online tools to work or stay in contact with relatives), and growing business confidence in automation. He also points to four counterarguments, two of which refer to labour force: many tasks are still better performed by humans than robots (which is in line with the Acemoglu and Restrepo concept of tasks in which people possess comparative advantage); the economic downturn caused by the COVID-19 pandemic resulted in higher unemployment and thus a higher availability of workers on the labour market, which should decrease the wage pressure and make labour relatively cheaper in comparison with capital.

This chapter aims to identify the influence of the COVID-19 pandemic on the Polish labour market, covering a 95-week period since the first COVID-19 case in Poland was reported and a similar period before the pandemic outburst (the 18th week of 2018 to the end of 2021). Thus, we can track if the COVID-19 crisis has significantly shifted the labour demand patterns (by task-content groups in line with taxonomy proposed by Autor et al. (2003), called hereinafter the ALM model, and required skills) in the Polish labour market. Our main research hypothesis posits that labour demand will shift towards non-routine versus routine task-content groups, enhancing labour polarisation, because of COVID-19.

Most recent studies focused on the initial impact of COVID-19 on labour markets, while our approach contributes to the literature by focusing on longer effects. The study refers to the literature on technical change and the task-content group approach (Acemoglu & Autor, 2011; Acemoglu & Restrepo, 2019; Autor et al., 2003), and skill requirements posted in online job offers (Deming & Kahn, 2018; Hershbein & Kahn, 2018; Marinescu & Wolthoff, 2020), putting these dimensions into one research framework. By incorporating the task-content approach, we can measure indirectly the extent to which COVID-19 enhanced automation and the robotisation processes, which translates into changes in the routine and non-routine mix of jobs available in the Polish labour market and point to changes in the skill-mix required from candidates. This is additional contribution, as no such analytical framework has been proposed yet in the studies on the COVID-19 impact on the labour market.

The empirical study is based on data on job vacancies posted online, retrieved from the System of Online Job Offers (SOJO), developed by the Institute of Labour and Social Studies in Warsaw. Changes in the demand for task content of jobs and skill-mix was analysed with the use of descriptive statistics, and multinomial logistic models that captured the impact of COVID-19 by introducing different measures: dummy variable, time variable, and a square trend t^2 variable.

The study revealed that after initial contraction, labour demand revived but to a different extent across task-content groups and skills. Increase in demand for non-routine, cognitive personal and routine, cognitive jobs was recorded, after temporary decline, while a more permanent decrease was observed in non-routine manual jobs, and especially routine manual jobs. This points to a structural shift which favours non-routine jobs and translates into more dynamic polarisation processes in the Polish labour market. Moreover, demand for self-organisation, communication, managerial, and office skills was negatively influenced by the COVID-19 pandemic, while employer interest in computer, mathematical, and cognitive skills increased noticeably.

The remainder of this chapter is organised as follows. We begin with an overview of literature on the utilisation of online job postings in labour market research. The following section describes the data and methodology used in the empirical analysis. Section 'Demand for tasks and skills during the COVID-19 pandemic' elaborates on COVID-19 driven changes in labour demand, presenting the results of our research approach and econometric modelling. The final section concludes.

Online job postings as a source for labour analysis – synthetic literature review

Recent developments in ICT, especially in artificial intelligence (AI) and machine learning (ML), enhanced empirical studies in labour economics, taking advantage of job advertisements posted online to analyse the labour demand and employer requirements towards candidates. Such data sources seem to be a reliable source for labour market analysis (Kurekova et al., 2015; Lovaglio et al., 2020).

There are two basic data collection approaches in studying online job postings – to retrieve data on vacancies from either one (first approach) or several (the other approach) job portals. Studies based on data retrieved from one job portal only are less popular, but even in this case the scope of research problems and empirical strategies is vast, with strong focus on required skills [Beblavý et al. (2016a) for low- and medium-skilled occupations in Slovakia; Marinescu and Wolthoff (2020) for the United States; Böhm et al. (2020) who identify the gender bias in job postings in IT sector in Germany]. A more popular approach is to retrieve and analyse information from different Internet sources; Burning Glass Technologies (BGT) is a key data provider in this respect. BGT retrieves job postings from many company websites and job portals worldwide which BGT believes to be 'the near-universe of jobs that were posted online' (Forsythe et al., 2020). The vast majority of studies based on BGT data are concentrated on the United States, using different analytical approaches with quite extensive focus on skills requirements (Brüning & Mangeol, 2020; Deming & Kahn, 2018; Deming & Noray, 2020; Hershbein & Kahn, 2018; Lyu & Liu, 2021; Modestino et al., 2020). More and more studies deal with demand for ICT and AI-related skills on the US market (Acemoglu et al., 2021; Alekseeva et al., 2021; Beblavý et al., 2016b) and in other countries (Samek et al., 2021; Squicciarini & Nachtigal, 2021).

Recently, online job postings have been utilised to analyse the impact of COVID-19 on labour demand. In general, perceptive contraction in the scale of job offers published online was reported at the outburst of the COVID-19 pandemic. OECD (2021) reported a decline in online job postings by more than

50% between January and May in Australia, Canada, New Zealand, the United Kingdom, and the United States. Moreover, the overall decline in job postings was distributed unevenly across sectors, educational level, and skills requirements with cross – country variation. The sectors that contracted the most were these which suffered largely from lockdowns (e.g., leisure and hospitability); while in healthcare and 'essential' sectors labour demand was relatively strong. As a result, there was an increase in demand for skills specific to healthcare and logistics sectors, but also transversal skills such as communication and teamwork. In Australia and the United Kingdom, demand for low-skilled jobs decreased significantly compared to high-skilled jobs, while in Canada and the United States these differences were much less perceptible (OECD, 2021). More detailed studies for the United States also confirmed a significant decrease in the number of online vacancies. Forsythe et al. (2020) reported a drop in the number of postings between February and April 2020 by 44%. Campello et al. (2020) found that in the first week of May 2020 the number of active job postings in the United Stated was circa 40% below its average in the same period in the years 2017–2019. Shuai et al. (2021) reported a decrease in the number of job postings between March and June 2020 by around 30% compared to the respective period in 2019. The scale of job posting contraction in the US market was distributed similarly across industries (except for 'essential' retail and nursing, where the contraction was smaller), and regarding the mode of work (working from home vs. non-working from home capacity) – see Forsythe et al. (2020). Moreover, the contraction in postings was concentrated more in high-skill jobs compared to low-skill jobs, in small enterprises, and in local labour markets characterised by a large extent of concentration and greater income inequalities (which implies that COVID-19 had a more profound negative impact on the disadvantaged local labour markets in the United States) – see Campello et al. (2020). These observations are in line with the results of Tsvetkova et al. (2020) for regional differences in vacancies contraction and recovery across Metropolitan Statistical Areas. They found that larger cities and more educated and more diverse locations (as for industrial structure) witnessed a larger decrease in online job postings between February and April 2020, as well as suffered from slower recovery in the number of online vacancies in May–June 2020. This may be explained not just by the spread pattern of COVID-19 but also by the fact that the pandemic had a major impact on 'non-essential jobs', which are concentrated mainly in larger cities. Marinescu et al. (2021) analysed vacancies (and job applications) between January 2018 and July 2020, showing the Federal Pandemic Unemployment Compensation (FPUC) programme had a negative impact on job search activity, but not on vacancies (even in June–July 2020 when lockdowns were eased), translating into decreased labour market tightness in March–July 2020 compared to January–February 2020. Shuai et al. (2021) revealed that anti-COVID measures introduced by public authorities suppressed labour demand in the United States, however specific measures (Paycheck Protection Program) played an important role in stabilising wages, which were at similar levels in job offers posted before and during COVID-19 pandemic.

In Sweden, job postings published on the largest online Swedish job board Platsbanken.se also dropped by 40% at the beginning of COVID-19 pandemic. The largest decline in vacancy postings was recorded in offers regarding low-paid jobs (contrary to the US situation reported by Campello et al. (2020)), while the increase in the number of home-based job offers was timid. The most resilient occupations encompassed these related to healthcare, teaching, and transportation industries, while the least resilient ones were concentrated in the hospitality and sales industries (Hensvik et al., 2021). A 38% drop in the job postings between February and May 2020 was recorded in Mexico, and despite the recovery symptoms, the number of vacancies posted online till September 2020 was still below the average recorded at the beginning of 2020 (pre-lockdown period). The structure of vacancies by occupations and wages returned to their pre-COVID levels as fast as in May. Interestingly, during the pandemic the share of job postings providing the opportunity to work remotely dropped compared to pre-pandemic period (Campos-Vazquez et al., 2021).

Data and methodology

Data on online job postings used in this study were retrieved from the System of Online Job Offers (SOJO), developed by the Institute of Labour and Social Studies in Warsaw, which is a public research institute. SOJO takes advantage of a web scraping technique to collect, parse, and categorise information on vacancies posted on the six most popular Polish job portals: pracuj.pl, gazetapraca.pl, praca.pl, careerjet.pl, gratka.pl, olx.pl. Each job posting is recoded according to dictionaries embedded into SOJO and other relevant data sources and assigned to the six-digit occupations in accordance with the Polish Classification of Occupations and Specialities for the needs of the labour market (consistent with ISCO-08 classification), and skills categories. Researchers implement different approaches to identify and measure skills in online job postings, including among others O*NET and ESCO classifications, pointing to the fact, that there is no established common standard (Pater et al., 2019). In this study, we adjusted the classification elaborated in the BHC study,[1] listing the following 'key' (general) skills: cognitive, mathematical, computer, technical, self-organisation, interpersonal, communication, office, managerial, availability, and artistic.

Since SOJO classifies online vacancies into occupations according to ISCO classification, we are able to recode them into task-content groups, which enables analysing the impact of technical change on the Polish labour market. We applied Acemoglu and Autor (2011) task-content classification, which is the most popular and utilised in research studies methodology, based on conceptualisation proposed by Autor et al. (2003) and referred as the ALM model. In this approach, all jobs can be assigned to respective five task-content groups according to the dominant task content of the jobs: non-routine cognitive analytical, non-routine cognitive personal, routine cognitive, routine manual, and non-routine manual. Originally, Acemoglu and Autor (2011) assigned occupations into respective task-content groups for the US labour market based on O*NET data. To adapt the mechanism of assigning occupations into task-content group to the specific features of the Polish labour market, we applied the approach by Hardy et al. (2018) who recoded the O*NET descriptions into the Polish Labour Force Survey dataset. As a result, job postings with an assigned occupational group at the three-digit code level of the Polish Classification of Occupations and Specialities are reliably classified into respective task-content groups.

The SOJO database contains job postings from January 2017. The collected job offers dataset was aggregated to a weekly frequency. The first registered COVID-19 case in Poland is dated on 4 March 2020 – thus the 10th week of 2020 was set as 'starting point' of the COVID-19 impact on the Polish labour market. To centralise the pandemic impact, we used a sample of observations starting from the 18th week of 2018 to the end of 2021. This evenly distributes the period to 95 weeks before and after the impact plus one week right before the impact. This gave us 4,402,058 observations in total.

We modelled the probability $\Pr(TC_{w,g})$ that a job advertisement offers a position for an occupation that includes one of the five task-content groups $g = 1,\ldots,5$. We applied a multinomial logistic model of a form:

$$\Pr(TC_{w,g}) = \Pr\left(TC_w = g \mid SG_{s,w}\right) = \frac{\exp\left(\mathbf{x}_g \beta\right)}{1+\sum_{k=2}^{5}\exp\left(\mathbf{x}_k \beta\right)} \tag{3.1}$$

Our qualitative dependent variable took five categories, one for each task-content group, and k alternatives measured across weeks $w = 1, \ldots, 191$. We assumed that $\sum_{g=1}^{5} TC_{w,g} = 1$. Our vector of variables $\mathbf{x}_g$ contains measures of skills $SG_{s,w}$ grouped in $s = 1, \ldots, 11$ categories (see Appendix). Our model relates the probability of a skill group $SG_{s,w}$ being in a task-content group k to the routine manual task-content group.

We tested the effects of the COVID-19 pandemic on task-content groups in a few ways. First, we included a dummy variable d_{96-191} that takes the value of 1 since the 96th week of the study, when we assumed that the pandemic started to take effect in Poland. This approach assumes that the effects of pandemic where stable across all periods since March 2020 till the end of 2021 and shows the aggregate effect. Second, we included a time variable $t = 1, \ldots, 95$ that represents the period since the COVID-19 shock. This assumes that the pandemic had a linear effect on the demand for task-content groups. Third, the model was supplemented with a squared trend t^2 variable. This tests whether the pandemic had temporary effect on the demand for jobs, either decreasing the demand for a certain period up to a minimum and then increasing again, or increasing the impact in the beginning, reaching a peak of this effect, and decreasing the demand afterwards. With this approach, we can estimate the week of the highest impact. Next, we introduced two variables separately that show the unfolding effects of pandemic. The first one was the number of new COVID-19 registered cases in Poland, and the second was the pandemic stringency index. The stringency index is defined as[2] 'a composite measure based on nine response indicators including school closures, workplace closures, and travel bans, rescaled to a value from 0 to 100 (100 = strictest)'. Next, we introduced interactions between skills $SG_{s,w}$ and variables d_{96-191}, t, and t^2. The newly formed variables inform us how the demand for skills changed in all task-content groups during the COVID-19 pandemic in comparison to pre-pandemic period.[3]

Demand for tasks and skills during the COVID-19 pandemic

Before the pandemic, the Polish economy was in the expansion phase of the business cycle. However, vacancy data already indicated prospects of an economic downturn. As Gałecka-Burdziak and Pater (2015) proved, online job offers are a good leading indicator for the labour market. Our data showed that the business cycle peak of online job offers occurred on the 47th week of 2018. After this date the number of job offers diminished slowly to the 34th week of 2019, and then faster till the end of 2020. This might be the result of the 'overheating' of the Polish economy with increasing wage pressure, permanent labour supply deficit in some sectors and occupations, and decreasing productivity. The first COVID-19 cases were registered in Poland in the 10th week of 2020. Consequently, the number of job offers rapidly decreased in the 12–15th weeks of 2020 (a 65% drop), showing even greater contraction than in the United States, Sweden, Mexico, and other highly developed countries (Campos-Vazquez et al., 2021; Forsythe et al., 2020; Hensvik et al., 2021; OECD, 2021).

Labour market reaction was driven to some extent by lockdowns aimed at mitigating the spread of COVID-19. The first restrictions were introduced in Poland on 10 March 2020 (cancelation of all public events) and were successively extended till mid-April 2020. The main lockdown measures included: a stay at home policy; remote schooling; limited number of clients in shops, shopping malls, and public transport; closure of fitness clubs, sport facilities, dance studios, cinemas, theatres, museums in the first stage, and hotels, beauty salons, and hairdressers in the next stage; restaurants could have operated only in the mode of take away delivery. Companies and institutions shifted to remote working where feasible to maximise social distancing. In mid-April the government announced the plan of reducing restrictions, which was implemented till June 2020. However, succeeding waves of COVID-19 resulting in increase of infections led to consecutive lockdowns (restrictions encompassing mostly traditional commerce, hotels, restaurants, sport and leisure facilities – captured by the stringency index). To counteract the negative effects of the COVID-19 pandemic, the Polish government introduced a set of measures called the 'Anti-crisis shield', which were modified numerous times.

The immediate impact of the COVID-19 pandemic may be calculated using a difference-in-differences (DiD) measure used by Chetty et al. (2020) and Shuai et al. (2021). We followed this approach and calculated a DiD measure of pandemic-induced changes in the number of job postings in 2020–2021 considering three periods:

January–February: in 2020, it was the time before the pandemic in Poland; and in 2021, it was the period of winter recurrence of the pandemic, resulting in a huge increase in new COVID-19 cases, followed by harsh economic activity restrictions (Figure 3.1);

March–June: in 2020, it was the time of pandemic shock and its immediate effects, and introduction of severe restrictions on economic activity; and in 2021, it was the period of slow economic recovery and repealing restrictions;

July–December: in 2020, it was the time of easing restrictions and the first wave of huge increase in demand for certain services (e.g., in tourism), but in the end of this period the restrictions were re-introduced; and in 2021, it was the period during which we observed stable restriction conditions and large adaptation to pandemic situation.

To compare changes in job offers between given periods, in the first step, we computed two types of differences for years 2019–2021:

$$\Delta_1 JO_{mj/jf,t} = JO_{mj,t} - JO_{jf,t},$$

$$\Delta_2 JO_{jd/jj,t} = JO_{jd,t} - JO_{jj,t},$$

where $\Delta_1 JO_{mj/jf,t}$ is a Difference (1) between the sum of job offers in March–June (mj) and January–February (jf), and $\Delta_2 JO_{jd/jj,t}$ is a Difference (2) between the sum of job offers in July–December (jd) and January–June (jj) for $t = 2019, 2020, 2021$.

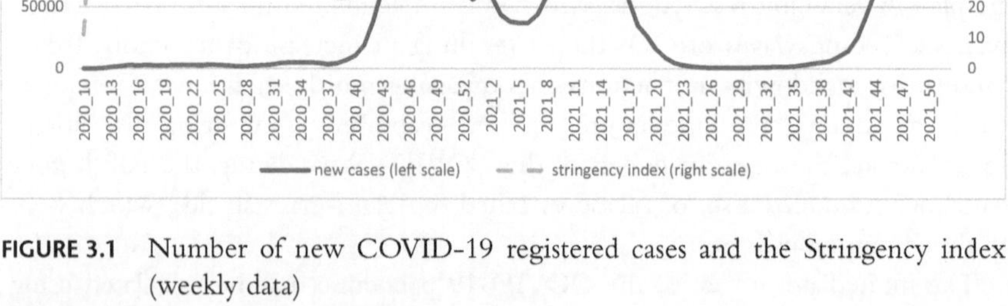

FIGURE 3.1 Number of new COVID-19 registered cases and the Stringency index (weekly data)

Source: Elaboration based on https://ourworldindata.org/coronavirus/country/poland#how-many-tests-are-performed-each-day.

In the second step, we calculated two types of DiD measures:

$$DiD_1(JO)_{t/t-1} = \Delta_1 JO_{mj/jf,t} - \Delta_1 JO_{mj/jf,t-1},$$

$$DiD_2(JO)_{t/t-1} = \Delta_2 JO_{jd/jj,t} - \Delta_2 JO_{jd/jj,t-1}.$$

$DiD_1(JO)_{t/t-1}$ and $DiD_2(JO)_{t/t-1}$ are differences between relative numbers of job offers calculated in the first step in two consecutive years. DiD_1 measures the relative effects in March–June, and DiD_2 measures the relative effects occurring in July–December (see Table 3.1).

We can see that in the Polish economy the decrease in the number of job offers already occurred before pandemic. In January–February 2020, the number of job offers was 14% lower than in the same period 2019, which is a clear difference between the Polish economy and the US economy. Due to a high demand for routine manual jobs before the pandemic, Poland faced a larger decrease in non-routine cognitive jobs in January–February 2020, which we estimate for 32%, than that for the rest job types.

The DiD_1 measure shows that the relative number of job offers $\Delta_1 JO_{mj/jf}$ between 2019 and 2020 decreased by 183.3 thousand, that is, by 78%. This decrease is huge, especially in comparison to the estimates of around a 30–40% decline in the United States (Campello et al., 2020; Chetty et al., 2020; Forsythe et al., 2020). However, it is also a result from the business cycle downturn that had been occurring before the pandemic. March–June 2020 brought a visibly milder decrease in

TABLE 3.1 Difference-in-differences measures of COVID-19 pandemic impact on the number of online job offers across task-content groups

	All jobs	*Routine manual*	*Routine cognitive*	*Non-routine manual*	*Non-routine cognitive personal*	*Non-routine cognitive analytical*
Difference (1) 2019	236431	110837	35024	18857	44498	27215
Difference (1) 2020	53146	12877	7438	6788	15146	10897
Difference (1) 2021	264342	103989	37759	24961	62166	35467
DiD1 2020–2019	−183285	−97960	−27586	−12069	−29352	−16318
DiD1 2021–2020	211196	91112	30321	18173	47020	24570
Difference (2) 2019	−340599	−106956	−54394	−27078	−89982	−62189
Difference (2) 2020	−41863	−51810	−7172	9313	−2030	9836
Difference (2) 2021	111132	43088	20327	−4059	49329	2447
DiD2 2020–2019	298736	55146	47222	36391	87952	72025
DiD2 2021–2020	152995	94898	27499	−13372	51359	−7389

Source: Own elaboration.

Note: The table presents differences in the number of job offers in given periods. Difference (1): between the sum of job offers in March–June and January–February; Difference (2): between the sum of job offers in July–December and January–July; DiD_1: difference in Differences (1) between indicated years; DiD_2: difference in Differences (2) between indicated years.

job offers for non-routine jobs (−64%) than for routine jobs (−86%), and the lowest decline was estimated for the cognitive analytical jobs (−60%).

The second half of a typical pre-pandemic year, for example, 2019, was characterised by a lower labour demand. In 2019, the number of job offers in July–December was 42% lower than in January–June. This decrease encompassed all job types. This visibly changed in 2020, when in July–December the number of job offers decreased only by 8% in relation to January–June of the same year. Two task-content groups even experienced increased number of job offers. These were: non-routine manual tasks (increase by 9.3 thousand job offers) and cognitive analytical tasks (increase by 9.8 thousand job offers). Therefore, the DiD_2 measure of $\Delta_2 JO_{jd/jj}$ changes between 2019 and 2020 was largely positive, with 298.7 thousand new job offers in the market. This means an enormous structural change in economic activity and labour demand in 2020.

All of 2020 ended negatively with a lower number of job offers by 18% than in 2019 (Table 3.2). The largest decrease was observed for routine cognitive (−26%) and non-routine cognitive personal jobs (−23%), while the lowest decrease occurred for non-routine manual (−8%) and non-routine cognitive analytical jobs (−12%).

During the first two months of 2021, the pandemic effects increased again. The number of job offers decreased by 26% annually. The exception was non-routine cognitive analytical jobs, for which the number of job offers increased by 13% in this period. However, their number was still lower by 23% than before the pandemic in January–February 2019.

A visible increase in job offers came in March–June 2021. Their number was higher by 49% in comparison to the same period of 2020. This resulted in 212.0 thousand new job offers measured by DiD_1 in relation to 2020. This means that the number of job offers increased three times, with a sixfold increase in offers of routine jobs and 2.7 times increase in non-routine jobs.

The second half of 2021 also resulted in positive changes. The number of job offers increased by 47% annually, and by 59% in comparison to pre-pandemic period in 2019. The DiD_2 measure indicates 153.0 thousand new job offers,

TABLE 3.2 The number of online job offers across years and task-content groups

	All jobs	*Routine manual*	*Routine cognitive*	*Non-routine manual*	*Non-routine cognitive personal*	*Non-routine cognitive analytical*
2019	1271371	497418	190506	98220	304022	181205
2020	1048841	424456	140748	90041	233302	160294
2021	1366860	483666	195769	108003	360513	218909
2020/2019	−18%	−15%	−26%	−8%	−23%	−12%
2021/2020	30%	14%	39%	20%	55%	37%
2021/2019	8%	−3%	3%	10%	19%	21%

Source: Own elaboration.

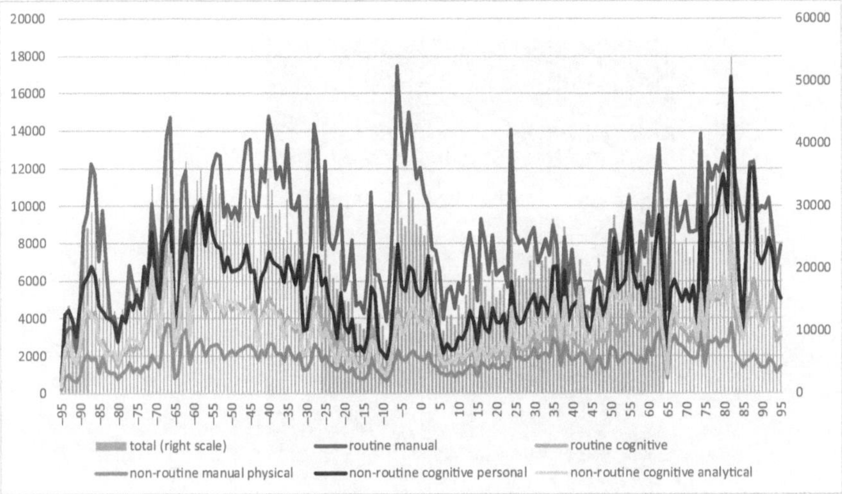

FIGURE 3.2 Job postings by task-content groups across 95 weeks before and after the start of COVID-19 pandemic in Poland

Source: Own elaboration.

however distributed unevenly. The number of vacancies for non-routine manual tasks and for non-routine cognitive analytical jobs decreased by 13.4 thousand and 7.4 thousand, respectively.

The year 2021 ended with 30% more job offers than 2020 and 8% more than 2019. In comparison to pre-pandemic 2019, the number of job offers for non-routine cognitive analytical tasks increased by 21% and for non-routine cognitive personal tasks by 19%. Demand for routine manual jobs was the only one that decreased (by 3%) (Figure 3.2).

Analysis of changes in the structure of job offers by task-content groups is another way to examine if COVID-19 enhanced technical change in the Polish labour market, and thus led to hollowing out routine jobs. As can be seen in Figure 3.3, even if there are weeks during which dynamic changes in the structure of demand across task-content groups take place, the structure is quite stable, with a dominant share of routine manual job postings. However, there is a trend showing the declining role of routine jobs and the growing importance of non-routine jobs in the Polish labour market. A comparison of the structure of job postings in the last and first week of observation yields a mild decrease of demand in routine manual and cognitive jobs (by 1.2 and 0.4pp, respectively) with very modest growth in non-routine cognitive analytical and personal jobs (0.8 and 0.7pp, respectively). This trend is even more clear when comparing the last week of 2021 and the first week of the COVID-19 pandemic – the share of routine manual postings dropped by 6.5pp, routine cognitive by 0.9pp, while the share of non-routine personal and analytical job offers increased by 5.4 and 1.8pp, respectively. This

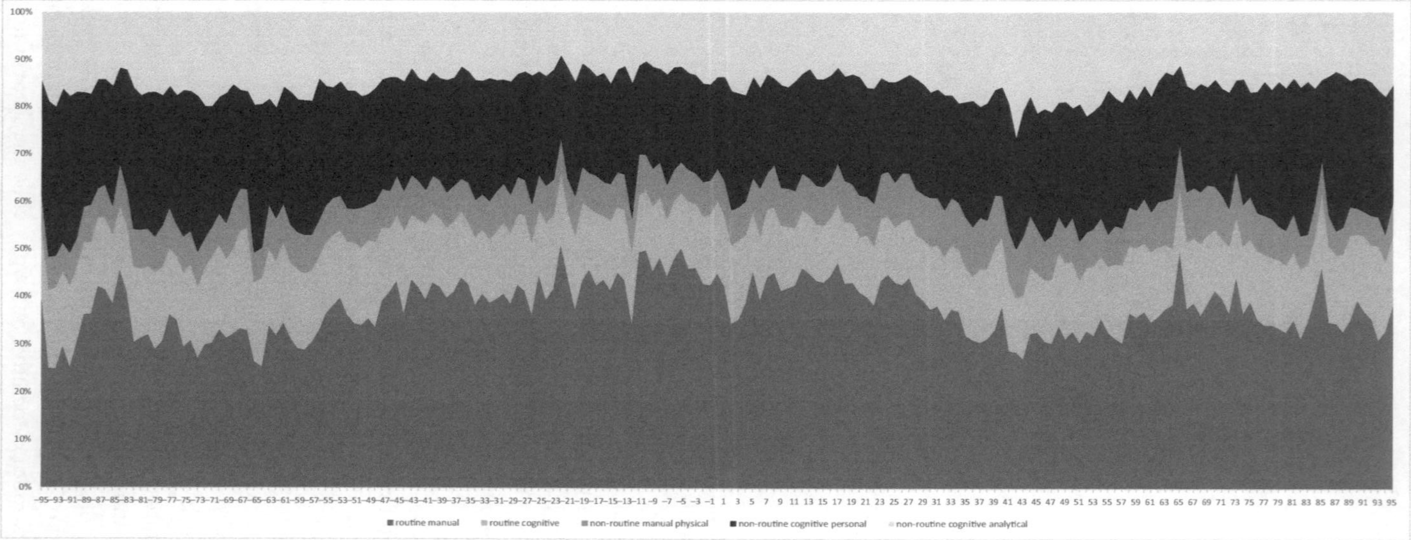

FIGURE 3.3 Tempogram – structure of job postings by task-content groups across 95 weeks before and after the start of COVID-19 pandemic in Poland

Source: Own elaboration.

points to polarisation-type shifts in the labour demand in Poland, fuelled by the COVID-19 pandemic.

To test how COVID-19 influenced the labour demand by task-content groups and skills, and if these changes are temporary or more persistent, multinomial logistic models in six different versions (all versions are based on equation 3.1) were estimated (Table 3.3 in the Appendix).

Models (1) and (4) show that the effect of the COVID-19 pandemic on the demand in each task-content group was significant, and in most cases positive relative to routine manual jobs,[4] with perceptible variation in skills demand – in some cases, this change was so large that it affected the sign of skill influence on demand for certain tasks from negative to positive or vice versa. The overall effect of the shock includes the initial impact, adjustments of the companies, and structural changes that the shock induced. As we have shown, only demand for manual routine jobs slightly decreased in effect of the pandemic. This means that after the first negative shock, the companies generally adjusted to the new reality and increased the demand for workers in these jobs.

The COVID-19 pandemic had a positive and the strongest effect on demand for non-routine manual jobs. These jobs are mostly supplemented by new technologies that enable transitioning into online mode, but also cover health personnel in hospitals and pharmacies. Seven skills in this task-content group were less required during the COVID-19 pandemic than before. Among them communication (with a significantly strong decrease in relation to routine manual jobs), managerial, self-organisation, technical, and artistic skills were the ones with non-negligible and negative coefficient. Demand for interpersonal skills increased perceptibly, and slightly for mathematical skills during the pandemic.

The demand effect for routine cognitive and non-routine cognitive analytical tasks was smaller, but also positive. Nevertheless, the effect of the pandemic on skill demand in the latter group was mostly negative. Lower demand was observed especially for technical, artistic, and self-organisation skills. In effect, demand for technical and artistic skills became like the one in the routine manual tasks group and the demand for artistic skills became even lower than in jobs with routine manual tasks. However, demand for individuals with strong mathematical and cognitive skills significantly increased to very high levels in the non-routine cognitive analytical jobs. This result means a huge effort from Polish companies to implement new technologies and online work. The routine cognitive jobs include financial and mathematical associate professionals, legal, social, and religious associate professionals, clerical support workers, childcare workers and teachers' aides. Such jobs can be executed online or provide offline support in managing business in times of restrictions. Overall, demand for five skills increased, and decreased for six during the pandemic. Mathematical skills became most demanded, followed by cognitive and interpersonal skills. Much less demanded were self-organisation skills (the overall effect of demand for these skills during pandemic became negative, that is, these skills became less demanded during the pandemic in routine cognitive tasks than in routine manual tasks, while before the pandemic the situation was the opposite).

The effect on the demand for the rest of the skills in routine cognitive jobs was lower and did not change the sign of the overall effect. Still, communication, managerial, and office skills were less often required than before the pandemic.

Demand for individuals performing non-routine cognitive personal tasks decreased during the COVID-19 pandemic, which can be interpreted as the effect of a major transition into remote work in Poland. This strongly affected skill requirements in this task-content group. Lower demand was observed mainly for technical, communication, office, and artistic stills. The most profound effect was observed for the technical skills, which before pandemic had been more often required than in occupations with routine manual tasks. The pandemic reversed this strong positive effect to weak negative. At the same time, demand for interpersonal, computer, mathematical (with largest positive inclination to hire individuals with these skills), and cognitive skills was significantly enhanced during the pandemic.

The number of new COVID-19 registered infections had three peaks in Poland (Figure 3.1). The first one occurred in the last months of 2020, the second occurred between the first and second quarter 2021, and the third was observed in the end of 2021. Models (1)–(3) indicate a significant impact of new COVID-19 case variability on the vacancies in all task-content groups. Demand for cognitive jobs increased with newly registered cases, while the demand for non-routine manual jobs decreased. These results may be explained by a general shift to remote work, which demands strong cognitive skills. Also, a decrease in economic activity, especially in tourism and manufacturing caused temporary lay-offs. The decrease of job offers for non-routine manual jobs (compared to manual ones) may be explained by the specificity of the Polish economy. For the last years, the economy has faced a lack in many vocational education workers in manual routine jobs mostly in building and construction, manufacturing, logistics. Some workers, who lost their jobs in sectors sensitive to pandemic conditions, sought work in other sectors. Some sectors were prospering during the pandemic: not only parcel transport being a good example, but also building and construction, which has a large share in labour demand. This, and sudden changes in market demand for goods and services, might have temporarily increased the demand for manual jobs.

While the impact of new COVID-19 cases might have had a temporary and short-lived effect on the demand for labour, governmental restrictions may have induced more lasting effects. Models (4)–(6) include the stringency index, which captures the impact of governmental restrictions on labour demand. The strongest restrictions in Poland were imposed after the first COVID-19 impact in the second quarter of 2020 (Figure 3.1). The second phase of harsh restrictions occurred in the last quarter of 2020 and the first quarter of 2021, after the pandemic's winter recurrence. The largest increase in the demand for individuals related to imposing restrictions was observed in non-routine analytical and non-routine manual jobs. The former includes highly specialised workers, among others: medical personnel (the deficit of which surged because of COVID-19), ICT specialists responsible for implementing digital solutions, or financial specialists, who shifted easily to remote working. The non-routine manual jobs also included the personnel for the above sectors, but on the level of technician, rather than a specialist. Routine cognitive and non-routine personal job offers were less frequent in the high-restrictions weeks.

Linear COVID-19-driven patterns of labour demand across task-content groups are captured in Models (2) and (5). The COVID-19 pandemic pushed a decrease in demand for non-routine cognitive analytical, non-routine manual, and routine cognitive jobs in comparison to routine manual tasks. Only non-routine cognitive personal jobs were characterised by a positively sloped trend. It may be explained by an especially fast increase in demand for these jobs during the lower-restriction period of the second half of 2021 and rebuilding the demand for personal tasks (91% increase compared to 2019, with an average increase of 59% for all task-content groups). The largest impact on skill trends during the pandemic was observed for non-routine cognitive personal jobs. A strong positive trend in demand for technical, communication, artistic, and managerial skills was reported. Even steeper but negatively sloped trends occurred for mathematical, interpersonal, and computer skills. Non-routine cognitive analytical jobs faced positive trends of office skills, and self-organisation skills. Negative trends (relative to routine manual tasks) were revealed in case of mathematical skills.

A possible nonlinear relationship between COVID-19 and demand for tasks and skills was studied in Models (3) and (6), which incorporate a parabolic function. Due to this approach, we were able to show that the effects of COVID-19 on non-routine manual jobs was small at the beginning of the pandemic, and then was strengthening till the 33rd week of the pandemic (mid-October 2020). After this peak, the demand diminished fast. Referring to skills required in non-routine manual jobs, the demand for managerial, artistic, computer, and mathematical ones increased temporarily (and exhibited a maximum temporary effect during the pandemic), while the demand for one skill (interpersonal) decreased temporarily (and exhibited a minimum temporary effect). The demand for routine and non-routine cognitive jobs was decreasing up to about the 40th week of the pandemic (December 2020), and then increased again. This means that the highest negative temporary effect of the COVID-19 on the demand for cognitive tasks emerged during the second large pandemic shock in Poland. During the pandemic, companies also temporarily increased the demand for interpersonal, cognitive, self-organisation, and computer skills in routine cognitive jobs. In non-routine cognitive jobs the temporary demand grow for office, interpersonal, self-organisation, technical, and computer skills, and temporary decline of demand for communication, managerial, mathematical, and cognitive skills was recorded. Negative temporary effects of COVID-19 were most persistent in non-routine cognitive analytical jobs – they ended in the 90th week of the pandemic (November 2021). However, this task-content group recorded more visible and important permanent positive effects. Among jobs with prevailing analytical tasks, a strong temporary increase in demand (relative to routine manual tasks) for technical skills, and a milder temporary increase for artistic and computer skills was observed, while demand for communication, availability, and self-organisation skills declined temporarily.

Conclusions

The COVID-19 pandemic has led to perceptible changes in all dimensions of socio-economic life. This study focused on how COVID-19 influenced the labour market in Poland by examining changes in labour demand by task-content groups and skill requirements, with the use of online job postings.

At the beginning of the COVID-19 pandemic, we witnessed significant contraction in the labour demand proxied by online job postings – the decline in the number of job offers in the first weeks of pandemic was deeper than in United States and other OECD countries. Then, the contraction was responding to fluctuations in restrictions posed by the Polish government, which were taken into account in modelling by introducing the stringency index into respective models.

The first conclusion stemming from this study states that companies generally adjusted to the new COVID-19 reality and finally reinforced the demand for workers in most jobs, however a decline in demand for routine manual jobs was observed (compared to the pre-COVID period). The biggest increase in online job offers was recorded in non-routine manual jobs, while the demand effect for routine cognitive and non-routine cognitive analytical jobs was smaller, but also positive.

The second conclusion points to an overall increase in demand for computer, mathematical, and cognitive skills, their being strongest in the non-routine task-content group. Not just self-organisation skills appeared to be much less demanded, but also communication, managerial, and office skills were negatively hit by COVID-19. However, the skill-mix required in non-routine cognitive personal jobs was most profoundly affected by the pandemic in terms of variability – some skills were affected negatively, while some positively.

Third, COVID-19-driven changes in the demand for task-content groups and skills have both a permanent or temporary nature – in the latter case some of them reversed when restrictions were eased, or companies had enough time to adjust to pandemic conditions. Renewal of demand for non-routine cognitive personal and routine cognitive jobs are good examples of such a reversed trend. A notable exception was the demand for non-routine manual jobs, which increased in the pandemic up to October 2020 and then declined. In the case of skills, we witnessed an initial decline and then a slow increase in demand for managerial, office, and self-organisation skills. The opposite situation was recorded for mathematical, cognitive, and computer skills, which were intensively demanded in the beginning of the pandemic. The permanent (and positive) effect of COVID-19 was recorded in non-routine cognitive analytical jobs.

Summing up, our multidimensional analysis reveals that although the initial impact of COVID-19 on labour demand in Poland was significant and negative, the pandemic effects appeared to be mostly temporary – after an initial shock and subsequent shocks related to lockdown restrictions, the demand across task-content groups and skills requirements revived to a large extent. However, considering the fact that the structural shift in demand towards non-routine versus routine jobs has accelerated since the outburst of the COVID-19 pandemic, we may expect deepening polarisation processes in the Polish labour market. Undoubtedly, this trend shall be analysed thoroughly in the future, when more extensive time series data will be available.

There are certain limitations of this study. The analysis was based on online job offers, which reflect any shocks, including pandemic related, almost instantly. Apart from the unarguable merits, online job postings have some limitations concerning the total vacancy population coverage. Moreover, even though almost two years have passed since the first pandemic shock hit the Polish economy and labour market, our study cannot identify all the effects of the COVID-19. We considered only the short- to medium-run effects. The pandemic continues, and still may induce longer-lasting effects. Finally, it would be also interesting to look for a causal inference, which was not included in this study.

Acknowledgements

We are grateful to the National Science Centre, Poland, for the funding provided within the project 'The polarisation of the Polish labour market in the context of technical change' (contract number 2016/23/B/HS4/00334), and the Institute of Labour and Social Studies in Warsaw for providing data on online job offers.

Notes

1 BHC is a research project launched in 2009 to monitor demand for skills on the Polish labour market.

2 The stringency index and the number of new COVID-19 cases were taken from https://ourworldindata.org/coronavirus/country/poland#how-many-tests-are-performed-each-day.

3 We also tested unrestricted fixed and random effects to account for possible COVID-19 time effects. Information criteria showed that the model with random effects was better, but the pattern of both fixed and random effects did not match the COVID-19 period. Thus, we did not report these results – they are available upon request.

4 The results of multinomial logistic models shall be always interpreted regarding routine manual task-content group as a reference group.

References

Acemoglu, D., & Autor, D. (2011). Skills, tasks and technologies: Implications for employment and earnings. In D. Card & O. Ashenfelter (Eds.), *Handbook of labor economics, 4B* (pp. 1043–1171). Elsevier.

Acemoglu, D., Autor, D., Hazell, J., & Restrepo, P. (2021). AI and jobs: Evidence from online vacancies. (*NBER Working Paper* 28257). National Bureau of Economic Research.

Acemoglu, D., & Restrepo, P. (2019). Automation and new tasks: How technology displaces and reinstates labor. *Journal of Economic Perspectives, 33*(2), 3–30. https://doi.org/10.1257/jep.33.2.3

Acemoglu, D., & Restrepo, P. (2020). The wrong kind of AI? Artificial Intelligence and the future of labour demand. *Cambridge Journal of Regions, Economy and Society, 13*(1), 25–35. https://doi.org/10.1093/cjres/rsz022

Alekseeva, L., Azar, J., Giné, M., Samila, S., & Taska, B. (2021). The demand for AI skills in the labor market. *Labour Economics, 71*. https://doi.org/10.1016/j.labeco.2021.102002

Arntz, M., Gregory, T., & Zierahn, U. (2016). The risk of automation for jobs in OECD countries: A comparative analysis. (*OECD Social, Employment and Migration Working Papers* 189). http://dx.doi.org/10.1787/5jlz9h56dvq7-en.

Autor, D., Levy, F., & Murnane, R. J. (2003). The skill content of recent technological change: An empirical exploration. *Quarterly Journal of Economics, 118*(4), 1279–1333. https://doi.org/10.1162/003355303322552801

Beblavý, M., Fabo, B., & Lenaerts, K. (2016b). Demand for digital skills in the US labour market: The IT skills pyramid. *CEPS Special Report* 154.

Beblavý, M., Mýtna Kureková, L., & Haita, C. (2016a). The surprisingly exclusive nature of medium- and low-skilled jobs. Evidence from a Slovak job portal. *Personnel Review, 45*(2), 255–273. https://doi.org/10.1108/PR-12-2014-0276

Böhm, S., Linnyk, O., Kohl, J., Weber, T., Teetz, I., Bandurka, K., & Kersting, M. (2020). *Analysing gender bias in IT job postings: A pre-study based on samples from the German job market* [Proceedings]. Proceedings of the 2020 Computers and People Research Conference (SIGMISCPR'20), June 19–21, 2020, Nuremberg, Germany. ACM, New York, NY, USA. https://doi.org/10.1145/3378539.3393862

Brüning, N., & Mangeol, P. (2020). What skill do employers seek in graduates? Using online job posting data to support policy and practice in higher education. (*OECD Education Working Paper* 231). Organisation for Economic Co-operation and Development.

Campello, M., Kankanhalli, G., & Muthukrishnan, P. (2020). Corporate hiring under COVID-19: Labor market concentration, downskilling, and income inequality. (*NBER Working Paper* 27208). National Bureau of Economic Research.

Campos-Vazquez, R. M., Esquivel, G., & Badillo, R. Y. (2021). How has labor demand been affected by the COVID-19 pandemic? Evidence from job ads in Mexico. *Latin American Economic Review, 30*(1). https://doi.org/10.47872/laer-2021-30-1

Chetty, R., Friedman, J. N., Hendren, N., & Stepner, M. (2020). *How did COVID-19 and stabilization policies affect spending and employment? A new real-time economic tracker based on private sector data*. Harvard Kennedy School. www.hks.harva rd.edu/cente rs/mrcbg /programs/growthpolicy/realtime-econo mics-new-platform-track-impacts-covid-19-people

Coombs, C. (2020). Will COVID-19 be the tipping point for the Intelligent automation of work? A review of the debate and implications for research. *International Journal of Information Management, 55*. https://doi.org/10.1016/j.ijinfomgt.2020.102182

Deming, D. J., & Kahn, L. B. (2018). Skill requirements across firms and labor markets: Evidence from job postings for professionals. *Journal of Labor Economics, 36*(S1), S337–S369. http://dx.doi.org/10.1086/694106

Deming, D. J., & Noray, K. L. (2020). Earnings dynamics, changing job skills, and STEM careers. *Quarterly Journal of Economics, 135*(4), 1965–2005. https://doi.org/10.1093/qje/qjaa021

Forsythe, E., Kahn, L. B., Lange, F., & Wiczer, D. G. (2020). Labor demand in time of COVID-19: Evidence from vacancy postings and UI claims. *Journal of Public Economics, 189*. https://doi.org/10.1016/j.jpubeco.2020.104238

Frey, C. B., & Osborne, M. A. (2017). The future of employment: How susceptible are jobs to computerisation? *Technological Forecasting and Social Change, 114*(C), 254–280. https://doi.org/10.1016/j.techfore.2016.08.019

Gałecka-Burdziak, E., & Pater, R. (2015). Ile jest wolnych miejsc pracy w Polsce? *Gospodarka Narodowa, 279*(5), 171–186. https://doi.org/10.33119/GN/100855

Hardy, W., Keister, R., & Lewandowski, P. (2018). Educational upgrading, structural change and the task composition of jobs in Europe. *Economics of Transition, 26*(2), 201–231. https://doi.org/10.1111/ecot.12145

Hensvik, L., Le Barbanchon, T., & Rathelot, R. (2021). Job search during the COVID-19 crisis. *Journal of Public Economics, 194*. https://doi.org/10.1016/j.jpubeco.2020.104349

Hershbein, B., & Kahn, L. B. (2018). Do recessions accelerate routine-biased technological change? Evidence from vacancy posting. *American Economic Review, 108*(7), 1737–1772. https://doi.org/10.1257/aer.20161570

Kurekova, L. M., Beblavy, M., & Thum-Thysen, A. (2015). Using online vacancies and web surveys to analyse the labour market: A methodological inquiry. *IZA Journal of Labor Economics, 4*, 18. https://doi.org/10.1186/s40172-015-0034-4

Lovaglio, P. G., Mezzanzanica, M., & Colombo, E. (2020). Comparing time series characteristics of official and web job vacancy data. *Quality & Quantity, 54*, 85–98. https://doi.org/10.1007/s11135-019-00940-3

Lyu, W., & Liu, J. (2021). Soft skills, hard skills: What matters most? Evidence from job postings. *Applied Energy, 300*. https://doi.org/10.1016/j.apenergy.2021.117307

Marinescu, I., Skandalis, D., & Zhao, D. (2021). The impact of the federal pandemic unemployment compensation on job search and vacancy creation. *Journal of Public Economics, 200*. https://doi.org/10.1016/j.jpubeco.2021.104471

Marinescu, I., & Wolthoff, R. (2020). Opening the black box of the matching function: The power of words. *Journal of Labor Economics, 38*(2), 535–568. https://doi.org/10.1086/705903

Modestino, A. S., Shoag, D., & Balance, J. (2020). Upskilling: Do employers demand greater skill when workers are plentiful? *The Review of Economics and Statistics, 102*(4), 793–805. https://doi.org/10.1162/rest_a_00835

OECD. (2021). *An assessment of the impact of COVID-19 on job and skills demand using online vacancy data* [Policy brief]. Organisation for Economic Co-operation and Development.

Pater, R., Szkoła, J., & Kozak M. (2019). A method for measuring detailed demand for workers' competences. *Economics: The Open-Access, Open-Assessment E-Journal, 13*(1), 1–29; http://dx.doi.org/10.5018/economics-ejournal.ja.2019-27

Samek, L., Squicciarini, M., & Cammeraat, E. (2021). The human capital behind AI: Jobs and skills demand from online job postings. (*OECD Science, Technology and Industry Policy Papers* 120). Organisation for Economic Co-operation and Development.

Shuai, X., Chmura, C., & Stinchcomb, J. (2021). COVID-19, labor demand, and government responses: Evidence from job posting data. *Business Economics, 56*, 29–42. https://doi.org/10.1057/s11369-020-00192-2

Squicciarini, M., & Nachtigal, H. (2021). Demand for AI skills in jobs: Evidence from online job postings. (*OECD Science, Technology and Industry Policy Papers* 3). Organisation for Economic Co-operation and Development.

Tsvetkova, A., Grabner, S., & Vermeulen, W. (2020). Labour demand weakening during the COVID-19 pandemic in US cities: Stylised facts and factors related to regional resilience. (*OECD Local Economic and Employment Development Papers* 2020/06). Organisation for Economic Co-operation and Development.

APPENDIX

TABLE 3.3 The results of the COVID-19 pandemic on the labour demand by task-content groups and skills; estimates of a multinomial logit regression

Task content	*Model 1*		*Model 2*		*Model 3*		*Model 4*		*Model 5*		*Model 6*	
	Coef.	*Std. Err.*	*Coef.*	*Std. Err.*	*Coef.*	*Std. Err.*	*Coef.*	*Std. Err.*	*Coef.*	*Std. Err.*	*Coef.*	*Std. Err.*
Routine cognitive												
communication	0.734	0.007	0.717	0.006	0.737	0.007	0.734	0.007	0.714	0.006	0.738	0.007
managerial	0.519	0.007	0.514	0.007	0.513	0.007	0.519	0.007	0.516	0.006	0.514	0.007
availability	−0.311	0.006	−0.303	0.006	−0.305	0.006	−0.311	0.006	−0.304	0.006	−0.305	0.006
office	0.165	0.005	0.149	0.005	0.123	0.005	0.165	0.005	0.147	0.005	0.122	0.005
interpersonal	0.223	0.005	0.285	0.005	0.208	0.005	0.223	0.005	0.280	0.005	0.207	0.005
self-organisation	0.169	0.005	0.219	0.005	0.190	0.005	0.169	0.005	0.223	0.005	0.190	0.005
technical	0.242	0.005	0.215	0.005	0.201	0.005	0.242	0.005	0.213	0.005	0.201	0.005
artistic	−0.126	0.005	−0.126	0.005	−0.107	0.005	−0.126	0.005	−0.125	0.005	−0.106	0.005
computer	2.145	0.010	2.174	0.010	2.124	0.010	2.145	0.010	2.177	0.010	2.125	0.010
mathematical	0.044	0.008	0.056	0.007	0.056	0.008	0.044	0.008	0.055	0.007	0.055	0.008
cognitive	0.492	0.006	0.567	0.006	0.500	0.006	0.492	0.006	0.564	0.006	0.500	0.006
_cons	−1.604	0.006	−1.689	0.005	−1.585	0.005	−1.604	0.006	−1.674	0.005	−1.587	0.005
covid	0.065	0.022					0.081	0.022				
trend			−0.002	1.3E-04	−0.031	4.9E-04			−0.001	1.3E-04	−0.031	0.001
trend2					3.6E-04	5.9E-06					3.7E-04	6.6E-06
new_cases	1.2E-06	4.0E-08	1.0E-06	4.1E-08	1.1E-06	4.2E-08						
stringency_index							0.001	1.2E-04	−0.001	7.2E-05	4.7E-04	1.1E-04
communication#covid	−0.127	0.010					−0.130	0.010				
managerial#covid	−0.168	0.010					−0.166	0.010				
availability#covid	0.050	0.009					0.050	0.009				
office#covid	−0.131	0.009					−0.115	0.009				
interpersonal#covid	0.140	0.007					0.140	0.007				
self-organisation#covid	−0.510	0.008					−0.511	0.008				

technical#covid	0.038	0.008					0.029	0.008				
artistic#covid	−0.070	0.007					−0.073	0.007				
computer#covid	−0.033	0.014					−0.036	0.014				
mathematical#covid	0.299	0.012					0.288	0.012				
cognitive#covid	0.131	0.009					0.129	0.009				
communication#c.trend			0.002	1.4E-04	−0.002	0.001			0.002	1.4E-04	−0.003	0.001
managerial#c.trend			0.003	1.6E-04	0.004	0.001			0.003	1.6E-04	0.004	0.001
availability#c.trend			−0.001	1.4E-04	0.000	0.001			−0.001	1.3E-04	0.001	0.001
office#c.trend			0.005	1.5E-04	0.007	0.001			0.005	1.5E-04	0.007	0.001
interpersonal#c.trend			−0.005	1.1E-04	0.013	4.3E-04			−0.005	1.1E-04	0.013	4.3E-04
self-organisation#c.trend			0.007	1.1E-04	0.021	4.6E-04			0.007	1.1E-04	0.021	4.6E-04
technical#c.trend			4.2E-040	1.1E-04	0.004	4.5E-04			0.001	1.1E-04	0.005	4.5E-04
artistic#c.trend			0.001	1.1E-04	−0.005	4.3E-04			0.001	1.1E-04	−0.005	4.4E-04
computer#c.trend			−2.7E-04	2.1E-04	0.012	0.001			-2.8E-04	2.1E-04	0.012	0.001
mathematical#c.trend			−0.007	1.9E-04	−0.003	0.001			−0.007	1.9E-04	−0.002	0.001
cognitive#c.trend			−0.005	1.4E-04	0.015	0.001			−0.005	1.4E-04	0.015	0.001
communication#c.trend2					4.7E-05	7.6E-06					0.000	0.000
managerial#c.trend2					−6.4E-06	7.8E-06					0.000	0.000
availability#c.trend2					−2.4E-05	6.6E-06					0.000	0.000
office#c.trend2					−1.5E-05	7.0E-06					0.000	0.000
interpersonal#c.trend2					−2.3E-04	5.2E-06					0.000	0.000
self-organisation#c.trend2					−1.7E-04	5.6E-06					0.000	0.000
technical#c.trend2					−5.4E-05	5.5E-06					0.000	0.000
artistic#c.trend2					7.0E-05	5.3E-06					0.000	0.000
computer#c.trend2					−1.5E-04	1.0E-05					0.000	0.000
mathematical#c.trend2					−5.3E-05	8.7E-06					0.000	0.000
cognitive#c.trend2					−2.5E-04	6.7E-06					0.000	0.000

(Continued)

TABLE 3.3 (Continued)

Task content	*Model 1*		*Model 2*		*Model 3*		*Model 4*		*Model 5*		*Model 6*	
	Coef.	*Std. Err.*	*Coef.*	*Std. Err.*	*Coef.*	*Std. Err.*	*Coef.*	*Std. Err.*	*Coef.*	*Std. Err.*	*Coef.*	*Std. Err.*
Non-routine manual												
communication	−0.054	0.010	−0.049	0.009	−0.044	0.010	−0.054	0.010	−0.040	0.009	−0.045	0.010
managerial	0.095	0.010	0.119	0.009	0.084	0.009	0.095	0.010	0.120	0.009	0.085	0.009
availability	0.303	0.007	0.295	0.006	0.310	0.007	0.303	0.007	0.298	0.006	0.310	0.007
office	−0.326	0.008	−0.369	0.007	−0.340	0.007	−0.326	0.008	−0.368	0.007	−0.339	0.007
interpersonal	0.502	0.007	0.356	0.006	0.448	0.007	0.502	0.007	0.371	0.006	0.446	0.007
self-organisation	0.058	0.007	0.078	0.006	0.074	0.006	0.058	0.007	0.073	0.006	0.074	0.006
technical	0.014	0.007	−0.015	0.006	0.001	0.006	0.014	0.007	−0.006	0.006	−0.001	0.006
artistic	0.104	0.006	0.190	0.006	0.144	0.006	0.104	0.006	0.189	0.006	0.145	0.006
computer	0.994	0.014	1.099	0.013	1.010	0.014	0.994	0.014	1.092	0.013	1.012	0.014
mathematical	0.807	0.009	0.878	0.008	0.836	0.009	0.807	0.009	0.875	0.008	0.835	0.009
cognitive	0.389	0.008	0.403	0.007	0.393	0.007	0.389	0.008	0.406	0.007	0.392	0.007
_cons	−2.232	0.008	−2.120	0.007	−2.223	0.007	−2.232	0.008	−2.174	0.007	−2.217	0.007
covid	0.443	0.028					0.235	0.029				
trend			−0.003	1.5E-04	0.015	0.001			−0.005	1.6E-04	0.016	0.001
trend2					−2.2E-04	7.4E-06					−2.4E-04	8.0E-06
new_cases	-1.7E-07	4.9E-08	4.6E-07	5.0E-08	-3.7E-07	5.2E-08						
stringency_index							0.004	1.5E-04	0.004	8.4E-05	−0.001	1.3E-04
communication#covid	−0.185	0.014					−0.199	0.014				
managerial#covid	−0.134	0.014					−0.135	0.014				
availability#covid	−0.057	0.010					−0.057	0.010				
office#covid	−0.050	0.012					−0.042	0.012				
interpersonal#covid	0.388	0.009					0.391	0.009				
self-organisation#covid	−0.220	0.009					−0.215	0.009				

technical#covid	−0.187	0.009					−0.180	0.009				
artistic#covid	−0.211	0.009					−0.212	0.009				
computer#covid	0.007	0.020					0.010	0.020				
mathematical#covid	0.153	0.013					0.153	0.013				
cognitive#covid	0.086	0.011					0.085	0.011				
communication#c.trend			0.002	2.0E−04	0.005	0.001			0.002	2.0E−04	0.005	0.001
managerial#c.trend			0.002	2.1E−04	0.013	0.001			0.002	2.1E−04	0.013	0.001
availability#c.trend			0.001	1.4E−04	−0.002	0.001			0.001	1.5E−04	−0.002	0.001
office#c.trend			0.003	2.0E−04	−0.002	0.001			0.003	2.1E−04	−0.002	0.001
interpersonal#c.trend			−0.003	1.3E−04	−0.016	0.001			−0.004	1.4E−04	−0.015	0.001
self-organisation#c.trend			0.004	1.4E−04	0.002	0.001			0.004	1.4E−04	0.002	0.001
technical#c.trend			0.004	1.4E−04	0.003	0.001			0.004	1.4E−04	0.003	0.001
artistic#c.trend			0.001	1.3E−04	0.011	0.001			0.001	1.3E−04	0.011	0.001
computer#c.trend			−0.004	2.9E−04	0.017	0.001			−0.003	2.9E−04	0.017	0.001
mathematical#c.trend			−0.005	2.0E−04	0.002	0.001			−0.005	2.1E−04	0.002	0.001
cognitive#c.trend			−0.002	1.7E−04	0.003	0.001			−0.002	1.7E−04	0.003	0.001
communication#c.trend2					-2.7E-05	1.1E-05					-2.7E-05	1.1E-05
managerial#c.trend2					-1.5E-04	1.0E-05					-1.5E-04	1.0E-05
availability#c.trend2					4.6E-05	7.0E-06					4.6E-05	7.0E-06
office#c.trend2					6.1E-05	9.3E-06					5.8E-05	9.3E-06
interpersonal#c.trend2					1.6E-04	6.4E-06					1.5E-04	6.4E-06
self-organisation#c.trend2					1.9E-05	6.6E-06					1.9E-05	6.6E-06
technical#c.trend2					1.8E-05	6.6E-06					1.8E-05	6.6E-06
artistic#c.trend2					-1.3E-04	6.5E-06					-1.3E-04	6.5E-06
computer#c.trend2					-2.6E-04	1.4E-05					-2.5E-04	1.4E-05
mathematical#c.trend2					-1.0E-04	9.9E-06					-1.0E-04	9.8E-06
cognitive#c.trend2					-6.1E-05	8.2E-06					-6.1E-05	8.1E-06

(Continued)

TABLE 3.3 (Continued)

Task content	*Model 1*		*Model 2*		*Model 3*		*Model 4*		*Model 5*		*Model 6*	
	Coef.	*Std. Err.*	*Coef.*	*Std. Err.*	*Coef.*	*Std. Err.*	*Coef.*	*Std. Err.*	*Coef.*	*Std. Err.*	*Coef.*	*Std. Err.*
Non-routine cognitive personal												
communication	1.026	0.006	0.989	0.005	1.031	0.006	1.026	0.006	0.992	0.005	1.033	0.006
managerial	0.837	0.006	0.801	0.005	0.829	0.006	0.837	0.006	0.801	0.005	0.829	0.006
availability	0.039	0.005	0.020	0.004	0.048	0.005	0.039	0.005	0.021	0.004	0.049	0.005
office	−0.277	0.005	−0.229	0.005	−0.294	0.005	−0.277	0.005	−0.230	0.005	−0.296	0.005
interpersonal	0.243	0.005	0.331	0.004	0.204	0.005	0.243	0.005	0.334	0.004	0.205	0.005
self-organisation	0.402	0.005	0.464	0.004	0.399	0.005	0.402	0.005	0.464	0.004	0.399	0.005
technical	0.301	0.005	0.326	0.004	0.328	0.005	0.301	0.005	0.329	0.004	0.331	0.005
artistic	0.318	0.004	0.320	0.004	0.347	0.004	0.318	0.004	0.321	0.004	0.347	0.004
computer	1.299	0.010	1.371	0.010	1.286	0.010	1.299	0.010	1.368	0.010	1.286	0.010
mathematical	0.225	0.007	0.177	0.006	0.221	0.007	0.225	0.007	0.173	0.006	0.221	0.007
cognitive	0.581	0.005	0.633	0.005	0.588	0.005	0.581	0.005	0.633	0.005	0.589	0.005
_cons	−1.693	0.005	−1.815	0.005	−1.697	0.005	−1.693	0.005	−1.832	0.005	−1.705	0.005
covid	−0.288	0.020					−0.310	0.021				
trend			0.001	1.1E-04	−0.025	4.5E-04			0.001	1.2E-04	−0.028	0.001
trend2					3.1E-04	5.5E-06					3.4E-04	5.9E-06
new_cases	7.2E-07	3.5E-08	8.9E-07	3.5E-08	6.4E-07	3.6E-08						
stringency_index							0.001	1.1E-04	0.001	6.2E-05	0.002	9.6E-05
communication#covid	−0.310	0.008					−0.314	0.008				
managerial#covid	−0.140	0.009					−0.139	0.009				
availability#covid	0.002	0.007					0.001	0.007				
office#covid	−0.296	0.008					−0.285	0.008				
interpersonal#covid	0.448	0.006					0.448	0.006				
self-organisation#covid	−0.010	0.007					−0.010	0.007				

technical#covid	−0.461	0.007					−0.465	0.007				
artistic#covid	−0.299	0.006					−0.301	0.006				
computer#covid	0.127	0.014					0.124	0.014				
mathematical#covid	0.928	0.011					0.922	0.011				
cognitive#covid	0.201	0.007					0.201	0.007				
communication#c.trend			0.005	1.2E-04	−0.005	0.001			0.005	1.2E-04	−0.005	0.001
managerial#c.trend			0.004	1.4E-04	−0.004	0.001			0.004	1.4E-04	−0.004	0.001
availability#c.trend			4.1E-04	1.0E-04	−0.006	0.000			0.000	1.0E-04	−0.006	4.2E-04
office#c.trend			0.006	1.5E-04	0.022	0.001			0.006	1.5E-04	0.022	0.001
interpersonal#c.trend			−0.010	9.3E-05	0.018	3.7E-04			−0.010	9.4E-05	0.018	3.7E-04
self-organisation#c.trend			−0.001	9.6E-05	0.017	3.9E-04			−0.001	9.6E-05	0.017	3.9E-04
technical#c.trend			0.007	1.0E-04	0.009	4.1E-04			0.007	1.0E-04	0.009	4.1E-04
artistic#c.trend			0.005	9.4E-05	−0.002	3.8E-04			0.005	9.4E-05	−0.003	3.8E-04
computer#c.trend			−0.004	2.2E-04	0.017	0.001			−0.004	2.1E-04	0.016	0.001
mathematical#c.trend			−0.016	1.8E-04	−0.031	0.001			−0.016	1.8E-04	−0.031	0.001
cognitive#c.trend			−0.006	1.1E-04	0.008	4.6E-04			−0.006	1.1E-04	o.008	4.6E-04
communication#c.trend2					1.2E-04	6.4E-06					1.2E-04	6.4E-06
managerial#c.trend2					1.1E-04	6.8E-06					1.1E-04	6.8E-06
availability#c.trend2					8.3E-05	5.2E-06					8.2E-05	5.2E-06
office#c.trend2					-2.1E-04	6.6E-06					-2.0E-04	6.6E-06
interpersonal#c.trend2					-3.4E-04	4.5E-06					-3.4E-04	4.5E-06
self-organisation#c.trend2					-2.2E-04	4.8E-06					-2.2E-04	4.8E-06
technical#c.trend2					-2.7E-05	5.0E-06					-2.9E-05	5.0E-06
artistic#c.trend2					9.4E-05	4.7E-06					9.4E-05	4.7E-06
computer#c.trend2					-2.6E-04	1.0E-05					-2.5E-04	1.0E-05
mathematical#c.trend2					2.1E-04	8.2E-06					2.0E-04	8.2E-06
cognitive#c.trend2					-1.7E-04	5.7E-06					-1.7E-04	5.6E-06

(Continued)

TABLE 3.3 (Continued)

Task content	*Model 1*		*Model 2*		*Model 3*		*Model 4*		*Model 5*		*Model 6*	
	Coef.	*Std. Err.*	*Coef.*	*Std. Err.*	*Coef.*	*Std. Err.*	*Coef.*	*Std. Err.*	*Coef.*	*Std. Err.*	*Coef.*	*Std. Err.*
Non-routine cognitive analytical												
communication	0.867	0.006	0.797	0.006	0.861	0.006	0.867	0.006	0.805	0.006	0.863	0.006
managerial	0.448	0.007	0.447	0.006	0.420	0.007	0.448	0.007	0.447	0.006	0.420	0.007
availability	−0.511	0.006	−0.544	0.006	−0.487	0.006	−0.511	0.006	−0.541	0.006	−0.486	0.006
office	−0.473	0.006	−0.538	0.006	−0.541	0.006	−0.473	0.006	−0.543	0.006	−0.544	0.006
interpersonal	0.240	0.006	0.186	0.005	0.204	0.005	0.240	0.006	0.196	0.005	0.206	0.005
self-organisation	0.125	0.006	0.018	0.005	0.101	0.005	0.125	0.006	0.015	0.005	0.101	0.005
technical	0.465	0.006	0.622	0.005	0.492	0.006	0.465	0.006	0.631	0.005	0.494	0.006
artistic	0.094	0.005	0.214	0.005	0.162	0.005	0.094	0.005	0.212	0.005	0.162	0.005
computer	2.053	0.010	2.100	0.010	2.037	0.010	2.053	0.010	2.093	0.010	2.036	0.010
mathematical	0.644	0.007	0.619	0.007	0.636	0.007	0.644	0.007	0.618	0.007	0.636	0.007
cognitive	0.954	0.006	0.981	0.005	0.967	0.005	0.954	0.006	0.984	0.005	0.969	0.005
_cons	−1.957	0.006	−1.973	0.006	−1.960	0.006	−1.957	0.006	−2.022	0.006	−1.970	0.006
covid	0.093	0.021					−0.151	0.022				
trend			−0.007	1.4E-04	−0.013	0.001			−0.009	1.4E-04	−0.017	0.001
trend2					7.3E-05	6.6E-06					1.1E-04	7.1E-06
new_cases	8.3E-07	3.9E-08	1.4E-06	4.0E-08	7.2E-07	4.1E-08						
stringency_index							0.005	1.2E-04	0.004	6.9E-05	0.002	1.1E-04
communication#covid	−0.059	0.009					−0.073	0.009				
managerial#covid	−0.043	0.010					−0.043	0.010				
availability#covid	0.021	0.009					0.021	0.009				
office#covid	−0.105	0.010					−0.090	0.009				
interpersonal#covid	0.069	0.007					0.075	0.007				
self-organisation#covid	−0.128	0.008					−0.122	0.008				
technical#covid	−0.472	0.008					−0.473	0.008				
artistic#covid	−0.300	0.007					−0.303	0.007				

computer#covid	0.084	0.014					0.085	0.014				
mathematical#covid	0.283	0.011					0.276	0.011				
cognitive#covid	0.123	0.008					0.122	0.008				
communication#c.trend			0.003	1.4E-04	−0.014	0.001			0.003	0.000	−0.014	0.001
managerial#c.trend			0.001	1.6E-04	0.008	0.001			0.001	0.000	0.008	0.001
availability#c.trend			0.001	1.3E-04	−0.015	0.001			0.001	0.000	−0.014	0.001
office#c.trend			0.006	1.6E-04	0.006	0.001			0.006	0.000	0.006	0.001
interpersonal#c.trend			-4.3E-04	1.1E-04	−0.001	4.3E-04			−0.001	0.000	−0.001	0.000
self-organisation#c.trend			0.006	1.1E-04	−0.012	4.4E-04			0.006	0.000	−0.012	0.000
technical#c.trend			0.004	1.3E-04	0.035	4.9E-04			0.004	0.000	0.035	0.000
artistic#c.trend			0.001	1.1E-04	0.013	4.3E-04			0.001	0.000	0.014	0.000
computer#c.trend			−0.003	2.1E-04	0.012	0.001			−0.003	0.000	0.012	0.001
mathematical#c.trend			−0.005	1.7E-04	−0.008	0.001			−0.005	0.000	−0.008	0.001
cognitive#c.trend			−0.003	1.2E-04	0.002	4.8E-04			−0.003	0.000	0.001	4.8E-04
communication#c.trend2					2.1E-04	7.2E-06					2.1E-04	7.2E-06
managerial#c.trend2					-9.6E-05	7.6E-06					-9.6E-05	7.6E-06
availability#c.trend2					1.9E-04	6.5E-06					1.9E-04	6.5E-06
office#c.trend2					-6.2E-06	7.4E-06					-2.9E-07	7.4E-06
interpersonal#c.trend2					5.1E-06	5.3E-06					6.3E-06	5.3E-06
self-organisation#c.trend2					2.3E-04	5.5E-06					2.3E-04	5.5E-06
technical#c.trend2					-4.0E-04	6.0E-06					-4.0E-04	6.0E-06
artistic#c.trend2					-1.6E-04	5.3E-06					-1.6E-04	5.3E-06
computer#c.trend2					-1.9E-04	1.0E-05					-1.8E-04	1.0E-05
mathematical#c.trend2					4.2E-05	8.1E-06					3.7E-05	8.1E-06
cognitive#c.trend2					-5.1E-05	6.0E-06					-5.0E-05	6.0E-06
Number of obs.	4,402,058		4,402,058		4,402,058		4,402,058		4,402,058		4,402,058	
Log likelihood	−6032603.5		−6026912.2		−6007252.0		−6032117.0		−6024996.9		−6007478.3	
LR chi2 (degrees of freedom)	1003877.4 (96)		1015259.9 (96)		1054580.2 (144)		1004850.4 (96)		1019090.4 (96)		1054127.7 (144)	
Prob > chi2		0.0		0.0		0.0		0.0		0.0		0.0
Pseudo R2		0.077		0.078		0.081		0.077		0.078		0.081

Source: Own elaboration.

Note: Routine manual task-content group is the reference group. # represents an interaction term.

4

POSTING OF WORKERS DURING THE COVID-19 PANDEMIC IN THE EUROPEAN UNION

The Case of Slovenia

Elizabeta Zirnstein, Klemen Širok, Suzana Laporšek, and Suzana Sedmak

Introduction

The free movement of services, one of the four fundamental freedoms of the European Union's (EU) internal market, allows companies to post their employees to other EU Member States. In Slovenia, the concept of cross-border posting became relevant after the country joined the EU in 2004. The number of posted workers in Slovenia has been growing steadily since then and is among the highest in the EU. An increase in postings has also been observed in the EU as well. One of the main reasons for the rapid increase in the number of workers posted to wealthier EU countries is the accession of ten new Member States in 2004, with significant differences in living standards between the 'new' and 'old' Member States. Focusing on Slovenia, an important reason for Slovenia's high numbers of posted workers is also its proximity to the countries of the former Yugoslavia and the strong migrant flows from these countries to the EU via Slovenian companies. As a result, the number of workers posted from Slovenia to other EU Member States has been one of the highest in the EU over the past decade.

In mid-March 2020, the World Health Organisation announced that Europe was considered an active centre of the COVID-19 pandemic. Consequently, national authorities began to impose restrictions and measures to contain infections. In the context of the fundamental freedoms of the EU, measures aimed at containing the spread of COVID-19 infections mainly concerned the free movement of workers and the freedom to provide services. The two freedoms suddenly became an exemption, approved only under strict conditions. In the context of the latter (freedom to provide services), the phenomenon of posting workers, as a form of cross-border service provision, was not left untouched by the health crisis.

The changes in business operations brought about by the pandemic depended largely on the type of business (sector) and the type of work performed by employees.

DOI: 10.4324/9781003326779-6

In some sectors, companies restructured and switched to telework shortly after the pandemic began. For them, the measures against the spread of COVID-19 did not present an important obstacle in carrying out their businesses. In others, however, telework was not an option, as jobs in some sectors cannot be performed remotely. Companies that fall into this category operate in sectors such as construction, international road transportation, agriculture, and installations. These are also the sectors in which the posting of workers is particularly widespread. On the other hand, some of these economic activities were (and are) considered essential and were not subject to pandemic restriction measures. Therefore, some workers (e.g., in health care, food industry, and drivers in international transport) were still able to move freely because they performed 'essential jobs.'

Studies have been published on the impact of the pandemic on migrant and/or posted workers in Europe (e.g., Stefanova-Behlert & Menghi, 2021; Fasani & Mazza, 2020; Anderson et al., 2021; Geyer et al., 2020; Rasnača, 2020), but no study has been conducted for Slovenia and the impact of the pandemic on Slovenian posting companies and workers. Our research seeks to fill this gap by focusing on the following questions:

- What were the consequences of the COVID-19 pandemic and containment measures for Slovenian posting companies?
- How did the COVID-19 pandemic and related containment measures affect the Slovenian posted workers?

The empirical research involved the collection of primary data through 18 semi-structured interviews with key stakeholders (posting employers, employer representatives, trade unions, and public authorities) and secondary (official and public authorities) data on the numbers of posted workers from Slovenia. Qualitative research was conducted in the second half of 2020 and at the beginning of 2022 (to obtain additional data two years after the pandemic outbreak); interviews were transcribed to facilitate content analysis. Secondary data were collected to determine the trends of posting workers from Slovenia in the first two years of the pandemic (2020 and 2021) and to compare it with the period before COVID-19.

Our findings provide new insights into how the COVID-19 pandemic affected posting processes in the EU and, in particular, the posting of workers from Slovenia. The obstacles faced by Slovenian posting employers and posted workers during the pandemic were numerous. Employers reported various barriers posed by protective measures to contain the spread of infections (more bureaucracy, higher financial burden due to quarantines and testing, constant changes in containment measures, and uncoordinated measures between the EU countries). At the same time, these measures had no impact on the absolute number of posted Slovenian workers at the EU level. On the contrary, the extent of posting increased during the first two years of the pandemic. On the other hand, the pandemic deepened and exposed the vulnerability of posted workers (the pandemic resulted in numerous lay-offs, high infection risk, limited access to medical treatment, undeclared work, and lack of wage compensation in case of illness).

This chapter is organised as follows: The next section provides a brief overview of the concept of posting of workers and an outline of posting legislation. The next subsection deals with the main features of posting workers from Slovenia to other EU countries. We continue by presenting the posting of workers in terms of COVID-19 containment measures, focusing on the obstacles faced by posting employers and posted workers during the COVID-19 pandemic. Later on, we present and discuss the research findings. Finally, we conclude with a discussion on future challenges that the pandemic may pose in the context of posting.

Posting of workers – a short regulative overview

The freedom to provide services is one of the fundamental economic freedoms in the EU. Companies providing services may temporarily send (post) their employees to another EU Member State. Such cross-border provision of services, where employees are sent to work in another Member State, gives rise to a special category of workers, known as 'posted workers'. The posting of workers is a form of labour migration. However, in comparison to labour mobility, which is based on the free movement of people, the posting of workers is based on the freedom to provide services. Unlike migrant workers, posted workers remain in the host country only temporarily and do not integrate into the labour market of that country. Keeping this in mind, research and studies on migrant workers apply, at least in a part, also to posted workers.

The legislation on posting of workers is very complex. It consists of EU directives and regulations, national implementing laws, collective agreements, and case law in various areas of law, such as labour law, social security law, company law, and tax law.

All the above-mentioned legislation can be divided (systematised) into two sets of content. The first set of regulations aims to ensure minimum rights for workers posted abroad. The main EU legislative act in this area is the Directive 96/71/EC (hereinafter referred to as the Posting of Workers Directive or the PWD)[1] and its implementing Directive 2014/67/EU.[2] One of the key requirements of PWD is that for posted workers, the host country legislation and collective agreements apply, at least those relating to working conditions such as minimum wage rates, maximum working hours and minimum rest periods, minimum paid annual leave, and health and safety regulations at the workplace.

As of 30 July 2020, the revised PWD is in force (Directive (EU) 2018/957),[3] which sets additional conditions that companies have to comply with. The most important of these is the equal pay condition.[4] This means that the remuneration of a posted worker must comply with the remuneration conditions set out in national law or in the generally applicable collective agreements of the host country. Not only must the minimum wage be complied with, but also the total remuneration, which consists of the basic salary plus performance bonuses, supplements for overtime work, for work under hazardous conditions, etc. The employee is also entitled to reimbursement of travel and accommodation expenses in the host country during the posting. The aim of these 'new rules' is to narrow the gap between the remuneration of posted workers compared to local workers.

The second set of regulations concerning the posting of workers deals with the coordination of the social security systems of the EU Member States. The main legal act in this area is Regulation (EC) No 883/2004[5] and its implementing Regulation (EC) No 987/2009.[6] The coordination of social security systems with non-EU countries (third countries) is regulated in bilateral social security agreements.

The main principle of the coordination of social security systems in the EU is that a worker pays social security contributions only in one country – usually, the country where he or she works. However, there is an exception that applies to posted workers – they remain insured in the country of employment (i.e., in the country from which they were posted). This special rule is intended to prevent employees working within the EU from having to switch frequently between social security systems. Before posting, the employer must apply for the portable document A1 (hereinafter, the PD A1), for each posted worker. With this certificate, the competent institution of the sending country declares that its social security system continues to apply to these workers.

The duration of the posting can be 12 months; in some cases, it can be extended to 18 months[7] (i.e., a one-time extension possibility of six months).

The posting of workers in Slovenia is regulated by several laws. The most important are the Employment Relationship Act[8] and the Transnational Provision of Services Act.[9] The latter was revised in July 2021, to implement the revised PWD directive. Employment and work of third-country nationals are regulated by the Employment, Self-employment, and Work of Foreigners Act.[10] The latter is important in the context of this chapter because it forms the basis for the employment of workers from the former Yugoslav countries (Bosnia and Herzegovina, Serbia, and North Macedonia) in Slovenia, who are later posted from Slovenia to other EU countries. The posting of workers can also take place through temporary employment agencies that provide workers to other companies based on The Labour Market Regulation Act.[11]

Posting of workers from Slovenia to the EU – characteristics

The number of posted workers from Slovenia in the last decade has been among the highest in the EU. Between 2010 and 2020 the increase in the issued PDs A1 was more than sixfold (23,944 and 146,157, respectively) (De Wispelaere et al., 2021; ZZZS, 2022). Since the same person can be posted several times in the same year, the number of posted workers is lower (compared to the number of the PDs A1). It is estimated that it represents approximately 60% of the total number of PDs A1 issued (De Wispelaere et al., 2021). Similarly, the growth of postings can be observed in the EU as well – there have been 1,058,314 PDs A1 issued in the EU in 2010, whereas in 2019 a fourfold increase has been registered (to 4,570,675 PDs A1) (ibid.).

Putting these numbers in another context, posted workers represent 1% of all the workers in the EU labour market. However, for Slovenia, this percentage is much higher, namely 3.1% (2019 data). More than 40% of all postings in the EU were in the construction sector, and this number is even higher for Slovenia – 54%. In 2019, more than 29% of Slovenian employees in the construction sector were posted to other EU countries (De Wispelaere et al., 2021). As will be shown later, these numbers continue to rise.

How can these relatively high numbers for Slovenia be explained? The concept of cross-border posting became relevant in Slovenia after the country joined the EU. In fact, the volume of postings in the EU increased significantly after the 2004 enlargement. One of the key reasons for the rapid increase in the number of workers posted to wealthier countries was a *significant difference in living standards and average incomes between the 'new' and 'old' Member States* (cf. Širok et al., 2021; Danaj & Geyer, 2020).

Focusing on Slovenia, another reason for Slovenia's high numbers of posted workers is crucial – namely, *a substantial share of posted workers from Slovenia are third-country nationals* (Danaj et al., 2020; EFBWW, 2019). They come mainly from the Western Balkans, more precisely from the countries that formed Yugoslavia in the past (together with Slovenia). Comparing the Western Balkan countries with the EU Member States, the differences in living standards and average income are even more striking. Expected income is several times higher in Slovenia than in Bosnia and Herzegovina (where most of the third-country nationals, employed in Slovenia, come from), Serbia, or North Macedonia (Eurostat, 2021). High unemployment rates and the general political and social situation in these countries, alongside the financial aspects, are strong push factors leading to migration flows to more prosperous parts of Europe. Due to the common history, geographical proximity, economic, and political ties, as well as family ties and friendships, Slovenia remains the destination country for many workers from the Western Balkans (as it used to be in the former Yugoslavia). Nowadays, however, Slovenia often serves as an 'intermediary' between the poorer countries of the Western Balkan and the wealthier EU Member States (cf. Tanasić & Jerkič, 2017; Danaj & Geyer, 2020). Indeed, many third-country nationals are very often hired by Slovenian companies only to be posted to other EU countries once the paperwork is done.

Bilateral agreements signed with Bosnia and Herzegovina and later with Serbia (2013 and 2019, respectively), which set the conditions for employment of citizens of these two countries and the procedures for issuing work permits, facilitate the process of employing their citizens. As of October 2019, 11% of the employed workers in Slovenia were foreigners (approximately 101,200). Most of them were citizens of Bosnia and Herzegovina (49%), Serbia (13%), and Kosovo (9%). The number of foreign workers increased by 81.4% (or approximately 45,400 people) between 2014 and 2019.[12] As mentioned earlier, a significant part of the foreign workforce is hired by Slovenian companies only to be posted abroad. This 'business model' has been heavily criticised nationally and internationally (cf. Krilić et al.,

2020; Danaj & Geyer, 2020). It has been associated with letter-box companies, exploitation of posted workers, violations of the law, abuse of workers' rights, etc.

As the Slovenian market is relatively small, many companies and business owners look for business opportunities beyond the borders, and in this way increase the *company's prospects for sustainable financial business performance* in the long run (cf. Furåker & Larsson, 2020).

It should be noted, however, that the profits of many Slovenian companies, providing services in foreign markets, can to a significant extent be attributed to the *regulation of social security contributions*. Slovenian employers deduct mandatory social security contributions from the income that the worker would have received for the same work in Slovenia – regardless of the minimum hourly rate (or the actual income the worker receives) in the host country. In practice, this often means that the mandatory social contributions are deducted from the Slovenian minimum wage. This practice, or more precisely, the underlying legislation, has been criticised by Slovene and foreign trade unions, foreign employer associations, and ministries and has been a reason for filing appeals against Slovenia in different institutions (cf. EFBWW, 2019; ETUC, 2019). The export of cheaper labour (due to generally lower wages, lower social contributions, posted third-country nationals with even lower wage expectations, and in some cases exploitative practices) has earned Slovenia accusations of *social dumping*.

Lack of control of posting employers has also been associated with high numbers of posted workers from Slovenia (Danaj et al., 2020). For example, if a company is accused of violating regulations, it cannot post its workers abroad.[13] However, as confirmed in our research, employers seeking to exploit the system in the ways described earlier, often establish or purchase another company to continue their illicit practices.

In addition, the Slovene Transnational Provision of Services Act,[14] which entered into force in January 2018, significantly tightened the conditions for obtaining PDs A1 under Article 12 of Regulation (EC) 883/2004. As a result, employers applied for PDs A1 under Article 13 of the Regulation (EC) 883/2004 and in this way tried to circumvent the stricter regulation, even though they were not entitled to obtain a PD A1 on this basis (Article 13), given the nature of the work performed abroad by their posted workers.

Pandemic and the posting of workers

The COVID-19 pandemic has significantly changed our lives. Work patterns have changed – some trends, such as remote working, automation, digitalisation, have been accelerated by the pandemic. Many employers have successfully adapted to the new conditions and integrated teleworking into their businesses. On the other hand, not all work can be done remotely, and, in some sectors, the pandemic posed a major challenge. This is the case in the construction sector, which accounts for most of the Slovenian workers posted abroad. Neither can international transport drivers nor assembly and maintenance workers, who represent another two substantially large groups of posted workers from Slovenia, perform their work remotely.

The pandemic reached Europe in early 2020, and measures to contain the spread of COVID-19 infections were introduced in most EU countries in mid-March. These measures (very often in the form of strict lockdowns, travel bans, and closures of internal EU borders) remained in place until April, and in May the measures were lifted in most EU countries.[15] In early fall 2020, the number of COVID-19 infections rose again, prompting several countries to reintroduce some of the measures in September and October, and to tighten them further in November 2020. Some EU countries (partially) lifted COVID-19 containment measures for the Christmas and New Year period, after which Europe generally saw a resurgence in infection rates. As a result, measures were reintroduced or strengthened in many countries in January and February 2021. In late December 2020, the COVID-19 vaccine deliveries began, but it took months for most of the EU population to have access to vaccines. Throughout Europe, the early 2021 lockdown remained in force until spring and was lifted in most countries in April/May. As the number of the vaccinated or recovered European population kept rising, it became easier to move between countries – complying with the 'vaccinated, recovered, or tested' requirement. In the fall and later in the winter of 2021, we experienced another COVID-19 wave, but given the relatively high immunity of the population and the less severe COVID-19 virus variant, borders were generally not closed as tightly, and lockdowns did not last as long as before (Figure 4.2 provides a rough sketch of the COVID-19 waves).

As mentioned earlier, during the first wave of the pandemic, European countries implemented controls at internal EU borders to limit the spread of COVID-19 disease. This restricted, and in some cases made impossible, the free movement of people, as well as the free movement of services. The posting companies faced unprecedented difficulties while trying to comply with the signed contracts. The difficulties faced by posted workers due to restrictions on free movement within the EU were addressed in a March 2020 communication from the European Commission (European Commission, 2020b), which called on EU countries to address the problem of border crossings in a coordinated manner. In a May 2020 communication, the European Commission reiterated the importance of the free movement of persons and called for the lifting of restrictions, which, it wrote, was *key for the economic recovery. Restricting free movement and reintroducing internal borders harm the Single Market and the smooth operation of supply chains* (European Commission, 2020a).

While the pandemic containment measures did not directly aim to restrain the posting processes (Stefanova-Behlert & Menghi, 2021), they did cause disruptions in labour markets. To mitigate these and facilitate the functioning of essential industries/sectors (indeed, a substantial share of posted workers falls into the category of 'key workers'), exemptions from travel bans were introduced. As a result, some workers (e.g., in health care, food industry, and drivers in international transport) have continued to be granted free movement on the grounds of performing 'essential' jobs (Anderson et al., 2021; Robin-Olivier, 2020; Salamońska et al., 2020).

What obstacles did posting employers and posted workers face during the COVID-19 pandemic? Migration flows in general were disrupted in the first months of the pandemic (cf. OECD, 2020b; Lange et al., 2020; Vladisavljevic et al., 2020). Focusing on posting of workers, recent EU data show a sharp decrease in PDs A1 issued in 2020 compared to 2019 (3,675,687 and 4,512,401, respectively, or −18.5%) (De Wispelaere et al., 2022).[16] This decrease could be attributed to pandemic containment measures. At this stage, exact numbers for EU postings in 2021 cannot be provided, but Slovenian trends in posting during the pandemic (years 2020 and 2021) will be presented later.

As mentioned earlier, due to travel bans and border closures imposed by many countries, the free movement of people and the freedom to provide services were hindered, which created major challenges for both the posting employers and their employees in reaching their destination and meeting contractual obligations. Another obstacle for the posting companies was the introduction of mandatory quarantine for the workers sent abroad, which was imposed by many European countries and could last up to 14 days. Consequently, short postings did not make (financial) sense anymore. Questions were raised regarding costs, salary, and insurance for the quarantined workers (Stefanova-Behlert & Menghi, 2021; Salamońska et al., 2020). The reluctance of some workers to be posted has been evidenced – fear that travelling and working abroad would increase the risk of infection (cf. Salamońska et al., 2020). In general, the cost of posting workers increased due to containment measures.

With regard to workers, there have been testimonies about the specific, vulnerable position of workers providing cross-border services during the pandemic period (cf. ETUC, 2020; Geyer et al., 2020; Rasnača, 2020). As Lange and co-authors (while referring to migration in general) put it: 'The COVID-19 pandemic is, among other crises, also a migration crisis: we have seen huge movements of migrant workers forced to return home, laid-off, or employed at workplaces that pose a high risk of infection' (Lange et al., 2020, p. 336). In the event that posted workers contracted COVID-19, isolating those with the disease in common housings proved to be very challenging (Salamońska et al., 2020). In some countries, the pandemic further complicated the paperwork that needed to be completed before posting workers, for example, some Polish workers were posted without obtaining the European Health Insurance Card due to the lengthy process for issuing A1 PDs in Poland (Salamońska et al., 2020). This could deny posted workers access to medical treatment and other health services in case of injury or illness.

Posting of workers from Slovenia during the pandemic

Methodology

The results of the qualitative research conducted in the second half of 2020 and in February and March 2022 are presented in this chapter. The research conducted in

2020 was carried out within the framework of the project 'POW-Bridge – Bridging the gap between legislation and practice in the Posting of Workers.' Although the POW-Bridge project aimed to examine the interplay between EU and national regulations on various aspects of the posting of workers, the results presented here focus only on the pandemic-related issues in posting. *More precisely, we are interested in how the COVID-19 pandemic and containment measures affected the posting process for Slovenian employers and what consequences they had for the posted workers*. The first part of the qualitative research was conducted when the pandemic had not yet subsided. In order to obtain more data, it was decided to continue the research in early 2022, two years after the beginning of the pandemic.

A total of 18 semi-structured interviews were conducted to collect primary data. The interviewees were public authorities' representatives (5 interviews), employee representatives (4 interviews), employer associations' representatives (4 interviews), and posting employers (5 interviews). This allowed us to get a comprehensive picture of the various aspects of posting and the challenges associated with posting workers. Due to pandemic constraints, most interviews took place online. With the consent of the interviewees, the interviews were recorded and later transcribed, which allowed for a more efficient content analysis of the primary data.

Secondary data on the extent of postings from Slovenia were provided by the Health Insurance Institute of Slovenia (ZZZS). These are regular quarterly statistics of PDs A1 issued for the 2019–2021 period. The data obtained allowed us to *identify the posting trend during the pandemic*.

In the first part of this subchapter, the results of the secondary data analysis are given and the posting trends from Slovenia are presented in numbers and discussed. Subsequently, the findings of the qualitative research are presented, and the consequences of the pandemic are discussed from the perspective of posting employers and posted workers.

Posting of workers during the COVID-19 pandemic in numbers

As EU data on postings in 2020 show,[17] the posting of workers decreased by 18.5% in the first year of the pandemic (De Wispelaere et al., 2022). Available data for Slovenia show a different trend. As it can be seen from Figure 4.1, the number of postings from Slovenia continued to increase throughout the pandemic period (2020 and 2021).

According to the available data (Figure 4.1), the volume of posted workers in Slovenia has increased, except for 2018, when (as explained earlier) the Transnational Provision of Services Act (ZČmIS) was introduced, which brought stricter conditions for posting. The increase can be seen in both the number of PDs A1 issued and the number of posted persons (data available only from 2018 onwards). From 2012 until the adoption of the ZČmIS, the average annual growth in the volume of issued PDs A1 in Slovenia was 24%. The adoption of the ZČmIS in 2018 resulted in an annual decline of 33%, while in the first year after

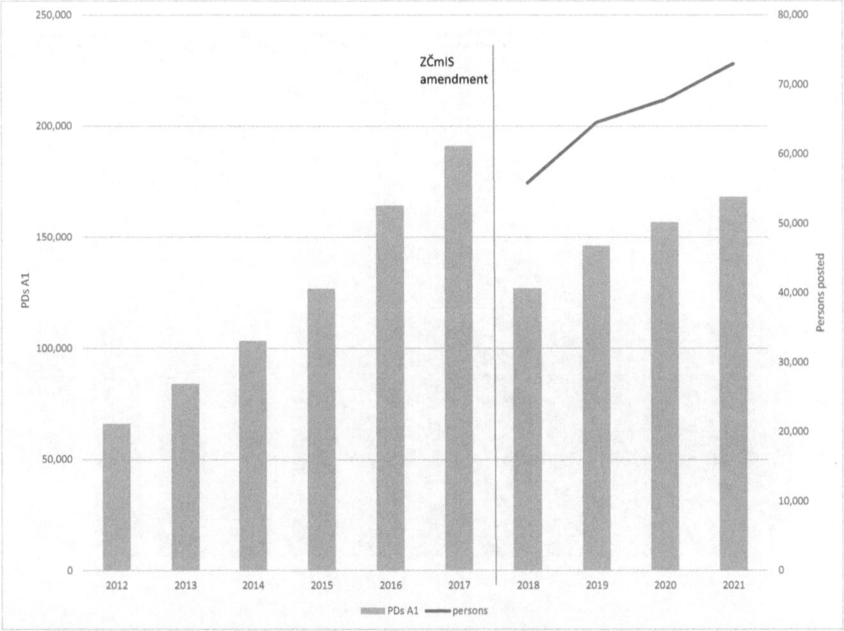

FIGURE 4.1 The volume of postings from Slovenia during 2012–2021 period

Source: Health Insurance Institute of Slovenia administrative data (ZZZS, 2022) and De Wispelaere et al., 2021; own calculation.

the introduction of the ZČmIS (until the outbreak of COVID-19), the annual growth in volume was 15%, which continued in the COVID-19 period with a 7% annual increase.

Analysis of data from the Health Insurance Institute of Slovenia (ZZZS, 2022) shows that – unexpectedly – during the pandemic, despite numerous COVID-19 containment measures, the number of posted workers from Slovenia increased steadily with minor fluctuation (Figure 4.2). This fluctuation could be attributed to the seasonal nature of the work. During the pandemic in Slovenia, we observed an increase in the number of postings abroad as well as an increase in the number of people who worked abroad. At the annual level, the number of postings in 2020 increased by 7.3% (number of PDs A1 issued) and 5.8% (number of workers posted) compared to 2019, despite the two waves of the pandemic that restricted free movement in the EU. In the first wave of the pandemic (March to April 2020) and in the second wave (September to December 2020), containment measures and lockdowns had a direct impact, while this was not the case in the third wave (January and February 2021). The period of the first wave of the pandemic coincides with a decrease in postings of 11.4% (number of PDs A1 issued) and 7.8% (number of workers posted). The second (fall) wave of the pandemic coincides with a decrease of 8.9% (number of PDs A1 issued) and 6.1% (number of workers

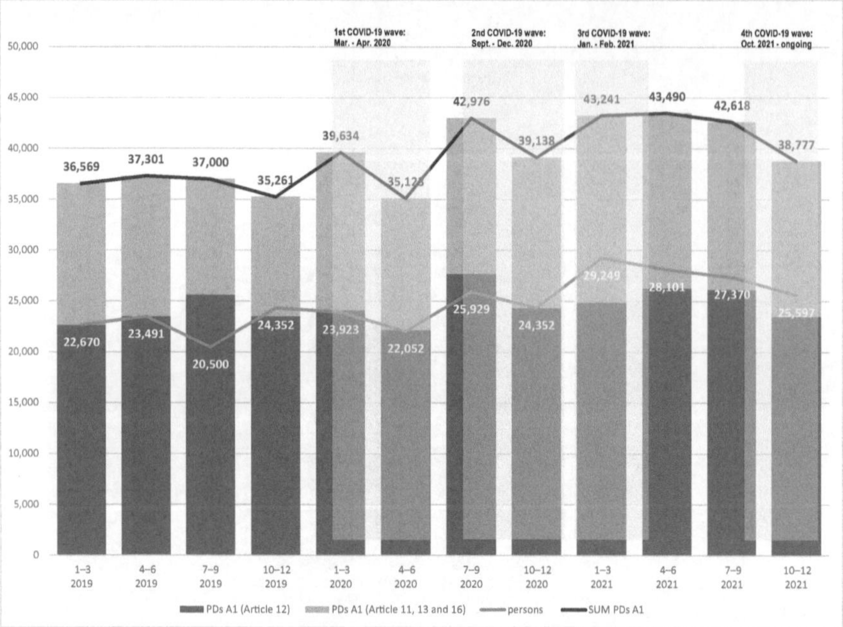

FIGURE 4.2 The volume of postings from Slovenia in the period 2019–2021 with marked waves of the pandemic

Source: Health Insurance Institute of Slovenia (ZZZS, 2022), own calculation.

posted). In contrast, the third wave of the pandemic brought an increase in worker mobility, both in absolute and relative terms. During the third wave of the pandemic in January and February 2021, the three-month volume of posted workers reached its highest level since 2017, with a 10.5% increase in the number of PDs A1 issued and a 20.1% increase in posted workers compared to the previous quarter; that coincided with the second wave of the pandemic. The impact of the fourth wave, which was by far the most severe in terms of detected cases and deaths and was not accompanied by lockdown measures, was comparable to the impact of the second wave.

What are the reasons that postings from Slovenia continues to increase despite the pandemic and related measures to contain it? One explanation could lie in the specifics of demand in the sectors where a significant share of posting from Slovenia occurs. The sectors with the largest share of posted workers are construction and transport. Data from the Slovenian Health Insurance Institute for 2018–2021 (ZZZS, 2022) show that more than 70% of postings, whether we look at the number of PDs A1 issued, or the number of persons posted, come from the construction, industry, installation/maintenance, and international road transport sectors. Construction and installation/maintenance together account for 42% of postings (in terms of both PDs A1 issued and persons posted). Industry and international road transport, on the other hand, vary according to the size of the indicator observed. The industry sector contributes 20% to PDs A1 and 9% to posted persons, while the transport sector contributes 10% to PDs A1 and 19% to posted persons. Over the 2018–2021 period, an increasing trend in postings (both PDs A1 issued and persons posted) is observed in the installation/maintenance sector. International road transport also shows an increasing trend (Figure 4.3).

The dynamics of posted workers described above indicate the demand-driven nature of the construction and transport sector. The reason for the lower number of posted workers could be (to some extent) ascribed to the stagnation of economic activity in the destination countries. However, since construction is not the activity essential to the functioning of society during the pandemic, the question arises as to what led to the increase in the number of posted construction workers and installers during the pandemic. The analysis of the situation of the construction sector in the target countries shows that Slovenian construction workers and installers performed their work while posted mainly to countries where the construction sector was least affected. The growth rates in the construction sector between April 2020 and February 2021 indicate an increase in production in the countries where most Slovenian workers are posted, that is, Austria (+ 27%) and Belgium (+ 8.6%), or a slight decrease in Germany (−3.2%).[18]

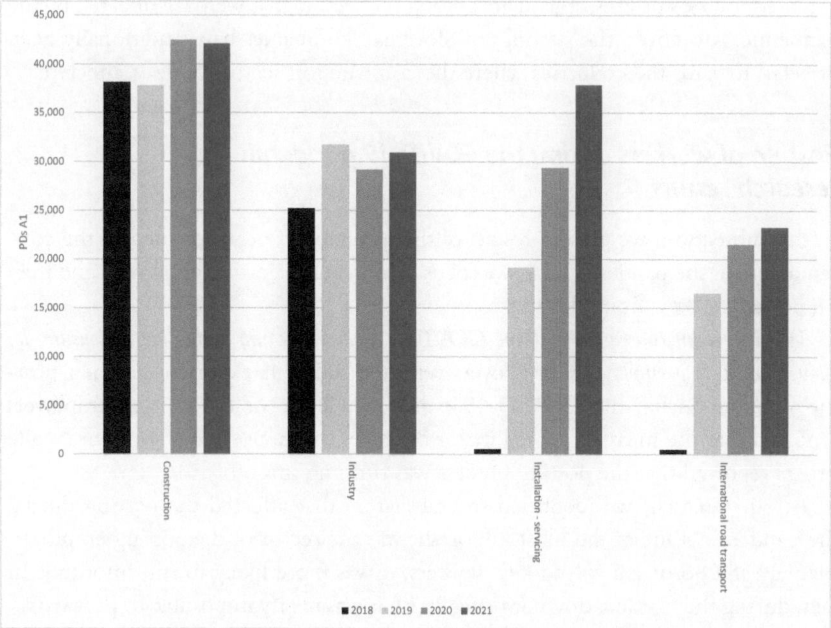

FIGURE 4.3 The volume of postings during the period 2018–2021 according to the sector (of employer)

Source: Health Insurance Institute of Slovenia (ZZZS, 2022).

A partial answer to the increasing number of postings in international road transport would be the categorisation of drivers as key workers, which is why demand in the transport sector did not decrease with the outbreak of the pandemic. The transport of goods and freight was necessary to avoid a general shortage in the event of stagnation of social life. Therefore, enormous (political) efforts were made to efficiently maintain the free movement of goods throughout the EU. The European Commission (European Commission, 2020a) issued recommendations on 23 March 2020, to implement 'green belts' aimed at lifting travel restrictions and mandatory quarantine of transport workers and at avoiding disruption of emergency travel. Thus, the pandemic did not seriously disrupt international freight traffic. However, regular passenger services, especially related to the tourism sector, were seriously affected.

Thus, the increase in the number of postings of Slovenian workers during the pandemic can be explained by a combination of factors. First, the need for movement of goods and capital, and hence labour, resisted the pandemic containment measures, which made cross-border travel to provide services much more difficult. Second, the characteristics of individual sectors also play an important role. It seems that, despite the impossibility of performing work at a distance, certain sectors experienced a decrease in demand to a lesser extent, which – based on the Slovenian case presented – is especially true for the construction sector and international road transport. Third, the segments of the Slovenian labour market that are most oriented towards posting abroad are among the sectors that were less affected by the pandemic. Moreover, the postings of Slovenian companies have traditionally been directed towards the countries where the construction sector was least affected.

Posting of workers during the COVID-19 pandemic – research results

In this subsection, we present results of the qualitative research related to the consequences of the pandemic; first we focus on Slovenian posting employers and then on posted workers from Slovenia.

What were the consequences of the COVID-19 pandemic and containment measures for Slovenian posting employers? Employers reported different experiences when posting workers during the COVID-19 pandemic. Some of the posting employers reported that the measures posed major obstacles to the posting of workers, while others reported that the posting process was running smoothly.

In our research, we identified several factors that affected the posting during the pandemic. One of the most important was the sector of the posting employer. Namely, if a posting involved key workers, it was more likely to run smoothly. In fact, during the first lockdown (Spring 2020) it was nearly impossible to post workers from non-essential sectors, whereas key workers resumed their work abroad relatively quickly. Another critical factor proved to be the size of the company. In the posting process – regardless of the pandemic – bigger employers reported fewer barriers in administrative procedures compared to medium or small-size companies. Medium- and, especially, small-size employers did not have their own resources and knowledge and therefore often found the posting process more complicated and lengthier. In addition, they often had to hire an agency or a representative to sort out bureaucratic requirements and comply with domestic and foreign regulations, which added to the costs of the posting. On the other hand, bigger companies had more resources (be it human and/or financial) to address these issues. Although bigger employers have reported lengthier and more scrupulous posting paperwork in the pandemic period, they did not perceive this as a major obstacle (given the resources available to them).

A representative of an employer association reported that its members (posting employers) most often needed their help with the following: information on relevant containment measures, posting documents, information on the 'vaccinated, recovered, tested' requirement, testing sites in destination countries, the validity of negative tests in different countries, the maximum length of stay in the host country without being subject to quarantine, etc. In the early months of the pandemic, there was a tremendous workload at the employer associations as employers sought their advice. The employer associations also acted as intermediaries between the employers and the state authorities, expressing the employers' requests and forwarding the employers' proposals to the authorities. Support was offered to the posting employers also by the Slovenian and foreign consulates.

The pandemic containment measures and their constant changes were the biggest obstacles in the posting process. For employers, the frequent (weekly, sometimes even daily) changes in regulations were confusing and time consuming, as they had to constantly keep track of and monitor the containment rules introduced in different EU countries. Sometimes changes occurred during a posting, which could make it difficult for posted workers to re-enter their home country. Employers complained about the uncoordinated measures taken by different countries, which also contributed to making the posting process even more complex than it already was.

Mandatory quarantines were a major obstacle for posting employers in 2020. According to the employer association representative, there were very few exemptions to the mandatory quarantines in the first pandemic wave.

All these measures resulted in higher costs for the employers. Mandatory quarantine measures were accompanied by accommodation costs, loss of income for the 10- or 14-day quarantine period, testing expenses, etc. Sometimes workers had to be quarantined upon their return to Slovenia – this also resulted in loss of income for a certain period. In some cases, the quarantine period could amount to one month per worker per posting (two weeks abroad immediately after entering the host country, followed by two weeks upon return to Slovenia). As one of the employers mentioned, this was especially difficult for smaller businesses, consequently some of them provided services abroad without reporting it to the local authorities, that is, they performed undeclared work. In addition to the financial burden, the pandemic has also caused more documentation work for the posting companies, so the 'bureaucratic' workload increased as well.

Sometimes workers (especially at the beginning of the pandemic in 2020) expressed reluctance towards being posted, stating concerns about their own health, or uncertainty about how the posting would proceed. After the vaccines introduction, some workers refused to be posted because they did not want to be vaccinated. Indeed, some European countries introduced the 'vaccinated or recovered' requirement (including Austria and Germany, the first two destination countries in terms of the number of posted workers from Slovenia). In some cases, there was a problem with a particular vaccine. Although workers were vaccinated, some vaccines were not accepted (e.g., Serbian workers vaccinated with the Sputnik vaccine did not meet requirements in many EU countries).

In some cases, containment measures conflicted with other regulations. The respondent from the transport sector reported the problem his drivers faced – the accommodation facilities remained closed in many European countries throughout different pandemic waves, so truck drivers could not comply with EU regulations (e.g., 45 hours of weekly rest outside the trucks).

As reported by a representative of the employer association, at the beginning of the pandemic there was 'panic' among posting employers, because of too many uncertainties. However, from a time distance, the representative cannot confirm a long-term detrimental effect of the pandemic containment measures on posting to other countries. After the initial shock and the first two waves of the pandemic, employers seemed to adjust to the change in business conditions. A significant difference could be noted after the vaccination started. After the 2021 introduction of the 'vaccinated, recovered, tested´ requirement, it became easier for employers to post workers. Although no research has been done, terminations of contracts due to the pandemic measures have not been seen as a trend, according to the employer association representative (due to the government measures and reimbursements); however, in some cases, there were delays in meeting the contractual deadlines.

How did the COVID-19 pandemic and related containment measures affect the Slovenian posted workers? As noted earlier, the COVID-19 pandemic has deepened the vulnerability of posted workers. Many of the findings on the worsening situation for posted workers during the pandemic can also be confirmed in the case of Slovenia. As in other EU countries, the pandemic was a very common and 'easily justifiable reason' for dismissing workers.

As has been reported, due to many unknowns and uncertainties at the beginning of the pandemic, workers at first felt reluctant towards being posted abroad. In fact, in March 2020, most of the posted workers left the sites abroad to return to Slovenia. In a few months, many services resumed and workers were re-posted. The testing of workers prior to the departure (and in host countries, if needed) was covered by employers in most cases. There were reports of tighter controls on documentation, which included proof of compliance with pandemic containment measures and other travel and work documentation when crossing borders. In some countries (e.g., Austria and Germany, according to interviewees), workers were even required to provide the employer's and contractor's declaration of compliance with containment measures. However, it has been reported this was just a 'dead letter on paper', since in practice the measures were very often ignored. Compliance with the containment measures, for example, on construction sites (where most of the Slovenian posted workers worked) and in common housings (where they lived) was often difficult and was therefore frequently disregarded.

One of the problems reported was the common housing of the posted workers. If someone caught the COVID-19 disease, it was almost impossible to isolate a person in a place where several workers shared the same sleeping room, bathroom, kitchen, etc. Even if an employer attempted to rent another accommodation, it was often impossible to get one, for fear of lending property to infected persons, while on the other hand, many accommodation facilities stayed closed during the pandemic period. These constraints led to more infections among posted workers.

If a company failed to monitor changes in containment measures, its workers could face fines for not complying with host country requirements. There have even been cases of entire groups of workers being fined at border crossings, because their employers were unaware that the duration of the 'vaccinated, recovered, tested' requirement had been shortened.

As mentioned above, a substantial share of posted workers from Slovenia are third-country nationals. According to our respondents, those workers often do not exercise their right to wage compensation for temporary absence from work in case of COVID-19 infection or other illness. Several reasons were given for this. First, many workers did not know their rights and how to exercise them. Second, many of the third-country nationals do not live in Slovenia and have not a Slovenian general practice physician/family doctor, which makes the exercise of workers' rights more complicated, in some cases even impossible. Third, many workers who were sent abroad did not have the social insurance arranged in Slovenia (and neither in any other country), meaning they were performing undeclared work and were not entitled to wage compensation in case of illness.

Another fraud was found in connection with undeclared work. In some cases, workers were given falsified PDs A1 by their employers, often presented as issued by a Slovak authority. PDs A1 issued by Slovenian authorities can be easily verified via the QR code, which is not the case with Slovak PDs A1, making them easier to falsify (and subsequently more difficult to verify at border controls). Such a worker – having no social insurance – would have to pay for his or her medical treatment by himself. Our interviewee reported a case of a Bosnian worker posted by a Slovenian company illegally (with a falsified PD A1) to Germany, where he contracted infection, got treated in a hospital, and later died. The bill for the hospital treatment was sent to his family (and was later paid by the employer). However, employers' ignorance of workers' rights and of unexpected situations that can occur, threatens workers' health and lives. Although this problem was known before the pandemic, additional issues arose in the event that a worker become ill and hospitalised due to coronavirus illness.

The Slovenian government introduced numerous measures and temporary legislative changes/adjustments to mitigate the negative impact of the pandemic on the economy. Many employers took advantage of this – including in relation to the posting of workers. There were documented violations of the 'crisis allowance' payments to workers for the March–May 2020 period, as well as for the last quarter of 2020. As it was reported, some employers withheld this allowance and workers did not receive the higher payments to which they were entitled. The amount they received was the same as before the allowance, that is, as in the pre-pandemic period. It must be noted that this amount was retained by employers, who – in order to pay the crisis allowance to their workers – were exempt from paying certain social security contributions during the epidemic.

Another typical abuse involved falsely declaring employees to be on furlough. During the epidemic in Slovenia (this period does not coincide with the globally declared pandemic), the government reimbursed employers for the wage costs of those employees who could not perform their jobs due to the epidemic, amounting to 80% of their wages. According to our respondents, many employers took advantage of this – they reported their workers on furlough, subsequently received the compensation for their salaries, however, the workers performed their jobs all that time. Needless to say, workers have not received higher wages because of this, in fact, there were cases reported they have received only 80% of their usual wage (the amount, subsidised by the government).

Conclusion

At first glance, the posting of workers seems to be a marginal issue. However, we maintain that it is a topical issue which will become even more important in the future. After all, there is a huge labour shortage in the EU, with structural disparities in the labour market. Adding to this the fact that the European population is ageing rapidly, labour mobility (and thus the posting of workers) is undoubtedly crucial for the European economy and will remain as such in the future. This is already evident from the trends in posting. In Slovenia, the concept of cross-border posting became relevant after the country joined the EU in 2004. The number of posted workers in Slovenia has been growing steadily ever since and is among the highest in the EU. This growth was not halted by the COVID-19 pandemic.

We assumed that the impact of the pandemic on the numbers and trends of posting in Slovenia would be negative. The analysis of secondary data did not confirm this. On the contrary, despite numerous COVID-19 containment measures, the number of posted workers from Slovenia increased steadily. This is due to a combination of factors. First, posting from Slovenia is mainly present in sectors where Slovenian companies are traditionally oriented towards countries where the COVID-19 containment measures did not have a significant negative impact on the economy and business. Second, the Slovenian sectors with the highest share of posted workers are construction and transport. Due to labour shortages in these sectors at the EU level, the posting of workers during the pandemic remained at a similar level as before. In addition, after the initial shock in March 2020, the borders of EU Member States were no longer hermetically sealed, and there were some exceptions to border crossings, which included posted workers. The need for free movement of goods and the demand for labour were obviously stronger than government measures to contain the pandemic.

The issues surrounding the posting of workers in Europe are numerous and have a long history. Although the EU has partially responded to some of them with the amended PWD, some remain unanswered. The COVID-19 pandemic has revealed many of them.

The pandemic has exposed the vulnerable position of posted workers. To mention just a few: many workers lost their jobs shortly after the outbreak of the pandemic. They were at a higher risk of getting infected due to living conditions abroad, which made it difficult for infected workers to isolate and not expose other workers to infection. Illegal posting, that is, without valid health insurance, could have had unforeseen financial consequences (for the worker or his/her employer) in the case a worker needed medical treatment.

The pandemic also put posting companies in a difficult position. Measures to contain the spread of infection made posting more difficult due to border restrictions, more paperwork, higher expenses due to quarantines, testing, etc. Containment measures changed frequently and there were significant differences between countries in this regard. For all these reasons, the posting process became even more complex than it has already been.

Although the pandemic is no longer at its peak at the time of writing, we are far from the end of it. It is not unlikely that we will see new waves in the near future. What have we learned from the first two years of the pandemic?

In the event of a pandemic or similar crisis, solutions must be found that lead to closer cooperation and joint action at the EU level. Due to the lack of experience with such crises, measures to contain the spread of the coronavirus varied significantly from country to country, but most importantly, they changed constantly, weekly, sometimes even daily. In the event of future health crises, EU Member States will need to find a way to better respond to similar situations, with uniform measures. The establishment of the so-called EU green belts can be mentioned as a good recent practice.

In terms of labour market changes, the pandemic altered work patterns, accelerating the shift to remote working in many sectors. In other sectors, such as transport, construction, or installation, telework was not an option, because the work in these sectors could not be performed remotely. These are also the sectors/jobs where the posting of workers is particularly widespread, due to the huge labour shortages. If we want these sectors to continue to function normally in the future, we need to pay more attention to the legal and practical challenges of posting in these sectors.

Acknowledgements

Some of the results presented in this paper were obtained in the course of the POW-Bridge project (Bridging the gap between legislation and practice in the

Posting of Workers, 2020–2021). The project received financial support from the EU Employment and Social Innovation Program 'EaSI' (2014–2020).

Notes

1 Directive 96/71/EC of the European Parliament and of the Council of 16 December 1996 concerning the posting of workers in the framework of the provision of services. OJ L 18, 21 January 1997, pp. 1–6.
2 Directive 2014/67/EU of the European Parliament and of the Council of 15 May 2014 on the enforcement of Directive 96/71/EC concerning the posting of workers in the framework of the provision of services and amending Regulation (EU) No 1024/2012 on administrative cooperation through the Internal Market Information System (the IMI Regulation). OJ L 159, 28 May 2014, pp. 11–31.
3 Directive (EU) 2018/957 of the European Parliament and of the Council of 28 June 2018 amending Directive 96/71/EC concerning the posting of workers in the framework of the provision of services. OJ L 173, 9 July 2018, pp. 16–24.
4 Article 3, para 3 of the Directive (EU) 2018/957.
5 Regulation (EC) No 883/2004 of the European Parliament and of the Council of 29 April 2004 on the coordination of social security systems. OJ L 166, 30 April 2004, pp. 1–123.
6 Regulation (EC) No 987/2009 of the European Parliament and of the Council of 16 September 2009 laying down the procedure for implementing Regulation (EC) No 883/2004 on the coordination of social security systems. OJ L 284, 30 October 2009, pp. 1–42.
7 Article 3, paragraph 1 (a) of the revised PWD.
8 Official Journal of Republic of Slovenia, no 21/2013 and following.
9 Official Journal of Republic of Slovenia, no 10/2017. English translation is available here www.pisrs.si/Pis.web/cm?idStrani=prevodi.
10 Official Journal of Republic of Slovenia, no 47/2015 and following.
11 Official Journal of Republic of Slovenia, no 80/2010 and following.
12 All data were obtained from the Statistical Office of the Republic of Slovenia (Https://www.stat.si/StatWeb/en).
13 Article 4 of the Transnational Provision of Services Act.
14 Official Journal of Republic of Slovenia, no 10/2017.
15 This rough and generalised timeline of the COVID-19 waves and containment measures in the EU is given for the reader to easier navigate through the consequences of the lockdowns described later.
16 It should be noted that the 2020 PDs A1 numbers are still higher than those of 2018 (3,675,687 and 2,884,994, respectively).
17 No data for postings in 2021 were available at the time of concluding this paper.
18 Eurostat data, 2021.

References

Anderson, B., Poeschel, F., & Ruhs, M. (2021). Rethinking labour migration: COVID-19, essential work, and systemic resilience. *Comparative Migration Studies*, *9*(1). https://doi.org/10.1186/s40878-021-00252-2

Danaj, S., & Geyer, L. (2020). *Here, not to stay – The posting of third-country nationals between Bosnia and Herzegovina, Slovenia, and Austria* (p. 12). European Centre for Social Welfare Policy and Research. www.euro.centre.org/publications/detail/3845

Danaj, S., Geyer, L., Krilić, S. C., Toplak, K., & Jevšnik, M. V. (2020). *Regional case study from Bosnia and Herzegovina to Austria via Slovenia: Migration and posting of third country nationals in the EU* (p. 62). European Centre.

De Wispelaere, F., De Smedt, L., & Pacolet, J. (2021). *Posting of workers. Report on A1 portable documents issued in 2019*. European Commission. https://lirias.kuleuven.be/retrieve/616238

De Wispelaere, F., De Smedt, L., & Pacolet, J. (2022). *Posting of workers – Report on A1 portable documents issued in 2020*. Publications Office of the European Union. https://doi.org/10.2767/048597

Directive 2014/67/EU of the European Parliament and of the Council of 15 May 2014 on the enforcement of Directive 96/71/EC concerning the posting of workers in the framework of the provision of services and amending Regulation (EU) No 1024/2012 on administrative cooperation through the Internal Market Information System (the IMI Regulation), Pub. L. No. OJ L 159, 28.5.2014, pp. 11–31. (2014). https://eur-lex.europa.eu/legal-content/EN/TXT/?uri=CELEX%3A32014L0067&qid=1647312131839

EFBWW. (2019, May 24). *Social irregularities in Slovenia*. www.efbww.org

ETUC. (2019, October 15). *Unions refer first exploitation cases to new European labour authority for investigation*. ETUC | European Trade Union Confederation. www.etuc.org/en/pressrelease/unions-refer-first-exploitation-cases-new-european-labour-authority-investigation

ETUC. (2020, May 20). *ETUC note on posted workers and the COVID-19 outbreak*. ETUC | European Trade Union Confederation. www.etuc.org/en/document/etuc-note-posted-workers-and-covid-19-outbreak

European Commission. (2020a). *Communication from the commission towards a phased and coordinated approach for restoring freedom of movement and lifting internal border controls – COVID-19 2020/C 169/03*. https://eur-lex.europa.eu/legal-content/EN/TXT/?uri=CELEX%3A52020XC0515%2805%29

European Commission. (2020b). *Covid-19 – Informacije za obmejne delavce in napotene delavce*. https://europa.eu/youreurope/citizens/files/Covid_FrontierPostedWorkers_sl.pdf

Eurostat. (2021, March 24). *Mean and median income by age and sex – EU-SILC and ECHP surveys*. https://appsso.eurostat.ec.europa.eu/nui/show.do?dataset=ilc_di03&lang=en

Fasani, F., & Mazza, J. (2020). Immigrant key workers: Their contribution to Europe's COVID-19 response. *SSRN Electronic Journal*. https://doi.org/10.2139/ssrn.3584941

Furåker, B., & Larsson, B. (2020). *Trade union cooperation in Europe: Patterns, conditions, issues*. Springer International Publishing. https://doi.org/10.1007/978-3-030-38770-9

Geyer, L., Danaj, S., & Scoppetta, A. (2020). *The impact of COVID-19 on the posting of workers and their workplace safety*. www.euro.centre.org/webitem/3752

Krilić, S. C., Toplak, K., & Jevšnik, M. V. (2020). *Posting of third country nationals* (p. 83). ZRC SAZU.

Lange, T. de, Mantu, S., & Minderhoud, P. (2020). Into the unknown: COVID-19 and the global mobility of migrant workers. *American Journal of International Law*, *114*, 332–336. https://doi.org/10.1017/aju.2020.62

OECD. (2020a). *COVID-19 and key workers: What role do migrants play in your region?* OECD. www.oecd.org/coronavirus/policy-responses/covid-19-and-key-workers-what-role-do-migrants-play-in-your-region-42847cb9/

OECD. (2020b). *Managing international migration under COVID-19*. OECD. www.oecd.org/coronavirus/policy-responses/managing-international-migration-under-covid-19-6e914d57/

Rasnača, Z. (2020). Essential but unprotected: Highly mobile workers in the EU during the Covid-19 pandemic. *SSRN Electronic Journal*. https://doi.org/10.2139/ssrn.3699377

Robin-Olivier, S. (2020). Free movement of workers in the light of the COVID-19 sanitary crisis: From restrictive selection to selective mobility. *European Papers – A Journal on Law and Integration*, *5*(1), 613–619. https://doi.org/10.15166/2499-8249/357

Salamońska, J., Brzozowska, A., & Matuszczyk, K. (2020). *Posting of workers from the Polish perspective – Overview and most recent trends*. Centre of Migration Research.

Širok, K., Sedmak, S., & Zirnstein, E. (2021). Izzivi pri napotitvi delavcev v okviru čezmejnega opravljanja storitev v EU v času epidemije COVID-19 (predstavitev rezultatov raziskovalnega projekta). *Izzivi managementu, III*(2), 34–41.

Stefanova-Behlert, S., & Menghi, M. (2021). *The impact of COVID-19 on posted workers: The new 'posting framework*. www.robert-schuman.eu/en/doc/questions-d-europe/qe-591-en.pdf

Tanasić, M., & Jerkič, L. (2017). *Problematika napotitve delavcev na delo v tujino iz Slovenije*. ZSSS. www.zsss.si/wp-content/uploads/2017/12/DanClovekovihPravic_Napotitve_2018.pdf

Vladisavljevic, A., Ciobanu, C., Kovacevic, D., Inotai, E., Gascón Barberá, M., German Sirotnikova, M., Kajosevic, S., Dragoljo, S., Todorov, S., & Gosling, T. (2020). *Pandemic disrupts southeast Europe labour flows*. BIRN. https://balkaninsight.com/2020/11/25/pandemic-disrupts-southeast-europe-labour-flows/

ZZZS. (2022). *Izdaja potrdil A1*. ZZZS; Internal document.

5

THE DETERMINANTS OF (NOT) HIRING MIGRANTS IN POLAND

The Pandemic Perspective

Olena Shelest-Szumilas and Marcin Woźniak

Introduction

The negative consequences of the pandemic crisis were particularly severe for migrant workers (Alaverdov, 2021; Enright et al., 2020; Fassani & Mazza, 2020; Guadagno, 2020), whose position is traditionally reported to be more vulnerable due to having less secure employment and less favourable working conditions as compared to natives. At the same time, in the European Union (EU) immigrants comprise 13% of workers employed in key occupations (Fassani & Mazza, 2020), while in the United States, the percentage of migrant workers working in essential industries was found to be even higher (Gelatt, 2020; Kerwin et al., 2020).

Migrant workers employed in the sectors most affected by the pandemic crisis were found in a particularly difficult and vulnerable situation. Consequently, the unemployment rate for this group has risen in many EU countries (European Commission, 2020; The Migration Observatory, 2021). Fassani and Mazza (2020) estimated that approximately 3.1 million EU-born and 6.1 million extra-EU migrants working in the EU14+UK area were at risk of losing their jobs due to the pandemic crisis. For many categories of migrants, job loss means limited access to social protection and higher uncertainty about their legal status, as well as deterioration of the economic situation of their families which are deprived of remittances (Moroz et al., 2020). Some of them had been stuck in the host country, living in poor conditions with no possibility of returning home (Tompson et al., 2020).

The decline of the migrant employment rate can be partly explained by the fact that these workers perform particular types of jobs (Borjas & Cassidy, 2020), most of which have suffered from social distancing measures and have become less demanded because of lower business activity. In Poland, migrants traditionally find employment in jobs that cannot be conducted remotely (construction, transportation, manufacturing industry) or in sectors that rely on interpersonal contacts

DOI: 10.4324/9781003326779-7

(accommodation and catering services, other services). As a result, in sectors where job tasks could not be performed at home, the incidence of job losses was higher.

The main purpose of the paper is to investigate and assess the determinants of hiring migrant workers during the COVID-19 pandemic in one of the largest Polish cities. We also use descriptive statistics to provide a general picture of immigrant employment in Poland. In the paper we seek an answer to the following research question: What are the key determinants of hiring migrant labour during the COVID-19 pandemic?

While negative consequences of the COVID-19 pandemic have been examined in different countries all over the world, relatively little attention has been paid to the impact of the crisis on migrants in regional labour markets so far. Our study also seeks to fill another research gap which arises from the fact that the majority of previous research has focused on the situation of economic migrants, whereas the demand for migrant labour under pandemic conditions has been overlooked.

The spatial scope of the study is Poznań agglomeration which is one of the main destinations for migrants in Poland.[1] The data were collected from October 13 to December 15, 2020, using CATI and CAWI techniques. The research sample contains 420 employers from the Poznań agglomeration. The empirical analysis focuses on companies that currently employ migrant workers or declared that employed ones within 12 months prior to the survey. To identify the factors that may increase or decrease the probability of hiring migrant workers by local companies in the 12 months following the survey, we developed three ordinal logistic regression models. The results show that factors that decrease the chances of the company to report the demand for migrant workers prevail. This suggests an overall negative impact of the pandemic on migrant workers in the local labour market and a reduced likelihood of reporting a demand for migrant labour in the following year. Although the research presents a local perspective on the situation of migrant workers, our findings may be valid for most Polish cities with the highest concentration of immigrants. The study gives a new insight into the employment of migrant employees during the pandemic shock and provides a better understanding of the demand side of the labour market which has been neglected so far in this type of research.

The remainder of the paper is organised in the following manner. The next section provides a short review of previous studies. Following that, the paper presents current statistical data on migrant workers in Poland. The subsequent two sections describe methods, the data collection procedure and research sample. The next section looks at the main empirical findings. The last section presents our conclusions and discusses limitations of the study.

Literature review

The negative impact of the COVID-19 pandemic on the labour market situation of migrants and ethnic minorities has been documented in several countries. Garrote Sanchez et al. (2020) focused on migrant workers in the EU. The authors identified jobs that were at higher risk depending on whether they belong to one of the essential sectors, whether they can be done from home, and whether they require any personal interactions. The study showed that migrants from outside of the EU were more likely to do jobs that were found to be most exposed to COVID-19-related lay-offs.

The analysis performed by Borjas and Cassidy (2020) for the US labour market confirms that the employment decline in the first several months of the lockdown was higher for migrant workers than for natives. At the same time, migrants were less likely to find new employment in the recovery months (from April to May 2020) compared to native workers. Montenovo et al. (2020) documented large declines of employment rate for Hispanics in the US who tend to work in jobs that cannot be done at home. Fairlie et al. (2020) explored the impact of the COVID-19 pandemic on job losses among minorities and confirmed the negative effect for African-American and Latin populations, showing that the latter was exposed to much higher rates of unemployment compared to other groups.

The study conducted by Enright et al. (2020) focused on the situation in Ireland. The authors presented evidence for greater employment decline among non-Irish nationals. Interestingly, the study provided evidence that in the case of Eastern European nationals the higher probability of job loss could not be explained by the fact that they work in jobs that cannot be done from home. Hu (2020) addressed the problem of ethnic and native – migrant inequalities of the COVID-19 impact in the United Kingdom. The study provides ample evidence that the migrant population was more likely to experience negative consequences of the pandemic.

Barker et al. (2020) investigated how the situation of migrant-dependent households has changed due to the COVID-19 in Bangladesh and Nepal. The authors demonstrated that the negative effect was due to the lower rates of migration as well as decreased remittances. They concluded that migrant families are particularly vulnerable to the crisis because of the close relationship between earnings and mobility opportunities that has been significantly reduced. Honorati et al. (2020) and Varshaver et al. (2020) formulated very similar conclusions investigating vulnerability of the migrant populations in Russia.

Using qualitative techniques, Bhandari et al. (2021) documented that the COVID-19 outbreak resulted in financial difficulties of Nepalese migrants residing in Japan, which were caused by job losses or reducing working hours. The research also revealed several cases of perceived discrimination that migrants faced during COVID-19 (e.g., in terms of the access to information). The newest report published by UNICEF (2021) explored economic and social implications of the pandemic focusing on the situation of migrant workers in South Asia. The authors stressed not only the problem of massive job losses and significant wage reductions but also wage thefts that resulted in lower remittance flows and deterioration of migrant family living conditions. Pizarro (2020) examined the impact of the COVID-19 pandemic on labour migrants in Argentina and found that recently arrived migrants were more likely to lose their jobs and income. The author also stressed the limited access to social protection, which was particularly acute for undocumented migrants. Strzelecki (2020) explored the impact of the COVID-19 on companies that employ migrant workers in Poland. He found that the fluctuation of migrant worker employment was much higher than that of overall employment.

Although negative consequences of the COVID-19 pandemic crisis on the labour market can be observed in many dimensions, its impact was found to be not the same for different job sectors and occupations. For example, several studies (e.g., Adams-Prassl et al., 2020; Montenovo et al., 2020) demonstrated that groups of workers who have been most hit by the pandemic include those employed in occupations with low share of tasks that can be performed from home. Also, Pagano et al. (2020) showed that some industries can be more or less resilient to the COVID-19 related crisis depending on the degree of teamwork, interaction with customers, and physical presence required at the workplace. Moreover, Mongey et al. (2020) observed that workers in low-work-from-home or high-physical-proximity jobs were found to be less educated, of lower income, have fewer liquid assets relative to income, and are more likely to be renters and, thus, more vulnerable to COVID-19. Another strand of literature is related to the situation of different populations of migrant workers. These papers document the impact of the COVID-19 on specific groups of migrants. Factors to be taken into account include age and gender (Enright et al., 2020), skill level (Montenovo et al., 2020) as well as legal and employment status of surveyed migrants (Borjas & Cassidy, 2020).

To sum up the literature review, we can conclude that the negative impact of COVID-19 on migrants has been well documented across different countries. However, previous work has only focused on the impact of type of jobs (occupations) performed by migrants and demographic characteristics of migrant workers on their situation on the labour market. Yet, insufficient attention has been paid to exploring the determinants that reflect companies' characteristics and may affect their demand for migrant labour. The functioning of regional labour markets during the pandemic have also rarely been in the focus of previous studies.

Migrant workers in Poland

Compared to many western economies, Poland has faced increased migration inflows relatively recently. The phenomena arose mainly as a result of the armed conflict in Donbass (Eastern Ukraine) that has been ongoing since 2014 and the general improvement of the economic situation in Poland. As a consequence, in 2018 Poland welcomed over one million temporary and seasonal workers from outside the European Union, most of whom were Ukrainian citizens (OECD, 2020). The general situation on the labour market in region and in Poland is presented in Figure 5.1.

It is worth noticing, that at the beginning of the XXI century Poland was characterised by a high and persistent unemployment rate which oscillated around 20%. After accessing the EU in 2004, the economic situation in Poland has radically improved. Th unemployment rate started to drop and the average wage increased

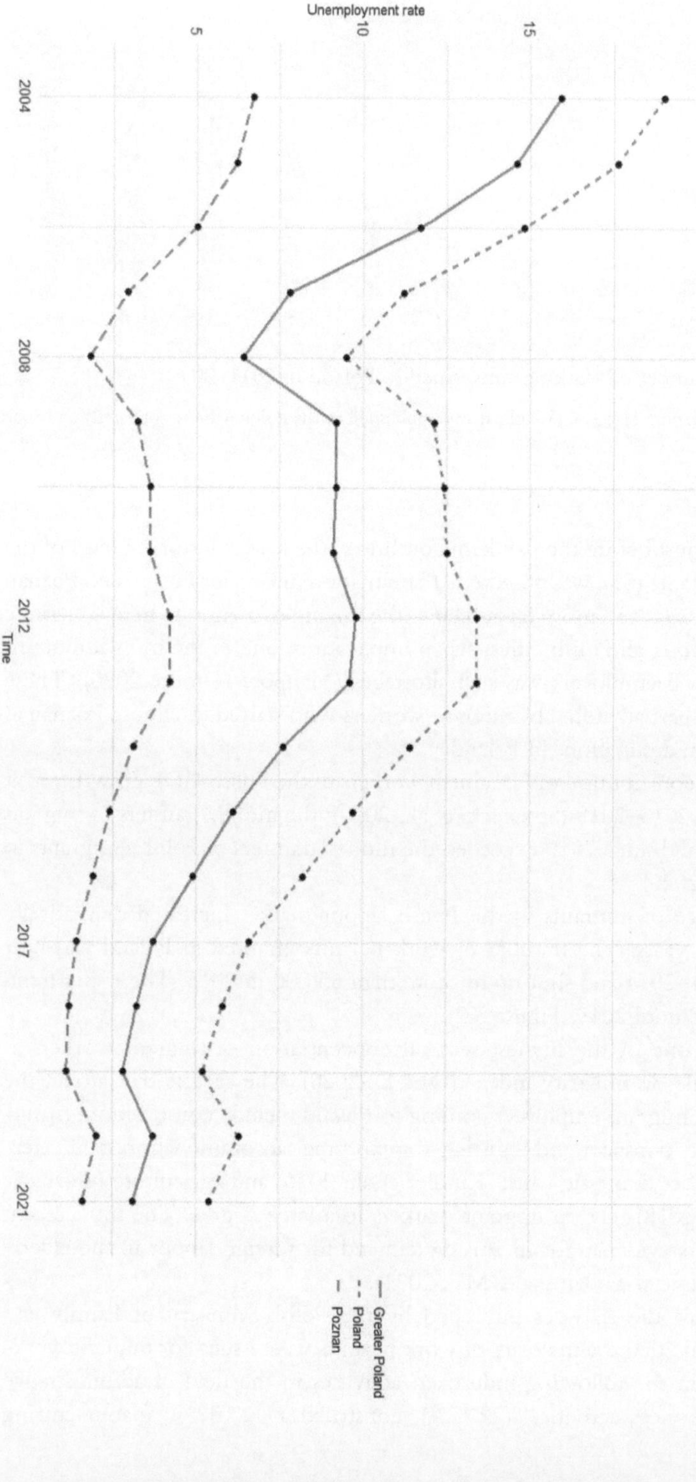

FIGURE 5.1 The unemployment rate in Poznań, Greater Poland, and Poland in 2004–2021

Source: Own elaborations based on the data provided by the Central Statistics Office.

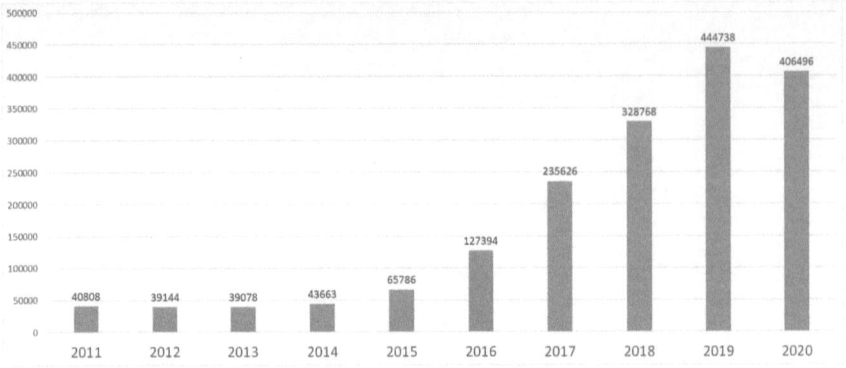

FIGURE 5.2 Number of work permits issued in Poland in 2011–2020

Source: Own elaborations based on the information published by the Polish Ministry of Family and Social Policy.

over the years. Just before the pandemic outbreak, the lowest historical level of the unemployment rate (5%) was observed. The situation in Greater Poland and Poznań agglomeration was even more favourable – the unemployment rate here was at the lowest level among all Polish cities. As an implication, one of the most important problems of local employers was staff shortages (ManpowerGroup, 2020). These shortages were partially filled by migrant workers who started to choose Poznań as one of the main destinations in Poland.

The overall contribution of Ukrainian workers to the Polish GDP growth was at around 13% in 2013–2018 (Strzelecki et al., 2020); the money transfers of migrant workers in Poland since 2019 exceeded the money transfers of Polish emigrants to Poland (NBP, 2020).

The presence of migrants in the Polish labour market increased dramatically in the last five years. The number of work permits[2] granted in Poland was near 40,000 in 2011–2014 and shot up to more than 65,000 in 2015. The rising trend was maintained until 2019 (Figure 5.2).

Poland has one of the highest sectoral concentration of migrant workers as measured by the dissimilarity index[3] (OECD, 2020). The sectors that attract the largest share of migrant employees coming to Poland include construction, manufacturing, trade, transport and logistics, warehousing, accommodation, and catering services. Also, domestic work (Kindler et al., 2016) and agriculture (Górny & Kaczmarczyk, 2018) rely on migrant workers to a large degree. The most recent research delivers evidence for increasing demand for foreign labour in the elderly care sector (Kubiciel-Lodzińska & Maj, 2021).

According to the statistics published by the Polish Ministry of Family and Social Policy, in 2020 the majority of work permits were issued for migrant workers employed in the following industries: activities in the field of administrative and support services activities[4] (22.12%), construction (23.52%), manufacturing

(23.34%), transport and storage (17.83%). The sectors that are less attractive but still rely on migrant labour are trade (3.14%) and accommodation and food services (3.35%) (MRPS, 2021). Not all these sectors have been exposed to the COVID-19 pandemic impact in the same way. Among sectors where the majority of migrant workers concentrate, the deepest fall in overall employment was reported in such industries as administrative and support service activities, agriculture, forestry and fishing, manufacturing, and accommodation and food services (GUS, 2021). When it comes to the situation of migrant workers, the impact of the pandemic on migrant inflows and employment varied between regions in Poland.

The Poznań agglomeration is one of the largest and most important metropolitan areas in Poland (Śleszyński, 2015). It is in the central-western part of the country as the driving force of the regional economy with dominant industries: construction, services, trade, and logistics. The area is also characterised by a high degree of internationalisation and favourable economic situation In general, the largest number of declarations of entrusting work to a foreigner[5] was condensed in central and western Poland, where the largest and wealthiest Polish cities are located. Warsaw was in first place with almost 88,000 work declarations, and Poznań came in second with almost 76,000 declarations. Other cities with a high number of work declarations were Wrocław, Łódź, Gdańsk, Kraków, Szczecin, and Bydgoszcz (Figure 5.3).

Data collection and research sample

The fieldwork was conducted from 13 October to 15 December 2020. From the research sample of 11,047 local enterprises, we gathered 420 computer-assisted telephone or web interviews. The CAWI questionnaire was sent to the respondent in either of the two cases: refusal to provide a telephone interview or lack of a telephone number in the database.

The REGON register[6] was used as the sampling operator. A sampling scheme defining two stratifying variables was adopted. The first one is the size of the enterprise (micro, small, medium, and large), the second one is the location of the company's registered office or its local branch (the city of Poznań or Poznań district). Interviews were conducted with the owner, co-owner, manager, or someone indicated by these persons. Generalisation of the study on the entire population is associated with statistical error equal to 4.78% at a 95% confidence level.[7]

For estimations we selected variables that could be of interest in terms of determinants of hiring migrants and were found important in some previous studies. Danzer and Dietz (2018) includes economic branches among determinants of migrants' well-being during the crisis. Ambrosini and Barone (2007) point that working conditions (e.g., type of contract, wages) are important factors diversifying migrant employment in both the EU and home countries. Likewise, Sterud et al. (2018) stresses the role of the conditions of employment. They also add discrepancy between a person's educational attainment, the job requirements and higher risk of poor self-reported health among migrant workers. Among rare Polish

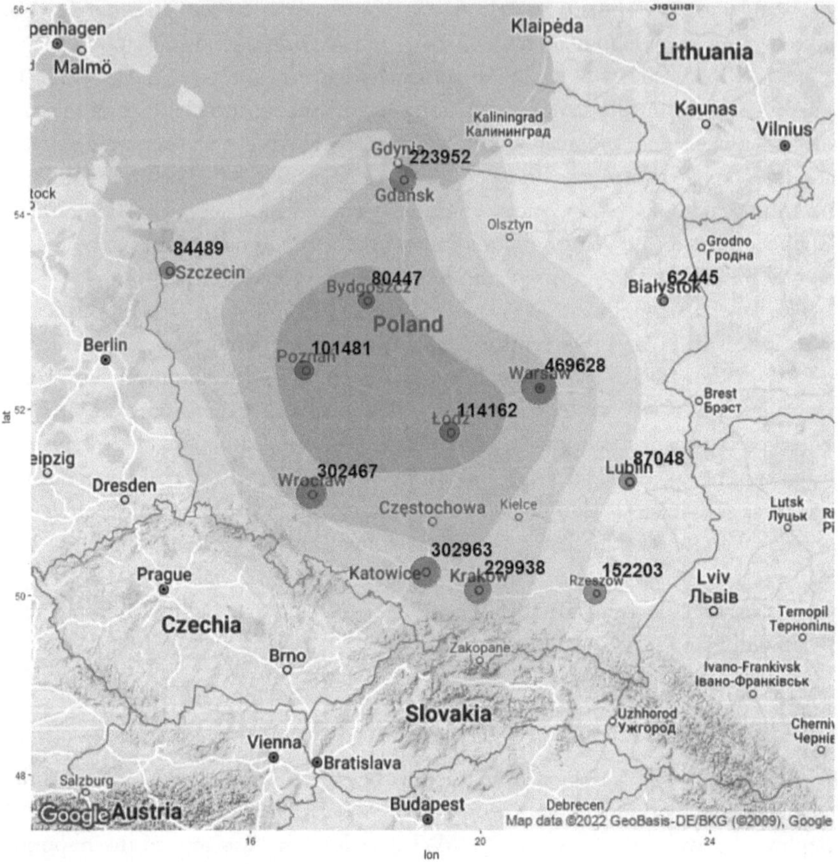

FIGURE 5.3 The number and density of declarations of entrusting work to foreigners in the largest Polish cities in 2020

Source: Own elaborations based on Public Employment Service data and Google (n.d.).

contributions, the study by Strzelecki (2020) also concerns working conditions, mainly the type of work contract as a factor that may impact the decision on hiring migrant workers in Poland.

Therefore, we extracted 15 variables that could explain the willingness to hire foreign workers by Polish entrepreneurs in the year following the survey. We sorted them according to the thematic areas (Table 5.1). The first seven variables from the top concerns the metric area, the second area (next 4 variables) is related to working conditions, and the third area (the final three variables) concerns questionnaire questions directly related to the COVID-19 pandemic. Table 5.1 also summarises descriptive statistics on the variables used in the regression analysis. We included categories with frequencies (raw and percentage count) and the number of missing values for each variable. 'It is hard to say' or 'I do not know' answers were treated as missing values and removed from the data set.

TABLE 5.1 Basic descriptive statistics of variables used in the regression models

Variable	*Categories with frequencies*	*Ordered**	*Missing values*
V12_hire (dependent variable)	Not likely – 36 (9.2%)	YES	30 (7%)
	Somewhat likely – 125 (32.1%)		
	Very likely – 229 (58.7%)		
V13_size	Very small/small – 324 (77.1%)	NO	0 (0%)
	Medium/large – 96 (22.9%)		
V14_branch**	Manufacturing industry – 146 (34.8%)	NO	0 (0%)
	Construction – 73 (17.4%)		
	Transport and warehouse services – 35 (8.3%)		
	Wholesale and retail trade; vehicle repair – 67 (16.0%)		
	Activities related to culture, entertainment, and recreation – 34 (8.1%)		
	Accommodation and catering services – 43 (10.2%)		
	Other services – 22 (5.2%)		
V15_stakes	Yes – 63 (15.0%)	NO	0 (0%)
	No – 357 (85.0%)		
V17_lok	Poznań – 224 (53.3%)	NO	0 (0%)
	Surrounding counties – 196 (46.7%)		
V18_ex	Yes – 203 (48.3%)	NO	0 (0%)
	No – 217 (51.7%)		
V2_share***	32 distinct values	n/a	*19 outliers were removed*
	Mean (sd): 20.3 (19.3)		
V3_year	17 distinct values	n/a	0 (0%)
	Mean (sd): 2017.1 (3.4)		
V1_activ	Yes – 269 (64.0%)	NO	11 (2.6%)
	No – 140 (33.3%)		
V5_job	Physical work – 368 (90.2%)	NO	12 (2.9%)
	Intellectual work – 40 (9.8%)		
V9_contract	Full- or part-time permanent contract – 231 (57.0%)	NO	15 (3.6%)
	Employment contract for a trial period – 24 (5.9%)		
	Full- or part-time contract on specific time – 70 (17.3%)		
	Temporary contact (contract of mandate, contract for specific job) – 80 (19.8%)		
V8_know	Lower than Poles – 73 (17.4%)	YES	0 (0.0%)
	Similar to Poles – 332 (79.0%)		
	Higher than Poles – 15 (3.6%)		
V4_C19	Decrease in employment – 128 (31.4%)	YES	13 (3.1%)
	No impact – 261 (64.1%)		
	Increase in employment – 18 (4.4%)		

(*Continued*)

TABLE 5.1 (Continued)

Variable	*Categories with frequencies*	*Ordered**	*Missing values*
V5_C19P	Decrease in employment – 95 (22.9%) No impact – 285 (68.8%) Increase in employment – 34 (8.2%)	YES	6 (1.4%)
V10_fut	Decrease – 65 (19.8%) No change – 174 (53.0%) Increase – 89 (27.1%)	YES	92 (21.9%)

Source: Own elaborations.

Note:

* Ordered variable is variable with meaningful order and has more than two categories.

** Economic branches are reported according to the Polish Classification of Business.

*** Nineteen outliers were removed from the dataset. They were classified according to the definition: each point below [quartile 1 – (1.5)*quartile range] or above [quartile 3 + (1.5)*quartile range].

Methods

Logistic regression is one of the regression analysis techniques and allows for estimating the relationship among variables. Logistic regression measures the relationship between the categorical dependent variable and one or more independent variables by estimating probabilities using a logistic function, which is the cumulative logistic distribution (Lee, 2018). Hilbe (2009) provides detailed description of several types of logistic regression models. Key terms in any type of logistic regression are odds which are defined as the division of the probability of success to the probability of failure. It can be simplified as the ratio of the frequency of one variable to the frequency of another variable (O'Connel, 2005).

Moving on, an ordinal variable is a categorical variable with a natural ordering to the categories. The example is our dependent variable, the chances of hiring migrant workers in the next year (V12) that are described as not likely, somewhat likely, and very likely. An ordinal response regression model describes the relationship between an ordinal response variable and explanatory variables. Ordinal logistic models are of particular interest because of their conceptual similarity to the commonly used binary logistic regression model (Fagerland & Hosmer, 2017).

In ordinal regression models, the relationship between response variable and its covariates is described by $c-1$ logits equations so that it can be written as:

$$log\left(\frac{P(Y \le j)}{P(Y \le j)}\right) = logit(P(Y \le j) \tag{5.1}$$

Each logit consists of intercepts and regression coefficients. Having this in mind ordinal logistic regression model for dependent variable Y can be defined as:

$$logit(P(Y \le j) = \beta_{j0} + \beta_{j1x_1} + \beta_{j2x_2} + \beta_{jpx_p} \tag{5.2}$$

where $x_1, x_2, \supset, x_n$ are explanatory variables; $\beta_{j0}, \beta_{j1}, \ldots, \beta_{jn}$ are model coefficients. According to the parallel lines assumptions, the parameters should not change for different categories (Arı & Yildiz, 2014). Moreover, in software implementation the coefficients are parametrised as $-\beta_i = \eta_i$ (Bilder & Loughin, 2014). For example, if we want to investigate the impact of size of company (V13_size) on response variable (V12 – *Chances of hiring migrant workers in the next year*), the equations for two categories of V13_size would be:

$$logit(P(Y \leq j \mid x_1 = 2) = \beta_{j1} - \eta_2 \tag{5.3}$$

$$logit(P(Y \leq j \mid x_1 = 1) = \beta_{j1} \tag{5.4}$$

So,

$$logit(P(Y \leq j \mid x_1 = 2) - logit(P(Y \leq j \mid x_1 = 1) = -\eta_2, \tag{5.5}$$

where $-\eta_2$ represents a one unit change in the log odds of hiring migrant workers by small and medium (first category) versus large and very large firms (second category).

In proportional odds logistic regression, the assumption is that the odds ratios are the same across $J-1$ categories. To obtain those ratios one has to exponentiate (1) and use the basic log rule: $log\left(\frac{a}{b}\right) = log(a) - log(b)$, so:

$$\frac{P(Y \leq j \mid x_1 = 2)}{P(Y > j \mid x_1 = 2} / \frac{P(Y \leq j \mid x_1 = 1)}{P(Y > j \mid x_1 = 1)} = exp(-\eta_2) \tag{5.6}$$

Each of the logits of the model compares the probabilities of two sets of response categories: an equal or smaller response versus a larger response. Accordingly, we developed three ordinal logistic regression models to identify what factors may impact hiring of migrant workers during COVID-19 pandemic.

To minimise the risk of model overfitting (van Smeden et al., 2016), we split our data into three thematic areas (as shown in Table 7.1). Accordingly, we estimated the models for chances of hiring migrants based on these three areas. In the first model, the probability of hiring migrants were explained by firm characteristics:

$$V12\_hire = V2\_share + V3\_year + V13\_size + V15\_stakes + V14\_branch + V17\_lok + V18\_ex \text{ (Model I)}$$

The second model considers mainly the impact of workplace conditions and perceived knowledge level of migrant workers on the probability of hiring. Thus, the specification is:

$$V12\_hire = V1\_actions + V6\_wage + V5\_job + V8\_know \text{ (Model II)}$$

Finally, the third model joins the variables that link to pandemic impact on employment level in enterprise. Two COVID-19 variables were combined with prospects about hiring the migrant workers. So, the third model is:

$$V12\_hire = V4\_C19 + V4\_C19P + V10\_fut \quad \text{(Model III)}$$

Results

The models were estimated with *proportional odds logistic regression* (*polr*) function from the MASS R package (Venables & Ripley, 2002). *Polr* allows for fitting a logistic or probit regression model to an ordered factor response according to the equations (1)–(4). Estimation results are presented in Table 5.2.

The Pulkstenis and Robinson (2004) and Lipsitz et al. (1996) are goodness-of-fit tests for ordinal logistic regression models. These tests are appropriate for models with categorical and numerical variables. Fagerland and Hosmer (2017) recommend that the Pulkstenis-Robinson tests be run in parallel with the Lipsitz test and the Hosmer-Lemeshow test. Due to different numbers of missing values, we could not use the latter. However, a comparison of the values and significance of the Pulkstenis-Robinson and Lipsitz tests indicates that the data used in the models are consistent. According to the Akaike Information Criterion (AIC), the fit of the third model is the best one, but this can also be explained by the least number of variables used in the last model.

Regarding the interpretation of the coefficients of Model I, the estimators of manufacturing (*V14_branch(9)*) and trade (*V14_branch(7)*) are highly significant and negative. This is interpreted as a reduction in the probability that firms operating in these branches will report demand for migrant workers in the next year. The Polish Agency for Enterprise Development (2021) study indicates these were the two industries that were most interesting to foreign workers before the COVID-19 pandemic. The vast majority of migrant workers looked for work in one of these two industries. The variables other service activities *(V14_branch(19)*) and arts, entertainment, and recreation activities (*V14_branch(10)*) also have significant negative coefficients. Similarly, it indicates a reduction in the odds of reporting demand for foreign labour in these two branches. The results may suggest that the chances of hiring migrant workers will decline over the next 12 months – none of the branch coefficients were both: positive and statistically significant.

In Model II, the coefficient of activities supporting migrants in the workplace (*V1_activ*) was significant and negative. The lack of such activities[8] decreases the chances that the firm will hire migrant workers in the future. In addition, the probability of hiring migrant workers is closely related to the form of employment. Temporary employment contracts (contract of mandate or contract for specific work – *V19_contr(4)*) is associated with a significantly higher probability of employment than any other type of contract (permanent – *V19_contr(1)*, fixed-term – *V19_contr(2)*, or substitute employment contract – *V19_contr(3)*). This suggests an evolution of employment relationships towards temporary contracts

TABLE 5.2 Result of ordinal logistic regression models

Var	*Model I*	*Var*	*Model II*	*Var*	*Model III*
V2_share	0.02** (0.03)	V1_activ	−1.20*** (0.000)	V4_C19(L)	1.02* (0.03)
V3_year	−0.133*** (0.000)	V7_know(L)	−0.93*(0.03)	V4_C19(Q)	0.42 (0.16)
V5_lok	0.52* (0.02)	V7_know(Q)	−0.33 (0.23)	V5_C19P(L)	−0.85* (0.02)
V13_size	0.42* (0.03)	V19_contr(1)	−0.02 (0.94)	V5_C19P(Q)	−0.20 (0.43)
V15_stakes	−0.62 (0.1)	V19_contr(2)	−0.12 (0.67)	V10_fut(L)	0.19 (0.44)
V18_ex	0.25 (0.26)	V19_contr(3)	−0.13 (0.64)	V10_fut(Q)	0.07 (0.70)
V14_branch(6)	−0.30 (0.23)	V19_contr(4)	1.32***(0.000)	–	–
V14_branch(7)	−1.56*** (0.000)	–	–	–	–
V14_branch(8)	−0.03 (0.89)		–	–	–
V14_branch(9)	−1.28*** (0.000)	–	–	–	–
V14_branch(10)	−0.63* (0.03)	–	–	–	–
V14_branch(19)	−0.83* (0.02)	–	–	–	–
Intercept: 1|2	−272.74*** (0.000)	Intercept: 1|2	−2.43*** (0.000)	Intercept: 1|2	−2.49*** (0.000)
Intercept: 2|3	−270.11*** (0.000)	Intercept: 2|3	−031 (0.2)	Intercept: 2|3	−0.57* (0.03)
Pulkstenis-Robinson test	640.14* (0.04)	Pulkstenis-Robin test	28.96 (0.13)	Pulkstenis-Robin test	44.064** (0.01)
Lipsitz test	9.11 (0.42)	Lipsitz test	10.78 (0.14)	Lipsitz test	20.03* (0.02)
AIC	651.587	AIC	623.084	AIC	521
No. of obs.	372/420	No. of obs.	366/420	No. of obs.	296/420

Source: Own elaborations.

during economic shocks. This is a natural consequence of unexpected fluctuations in demand for goods and services. Employers protect themselves against potential loss of profit and flexible job contracts allow them to quickly reduce employment.

Interestingly, the chances of hiring migrant workers decrease as the employers' perceived level of her or his knowledge increases (*V7_know*). This result may indicate that Polish entrepreneurs prefer low-skilled (i.e., low paid) rather than high-skilled workers that typically associate with higher wages. These findings may reflect the stereotypical perception of employees from Ukraine (Wysieńska-Di Carlo & Klaus, 2018) which has existed in Polish society for a long time. As a result, employers may offer lower wages at the expense of the applicant competencies. Consequently, an employee with a lower level of skills accepts worse working conditions and wages as pointed out by Carrillo-Tudela (2012).

Model III identifies two statistically significant variables, that is, the effect of COVID-19 on hiring foreign workers in the firm in the last year (*V4_C19*) and the effect of COVID-19 on hiring Polish workers in the firm in the last year (*V5_C19P*). Precisely, lay-offs of foreign workers in the past year are a significant factor that increases the chances that firms will report a demand for them. In turn, lay-offs of Polish workers decrease the likelihood that the company will report a demand for migrant workers.

Below we present the in-depth analysis of significant covariates of Model I – III performed with *effects* R library (Fox & Weisberg, 2019). We also investigated interaction effects between selected variables.

Figure 5.4 shows the effect of the firm size (*V13_size*), and the share of employed migrant workers (*V2_share*) on the probability that such a firm will report a demand for migrant workers.

The probability of hiring migrant workers rises together with the size of firms. It is about 10% higher among large and very large enterprises compared to small and medium firms. The odds of hiring foreigners rises together with the share of already-employed migrant workers. The difference in hiring probability between companies with the least and the most migrant workers reaches as much as 30% (in favour of companies employing more foreigners).

Figure 5.5 presents the effect of the perceived level of knowledge of migrant workers (*V8_know*) on the dependent variable. The same figure also illustrates the relationship between activities supporting migrants in the workplace (*V1_activ*) and the dependent variable.

The probability of hiring migrant workers decreases as the (perceived) knowledge level of the foreigners increases. Accordingly, the migrant workers with lower level of knowledge compared to Polish workers have a higher chance of being hired. The odds of hiring migrant workers are much lower in firms that do not undertake activities supporting migrants in the workplace. Two interaction plots are shown in Figure 5.6. The first is the effect between the size of the firm (*V13_size*) and the share of migrant workers (*V2_share*). The second is interaction between the knowledge level of migrant workers (*V8_know*) and activities supporting the foreigners in the workplace (*V1_activ*).

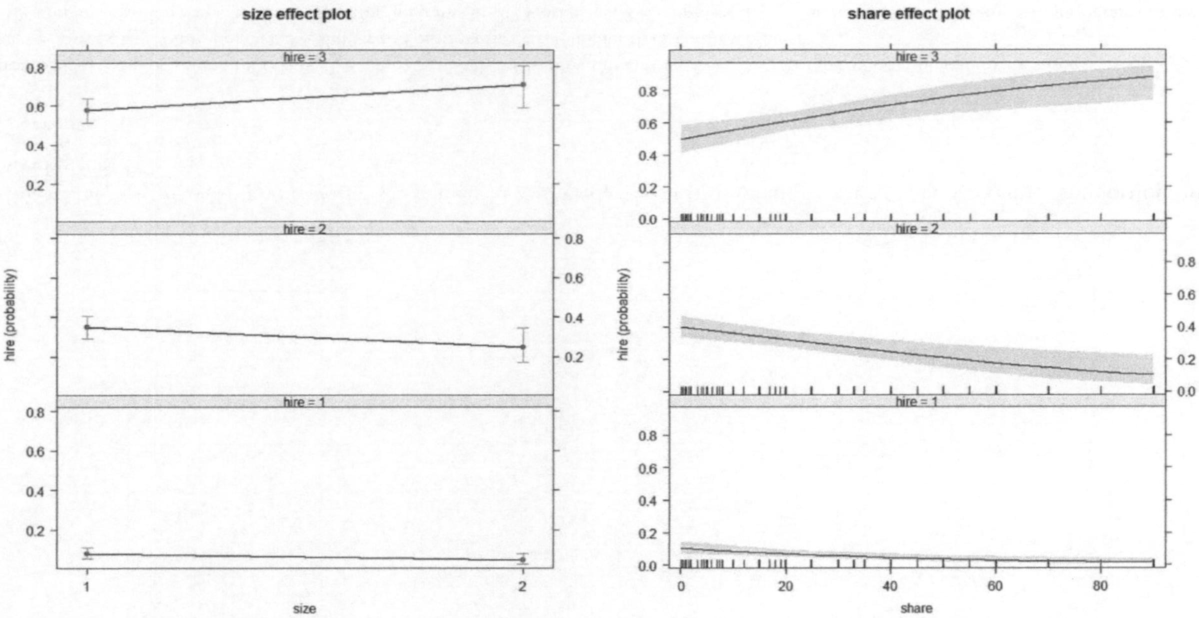

FIGURE 5.4 Probability of hiring migrant workers*, size of enterprise**, and the share of employed migrants***

Source: Own elaborations.

Note:

* Hire: 1 – not likely to employ migrants; 2 – somewhat likely to employ migrants; 3 – very likely to employ migrants;

** Size: 1 – very small and medium; 2 – large and very large;

*** Share is numerical continuous variable with min = 0.05 and max = 0.60.

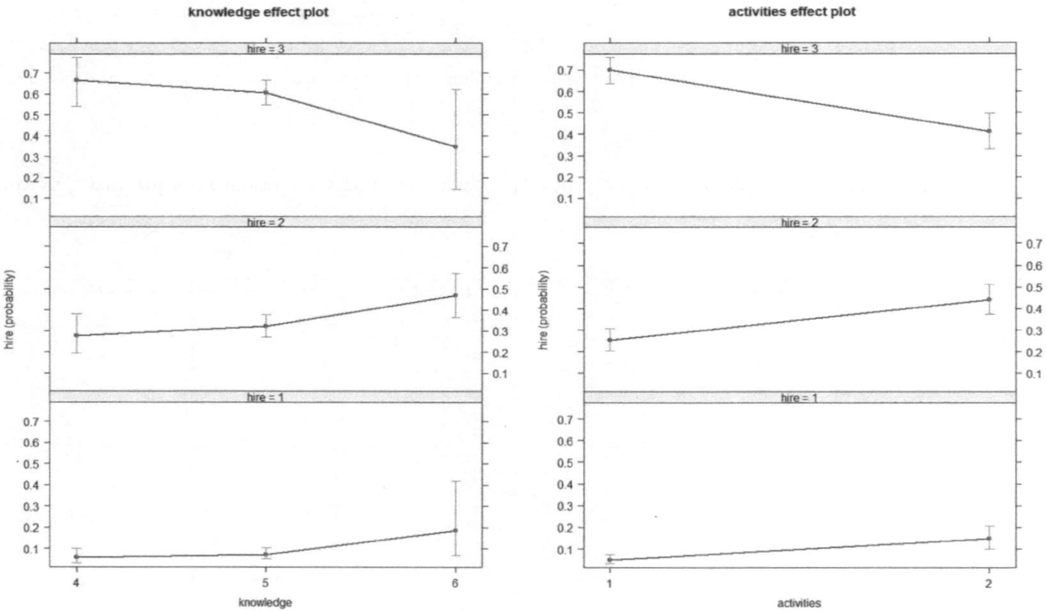

FIGURE 5.5 Probability of hiring migrant workers*, perceived knowledge level of migrant workers**, and activities supporting migrants in the workplace***

Source: Own elaborations.

Note:

* Hire: 1 – not likely to employ migrant workers; 2 – somewhat likely to employ migrant workers; 3 – very likely to employ migrant workers;

** Knowledge: 4 – lower than Polish workers; 5 – similar to Polish workers; 6 – higher than Polish workers;

*** Activities: 1 – employer undertakes activities supporting migrants in the workplace; 2 – employer doesn't undertake activities supporting migrants in the workplace.

Regarding the former, larger firms with a higher percentage of employed migrant workers report a higher probability of hiring another foreign worker in the future. When it comes to the latter, the probability of hiring drops together with the increase of perceived level of knowledge of migrant workers. It is visible in both types of enterprises. However, the probability of hiring high-skilled migrant workers (with higher level of knowledge) is higher in enterprises that undertake activities supporting migrants in the workplace. Accordingly, the firms that do not undertake such actions are much less interested in hiring migrant workers with higher skill levels.

In Figure 5.7, we plotted the COVID-19 impact on employment of foreign (*V4_C19*) and domestic (*V5_C19P*) workers in the last year. The figure shows the impact of these two factors on the dependent variable.

The firms that declared a negative COVID-19 impact on employment of foreign workers are characterised by a higher probability of hiring migrants in the next year. On the contrary, the firms that declared a positive COVID-19 impact on employment of Polish workers are also characterised by a higher probability of hiring migrant workers in the next year. The enterprise that laid-off foreigners because of the pandemic may fill the staff shortages with the workers of the same type. Enterprises that increased Polish staff during the pandemic may also seek for migrant workers in the future. The Figure 5.8 illustrates the interaction effect between these two COVID-19 variables and their combined effect on the probability of hiring migrant workers.

The multiplying effect of these two variables was identified: the probability of hiring migrant workers rises among firms that declared a reduction of employment in both groups of workers: Polish and foreigners (left upper graph). The situation may be the result of increased labour demand caused by the redundancies in 2020. The overall economic situation in such enterprises may somehow recover as they are interested in hiring staff. On the other hand, the probability of hiring migrant workers in firms that did not lay off workers during the pandemic is very small and oscillates at about 5%.

Discussion and conclusions

Negative consequences of the COVID-19 pandemic crisis on the labour market can be observed in many dimensions and have attracted attention of researchers and institutions. On the basis of the conducted regression analysis, we were able to identify factors that increase and factors that decrease the likelihood of firms from Poznań agglomeration to report the demand for foreign labour. However, it must be remembered that collected data relates to the particular point in time which is the COVID-19 pandemic (Table 5.3). Our findings indicate that, if we consider the severity and scope of the impact, the factors that decrease the chances of the company to report the demand for foreign workers prevail. This suggests an overall negative pandemic impact on foreigners in the local labour market and a reduced likelihood of reporting a demand for their labour in the following year.

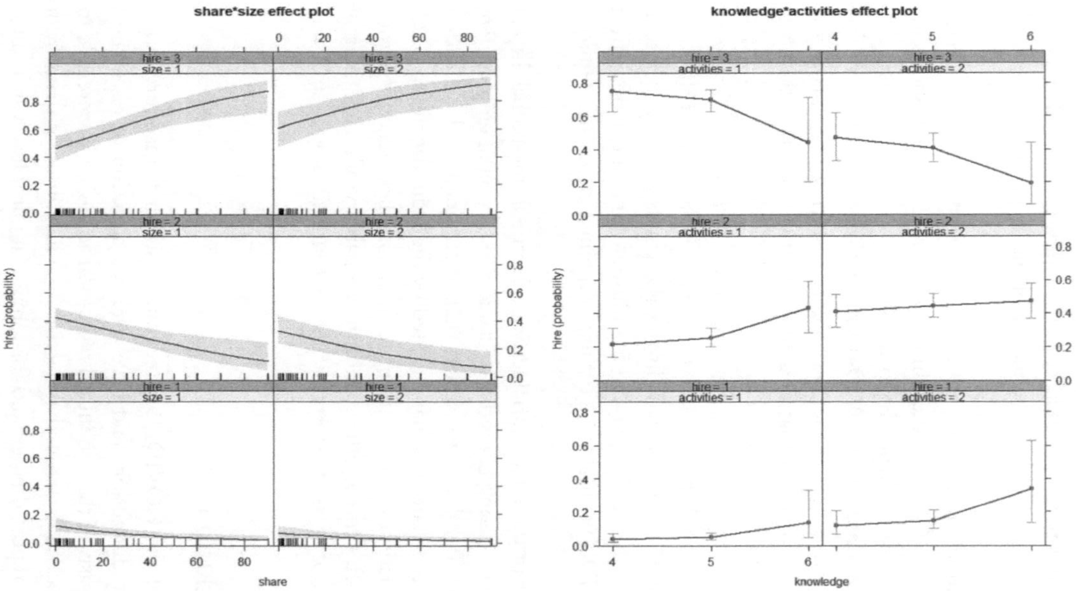

FIGURE 5.6 Joint effect of share of employed migrants with firm size* (left) and perceived migrants' knowledge level with activities supporting migrants** (right) on hire probability of foreign workers***

Source: Own elaborations.

Note:

* Size: 1 – very small and medium; 2 – large and very large; hire: 1 – not likely to employ migrants; 2 – somewhat likely to employ migrants; and 3 – very likely to employ migrants.

** Activities: 1 – not likely to employ migrants; 2 – somewhat likely to employ migrants; and 3 – very likely to employ migrants.

*** Hire: 1 – not likely to employ migrant workers; 2 – somewhat likely to employ migrant workers; and 3 – very likely to employ migrant workers.

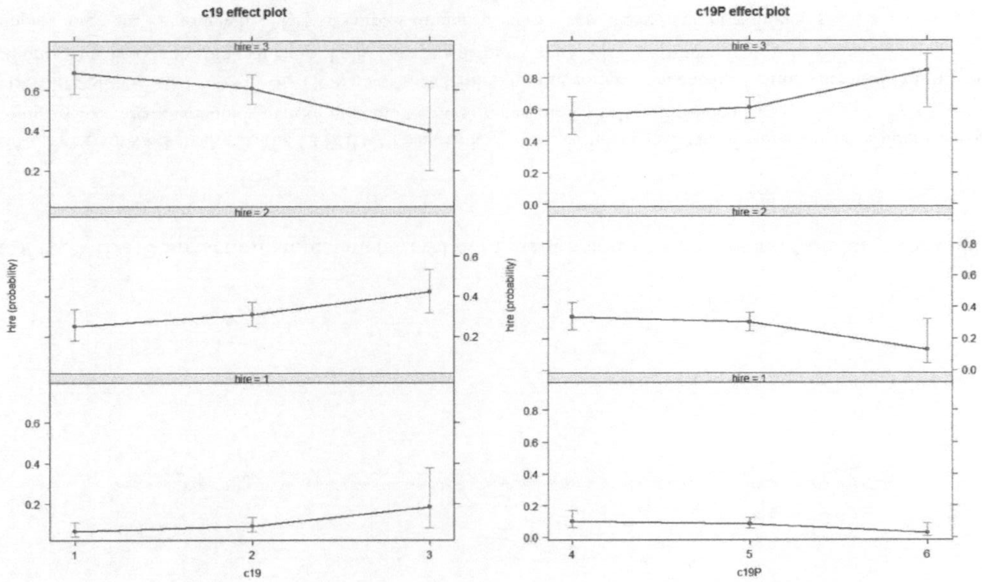

FIGURE 5.7 Probability of hiring migrant workers* and pandemic impact on migrants (c19)** and Polish workers (c19P)***

Source: Own elaborations.

Note:

* Hire: 1 – not likely to employ migrants; 2 – somewhat likely to employ migrants; 3 – very likely to employ migrants;

** c19: 1 – the company laid-off migrant workers due to the COVID-19 pandemic; 2 – the company maintained employment of migrant workers despite the COVID-19 pandemic; and 3 – the company increased the employment of migrant workers despite the COVID-19 pandemic;

*** c19P: 4 – the company laid-off Polish workers due to the COVID-19 pandemic; 5 – the company maintained employment of Polish workers despite the COVID-19 pandemic; and 6 – the company increased the employment of Polish workers despite the COVID-19 pandemic.

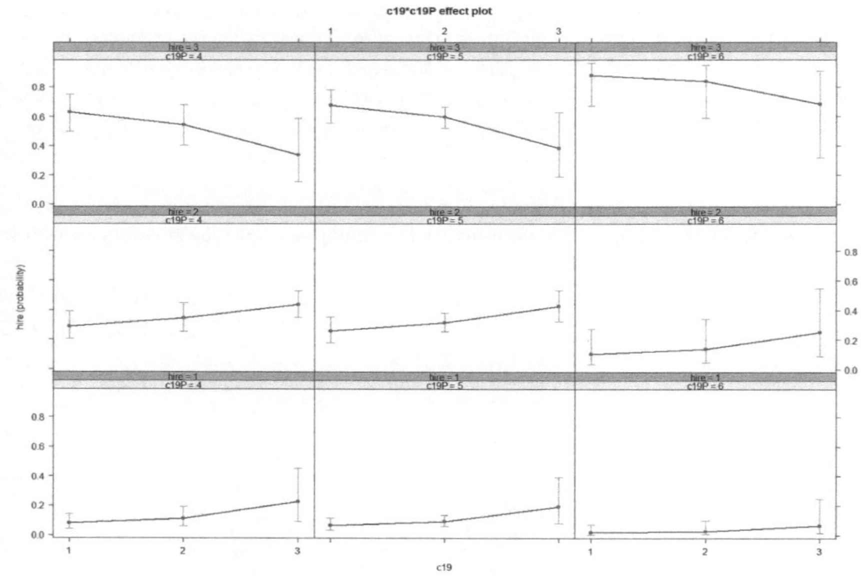

FIGURE 5.8 Joint effect of COVID-19 impact on employment level of migrants* and Polish workers** on hire probability of foreign workers***

Source: Own elaborations.

Note:

* c19: 1 – the company laid-off migrant workers due to the COVID-19 pandemic; 2 – the company maintained employment of migrant workers despite the COVID-19 pandemic; and 3 – the company increased the employment of migrant workers despite the COVID-19 pandemic;

** c19P: 4 – the company laid-off Polish workers due to the COVID-19 pandemic; 5 – the company maintained employment of Polish workers despite the COVID-19 pandemic; and 6 – the company increased the employment of Polish workers despite the COVID-19 pandemic;

*** Hire: 1 – not likely to employ migrants; 2 – somewhat likely to employ migrants; and 3 – very likely to employ migrants.

TABLE 5.3 The factors that may increase and decrease the chances of reporting demand for migrant labour during COVID-19 pandemic

+	-
Lay-offs of migrant workers in the last 12 months	Lay-offs of Polish workers in the last 12 months
Greater share of migrant workers in the overall employment in the enterprise	Seeking for a job opportunities in the industrial production, trade, cultural, entertainment, and recreation activities, or other service activities
Firm size (large and very large company)	Firms that don't undertake activities supporting migrants in the workplace
Temporary rather than permanent work	Longer history of migrants employment in the firm
Localisation of the firm in the surrounding counties rather than core metropolitan area	Perceiving migrant workers' knowledge level as higher than Polish workers

Source: Own elaborations.

The factors are often connected to the increased instability of employment. For example, increased odds of gaining a temporary job contract may be perceived as a reluctance to commit to a permanent employee and precarisation of employment (Thelen, 2019). Flexible forms of employment may also carry a number of psychological consequences related to persistent uncertainty in the economic sphere (Inanc, 2018). In the absence of institutional forms of support for such employees, it is difficult to speak of stability or prospects for professional development. Past lay-offs of migrant workers may somehow increase the demand for them in the future, however, together with temporary work character may create a situation of high insecurity of migrant workers. This uncertainty is higher compared to native employees in Poland.

We found that firm size has a significant effect on the probability of hiring migrant workers in the next 12 months (i.e., the larger the firm, the probability also rises). This is consistent with the results of some previous studies indicating that employment losses were disproportionately concentrated among smaller firms (e.g., Cajner et al., 2020).

The results of the regression analysis suggest that firms with longer employment histories of migrants will be less likely to report a demand for a new foreign worker in the future. This may be related to several factors, such as lower turnover in such enterprises and saturation of demand for migrant labour. In contrast, firms employing a higher proportion of foreigners are also more likely to recruit them in the future. In this case, the situation may be explained by higher turnover: a greater number of foreigners employed in the company also means a potentially more frequent replacement of staff. Slightly more likely is that the demand for foreigners will be reported by companies from the neighbourhood counties (rather than the city core area). The explanation may be the fact that a significant number of large companies representing industries most often chosen by foreigners are located outside the city of Poznań.

As already mentioned, the regression results clearly indicate which economic branches were particularly affected by the pandemic. These are manufacturing, wholesale and retail trade, cultural and recreational activities, and other service activities. The first two are industries in which foreigners most often took up employment in agglomerations. This leads to the conclusion of a general decrease in the demand for foreign labour in the perspective of the next 12 months.

The findings presented above stand in contrast to those of Strzelecki (2020) who suggest that reduced recruitment of new workers and lay-offs affected migrants less than native workers. However, the research on the COVID-19 impact on the demand for migrant labour is scarce, so it is not possible to compare the results obtained in this study with the results of other similar studies (e.g., for other countries).

Our research enriches rare, existing contributions by new knowledge about the mechanisms of hiring foreigners during the pandemic crisis. Still the study suffers from some inevitable limitations. A major drawback is due to the lack of representativeness of the research sample. The survey is a cross-sectional study and covers only one period. Therefore, future research efforts should include examining the effect of the pandemic shock on the demand for migrant work with a focus on sector-specific factors as well as identifying changes that have occurred in the sectoral concentration of migrant workers.

Acknowledgements

The authors greatly appreciate the financial support received from the City of Poznań.

Notes

1 For example, according to the data of poviat labour offices, among the largest cities, Poznań was ranked second in terms of the number of registered declarations of entrusting work to a foreigner in 2020.
2 In Poland, a foreigner may take up employment on the basis of a residence permit, work visa, work permit or under a simplified procedure (on the basis of an employer's declaration of entrusting work to a foreigner). There are also certain groups of migrants who are released from the obligation to have a work permit (e.g., citizens of EU countries, refugees, graduates of Polish secondary schools and universities).
3 The dissimilarity index is calculated as half the sum of the absolute values of the differences between the distribution of the foreign workers across industries and the distribution of the natives across industries (OECD, 2020).
4 This section includes temporary employment agencies as well as activities related to building and landscape maintenance and management of green areas.
5 According to the simplified procedure, the citizens of Armenia, Belarus, Georgia, Moldova, Ukraine, and Russia do not need to apply for a work permit to undertake employment up to six months during 12 consecutive months.

6 The REGON register is a collection of data on national economy entities in the form of a central database, available at: https://wyszukiwarkaregon.stat.gov.pl/.
7 The statistical error were computed according to the equation: 1.96*sqrt(1-(n/N)*1/(4(n-1)), where n is the size of the research sample, N is the size of the sampling operator.
8 These activities may have a wide spectrum, for example, support for educational or career counseling; hiring employees trained in immigration law; assign native mentors (tutors) to employed migrant workers; foreign language lessons; and integration meetings

References

Adams-Prassl, A., Boneva, T., Golin, M., & Rauh, C. (2020). *The large and unequal impact of COVID-19 on workers*. Retrieved May 14, 2021, from https://voxeu.org/article/large-and-unequal-impact-covid-19-workers

Alaverdov, E. (2021). The impact of COVID-19 on the vulnerable groups: Refugees and labor migrants-based view. In E. Alaverdov & M. W. Bari (Eds.), *Impact of infodemic on organizational performance* (pp. 10–23). IGI Global.

Ambrosini, M., & Barone, C. (2007). *Employment and working conditions of migrant workers*. European Foundation for the Improvement of Living and Working Conditions. Retrieved May 28, 2021, from www.eurofound.europa.eu/publications/report/2007/employment-and-working-conditions-of-migrant-workers

Arı, E., & Yildiz, Z. (2014). Parallel lines assumption in ordinal logistic regression and analysis approaches. *International Interdisciplinary Journal of Scientific Research, 1*, 8–23.

Barker, N., Davis, C. A., López-Peña, P., Mitchell, H., Mobarak, A. M., Naguib, K., Reimão, M. E., Shenoy, A., & Vernot, C. (2020). Migration and the labour market impacts of COVID-19. (*WIDER Working Paper* 2020/139). The United Nations University World Institute for Development Economics Research (UNU-WIDER), Retrieved May 14, 2021, from EconStor: Migration and the labour market impacts of COVID-19

Bhandari, D., Kotera, Y., Ozaki, A., Abeysinghe, S., Kosaka, M., & Tanimoto, T. (2021). COVID-19: Challenges faced by Nepalese migrants living in Japan. *BMC Public Health, 21*, 752. https://doi.org/10.1186/s12889-021-10796-8

Bilder, Ch., & Loughin, T. (2014). *Analysis of categorical data with R*. Chapman and Hall/CRC.

Borjas, G. J., & Cassidy, H. (2020). The adverse effect of the COVID-19 labor market shock on immigrant employment. (*NBER Working Paper* 27243). The Adverse Effect of the COVID-19 Labor Market Shock on Immigrant Employment. Retrieved May 14, 2021, from nber.org

Cajner, T., Crane, L. D., Decker, R. A., Grigsby, J., Hamins-Puertolas, A., Hurst, E., Kurz, Ch., & Yildirmaz, A. (2020). The US labor market during the beginning of the pandemic recession. (*NBER Working Paper* 27159). Retrieved May 18, 2021, from w27159.pdf (nber.org)

Carrillo-Tudela, C. (2012). Job search, human capital and wage inequality. (*CESifo Working Paper Series* 3979). CESifo. Retrieved June 14, 2020, from http://ftp.iza.org/dp6949.pdf

Danzer, A. M., & Dietz, B. (2018). The economic and social determinants of migrants' well-being during the global financial crisis. (*IZA Discussion Papers* 11272). Institute of Labor Economics (IZA).

Enright, S., McGinnity, F., Privalko, I., & Russell, H. (2020). *COVID-19 and non-Irish nationals in Ireland*. The Economic and Social Research Institute. Retrieved May 14, 2021, from www.researchgate.net/profile/Helen-Russell-6/publication/347327948_COVID-19_AND_NON-IRISH_NATIONALS_IN_IRELAND/links/5fd9da7f299bf1408811f9bc/COVID-19-AND-NON-IRISH-NATIONALS-IN-IRELAND.pdf

European Commission. (2020). *Spain: Migrant unemployment rate rises after COVID-19*. Retrieved May 14, 2021, from https://ec.europa.eu/migrant-integration/news/spain-migrant-unemployment-rate-rises-after-covid-19

Fagerland, M. W., & Hosmer, D. W. (2017). How to test for goodness of fit in ordinal logistic regression models. *The Stata Journal*, *17*(3), 668–686. https://doi.org/10.1177/1536867X1701700308

Fairlie, R. W., Couch, K., & Xu, H. (2020). The impacts of COVID-19 on minority unemployment: First evidence from April 2020 CPS microdata. (*NBER Working Paper* 27246). Retrieved April 24, 2021, from w27246.pdf (nber.org)

Fassani, F., & Mazza, J. (2020). *A vulnerable workforce: Migrant workers in the COVID-19 pandemic* (JRC Technical Report). Publications Office of the European Union. Retrieved April 24, 2021, from https://respect.international/wp-content/uploads/2020/07/a-vulnerable-workforce-migrant-workers-in-the-covid-19-pandemic.pdf

Fox, J., & Weisberg, S. (2019). *An R companion to applied regression* (3rd ed.). Retrieved April 10, 2021, from https://socialsciences.mcmaster.ca/jfox/Books/Companion/index.html

Garrote Sanchez, D., Gomez Parra, N., Ozden, C., & Rijkers, B. (2020). *Which jobs are most vulnerable to COVID-19? what an analysis of the European Union Reveals*. Retrieved April 25, 2021, from https://elibrary.worldbank.org/doi/abs/10.1596/33737

Gelatt, J. (2020). *Immigrant workers: Vital to the US COVID-19 response, disproportionately vulnerable*. Migration Policy Institute. Retrieved April 21, 2021, from Research: Immigrant Workers: Vital to the U.S. COV. | migrationpolicy.org

Główny Urząd Statystyczny. (2021). *Zatrudnienie i wynagrodzenia w gospodarce narodowej w 2020 roku*. Retrieved May 7, 2021, from https://stat.gov.pl/obszary-tematyczne/rynek-pracy/pracujacy-zatrudnieni-wynagrodzenia-koszty-pracy/zatrudnienie-i-wynagrodzenia-w-gospodarce-narodowej-w-2020-roku,1,41.html

Google. (n.d.). *Google Maps for Poland*. Retrieved June 14, 2021, from with Google API Console.

Górny, A., & Kaczmarczyk, P. (2018). A known but uncertain path: The role of foreign labour in Polish agriculture. *Journal of Rural Studies*, *64*, 177–188. https://doi.org/10.1016/j.jrurstud.2017.12.015

Guadagno, L. (2020). *Migrants and the COVID-19 pandemic: An initial analysis*. Migration Research Series N°60. International Organization for Migration (IOM). Retrieved April 28, 2021, from https://publications.iom.int/system/files/pdf/mrs-60.pdf

Hayward, S. E., Deal, A., Cheng, C., Crawshaw, A., Orcutt, M., Vandrevala, T. F., . . . & Hargreaves, S. (2021). Clinical outcomes and risk factors for COVID-19 among migrant populations in high-income countries: A systematic review. *Journal of Migration and Health*, 100041.

Hilbe, J. (2009). *Logistic regression models*. Chapman and Hall/CRC.

Honorati, M., Yi, S., & Choi, T. (2020). Assessing the vulnerability of Armenian temporary labor migrants during the COVID-19 pandemic. (*The World Bank Discussion Paper* 2003). Retrieved April 30, 2021, from https://openknowledge.worldbank.org/bitstream/handle/10986/34359/Assessing-the-Vulnerability-of-Armenian-Temporary-Labor-Migrants-during-the-COVID-19-Pandemic.pdf?sequence=1&isAllowed=y

Hu, Y. (2020). Intersecting ethnic and native – Migrant inequalities in the economic impact of the COVID-19 pandemic in the UK. *Research in Social Stratification and Mobility, 68*, 100528. https://doi.org/10.1016/j.rssm.2020.100528

Inanc, H. (2018). Unemployment, temporary work, and subjective well-being: The gendered effect of spousal labor market insecurity. *American Sociological Review, 83*(3), 536–566. https://doi.org/10.1177/0003122418772061

Kahle, D., & Wickham, H. (2013). ggmap: Spatial visualization with ggplot2. *The R Journal, 5*(1), 144–161. http://journal.r-project.org/archive/2013-1/kahle-wickham.pdf

Kerwin, D., Nicholson, M., Alulema, D., & Warren, R. (2020). *US foreign-born essential workers by status and state, and the global pandemic. CMS Report.* Center for Migration Studies. Retrieved May 21, 2021, from https://cmsny.org/publications/us-essential-workers

Kindler, M., Kordasiewicz, A., & Szulecka, M. (2016). *Care needs and migration for domestic work: Ukraine-Poland.* International Labour Organization.

Kubiciel-Lodzińska, S., & Maj, J. (2021). High-skilled vs. low-skilled migrant women: The use of competencies and knowledge – Theoretical and political implications: An example of the elderly care sector in Poland. *Journal of International Migration & Integration.* https://doi.org/10.1007/s12134-021-00813-5

Lee, H. C., Yoon, S. B., Yang, S. M., Kim, W. H., Ryu, H. G., Jung, C. W., Suh, K. S., & Lee, K. H. (2018, November 8). Prediction of acute kidney injury after liver transplantation: Machine learning approaches vs. logistic regression model. *Journal of Clinical Medicine*, 7(11), 428. https://doi.org/10.3390/jcm7110428.

Lipsitz, S. R., Fitzmaurice, G. M., & Molenberghs, G. (1996). Goodness-of-fit tests for ordinal response regression models. *Journal of the Royal Statistical Society, 45*(2), 175–190.

ManpowerGroup. (2020). *Rozwiązanie problemu niedoboru talentów: Dowiedz się, czego chcą pracownicy*. Retrieved February 11, 2021, from https://www.manpowergroup.pl/wp-content/uploads/2020/01/Rozwiazanie_problemu_niedob oru_talentow_PL.pdf

The Migration Observatory. (2021). *Migrants in the UK labour market: An overview.* Retrieved May 14, 2021, from https://migrationobservatory.ox.ac.uk/resources/briefings/migrants-in-the-uk-labour-market-an-overview/

Ministerstwo Rodziny i Polityki Społecznej. (2021). *Zezwolenia na pracę cudzoziemców.* Retrieved April 17, 2021, from https://psz.praca.gov.pl/web/urzad-pracy/-/8180075-zezwolenia-na-prace-cudzoziemcow

Mongey, S., Pilossoph, L., & Weinberg, A. (2020). Which workers bear the burden of social distancing policies? (*NBER Working Paper* 27085). Retrieved May 14, 2021, from www.nber.org/system/files/working_papers/w27085/w27085.pdf

Montenovo, L., Jiang, X., Lozano Rojas, F., Schmutte, I. M., Simon, K. I., Weinberg, B. A., & Wing, C. (2020). Determinants of disparities in Covid-19 job losses. (*NBER Working Paper* 27132). Retrieved May 14, 2021, from COVID19LaborMarketsCPSPaper.pdf (nber.org)

Moroz, H. E., Shrestha, M., & Testaverde, M. (2020). Potential responses to the COVID-19 outbreak in support of migrant workers. (*COVID-19 Living Paper*). World Bank Group. Retrieved April 21, 2021, from http://documents.worldbank.org/curated/en/428451587390154689/Potential-Responses-to-the-COVID-19-Outbreak-in-Sup port-of-Migrant-Workers-June-19–2020

NBP. (2020). Statystyka bilansu płatniczego. Retrieved from https://www.nbp.pl/home.aspx?f=/statystyka/bilans_platniczy.html.

O'Connel, A. (2005). *Logistic regression models for ordinal response variables.* SAGE Publications, Inc.

OECD. (2020). *International migration outlook 2020*. OECD Publishing. https://doi.org/10.1787/ec98f531-en

Pagano, M., Wagner, C., & Zechner, J. (2020). COVID-19, asset prices, and the great reallocation. *VoxEU.org*, 11. Retrieved May 20, 2021, from https://voxeu.org/article/covid-19-asset-prices-and-great-reallocation

Pizarro, C. A. (2020). The impact of the COVID-19 pandemic on labor migrants in Argentina. *Научное обозрение. Серия 1. Экономика и право*, *3*, 113–120. https://doi.org/10.26653/2076-4650-2020-3-10

Polish Agency for Enterprise Development. (2021). Zagraniczni pracownicy na polskim rynku pracy. *Raport tematyczny*. Retrieved from https://www.parp.gov.pl/storage/publications/pdf/Zagraniczni-pracownicy-na-polskim-rynku-pracy_last.pdf

Pulkstenis, E., & Robinson, T. J. (2004), Goodness-of-fit tests for ordinal response regression models. *Statistics in Medicine, 23*, 999–1014. https://doi.org/10.1002/sim.1659

Singh, S. V., & Singh, K. (2020). Migrants workers in tourism and hospitality industry: Effect of COVID-19. In V. Zutshi, N. Chowdhary, A. Kumar Singh, & P. Lakhawat (Eds.), *Covid-19 crisis: Policy solutions and way forward to rebuild travel, tourism & hospitality sector 2020*. Bharti Publications. SSRN: https://ssrn.com/abstract=3846906

Śleszyński, P. (2015). Problemy delimitacji miejskich obszarów funkcjonalnych w Polsce. *Rozwój Regionalny i Polityka Regionalna*, 37. 10.14746/rrpr.2015.29.04.

Sterud, T., Tynes, T., Mehlum, I. S., Veiersted, K. B., Bergbom, B., Airila, A., Johansson, B., Brendler-Lindqvist, M., Hviid, K., & Flyvholm, M. A. (2018). A systematic review of working conditions and occupational health among immigrants in Europe and Canada. *BMC Public Health*, 18. https://doi.org/10.1186/s12889-018-5703-3

Strzelecki, P. (2020). *Imigranci w polskiej gospodarce – raport z badań ankietowych*. Retrieved May 5, 2021, from Imigranci w polskiej gospodarce – raport z badań ankietowych (nbp.pl)

Strzelecki, P., Growiec, J., & Wyszyński, R. (2020). *The contribution of immigration from Ukraine to economic growth in Poland*. Retrieved April 24, 2021, from www.nbp.pl/publikacje/materialy_i_studia/322_en.pdf

Thelen, K. (2019). The American precariat: U.S. capitalism in comparative perspective. *Perspectives on Politics*, *17*(1), 5–27. https://doi.org/10.1017/S1537592718003419

Tompson, W., Lecomte, G., Pretet, A., & Mackle, L. (2020, November 16). *COVID-19 crisis response in central Asia*. Retrieved May 11, 2021, from www.oecd.org/coronavirus/policy-responses/covid-19-crisis-response-in-central-asia-5305f172/#contactinfo-d7e3334

UNICEF Regional Office for South Asia. (2021). *COVID-19 and migration for work in south Asia: Private sector responsibilities*. UNICEF. Retrieved May 28, 2021, from www.unicef.org/rosa/media/12656/file/Report%20-%20COVID-19%20and%20Migration%20for%20Work%20in%20South%20Asia%20Private%20Sector%20Responsibilities.pdf

Varshaver, E., Ivanova, N., & Rocheva, A. (2020, July). *Polozhenie migrantov v Rossii vo vremya pandemii koronavirusa (COVID-19): rezultaty oprosa* [The situation of migrants in Russia during the coronavirus (COVID-19) pandemic: Survey results]. Russian Academy of National Economy and Public Administration Under the President of the Russian Federation. Retrieved April 11, 2021, from http://mer-center.ru/_ld/1/169_06-07-2020-vars.pdf (in Russian).

van Smeden, M., de Groot, J. A., Moons, K. G., Collins, G. S., Altman, D. G., Eijkemans, M. J., & Reitsma, J. B. (2016). No rationale for 1 variable per 10 events criterion for binary logistic regression analysis. *BMC Medical Research Methodology*, *16*(1), 1–12.

Venables, W. N., & Ripley, B. D. (2002). *Modern applied statistics with S.* (4th ed.). Springer. ISBN 0-387-95457-0

Wysieńska-Di Carlo, K., & Klaus, W. (2018). Pracodawcy i pracodawczynie a zatrudnianie cudzoziemców i cudzoziemek. Retrieved May 12, 2022, from www.interwencjaprawna.pl/wp-content/uploads/2018/06/RAPORT_PRACODAWCY_I_PRACODAWCZYNIErev-1.pdf

6

IMPACT OF THE COVID-19 PANDEMIC ON LABOUR PRODUCTIVITY AND BUSINESS ACTIVITY IN THE CZECH REPUBLIC

Petr Suchánek, Tomáš Ondráček, Ladislava Kuchynková, Pavla Marciánová, Petr Pirožek, and Peter Mikuš

Introduction

The COVID-19 pandemic crisis has been associated with a range of challenges for society, the economy, and business in particular. The unexpected crisis has raised a range of different questions about how to deal with a new situation, and what is the impact of the changing circumstances on the labour market's outcome. The main goal of this chapter is to assess how Czech companies dealt with the COVID-19 crisis at the beginning of the pandemic and how this crisis impacted labour productivity in select sectors of the Czech economy. We used two methods to measure LP: first as hours worked, then as the ratio of total sales to the number of employees.

As a background for this study, we will use the concept of organisational crisis (Pearson and Clair, 1998; Huang, 2008). We understand this phenomenon as an event that threatens the existence of an organisation and that is characterised by ambiguity in cause, effect, and resolution, as well as the belief that decisions must be made quickly. It is important to examine how businesses were able to respond to the crisis, how they responded to the sudden change in conditions and related difficulties under the government-declared state of emergency, and whether they were able to maintain performance (including labour productivity) at the originally expected level.

In the literature concerning the Czech Republic, we can find analyses of the impact of COVID-19 on the economy of the Czech Republic (Andoh, 2020), the social impact analysis of COVID-19 (Kavan, 2021) and analysis of the impact of COVID-19 on various economic sectors, especially heavily affected ones such as tourism (Fialova and Vasenska, 2020; Novotny and Pellesova, 2021), fashion (Pelikánová et al., 2021) or the automotive industry (Klein et al., 2021).

So far, the literature does not deal with human resource management during the crisis in the context of qualitatively measured labour productivity. The available

DOI: 10.4324/9781003326779-8

research of the Czech setting has been conducted on the impact and influence of the COVID-19 pandemic on the whole economy or its various sectors, but not primarily on labour productivity (cf. Vrchota et al., 2020; Urbancová and Depoo, 2021; Ciobanu et al., 2020). Thus, there is a lack of research concerning the Czech Republic in this respect, as the impact of COVID-19 on labour productivity has been studied worldwide (see e.g., Bloom et al., 2020; Andrews et al., 2021).

Due to the negative impact of the pandemic on the economy and industries of the Czech Republic, a negative impact on labour productivity (however measured) can also be expected. However, this is not borne out by the research of Bloom et al. (2020), who report that hourly labour productivity (as measured by hours worked) in the United Kingdom increased between 2019 and 2020, due to a lower fall in capital inputs and a lower overall fall in revenue than the fall in hours worked. However, the reduction in working hours that occurred in the United Kingdom, the United States, and the EU were largely unaffected by unemployment in both the United States and the EU, due to most employees retaining their jobs through support programmes (EU) or by shifting to part-time work (US) (Gros and Ounnas, 2021). There has also been a decline in hours worked in Australia (Borland and Charlton, 2020).

Our study is based on two data sources and examines the years 2019–2020. First, we will assess changes in labour productivity calculated based on data from Bisnode database describing the interval between 2019 and 2020. The second source of data is an online questionnaire survey that was used to establish a baseline to study businesses' responses to the COVID-19 pandemic. We examined 95 companies primarily from the manufacturing and service sectors via LimeSurvey between October and November 2020.

Our findings show that in terms of labour productivity the situation is not clear-cut. Labour productivity measured in hours worked has increased (Zubíková and Smolák, 2022), but labour productivity measured in terms of sales has decreased (see Table 4.1). How labour productivity is measured is therefore important. If government interventions in the event of a pandemic lead to employment being maintained (CR situation) and employees continue working (reporting hours worked), hourly labour productivity will rise. However, if the firm does not sell its products (at all or to a limited extent), labour productivity as measured by sales falls.

Supplementary data from online surveys showed that manager and owner solutions were generally targeted to achieve the interests of the business or the interests of customers. Our primary finding is that during the pandemic, companies prioritised solving pandemic-related problems in ways that were perceived as fair to the employees by the employees themselves.

The chapter is structured as follows: in the first part we deal with the situation in the Czech Republic during the pandemic, then we examine labour productivity in the Czech Republic (especially in the context of employment), thus creating the context for the questionnaire survey. We present the data collected via this questionnaire in the third part of the chapter. That is followed by the results of the questionnaire research and discussion conducted in the context of labour productivity, and the whole chapter ends with a conclusion.

The COVID-19 pandemic in the Czech Republic

The COVID-19 pandemic has brought unprecedented interference in the lives of employees, with serious behavioural impacts and negative effects not only on the labour market (Huang et al., 2020) but also on businesses themselves (Shen et al., 2020). In the Czech Republic, a state of emergency had been in force from March (12 March 2020) to May (17 May 2020) and then from October (5 October 2020) to the end of 2020 (specifically until 14 February 2021), which in terms of the events in question and related interventions can be described as an organisational crisis with an impact on business performance.

During this period, performance of all activities falling under the sectors of accommodation, real estate, education, and culture was significantly reduced (with some softening in the May–September period, when, for example, it was compulsory to wear masks, the number of guests in restaurants and at cultural events was limited, but hotels, restaurants, and all shops were open). Businesses in the wholesale sector also saw a reduction in bricks-and-mortar operations and a shift of business (at least in part) to the Internet. National borders were also closed in March (16 March), with restrictions within the tourism sector lasting until the end of 2020 and remaining basically in place until the end of 2021. Since October 2021, the interventions had been tightened again (including limits on the number of people shopping in grocery stores, with other stores being closed entirely) including a curfew which has again mainly affected the accommodation, education, culture, and to some extent also wholesale sectors.

The above-mentioned interventions in the business environment can be described as unprecedented. Businesses were confronted with major restrictions and limitations on their operations. The impact of the crisis on sector performance, however, needs to be assessed on an individual basis, as for some sectors and organisations the crisis represented a significant opportunity (e.g., the move into e-commerce), and for others, it was a major threat.

Baniamin et al. (2020) identify factors critical to success in pandemic management, which they divide into state-centric (policy learning, implementation structure, and technological and administrative readiness) and socio-demographic (e.g., age, family structure, and cultural attributes). Obrenovic et al. (2020) found that businesses that have distributed leadership, workforces, and adaptive cultures will sustain the business during a pandemic, while resilient businesses further enable more informed and decentralised decision-making, and thriving businesses use information and communication technologies (ICT) and can integrate intranets, social media, and online communication platforms into their daily business routines. The pandemic has also driven businesses to go digital, with effective digitalisation's enabling businesses to succeed in dealing with pandemic crises (Penco et al., 2022). Home office, which allows employees to work from home despite government-imposed restrictions, was also an important factor in managing the pandemic crisis (Alves et al., 2021; Nový and Nováková, 2022).

To deal with the consequences of the pandemic, the Czech government introduced several programmes to help businesses including a compensation bonus (according to Act No. 159/2020 Coll.), 'Antivirus' programme (Section 120 of Act No. 435/2004 Coll., on Employment), COVID-rent (Ministry of Industry and Trade of the Czech Republic, 2021) and waiver of payment of minimum advances for health and social insurance (Ministry of Labour and Social Affairs, 2021). The compensation bonus mitigated the negative financial situation of operationally constrained or closed enterprises. The 'Antivirus' programme prevented lay-offs and unemployment increases despite the (partial) closure of several enterprises by essentially compensating the wages of their employees. The COVID-rent programme compensated the rents of businesses that were forced to temporarily close their establishments. The waiver of the payment of the minimum health and social security contributions covered all entrepreneurs (natural persons) between March and August 2020. These measures prevented redundancies or more massive lay-offs despite the reduction of operations or closure of enterprises in certain sectors (mainly trade and services).

A measure that rather negatively affected the labour market (its supply) is the restriction of mobility of employees – foreigners (Reichelt et al., 2021). This negatively affected mainly the construction sector and indirectly also the real estate sector (Hromada, 2021). Reduced employee mobility, especially of foreign workers, resulted in the low unemployment rate in 2020, due to increased demand for domestic workers in the construction sector. This was also probably the cause of the slight year-on-year wage growth (average wage increased by about EUR 43.4 to EUR 1,427 – exchange rate 25 CZK/EUR), as employment fell slightly year-on-year (by 82,500 persons to 3,979,200 persons) (Czech Statistical Office, 2021a).

Sectoral labour productivity in the Czech Republic

The impact of the COVID-19 pandemic on labour productivity may be measured for the whole economy or for a specific business. The two areas are interrelated, as the economic situation of enterprises is reflected in the economic situation of the whole economy. Generally, it could be assumed that the impact of the COVID-19 pandemic on the economy (or on businesses) would be negative, as the pandemic, or the government's response to it (restrictions), has caused a reduction or even an interruption of business activity for a large number of companies (Lustig and Mariscal, 2020; Brown et al., 2020).

In practice, in 2020, the unemployment rate in the Czech Republic was the lowest (2.6%) in the entire EU, thanks to the interventions of the Czech government (Hedvičáková and Kozubíková, 2021), even though it increased sharply year on year from 2.0% in 2019 (Czech Statistical Office, 2021b). The decrease in employment in 2020 can be seen in Figure 4.1. However, this decrease in employment has not increased labour productivity, as there has been a fall in sales (and consequently profits) due to the government's restrictions in the wake of the COVID-19 pandemic. The same mechanism in other countries was confirmed by the research of Gandy and Mulhearn (2021) and Andrews et al. (2021), but Bloom et al. (2020) found that labour productivity increased due to a lower rate of decline in sales (see Figure 6.1).

The government measures have only been able to compensate for part of the costs of enterprises (mainly fixed costs – e.g., rent) and have not been able to stimulate demand. On the contrary, state border closures, restrictions on the number of people in shops, and curfews significantly limited demand and were the cause of the aforementioned drop in sales.

The impact of the COVID-19 pandemic on labour productivity and the unemployment rate is ambiguous, due to the different impacts of the pandemic on different sectors of the economy, and due to the role of the remote work (cf., Bloom et al., 2020; Gros & Ounnas, 2021; Gandy & Mulhearn, 2021; Andrews et al., 2021). Generally, sectors with lower productivity and lower-skilled workers were more affected (e.g., tourism), and sectors with higher productivity and higher-skilled workers were less affected (Gandy & Mulhearn, 2021). For example, Andrews et al. (2021) found that in New Zealand, Australia, and the United

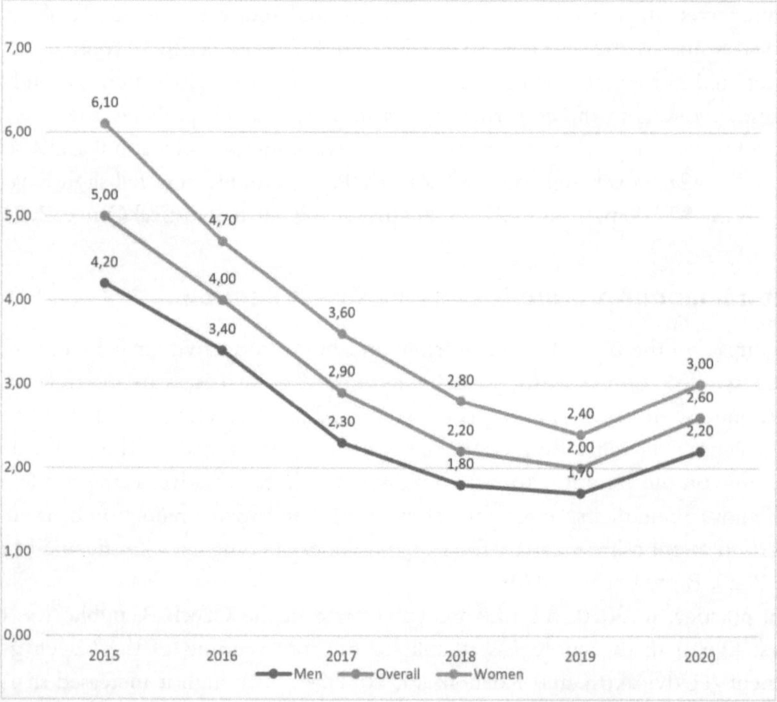

FIGURE 6.1 The unemployment rate in the Czech Republic in the years 2015–2020

Source: Own elaboration based on Czech Statistical Office (2021c).

Kingdom, 'firms with high productivity were more likely to expand and firms with low productivity were more likely to contract'.

The above research is based on indicators of labour productivity based on hours worked (Gros & Ounnas, 2021; Borland & Charlton, 2020). The evolution of this labour productivity in select European countries is presented in Table 6.1. The

TABLE 6.1 Change in labour productivity in European countries (2015 = 100%)

	2015	*2016*	*2017*	*2018*	*2019*	*2020*	*2021*
European Union – 27 countries	100	100.3	101.4	103.12	104.76	108.69	109.24
Belgium	100	100.2	101.92	103.21	104.71	106.65 p	:
Bulgaria	100	103.24	112.98	120.58	124.36	135.65	143.34 p
Czech Republic	**100**	**102.87**	**106.75**	**113.35**	**117.72**	**126.15**	**129.21**
Denmark	100	99.41	99.63	100.60	101.32	105.4	106.61
Germany	100	101.14	102.18	105.25 p	108.51 p	112.20 p	113.09 p
Estonia	100	104.02	107.64	113.81	120.01	126.31	124.08
Ireland	100	103.78	101.58	98.33	99.59	94.02	88.92
Greece	100	99.28	100.09	98.7	97.71 p	105.39 p	99.02 p
Spain	100	99.14	99.33	100.94	104.06 p	108.8 p	110.48 p
France	100	100.52	101.16	101.9	101.15 p	105.46 p	105.22 p
Croatia	100 p	97.71 p	97.31 p	100.98 p	100.99 p	111.16 p	107.80 p
Italy	100	99.93	99.59	101.21	102.51	103.78	105.03
Cyprus	100	97.14	98.17	98.84	101.71	103.24 p	103.46 p
Latvia	100	104.55	108.86	114.18	120.17	127.97	132.36
Lithuania	100	105.77	110.32	116.05	123.31	129.4	138.75
Luxembourg	100	98.82	103.98	108.68	110.94	114.44	116.16
Hungary	100	103.67	108.17	111.4	114.75	121.78 p	127.41 p
Malta	100	105.40	104.85	109.49	114.47	126.49	124.76
Netherlands	100	101.02	101.6	103.86	106.66 p	115.63 p	113.01 p
Austria	100	101.67	102.84	105.29	107.71	115.95	116.34
Poland	100	102.49	104.65	107.81	110.46	118.73	120.72 b
Portugal	100	101.06	103.01	106.66	110.00	119.87 p	120.38 p
Romania	100	109.90	120.17	129.63	138.62	145.38 p	134.63 b
Slovenia	100	102.24	103.3	105.72	110.4	118.16	116.32
Slovakia	100	102.73	107.31	111.79	117.83	124.5	126.85
Finland	100	98.53	95.25	97.8	99.44	100.12	103.48
Sweden	100	102.25	104.32	107.91	109.62	114.12	114.59
Iceland	100 p	105.04 p	110.41 p	115.98 p	116.62 p	122.87 p	129.22 p
Norway	100	100.48	101.21	104.87	109.86	110.77	112.71
Switzerland	100	98.97	98.45	97.9	99.10	100.42	:

Source: Own elaboration based on https://ec.europa.eu/eurostat/databrowser/view/nama_10_lp_ulc/default/table?lang=en

Note: Labour productivity is measured as the nominal unit labour cost based on hours worked

b – break in time series, p – provisional

results confirm the growth of labour productivity in the Czech Republic in the years under consideration (including 2021). The other V4 countries (Hungary, Slovakia, and Poland) recorded the same labour productivity growth as the Czech Republic. This productivity growth was quite strong (more than 20% in 2021 compared to 2015, and even more than 26% in the case of Slovakia, Hungary, and the Czech Republic). Meanwhile, labour productivity in the EU-27 also grew continuously, but only by 9% (in 2021 compared to 2015). The results of the core EU members are mixed, with relatively weak growth in France and Belgium (growth of about 6%), approaching (surpassing) 16% in Germany, the Netherlands, and Luxembourg, and 20% in Portugal (i.e., comparable to Poland). The highest-ever labour productivity growth was achieved by Bulgaria (43%), followed by Lithuania (almost 39%), Romania (almost 37% – but here labour productivity declined in 2021), and Latvia (32%). On the contrary, only Ireland (almost −11.08% – fluctuations with a negative trend) and Greece (−0.8% – fluctuations with a relatively constant trend) recorded a decline in labour productivity.

Labour productivity can also, however, be measured in terms of the number of employees relative to output (sales) (Yu and Park, 2006; Ahangar, 2011). There are some concerns about the comparability of these two methods. However, Ahmad et al. (2003) argued that, while maintaining internal consistency in the measurement of hours worked and the number of employees relative to sales, that is, ensuring (verifying) the accuracy of the data used, the two measurement methods are comparable. This is confirmed by the research of Grześ (2019), who compared the results of the two aforementioned indicators in Poland and found that although the two indicators reach different values, they follow the same trend of development. That means that they can assess labour productivity in the same way.

We applied the method of measuring productivity as the ratio of total sales to the number of employees (reported by the firm for a given year) in line with Yu and Park (2006), and Ahangar (2011). Labour productivity in each sector was calculated using the Bisnode database, which contains financial statements of companies. The relevant sectors were chosen in correspondence to our survey conducted in the enterprises.

Data in Table 6.2 confirm that labour productivity (measured in terms of the number of employees relative to sales) declined between 2019 and 2020 in the Czech Republic in most of the assessed sectors. A similar study (in terms of measuring labour productivity in selected sectors in the Czech Republic) was conducted by Zubíková and Smolák (2022). They found, however, that labour productivity (measured on hours worked) increased in this period. We can still indirectly assume that faster growth in nominal wages (compared to hourly labour productivity), with the decline in sales (for most firms in studied sectors), leads to lower (total or average) labour productivity (Zubíková and Smolák, 2022).

The decline in employment observed in the Czech Republic in 2020 should be reflected in labour productivity growth. In most sectors, however, productivity has fallen in line with the decline in sales. Sales decreased especially in sectors

TABLE 6.2 Change in labour productivity in select sectors in the Czech Republic

Sector	*LP*		*Δ LP*	*Total*
	2019	2020		
Agriculture, forestry, fishing	2714.47	2873.48	159.01	+
Manufacturing	2398.03	2292.80	−105.23	-
Water supply, waste, sanitation	2796.74	2551.50	−245.24	+
Construction	2163.47	2394.98	231.51	-
Wholesale and retail trade	1542.45	1329.38	−213.07	-
Accommodation, catering, hospitality	1223.35	837.99	−385.35	-
Information and communication activities	2855.03	2746.07	−108.96	-
Monetary and insurance activities	5407.14	4878.93	−528.21	-
Real estate activities	4032.47	3359.89	−672.58	-
Administrative and support service activities	3224.99	2218.10	−1006.89	-
Education	866.41	648.67	−217.74	-
Health and social work activities	1038.93	1096.77	57.84	-
Cultural, entertainment and recreation activities	2913.63	1941.93	−971.70	-
Other activities	1079.74	1035.69	−44.05	-
Average	2446.18	2157.584	−289.33	-

Source: Own calculations based on data from Bisnode database.

Note: Labour productivity is measured as the number of employees relative to output (sales).

severely affected by government restrictions, such as manufacturing, wholesale trade, accommodation, information technology, financial services, administration, education, or culture.

Survey data

Our first survey focused on employers, representatives, or owners of businesses. The second survey addressed employees. Both surveys were preceded by pilot surveys in three select enterprises to find key areas and eliminate possible inconsistencies in the questions. The goal of these surveys was to obtain baseline data related to the new phenomenon of the COVID-19 pandemic and its impact on businesses. The first survey was conducted in October–November 2020, the second from November 2020 to February 2021.

The first survey was conducted primarily in businesses in the South Moravian region. Approximately one-third of the responses were obtained from Prague, the second most represented region with ten business entities. The structure of the research sample was as follows: 15 micro-enterprises, 16 small enterprises, 20 medium-sized enterprises, and 21 large enterprises (the size of two enterprises was taken out of the company public information). The predominant activity of 24 enterprises was manufacturing, 9 enterprises were engaged in wholesale or retail trade, and 6 enterprises were engaged in information and communication activities. Other activities of 33 enterprises were variable, for example, agriculture, buildings, and hospitality. A total of 72 enterprises completed the questionnaire; however, due to incomplete or inconsistent responses, only a total of 49 questionnaires could be used for further processing related to the evaluation of the impact of COVID-19 on enterprises.

The second survey collected data from 45 employees, but only 34 responded to all questions. Regarding businesses where they were employed, the sample structure was as follows: 4 micro-enterprises, 7 small enterprises, 12 medium-sized enterprises, and 11 large enterprises. The predominant activity of these businesses was manufacturing with 6 employees, 5 enterprises were engaged in wholesale or retail trade, and enterprises engaged in IT, education, and health were represented each by 3 employees. Other activities of 20 enterprises were variable, for example, culture and financial.

The questionnaires used Likert scales to find out what pandemic-related problems businesses faced.

To determine attitudes towards the justification of solutions, Likert scales were used in both surveys, always with the appropriate sizes of scales, which are described in the survey results. Respondents were asked whether they considered solutions to problems fair. The data from the survey was evaluated through exploratory research using descriptive statistics methods.

General findings from the surveys

Given the still ongoing significant constraints not only in the personal but especially also in the business sphere, we have received responses from companies and employees, with a link to the problems and their possible solutions and the implications for firm performance. Despite the low number of respondents, this is a survey with real representatives of businesses and employees who have come into real contact with problems. Thus, although they may not present all problems and all areas, we can say that they are showing real cases of negative impacts of COVID-19 restrictions on enterprises and the relationship between management/owners and employees reflected in financial performance.

The examined problems were formulated based on a news review and a preliminary questionnaire. We pointed out five main issues: (1) a shortage of protective equipment, (2) uncertainty regarding wages, (3) scheduling of employees, (4) meeting agreements with suppliers, and (5) customer satisfaction. These types of problems were accepted by representatives as well as by employees.

The results show that the views of employees and managers/owners on the causes of the situation are different. Regarding the managers' and owners' perspectives, their responses identified the current resources of the enterprise as a significant cause of problems, as well as the governmental and institutional interventions. The demands of employees, customers, and suppliers were perceived as less important in more than half of the cases. From the employees' perspective, customer demands play a more critical role. Solutions presented by managers and owners were generally oriented towards the interests of the business or customers.

Regarding employees, the main goal of the business was to satisfy government regulations.

What was key and surprising was that businesses chose an approach to solve problems, such that all stakeholders ended up considering the solution fair. Although the primary orientation of businesses was its own interests and customers, the solution was still chosen with all stakeholders in mind. Businesses were not primarily oriented towards obtaining new profits but rather towards survival without unnecessarily hurting any other party. In most cases, employees considered the presented solutions fair, and they understood them. In fact, employees were even willing to adapt to changes in scheduling and, more specifically, move to home office if possible.

The perception of the problems of the COVID-19 pandemic is mainly linked to the behaviour of companies towards employees or how fair the proposed solutions are to employees. In this respect, it is surprising that about 10% of respondents, that is, five managers or owners, state and admit that some decisions were unfair. In a few cases, all decisions were identified as unfair. Here, however, one must also acknowledge the emotional impact of the COVID-19 pandemic on the running of businesses and the fact that their representatives necessarily act in an ambiguous role, representing their own interests and those of the company. The small sample size should also be considered.

From the employees' perspective, various problems were identified, mainly related to the distribution of working hours and delays in the payment of wages. The employees perceived the cause of these problems to be mainly government interventions and requirements. However, even when they encountered these problems, they considered their solutions to be understandable and fair in most cases. Thus, from this perspective, the crisis response by managers and owners to the organisational crisis can be described as successful.

Overall, the impacts on the examined areas can be evaluated as follows. Regarding the requirements for the procurement of protective equipment, it was found that the surveyed companies mostly encountered the problem once or several times during the period under review. However, not all surveyed businesses encountered problems with the procurement of protective equipment. For those enterprises that had faced this problem, the solution had been tailored to avoid negative consequences for any of the parties involved and to satisfy primarily the interests of the enterprise as well as government regulations or the interests of the employees. Such a solution was largely considered by the enterprise representatives to be fair and understandable.

The situation relating to the payment of wages was perceived differently by the managers or owners and the employees. From the managers' and owners' point of view, most surveyed enterprises did not experience a problem with wages in the period under review (Spring 2020). This may be because the representatives of the enterprises state that they have prevented negative consequences. They tried to prevent a possibly problematic situation, and they were focused on satisfying the interests of the enterprise. However, this aspect was cited by the employees as problematic. This seems to be related to the prioritisation of company interests over those of the rank and file. Thus, the overall prevailing fairness of the solution seems to be based on the clear communication of the solution. It needs to be stressed that the cause of the problem is an external crisis beyond the control of the company's management. Since this was a critical time for the whole society, employees seemed to be more sensitive in securing their life situations.

Concerning work schedule: the surveyed enterprises faced problems once or more than once during the period under review. There was again a minority of businesses that did not encounter this problem. In the case of work scheduling problems, the solution was mainly based on preventing negative consequences and an agreement between the employer, employees, customers, or suppliers. As can be seen, this was a comprehensive solution involving all stakeholders, including government regulations, which were also satisfied by this measure. This solution is also considered in most cases to be fair and understandable, both by employees and by managers and owners. Employees actively help with adapting to working from home or changes in work hours. Some businesses needed to divide their workforce into more groups, so there would be as few employees together in one place as possible.

The surveyed enterprises had encountered issues related to suppliers on one or more occasions during the period under review. As was the case with other problems, there was a minority of businesses that did not encounter problems with suppliers. There is a surprising consistency in the causes of problems and justifications of solutions, where the resolution process was linked to avoiding negative consequences for any of the stakeholders. The approach taken to the solution was to satisfy primarily the demands of customers or the self-interest of the companies concerned. The solution was assessed by the representatives of the enterprises and their employees as fair and understandable.

There were problems that affected the enterprises' customers. These problems were similar to those which affected suppliers, with the enterprises concerned experiencing problems one or more times during the period under review. There was again a minority of enterprises that did not encounter these problems. The causes behind these problems were primarily addressed in terms of avoiding negative consequences for any of the stakeholders. In a few cases, there has been an agreement between the stakeholders to resolve the problem. This corresponds to the prioritisation of reassuring customers or, in a marginal way, the company's interests. In the evaluation, both groups of respondents perceived the solutions as fair and clear.

It should also be added that we did not address the issue of government subsidies or compensation, as the situation with these was inconsistent and uncertain at the time we conducted the survey. However, it can be assumed that they will have a significant impact on the whole issue.

In conclusion, therefore, it can be said that the surveyed enterprises at the time of the COVID-19 pandemic in the spring of 2020 were affected to varying extent by problems related to the procurement of protective equipment, government interventions, financial provision of wages, distribution of working hours, and negative impacts on their suppliers and customers. However, they were able to cope with and solve these problems in a way that solutions were mostly perceived as fair. Affected enterprises were able to manage problems regarding prevention, that is, primarily preventing negative consequences towards stakeholders, and monitoring stakeholder interests, all in line with the interests of the business itself. Finally, it is also gratifying that most enterprises took direct responsibility for the COVID-19 pandemic that hit their enterprise in the context of the organisational crisis and the fair handling of the situation associated with it, which can be considered a successful level of crisis response.

Discussion of survey results in the context of labour productivity

The survey findings demonstrate that in companies that successfully managed the COVID-19 crisis by minimising the negative impact on financial transformation, it was important to implement systemic measures based on public regulations to prevent the spread of COVID-19 and coordinated by a qualified person in accordance with government interventions. The new phenomenon of digitalisation in the form of employee connectivity through electronic media operating both in the workplace and within the established home office emerged prominently in enterprises. These measures mostly used a rotation of workers who were not directly involved in the production and could thus use electronic tools and home office. Employees without the possibility of using the home office (mainly production and retail) were trained to perform work according to government recommendations, and work was carried out using protective equipment. All these phenomena led to preserving employment, discovering new ways of organising and performing work, and learning lessons in the context of the crisis caused by the COVID-19 pandemic (Stuart et al., 2021).

Managers and employees are already experiencing select negative phenomena such as the lack of social contact in the context of human resource development or the impacts associated with higher future home office usage with a link to the underutilisation of all existing corporate spaces. In many cases, these are proving to be less necessary or even unnecessary in terms of intellectual work. The COVID-19 pandemic and the associated need for accessibility via web interfaces have demonstrated the importance of digitisation and the associated level of government infrastructure in this area. Overall, it became clear that in organisational crises covering the issues, both dispositional and executive labour responded quite promptly to the state and governmental regulations (Janssen & Van Der Voort, 2020). The solutions chosen were considered understandable and mostly fair by employees across the board. If we consider this behaviour in terms of crisis response, it can be described as adequate (Raithel & Hock, 2021).

On the one hand, the decline of the accommodation, real estate, education, and cultural sectors can be justified by measures associated with the fight against the COVID-19 pandemic, especially in the area of limiting people-to-people contact, that is, limiting trade and services (Stuchlíková & Botlíková, 2021). On the other hand, the water supply sector was not affected at all by the pandemic or the fight against it, as water supply, waste and sanitation are not directly related to the COVID-19 pandemic and the fight against it, yet labour productivity declined even in this sector. Also, the sector of agriculture was not affected by the pandemic, which in the case of agricultural, forestry, and fishery enterprises is probably related to the considerable degree of mechanisation of labour and the fact that these activities are still mainly carried out by workers from the Czech Republic, with an increased orientation towards domestic production during the pandemic (Švecová et al., 2020). The wholesale sector has also been more significantly affected, which is probably related to the fact that the shift of trade to online stores, which is confirmed by the research of Švecová et al. (2020), had probably not yet been fully realised in 2020. Thus, the losses of businesses in bricks-and-mortar stores had not yet been sufficiently offset by the gains of businesses on the Internet.

Somewhat surprisingly, there was a decline in the manufacturing sector, which seems to have experienced disruptions in supply chains within national and international flows (of production factors and products) and forced organisational and management changes. It is uncertain to what extent the outflow of labour and subsequent labour shortages is related to the closing of borders to foreigners, or the restriction of employee mobility as described by Reichelt et al. (2021). This relationship has not been reflected in the construction sector, where labour productivity has increased.

In the health sector, health enterprises have been enormously burdened by the COVID-19 pandemic, which has led to a reduction in health activities focused on other diseases (Sedova et al., 2021) and a reduction in social service enterprises. Despite or because of this, there has been an increase in labour productivity in this sector. For health enterprises, there has been a huge increase in their workload (including the interventions performed), which has not been sufficiently compensated by increased staffing (also due to the considerable rigidity of the health system).

On the one hand, the decline in the money sector seems to indicate a successful digitalisation and transition to a virtual environment, and the COVID-19 pandemic has only accelerated this transition. Yet there has been a significant decline in labour productivity. Similarly, the administrative and support activities sector has successfully managed digitisation and the transition to a virtual environment but has failed to maintain adequate labour productivity.

The causes of the reduction in labour productivity (especially in the information, monetary, real estate, administrative, education, and other sectors) may be due to the introduction of teleworking or home working. Studies focusing on teleworking during the COVID-19 crisis compared to the pre-crisis period show that the exceptional conditions (here a pandemic) under which telework was introduced in firms reduced the productivity of employees who could work from home (Gorlick, 2020). However, our research shows that telecommuting has helped to address the substantive problems caused by the COVID-19 pandemic, although in economic terms its benefits are rather negative. In the long run, however, labour productivity can be expected to increase, as wider and smarter adoption of efficient teleworking practices can be expected because of the acceleration of the resolution of the crisis (Gibbs et al., 2021) caused by the pandemic.

Conclusion

Our research has shown that while the beginning of the COVID-19 crisis has brought several problems, most of these problems seem to be solvable from the point of view of firms and employees. Despite the many contradictory governmental regulations, arising problems were manageable and managed by businesses. There has been a mutual interaction where especially the implementation of the recommendations of experts has resulted in many cases in the continued operation of businesses. This prevented negative impacts on employment that would otherwise have resulted from businesses shutting down. Standard tools such as staff rotation at workplaces and the use of home office resulted in dealing with the COVID-19 pandemic between employees and managers/owners without significant conflicts or social upheaval.

On the contrary, the opportunity of using home office for some jobs to save space and associated costs is surprising. This also helped in dealing with uncertainty regarding wages and scheduling since employees were able to continue working in a safer environment. It also demonstrates the importance of digitalisation and the importance of adequate and functional infrastructure in the successful management of the crisis. This was particularly evident in employee work schedule, which was subject to government interventions and regulations. Despite the challenging conditions, businesses were able to coordinate and communicate so that the final decision was not only understandable but also considered fair.

The research on labour productivity showed that all the examined sectors (except agriculture, construction, and health and social work activities) were negatively affected by the COVID-19 pandemic, that is, there was a decline in labour productivity of these sectors for reasons explained deeper in the previous part. It appears that the negative impact on this productivity was mainly due to the government's demand (and therefore revenue) restriction measures aimed at containing the pandemic, that is, restricting the movement of people and closing borders. Some of these measures also caused labour shortages, which translated into an increase in average wages and counteracted the fall in wage costs caused by the loss of employees. However, the government's measures have also had an impact on business supply, as the reduction in people-to-people contacts has significantly dampened (or eliminated) the activity of businesses in sectors mainly focused on trade and services. These measures have thus harmed labour productivity.

Although the literature suggests that the two methods of productivity measurement used in this study are equivalent, this was not confirmed by our research. We found that labour productivity measured in terms of hours worked and the ratio of sales to the number of employees may show different trends and results.

Interestingly, the government's restrictive interventions did not translate significantly into the labour market, regarding a rise in unemployment. Although the unemployment rate has risen year-on-year, the figure of 2.6% in 2020 can still be considered low (considering the other EU member states). In this respect, the steps taken by the government through several programmes explained in the previous part are proving positive. However, it is unknown to what extent these measures have artificially maintained employment in enterprises that have subsequently closed (or will close) thus hindering the development of more successful enterprises (inability to find employees).

There are some limitations to our research that must be mentioned due to the nature, scope, and way the research was conducted in the context of the ongoing COVID-19 pandemic. Specifically, this was not a representative survey, and data were only collected during the first wave, which makes it impossible to generalise to later waves of the pandemic. The overall impact of the pandemic will need to be further studied on a larger number of enterprises and with a longer time lag.

Based on our findings, it is evident that in the context of an organisational crisis, businesses themselves were able to respond in a way that did not fundamentally disrupt their operations, and that this response was perceived to be understandable and fair. Businesses were able to respond to a new and unforeseen situation and, although it is questionable what the long-term consequences will be for society, businesses perceived their response as appropriate.

References

Act No. 159/2020 Coll.

Act No. 435/2004 Coll., on Employment.

Ahangar, R. G. (2011). The relationship between intellectual capital and financial performance: An empirical investigation in an Iranian company. *African Journal of Business Management*, *5*(1), 88–95.

Ahmad, N., Lequiller, F., Marianna, P., Pilat, D., Schreyer, P., & Wölfl, A. (2003). Comparing labour productivity growth in the OECD area: The role of measurement. https://doi.org/10.1787/18151965

Alves, T. L. D. L., Amorim, A. F. A., & Bezerra, M. C. C. (2021). "Not one less"! Adaptation to the home office in times of COVID-19. *Revista de Administração Contemporânea*, *25*, 1–15. https://doi.org/10.1590/1982–7849rac2021200234.en|

Andoh, R. (2020). The impact of COVID-19 on global economy: The case of the Czech Republic. *International Journal of Multidisciplinary Sciences and Advanced Technology*, *1*, 22–29.

Andrews, D., Charlton, A., & Moore, A. (2021). COVID-19, productivity and reallocation: Timely evidence from three OECD countries. https://doi.org/10.1787/18151973

Baniamin, H. M., Rahman, M., & Hasan, M. T. (2020). The COVID-19 pandemic: Why are some countries coping more successfully than others? *Asia Pacific Journal of Public Administration*, *42*(3), 153–169.

Bloom, N., Bunn, P., Mizen, P., Smietanka, P., & Thwaites, G. (2020). *The impact of COVID-19 on productivity* (No. w28233). National Bureau of Economic Research.

Borland, J., & Charlton, A. (2020). The Australian labour market and the early impact of COVID-19: An assessment. *Australian Economic Review, 53*(3), 297–324. https://doi.org/10.1111/1467–8462.12386

Brown, R., Rocha, A., & Cowling, M. (2020). Financing entrepreneurship in times of crisis: Exploring the impact of COVID-19 on the market for entrepreneurial finance in the United Kingdom. *International Small Business Journal, 38*(5), 380–390. https://doi.org/10.1177/0266242620937464

Ciobanu, R., Şova, R. A., & Popa, A. F. (2020). The impact of FDI on economic growth and how the COVID-19 crisis can impact the CEE economies. *CECCAR Business Review, 4*, 64–72. https://doi.org/10.37945/cbr.2020.04.08

Czech Statistical Office. (2021a). *Počet zaměstnanců a průměrné hrubé měsíční mzdy*. Retrieved October 25, 2021, from https://vdb.czso.cz/vdbvo2/faces/cs/index.jsf?page=vystup-objekt&pvo=MZD01-A&z=T&f=TABULKA&skupId=855&filtr=G%7EF_M%7EF_Z%7EF_R%7ET_P%7E_S%7E_null_null_&katalog=30852&pvo=MZD01-A&evo=v208_!_MZD-LEG4_1

Czech Statistical Office. (2021b). *Základní charakteristiky ekonomického postavení obyvatelstva ve věku 15 a více let*. Retrieved October 25, 2021, from https://vdb.czso.cz/vdbvo2/faces/cs/index.jsf?page=vystup-objekt&pvo=ZAM01-B&skupId=426&katalog=30853&pvo=ZAM01-B&str=v467&u=v413__VUZEMI__97__19

Czech statistical office. (2021c). *Obecná míra nezaměstnanosti v ČR a krajích*. Retrieved October 25, 2021, from www.czso.cz/csu/czso/obecna_mira_nezamestnanosti_v_cr_a_krajich

Fialova, V., & Vasenska, I. (2020). Implications of the COVID-19 crisis for the sharing economy in tourism: The case of Airbnb in the Czech Republic. *Ekonomicko-manazerske spektrum, 14*(2), 78–89.

Gandy, R., & Mulhearn, C. (2021). Allowing for unemployment in productivity measurement. *SN Business & Economics, 1*(1), 1–38. https://doi.org/10.1007/s43546-020-00008-7

Gibbs, M., Mengel, F., & Siemroth, C. (2021). Work from home & productivity: Evidence from personnel & analytics data on IT professionals. (*Becker Friedman Institute for Economics Working Paper* 1–39). University of Chicago.

Gorlick, A. (2020). The productivity pitfalls of working from home in the age of COVID-19. *Stanford News*, 1–4.

Gros, D., & Ounnas, A. (2021). Labour market responses to the COVID-19 crisis in the United States and Europe. *CEPS Working Document* 2021–01. https://doi.org/10.2139/ssrn.3832568

Grześ, A. (2019). The measurement of labour productivity in the enterprise sector. The example of Poland. *Optimum. Economic Studies, 98*(4), 44–55. https://doi.org/10.15290/oes.2019.04.98.04

Hedvičáková, M., & Kozubíková, Z. (2021). Impacts of COVID-19 on the labour market-evidence from the Czech Republic. *Hradec Economic Days, 11*(1), 232–241.

Hromada, E. (2021). Impacts of COVID-19 on the real estate market in the Czech Republic. In *SHS web of conferences* (Vol. 91). EDP Sciences. https://doi.org/10.1051/shsconf/20219101028

Huang, A., Makridis, C., Baker, M., Medeiros, M., & Guo, Z. (2020). Understanding the impact of COVID-19 intervention policies on the hospitality labor market. *International Journal of Hospitality Management, 91*. https://doi.org/10.1016/j.ijhm.2020.102660

Huang, Y. H. (2008). Trust and relational commitment in corporate crises: The effects of crisis communicative strategy and form of crisis response. *Journal of Public Relations Research, 20*(3), 297–327. https://doi.org/10.1080/10627260801962830

Janssen, M., & Van Der Voort, H. (2020). Agile and adaptive governance in crisis response: Lessons from the COVID-19 pandemic. *International Journal of Information Management*, *55*, 102180. https://doi.org/10.1016/j.ijinfomgt.2020.102180

Kavan, S. (2021). Selected social impacts and measures resulting from the Covid-19 epidemic in the Czech Republic on the specific example of the South Bohemian Region. *Health & Social Care in the Community*, *29*(5), e224–e231.

Klein, C., Høj, J., & Machlica, G. (2021). The impacts of the COVID-19 crisis on the automotive sector in Central and Eastern European Countries. *OECD Economics Department Working Papers* 1658, 1–18. OECD Publishing.

Lustig, N., & Mariscal, J. (2020). How COVID-19 could be like the global financial crisis (or worse). In Richard Baldwin & Beatrice Weder di Mauro (Eds.), *Mitigating the COVID economic crisis: Act fast and do whatever it takes* (pp. 185–190). CEPR Press

Ministry of Labour and Social Affairs. (2021). OSVČ. Retrieved October 25, 2021, from www.mpsv.cz/osvc-info

Ministry of Industry and Trade of the Czech Republic. (2021, October 25). Program COVID – Nájemné. Retrieved October 25, 2021, from www.mpo.cz/cz/podnikani/zivnostenske-podnikani/covid-19-najemne – 255305/

Novotny, L., & Pellesova, P. (2021). Impact of the COVID-19 crisis on the regulation to tourism in the Czech Republic. *Central European Public Administration Review*, *19*, 199.

Nový, M., & Nováková, J. (2022). Impact of the COVID-19 pandemic on construction companies in the Czech Republic. *Procedia Computer Science*, *196*, 717–723.

Obrenovic, B., Du, J., Godinic, D., Tsoy, D., Khan, M. A. S., & Jakhongirov, I. (2020). Sustaining enterprise operations and productivity during the COVID-19 pandemic: "Enterprise effectiveness and sustainability model". *Sustainability*, *12*(15), 5981.

Pearson, C. M., & Clair, J. A. (1998), Reframing crisis management. *Academy of Management Review*, *23*(1), 59–76. https://doi.org/10.5465/amr.1998.192960

Pelikánová, R. M., Němečková, T., & MacGregor, R. K. (2021). CSR statements in international and Czech luxury fashion industry at the onset and during the COVID-19 pandemic – Slowing down the fast fashion business? *Sustainability*, *13*(7), 3715.

Penco, L., Profumo, G., Serravalle, F., & Viassone, M. (2022). Has COVID-19 pushed digitalisation in SMEs? The role of entrepreneurial orientation. *Journal of Small Business and Enterprise Development*. https://doi.org/10.1108/JSBED-10–2021–0423

Raithel, S., & Hock, S. J. (2021). The crisis-response match: An empirical investigation. *Strategic Management Journal*, *42*(1), 170–184. https://doi.org/10.1002/smj.3213

Reichelt, M., Makovi, K., & Sargsyan, A. (2021). The impact of COVID-19 on gender inequality in the labor market and gender-role attitudes. *European Societies*, *23*(sup1), 228–245. https://doi.org/10.1080/14616696.2020.1823010

Sedova, P., Brown R. D., Jr., Bryndziar, T., Jarkovsky, J., Tomek, A., Sramek, M., Skoda, O., Sramkova, T., Littnerova, S., & Mikulik, R. (2021). Treat COVID-19, but not only COVID-19: Stroke matters as well. *Cerebrovascular Diseases*, 1–8. https://doi.org/10.1159/000517968

Shen, H., Fu, M., Pan, H., Yu, Z., & Chen, Y. (2020). The impact of the COVID-19 pandemic on firm performance. *Emerging Markets Finance & Trade*, *56*(10), 2213. https://doi.org/10.1080/1540496X.2020.1785863

Stuart, M., Spencer, D. A., McLachlan, C. J., & Forde, C. (2021). COVID-19 and the uncertain future of HRM: Furlough, job retention and reform. *Human Resource Management Journal*. https://doi.org/10.1111/1748–8583.12395

Stuchlíková, J., & Botlíková, M. (2021). The impact of the global pandemic on selected aspects of sustainable tourism in the Czech Republic. In *SHS web of conferences* (Vol. 92). EDP Sciences. https://doi.org/10.1051/shsconf/20219201046

Švecová, L., Ostapenko, G., & Veber, J. (2020). *Impact of global trends and the coronavirus challenge on consumer behavior* [Conference]. 2020 6th International Conference on Social Science and Higher Education (ICSSHE 2020), 1005–1009. Atlantis Press. https://doi.org/10.2991/assehr.k.201214.193

Urbancová, H., & Depoo, L. (2021). Factors affecting strategic types of organizational culture: Evidence from organizations and managers operating in the Czech Republic. *Management and Production Engineering Review*, 48–59. https://doi.org/10.24425/mper.2021.136871

Vrchota, J., Maříková, M., & Řehoř, P. (2020). Teleworking in SMEs before the onset of coronavirus infection in the Czech Republic. *Management: Journal of Contemporary Management Issues*, *25*(2), 151–164. https://doi.org/10.30924/mjcmi.25.2.8

Yu, G. C., & Park, J. S. (2006). The effect of downsizing on the financial performance and employee productivity of Korean firms. *International Journal of Manpower*, *27*(3), 230–250.

Zubíková, A., & Smolák, P. (2022). Macroeconomic impacts of the COVID-19 pandemic in the Czech Republic in the period of 2020–2021. *International Journal of Economic Sciences*, *11*(1), 117–145.

7

PRESERVING JOBS IN COVID-19 TIMES IN CEE COUNTRIES

Social Partners' Responses and Actions

Vassil Kirov, Lucia Kováčová, Martin Guzi, Jan Czarzasty, Dragoș Adăscăliței, and Martin Kahanec

Introduction

Eleven Central and Eastern European (CEE) countries joined the European Union in 2004, 2007 and 2013. While one of the objectives of European integration – economic convergence – has been at least partly achieved between new and old member states, it has not been accompanied by convergence in industrial relations systems (Delteil & Kirov, 2016). In fact, the characteristics of Eastern European capitalism and its subtypes vary across new member states (Bohle & Greskovits, 2012). Nevertheless, most of these countries share the common trend of eroding trade union membership and influence. Despite these trends, the social models in CEE countries were able to generate some compromises and responded to economic crises in the post-enlargement period, such as the Great Recession of 2008. Political responses to these crises reflected national institutional settings (Johnstone et al., 2019), and the role of trade unions in shaping anti-crisis measures varied across EU countries and industrial relations systems (e.g., Geary, 2015; Kahancová, 2013). During the COVID-19 pandemic, social partners in CEE have been active in efforts to mitigate the negative consequences of the economic downturn; however, evidence on the scope, scale, and effects of their roles in shaping policy responses to the pandemic remains scant.

Our study relates and contributes to an emerging literature on the roles of social partners in policy responses during the COVID-19 pandemic in 2020. Podvršič et al. (2020) study policy responses in the early stages of the pandemic in the export-oriented Central European countries including countries in this chapter. Their study finds that social actors were selectively integrated in the creation of policy responses to the pandemic, depending on the political composition of the ruling coalition as well as the nature of the extant tripartite framework. The adopted policy responses deployed similar instruments (including short-time work

DOI: 10.4324/9781003326779-9

provisions and tax and social security payment deferrals), and they varied in their scale and scope. Müller and Schulten (2020) study short-time work arrangements across Europe and identify key criteria for their success in preserving jobs and maintaining decent incomes. We add to this literature by studying job-preserving policies in the under-researched CEE region.

This chapter provides early evidence on the role of social partners in shaping job preservation policies, focusing on three main types: short-time working arrangements (e.g., *Kurzarbeit*); wage subsidies; and flexible work arrangements (e.g., teleworking). We present the main characteristics of the industrial relations systems and main social partners is five CEE countries: Bulgaria, the Czech Republic, Poland, Romania, and Slovakia. More specifically, we critically explore how social partners in these countries have been involved in designing and adopting job preservation policies responding to the COVID-19 economic crisis and increasing unemployment rates during 2020. We also focus on teleworking since this is a novel form of work organisation in the CEE countries as well as an important policy for preserving jobs during the current crisis (European Commission, 2020). However, while telework has been increasing massively since the beginning of the pandemic, social partners have had little to do with this process. At best, there have been cases of social dialogue at the company level.

The industrial relations systems in the CEE countries are characterised by a high fragmentation of social partners. In this chapter we study whether the COVID-19 pandemic provided an opportunity for social partners to revitalise tripartite arenas and effectively engage in the preparation of job preservation schemes. We take insights from interviews with national-level social partners and desk research carried out in each country. Our findings indicate strong involvement of social partners in the design of short-term working schemes but less engagement in the introduction of teleworking as a novel form of work organisation in CEE countries.

The remainder of this chapter is organised as follows. First section begins with a preview of theoretical literature that provides background for our empirical strategy and to which we contribute. In next section we elaborate a mixed-method empirical framework based on case studies to map these very recent developments and triangulate the roles of social partners. Next section introduces the context, presents the case studies, and comparatively evaluates them. We conclude by discussing the lessons learned and outlining key questions for further research.

Theoretical background and literature review

This chapter builds on theories of institutional change (Ost, 2000; Ost & Crowley, 2001) and restructuring regimes (Gazier, 2008; Bergström, 2019) to explore how, in the context of the COVID-19 pandemic, social partners in CEE have reacted to job preservation policies. In a broader sense, our study details industrial relations experiences from CEE countries in the context of the crisis. It also builds on punctuated-equilibrium theory (Baumgartner & Jones, 1993), postulating that the policy-making process is typically characterised by incrementalism, but when an era of policy stability is disrupted by a crisis (such as a pandemic), it may result in novel policies and new policy paradigms, including in employment and work organisation.

Institutional factors played an important role in shaping the evolution of social dialogue in the post-socialist countries of CEE aspiring to EU membership from the 1990s onwards. Implementation of tripartite institutions was a part of the *acquis* and as such had to be endorsed by the CEE countries (Vaughan-Whitehead, 2000). In a number of countries, for instance, Poland, the process dragged on (cf. Gardawski, 2009), and in all required a *de facto* creation of employer organisations in a top-down manner. The results of such imitational institutional change have been assessed critically, with the famous 'illusory corporatism' thesis (Ost, 2000, 2011; Woolfson & Kallaste, 2011) depicting tripartite bodies conceived under external pressure as a *façade* being frequently cited. The superficial nature of institutional change is well illustrated by the continuous crisis of collective bargaining, suffering from diminishing coverage rates and decentralisation, as well as on-going de-unionisation. In the accession states of CEE, which are portrayed as cases of 'neoliberal' (Baltic States) or 'embedded neoliberal' capitalism (Bohle & Greskovits, 2013), employer organisations have largely failed to become more than just business associations due to their inability to engage in genuine collective bargaining (cf. Müller et al., 2019). In all CEE countries, trade unions were losing their associational and structural power, partly due to historical legacies (cf. Crowley, 2004), partly due to inadequate capacity for re-inventing themselves in the context of rapid economic change (restructuring) (cf. Czarzasty et al., 2014), and partly due to enduring 'labour quiescence' after the fall of self-proclaimed worker-states (Crowley & Ost, 2001). Given the circumstances, tripartite bodies became an institutional prosthesis for weak social partners who could exercise via that channel – albeit in an increasingly symbolic way – some impact on public policies.

This weak impact on public policy was also demonstrated during the post-communism period and during the economic crisis of 2008. However, according to Bergström (2019), some changes in restructuring regimes[1] were observed in CEE countries such as Bulgaria and the Czech Republic in the 2008–2009 period. These countries introduced short-term working schemes, mainly funded by the European Social Fund (ESF). In 2020, the role of the state in all the examined countries has changed in terms of restructuring regimes with the massive use of short-time work in the context of the COVID-19 pandemic. This major policy change in CEE, compared to previous periods, has opened several opportunities for social partners, despite their relative weakness, to negotiate short-time work arrangements.

These recent developments may cause a major disruption in the industrial relations realities. During the three decades following the fall of communism, the role of social partners to shape policies was additionally restrained by austerity policies promoted by the European Union and/or international financial institutions and the limited budgets of national governments. However, the situation in the context of the pandemic has suddenly changed. Governments in the region have mobilised European and some national resources and invested massively, as illustrated by the country cases below. Indeed, we hypothesise that the role of social partners in national politics was suddenly disrupted, providing them with new tools to impact policymaking. In this context, the theory of incrementalism may be useful. It postulates that policymaking is based on minor adjustments made by policymakers to respond to societal problems rather than on grand changes in policy designs or even implementing novel policies that would significantly differ from the status quo (Hayes, 2001; Lindblom, 1959). As a result of the uncertainty of outcomes and lack of agreement over fundamental values, policymakers opt for an incrementalistic strategy in policymaking and seek local solutions. Thus, given the complexity of problems and lack of information and knowledge, policymakers decide to adopt policy measures that are possible and practical, and whose consequences are more predictable (Atkinson, 2011). Eventually, policy agendas become stable and major policy changes thus occur as an outcome of the accumulation of smaller adaptations to policies. Baumgartner and Jones (1993) further postulate that the policymaking process is typically characterised by incrementalism, but the era of policy stability is disrupted by a crisis (such as armed conflicts, epidemics, and terrorist attacks), which results in novel policies and new policy paradigms. In this context, policymakers irregularly respond to new information and overcome institutional obstacles (Baumgartner et al., 2009), and then major policy changes occur as a response to extraordinary circumstances. Nevertheless, not all exogenous disruptions result in large-scale policy actions (such as a slow response to climate change), as institutional settings, and especially frictions within institutions, have an impact on the variation and strength of policy changes (Baumgartner et al., 2009; Lundgren et al., 2017). Therefore, the current health and economic crisis plays a pivotal role in shaping new policy paradigms in job preservation employment policies and speeding up both the massive use of government funded job preservation schemes and the introduction of novel forms of work organisation (such as teleworking) that enable private companies and public entities to adjust to adverse economic circumstances and to address different restrictions relating to business venues, lockdowns, and school closures affecting the childcare responsibilities of working parents.

Methodology

To study institutional developments in CEE countries we employ mixed methods of analysis. The input from qualitative research (interviews with national-level social partners and desk research carried out in each country) provides insights about the role of social partners in policymaking for preserving jobs, at the macro and mezzo levels. We carried out 13 semi-structured interviews with representatives of trade union confederations and employer organisations in five countries (three in Bulgaria (BG), two in Poland (PL), two in Slovakia (SK), two in the Czech Republic (CZ), and four in Romania (RO)).

The context of job preservation

Between 2015 and 2019, CEE countries encountered a positive economic growth accompanied with a decreasing unemployment rate. The COVID-19 pandemic has reverted these positive trends. Figure 7.1 depicts the varying patterns in unemployment development between countries in 2020. In Poland, unemployment essentially remained flat throughout the year. In contrast, unemployment grew most in the Czech Republic: from the low base of 1.9% in March to 3.1% in December, that is, by 1.2 percentage points or 60% over nine months. In Bulgaria, the rise in unemployment spiked from 4.8% in March to above 6% in April and May 2020 but remained below 5% until the end of the year. In the Czech Republic, Romania and Slovakia, the increase in unemployment was gradual and spread over several months.

The COVID-19 pandemic has forced many employers to adopt remote work arrangements as a common form of work. However, surprisingly, policy measures to develop and implement effective teleworking arrangements have not been on the agenda of social partners in CEE countries. Teleworking has been left to individual bargaining or, in rare cases, social dialogue at the establishment level. Nevertheless, the spread of teleworking due to the outbreak of COVID-19 among workers in CEE countries was massive, in stark contrast to its low prevalence before 2020.

The share of jobs that could be done from home with existing technologies (Dingel & Neiman, 2020) in CEE countries is below the EU average of 36% (see Column 1 in Table 7.1). In Romania, only 22% of jobs are estimated to be plausibly performed at home, while the fraction of tele-workable employment ranges between 29% and 33% in other studied countries. Access to teleworking is greater among workers who use computers or electronic devices. Data from the EU survey on the use of information and communication technologies (ICT) among workers show that two-thirds of EU workers use ICT equipment at work but only a

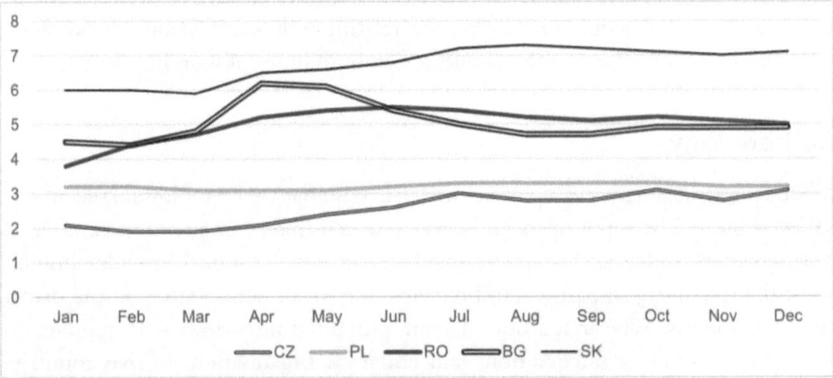

FIGURE 7.1 Monthly unemployment rates (seasonally unadjusted), 2020

Source: Own elaboration based on (Eurostat, 2021).

TABLE 7.1 Teleworkability and use of ICT at work (%)

Country	*Employment tele-workability*	*Use of ICT at work*	*Prevalence of teleworking in 2019*	*Teleworking in April 2020*	*Work from home in June/ July 2020*
	(1)	*(2)*	*(3)*	*(4)*	*(5)*
BG	29	39	1.2	27	27
CZ	33	56	10.3	37	45
EU-27	36	67	15.2	39	46
PL	33	52	15.0	31	38
RO	22	32	1.4	20	31
SK	29	52	9.7	31	32

Source: Own elaboration based on (Dingel & Neuman, 2020; Eurostat, Eurofound, 2020a).

Note: (1) Figures adopted from Dingel and Neiman (2020); (2) the share of individuals who use computers, laptops, smartphones, tablets or other portable devices at work from Eurostat (variable isoc_iw_ap); (3) the share of employed working from home from Eurostat (variable lfsa_ehomp); (4) the share of workers who started to work from home as a result of the COVID-19 situation from Eurofound (2020a); and (5) the share of workers indicating working from home from Eurofound (2020a). All shares in percentages. Individual weights are applied.

third of workers in Romania and Bulgaria and slightly over half of workers in the Czech Republic, Poland, and Slovakia (see Column 2 in Table 7.1). The share of employed working from home regularly or at least sometimes before 2020 was 15% in Poland, around 10% in the Czech Republic and Slovakia, but below 2% in Bulgaria and Romania (see Column 3 in Table 7.1).

The spread of COVID-19 acted as an exogenous shock to work organisation and increased the prevalence of teleworking. The Eurofound's Living, Working and COVID-19 survey (Eurofound, 2020a) identified 39% of workers in the EU working from home during the peak of lockdown restrictions. Rates below 30% were recorded only in four Member States, including Bulgaria (27%) and Romania (20%) (see Column 4 in Table 7.1). The follow-up survey found that working from home had increased to 46% in the EU in June/July 2020. The range of incidence in the CEE countries remains below the EU average and ranges between 27% in Bulgaria and 45% in the Czech Republic (see Column 5 in Table 7.1). The findings point to the lower use of ICT at work and lower prevalence of teleworking in CEE countries relative to the EU average.

We next summarise the main characteristics of the industrial relations systems and main social partners of the five countries (Table 7.2). While there are significant differences in terms of the fragmentation of social partners, the situation regarding power, measured by trade union density and collective bargaining coverage, clearly indicates a decrease compared to the situation ten years ago. Finally, there is a decentralisation trend taking place in all the countries, and national level tripartism loses ground. Will the current crisis related to COVID-19 reinforce these trends? Or can it be an opportunity for social partners to revitalise tripartite arenas and impact public policies tackling job preservation?

TABLE 7.2 Industrial relations key characteristics

Country	*Bulgaria*	*Czech Republic*	*Poland*	*Romania*	*Slovakia*
Collective bargaining coverage (%)	28 (2018)	50 (2016/2017)	13 (2019)	15 (2017)	24 (2015)
Trade union density	15 (2016)	11 (2018)	13 (2017)	21 (2018)	11 (2018)
Actors	two main trade union confederations and five EO	one main confederation and one EO	two confederations and five EO	five TUs confe derations and six EO	one main confederation and three EOs, and the Federation of towns and municipalities
Bargaining	Bargaining at company and industry level. Company-level bargaining prevails	Sectoral (setting general points) and enterprise (more specific), but only one level applies in many workplaces	Single-employer level dominates	Company bargaining the most important Cross-industry bargaining prohibited	Collective bargaining alternates between company, multi-employer, and sectoral bargaining. The latter two are still dominant but the company level is increasingly important.

Source: Adapted from (Müller et al., 2019; Visser, 2021).

Country cases

Bulgaria

Since the COVID-19 outbreak, social partners in Bulgaria have engaged in an intensive social dialogue leading to national-level agreements and have actively taken part in the formulation of job preservation measures. As is well documented elsewhere (Kirov, 2019; Adascalitei & Kirov, forthcoming), in previous crisis situations, such as in 1996–1997 or 2008, the social dialogue in Bulgaria intensified and improved due to government efforts to legitimise its policy and employers' will to engage in dialogue.

The larger measure to address the pandemic, in terms of budget and impact, has been tailored to support job preservation: 'COVID-19: Income support for workers 60/40'. The so-called '60/40' measure was introduced by the Bulgarian government as early as March 2020 to cover 60% of the wages of employees in affected sectors who would otherwise have been laid off (the overall amount of this measure has been estimated to be over 1.2% of 2019 GDP). In March–April 2020, '60/40' intended to cover companies whose activities were prohibited by restrictive measures related to COVID-19 and companies whose turnover decreased by 20% compared to the same period in 2019.[2] During the second wave of the programme (1 July–30 September 2020), the measure focused on the hospitality industry, in particular targeting seasonal workers. The third wave of the '60/40' measure, which started in October 2020, covered almost all sectors, and continued throughout 2021 and the beginning of 2022.

Along with the more general '60–40' measure, Bulgaria introduced another measure targeted at supporting short-time work in tourism and travel: 'Measures for maintaining employment in transport and tourism'. This measure has been aimed at employers and self-employed in the transport and tourism sectors. Eligible applicants must prove at least a 20% drop in sales revenue and to pay taxes and social security contributions for 2019. Initially, the measure was set to last six months and to preserve the employment of at least 22,000 people. The total budget allocated to this measure was BGN 40 million (€20 million). This measure might be combined with measure '60/40' to increase support to '80/20'. These measures are funded by the state budget and through ESF, by re-orientating other measures. Above all, the main instrument to tackle the crisis and preserve jobs has been through short-term unemployment schemes.

From the beginning, social partners took an active role in drafting measure '60/40'. This measure was discussed in detail within the National Council for Tripartite Cooperation (including government and representatives of the nationally representative employers' and trade union organisations). '60/40' was supported by all social partners. Social partners not only provided opinions, but also initiated solutions such as the measure for the support of jobs in travel and tourism, which was proposed by the unions, supported by all social partners, and then adopted and implemented.

As early as March 2020,[3] the largest trade union confederation (Confederation of Independent Trade Unions of Bulgaria – CITUB), supported the efforts of the Government and the Parliament of the Republic of Bulgaria to take urgent action in the state of emergency to protect the health and life of the nation and to preserve employment and production, as reasonably as possible, while ensuring conditions for survival. Employer organisations, alone or within their umbrella organisation the Association of Bulgarian Employer Organisations (AOBR), also supported the government measures.

Although social partners supported the measures for job preservation in general, they have been critical of certain aspects of the employment preservation policy. For example, CITUB underlined in late March that measures adopted by the government have been extremely insufficient in terms of scope and monetary value. According to the trade unions, a larger package of measures is needed to target all the affected sectors and categories of employees. Therefore, trade unions have lobbied not only for expanding the scope of the measures, but also for revising some relevant laws, for example, to increase the minimum unemployment benefit (from BGN 9 per day to BGN 17) or to permanently establish it at 60% of the minimum wage.

As early as 17 March 2020, the largest employer organisation, the Bulgarian Industrial Association (BIA), published a position on the Draft Law on measures during the emergency, requesting state support for different compensations that will allow companies to preserve jobs.[4] In April 2020, the employer association in Bulgaria published a joint statement of AOBR,[5] requesting a 'better formulation of the "60/40" measures' and pushing for additional working time flexibility, for example, that 'the employer may establish, for the whole period of the state of emergency, or part of that period, part-time work for full-time employees'.

At the beginning of April, CITUB, and other employer and trade union organisations, proposed new measures targeted at specific groups affected by the crisis to enter the second socio-economic package.[6] All the proposals submitted to the National Council for Tripartite Cooperation by the other social partners for new social and economic measures were compiled in a common package at the end of April 2020. Those proposals were then discussed with the government.

The high-level format of the social partners' involvement is illustrated also by the relatively regular meetings of the social partners' heads with the prime minister and the minister of finance to discuss the proposals for additional support for social groups affected by the crisis.[7]

On 10 June 2020, the social partners issued a joint statement asking the prime minister to discuss the economic and social measures to overcome the consequences of the COVID-19 pandemic, on which a consensus was reached between the social partners within the National Council for Tripartite Cooperation (the decision was taken at a meeting of the NCTS held on 21 May 2020).[8]

As in previous crises, the COVID-19 pandemic has stimulated a social dialogue leading to wide national agreements. On 17 June 2020, social partners signed a national tripartite agreement[9] covering five main areas: business environment and economics, energy, the European Green deal, demography, and education and social protection. While these areas have not been directly related to the COVID-19 situation, the broad consensus was possible because of the crisis; rarely in the context of Bulgarian industrial relations has such a national agreement been reached.

After the summer of 2020, social partners maintained their consensus regarding the general approach to address COVID-19. They continued to negotiate specific details about the coverage, scope and application of the job preservation measures and other actions. For example, in November 2020, the largest Bulgarian employer organisation, BIA, again advocated for measures to timely support the impacted businesses, such as the establishment of a National Program for Support of Bulgarian Business Affected by Restrictive Measures, providing an opportunity to quickly receive compensation from the state.[10] One of the measures that should be covered by the National Programme may be support for companies' fixed costs.

Regarding telework, there have been limited collective bargaining and specific agreements at company level and no regulations introduced at the sectoral or national level.

The Czech Republic

In March 2020, the Czech Ministry of Labour adopted an employment protection programme, called *Antivirus*,[11] as a temporary short-time work scheme until the introduction of permanent legislation. Employers could apply for compensation in two programmes. The first programme granted partial compensation of payroll expenses (80%) due to reasons on the employee's side (quarantine order) or full compensations of payroll expenses to employers who had to close or significantly limit their operations because of a government order. To qualify for the compensation, the employer was required to strictly adhere to the Labour Code, pay a wage and mandatory contributions, and the employment contract could not be terminated. Employees with temporary work contracts were not eligible for compensation. The maximum compensation per employee per month was initially set at EUR 1,470 and increased to EUR 1,890 on 1 October 2020. Under the second regime, employers could apply for compensation of payroll expenses for obstacles to work due to the spread of coronavirus (e.g., restricted supply of materials, reduction in demand for services, worker absence due to a school closure). The amount of compensation ranged between 60 and 100% with a maximum threshold of EUR 1,100 per employee per month. In the Czech Republic, compensations are paid to employers after the end of the calendar month. In 2020, the *Antivirus* programmes paid more than EUR 8.2 billion in compensation to a quarter of employees in the Czech Republic. To further support employment, the government waived the social security payments by the employer (24.8% of the assessment base) for the months of June, July, and August in 2020. This programme was open to companies with less than 50 employees that had not reduced their staff by more than 10% relative to the situation at the end of March 2020. The *Antivirus* was a temporary short-time work scheme, but ultimately remained in operation for the maximum period of one year until February 2021. The Czech Government has yet to enact a permanent short-time work scheme that would define universal compensation rules for preserving employment whenever the Czech economy suffers a crisis similar to COVID-19.

According to the Czech Labour Code, telework can be established after mutual agreement between the employer and the employee. Only for one week in November was telework mandated by Government Decree 1102/2020; no other provisions on telework were made in 2020.

The short-time work scheme is acknowledged by all social partners in the Czech Republic as a more effective policy measure than unemployment insurance as it helps enterprises during periods of temporary economic downturn to maintain employment. Trade union associations and employer associations at the tripartite level actively participated in the law-making process coordinated by the Ministry of Labour and Social Affairs. The employer representatives proposed the following changes in the design of short-time work scheme introduced by the Ministry in September 2020: a minimum replacement rate of 70% (60% proposed by the Ministry); a compensation cap defined by 150% (100% proposed by the Ministry) of the average national wage; higher flexibility in hours worked per employee with a possible reduction of up to 80% in the calendar month; the assessment base defined by the average salary in the previous 3 (or more) months (1 month proposed by the Ministry).[12] Social partners mainly refer to the German experience and the provision of the German *Kurzarbeit* scheme in the adoption process.

In September 2020, the Act on Employment was adopted by the Czech Government, and the Lower House approved the first reading in October 2020. The legislative process regarding the short-time work scheme, originally planned to be effective from 1 January 2021, was hampered by disputes within the coalition parties[13] concerning the level of replacement rate and other provisions. The final version of the legislation remains uncertain. In December 2020, representatives of both trade unions and employer associations jointly called on lawmakers to adopt the short-time work scheme given that the *Antivirus* programme could run for a maximum of one year, at which point compensation to employers would end.[14]

Regarding telework, the Czech-Moravian Confederation of Trade Unions claims that working from home has reduced operational costs to employers during the pandemic, and it initiated a dialogue with employers concerning lump-sum compensation to employees for teleworking. There is no regulation proposed or adopted at the national level.

Poland

In the first months since the initial outbreak of COVID-19, the social dialogue in Poland was side-lined with little involvement of the social partners. In late 2020 and throughout 2021, the attitude of the government towards social partners became more cooperative and the general climate in social dialogue improved albeit not to the point marking any qualitative change. In general, all anti-COVID-19 policy measures have been designed and implemented single-handedly by the government. In symbolic terms, the attitude of the government towards social dialogue in 2020 was best exemplified by a clause included in the Anti-crisis Shield 1.0[15] (Article 46) adopted in March 2020, by virtue of which the Prime Minister would gain the right to dismiss any member of the Social Dialogue Council (RDS), the central level tripartite body, if they commit an act of 'misappropriation of the Council's activities, leading to the inability to conduct transparent, substantive and regular dialogue between employee and employer organisations and the government'. All national-level social partners protested the new regulations in a joint protest signed by all eight representative organisations. Social partners claimed that the new regulations violated the autonomy of the RDS and of social partners themselves (Protest, 2020). The controversy stirred by the regulations prompted the President of Poland to request the Constitutional Court to review their legality. Thus, while the regulation has been put on hold, the future of tripartism is still unclear. Furthermore, according to an advisor of one of the national trade union confederations, bipartite social dialogue in the age of pandemics can be described as 'being in shambles': there are no pandemic crisis-related accords above the enterprise level, even in the form of 'soft' recommendations or declarations.

Even before the relapse of the early pandemic phase in the summer of 2020, some signs of revival of the tripartite social dialogue could be seen. First and foremost, the government made some concessions to trade unions in April 2020 as a result of informal negotiations between the government and NSZZ Solidarność. In particular, the initial anti-union and anti-employee provisions of the draft Anti-crisis Shield 3.0 such as suspending collective agreements and company social funds due to 'economic hardship' experienced by the employer or giving employers the right to dismiss employees if the latter are known to have any other source of income apart from the contract of employment were dropped from the law which was eventually adopted. Moreover, in late September 2020, RDS met for the first time since the pandemic's initial impact, and nation-wide representative social partners were able to agree on several issues that translated into four bipartite (no countersignature of the government side) resolutions, concerning public aid to be provided to transport companies (Resolution 87), hardships faced by food-processing and tourism industries (Resolution 88), possible redundancies in the public administration (Resolution 89), automotive sector (Resolution 90), and changes in income tax regulations (Resolution 91). While this could be read as a sign of the social partners' capacity to speak with one voice, no impact on public policy ensued due to the government's lack of interest in endorsing the bipartite initiatives. This tendency was further reinforced by the fact that – according to social partners – the government ignored their proposals while drafting amendments to the Act on Social Dialogue Council (RDS).

In 2021, there were short-lived signs of the climate surrounding social dialogue improving such as the idea for a new social pact emerging in the middle of the year, with negotiations on permanent regulations concerning remote work being the point of departure. Nevertheless, the negotiations collapsed following the ousting of Deputy Prime Minister (Jarosław Gowin) – who had endorsed the idea with the intention of turning it into his own political vehicle – from the government in the summer of 2021. On the other hand, there were also numerous signs of deepening impasse in tripartism such as growing discontent of trade unions translating into relatively huge protests (by nurse unions and energy sector workers) in May and June or side-lining of the social partners in the process of drafting the National Recovery Plan.

As far as the enacted anti-crisis policy measures are concerned, there are some – relatively weak but nevertheless present – references to social dialogue in the legal text, enabling employee representation to make impact on the new arrangements being introduced at the company level. For example, the short-time work scheme introduced in April 2020 states that a relevant agreement must be reached with 'employee representation' (which means not only trade unions/works council, but also a representative appointed in a 'way customary for the employer', if the former bodies are not present) in order to launch such a work-time arrangement. As for short-time working schemes, employers enduring economic difficulties (decrease in sales by at least 15% experienced over two consecutive months after 1 January 2020 due to the COVID-19 outbreak or by at least 25% experienced on a month-to-month basis after 1 January 2020 with no specific reason required) could request public aid due to the introduction of reduced working time (up to 20%, employee's reduced working time, still no less than 0.5 full-time working time, and the pay would not fall below the minimum wage). With the conditions met, the state would supplement wages up to 40% of the national average wage in Poland in the previous quarter.

Teleworking in Poland has been debated since the spring outbreak of COVID-19. The issue was temporarily regulated by the earliest, emergency regulation (preceding the Anti-Crisis Shield 1.0) at the beginning of March 2020. As remote work was generally well-received by both employees and employers, the idea of making the temporary solution permanent emerged. With the arrival of the second wave of the pandemic, the issue became even more urgent. The government stepped in with a proposal to integrate remote work and relevant regulations into the Labour Code. Initially, the idea was to replace the chapter on telework with a new set of provisions on remote work. According to national statistics (GUS, 2020), as of October 2020, some 25% of the workforce stated they were engaged in remote work. The share of the workforce with home offices would not fall over time but grew even further: in November 2021 nearly 30% of working people inquired admitted to be doing their jobs remotely (COV-WORK, 2022). Given that remote work is defined in vague terms – as the law stipulates only that an 'employer may request that the employee performs, for a definite period, work away from its permanent site (remote work), as long as the state of pandemic emergency or state of pandemics is in force for an additional three months after it ends' – a decisive resolution of the issue seems very urgent. It seemed that regulating remote work would propel negotiations on the social pact. Still following the collapse of the social pact idea, the issue of remote work (even though it has become a widespread phenomenon) has remained unresolved. As a result, the issue of remote work has not been regulated on permanent basis, so there is an essential question to be raised: what is going to happen when the state of pandemic is revoked, deactivating the provisional regulations?

Romania

The technical unemployment indemnity was introduced on 18 March 2020, during the early phase of the lockdown and was implemented in response to the unprecedented impact of the pandemic on the labour market and to calls from social partners for government support. A concerted effort by social partners called for 'urgent and exceptional policies to maintain the vital functioning of the economy and protect employees' (Cartel-Alfa.ro, 2020). Furthermore, a petition initiated on 13 March and signed by 50,000 employers called for the government to provide fiscal facilities and grants to firms who faced challenges due to the COVID-19 crisis. One of the key demands of employers was for the government to step in and subsidise companies that would maintain employment contracts during the pandemic (SmartBill.ro, 2020). Several days later, the two automotive manufacturers that operate in Romania, Ford, and Dacia, announced a temporary suspension of their operations as a result of the pandemic, and the move of their 20,000 workers to 'technical unemployment' (Mediafax, 2020a, 2020b). In addition, the government sought to avoid mass lay-offs and prevent companies from losing their skilled labour force.

The measure builds on the experience accumulated during the global financial crisis when a similar policy was adopted by the government to support employment levels. At the time, the government waived social security contributions and income tax for employees whose activity was interrupted because of the crisis. However, a similar measure during the recent pandemic was deemed insufficient as many of the companies in the sectors most impacted by the pandemic, such as retail and hospitality, are undercapitalised and therefore would have been unable to pay the benefits. Furthermore, interviews suggest that the government saw it necessary to step in as business activity was rescued because of the lockdown measures it adopted and not by a financial crisis.

The technical unemployment indemnity was followed up by a short-time working scheme which was put in place as of September 2020 for a period of three months. The scheme applies to establishments where at least 10% of the workforce is impacted and allows for a maximum 50% reduction of working time. Although hailed as a measure that could help protect employment by both unions and employers, its effectiveness at the time of writing is doubtful as subsidies through the scheme face significant delays.

Both trade unions and employer confederations reported that they have been consulted over various aspects of the design and implementation of the policy. However, evidence shows that the government was selective as to which of the suggestions from employers and trade unions to include.

Trade unions have been involved in the design of several elements of the policy. For example, at the request of the trade unions, a derogation from the Social Insurance law was introduced which stipulated that the entire time when the activity of an employee was discontinued is considered the contributory period for the unemployment insurance system. This was an important update of the policy as the generosity of the unemployment benefits in Romania is conditional on the length of the contributory period. Furthermore, social partners have been involved in re-designing the rules for implementing the policy. To apply for the technical unemployment indemnity, the initial policy required employers to submit a certificate of emergency from the Ministry of Economy and to prove a decrease in income in March of at least 25% compared to the average of the previous two months. The policy also capped the number of employees who could receive the allowance to 75%. These requirements were removed following discussions between social partners and the government. At the same time, consultations with social partners led to a reduction in the term set for the payment of benefits in the accounts of the employer for 30 to 15 days and the introduction of the requirement that employers transfer the net benefits into employees' accounts no later than 3 days after receiving the transfers.

Nevertheless, other demands by social partners have not been implemented. For example, both employer confederations and trade unions have advocated for introducing a requirement for employers to uphold employment contracts during or immediately after the temporary suspension of activity – a demand which was not adopted by government for the technical unemployment indemnity but was later added as a requirement to the newly established short-term working scheme (BNS, 2020a). Another trade union demand that was not implemented by government concerned the harmonisation of technical unemployment and unemployment benefits so that the unemployment benefit levels would not fall below 50% of the value of the basic salary in the past six months. Furthermore, in April, trade unions pursued the extension of the coverage of the scheme to public sector employees, a demand which was rejected by the government.

On the employer side, two of the key suggestions were incorporated in the update of the policy. First, GEO 32/2020 (the first update of the GEO 30/2020) eliminated the threshold which specified that only 75% of the employees of the company can benefit from the measure. Second, GEO 32 also clarified that employers have the freedom to top up the allowance paid by the state from their own funds. However, other suggestions, such as the payment of net instead of gross benefits, have not been incorporated in the law.

Overall, social partners have evaluated the level of social dialogue and their involvement in policy design and implementation to be more extensive than usual. Trade unions reported that the government has broadly relied on their expertise and knowledge of the labour market to ensure that the crisis responses are effective. They also reported that ongoing consultation with the government has broadened the coverage and generosity of the technical unemployment policy. Employers also reported that the government has involved them in consultations regarding the design of the scheme but that their feedback was included in minor, technical details of the scheme.

Slovakia

The Slovak Government has adopted a set of measures as a response to the current health and economic crisis that provided financial incentives to employers and self-employed with a purpose to preserve jobs (known as First Aid, First Aid +, and First Aid ++). Wage subsidies presented a main policy tool to mitigate the adverse impact of the pandemic on the job market in Slovakia. The wage subsidy measures adopted as a response to the COVID-19 pandemic consists of two types of policy measures: (1) a financial allowance for preserving jobs at companies covering 80% of the gross wage for employees (in October 2020 changed to 80% of the labour costs) who do not work due to pandemic-related restrictions in business operations (based on a government order) or due to a decline in revenue encountered by the company, and (2) financial contributions to compensate a loss of income for self-employed persons whose income has been reduced. The measures aspired to preserve already-existing jobs with standard employment contracts, while non-standard workers (workers with temporary contracts, seasonal or platform workers) were supported only poorly by the anti-pandemic measures.

These wage subsidy provisions are considered simplified versions of a short-time work scheme, responding to the consequences of the current crisis. The pandemic's impact on the Slovak labour market has triggered a discussion about the implementation of the German model of *Kurzarbeitsgeld* into Slovak law. In May 2021, the Act on Short-time Work Support was passed (to become effective from January 2022) to mitigate adverse economic impacts on companies and to preserve jobs in future crises. The financial support will be granted when business operations are restricted by external temporary factors preventing the work of at least one third of employees and for at least 10% of the weekly working time. The fund intends to compensate 60% of the average hourly gross wage for a maximum duration of 6 months within 24 consecutive months. Self-employed persons and public sector employees are excluded.

As a response to the pandemic and the need to facilitate teleworking, the amendment of the Labour Code in March 2020 (entered into force in April 2020) introduced occasional teleworking that may be temporarily ordered by the employer regardless of the employee's consent. The order must meet two conditions: (i) the employee can perform job tasks from home, and (ii) job tasks do not have to be carried out at the official workplace or carrying out job tasks at the official workplace is risky. Nevertheless, teleworking may be ordered for a limited time. The employee also acquired the right to teleworking; the employee may ask for permission to telework unless there are no operational restrictions. Before the amendment, the law recognised solely permanent teleworking, which was based exclusively on a mutual agreement between the employee and the employer.

The amendment to the Labour Code in March 2020 also established other minor provisions relating to flexible work arrangements, specifically regarding (i) planning a work-schedule and (ii) scheduling vacation time. The employee must be informed about the altered work time-schedule at least two days beforehand, a time-schedule must then be valid for at least ten days. Regarding vacation time, the employer has the right to order vacation time for the employee at least 7 days before the vacation starts, instead of 14 days as before the 2020 amendment, but solely during the state of emergency.

The Confederation of Trade Unions (*Konfederácia odborových zväzov*) criticised the nature of several policies that have been adopted to mitigate negative consequences of the pandemic on the labour market, mainly (1) discriminatory features of the current wage subsidies; and (2) a provision to preserve a job was not included in the conditions of the *Kurzarbeitsgeld* policy.

Regarding wage subsidies, the representative of the Confederation pointed out that individuals taking care of children younger than 11 due to school closure received the pandemic caregiver's allowance amounting to 70% of a net wage, while not-working employees received 80% of a gross wage.[16]

In general, the Confederation does not consider current job preserving policy tools as effective, and support introducing short-time work in the Slovak legislative framework. Nevertheless, it objected that a provision to preserve jobs was not included in the regulation, which means that employers will not be obliged to preserve jobs, and, consequently, no time limit was established during which the employee cannot be dismissed.[17]

Representatives of employers at the tripartite level criticised mainly the speed of aid provision and administrative costs incurred by companies in the process of applying for financial aid. From the beginning, the National Union of Employers supported introducing short-time work as a sustainable policy tool, given that the amount of social insurance contributions will not be increased.[18] In this respect, it seems that the employers' organisations representing especially the automotive industry, as a dominant industry in the country, played a pivotal role in dialogue over the adoption of a short-time work scheme. On the other hand, as part of the Economic Crisis Staff, the National Union of Employers pointed out that many companies did not apply for the wage subsidy due to administrative costs.[19]

Additionally, the Confederation also objected to the legislative process and the lack of involvement of trade unions. According to the representative of the Confederation, specifically the policy measures adopted during the first wave of the pandemic were not discussed with the trade unions. In addition, in November 2020, the government approved short-time work without discussing it at the tripartite level and, although the proposal was about to be discussed at the Steering Committee on Pension Reform, Social Insurance and Short-time Work (before the tripartite meeting), the Committee did not take place. Subsequently, the Confederation refused to participate in the tripartite meeting, claiming that the Ministry of Labour had excluded the Confederation of Trade Unions from a standard legislative process. As a response to the conflict, the Confederation launched a series of protest actions, including protest marches, open letters to representatives of the government and parliament, and an online campaign via social media channels.[20]

A deepening conflict between the trade unions at the national level on one side, and the government and employer associations on the other has resulted in attempts by the government to diminish the role of the Confederation by amending the Labour Code. The objective of the amendment (approved only by the government so far) should be to involve other organisations representing the rights of employees (trade unions and other non-governmental organisations) in social dialogue at the national level. At the same time, a condition of representativeness does not have to be met and the duration of membership is limited to one year.[21] In November 2020, the Confederation informed the European Commission about the steps taken by the government.[22] The Federation of Employer Associations of the Slovak Republic, as a tripartite partner, backed the position of the Ministry of Labour in this respect. Importantly, the conflict between social partners was accelerated during negotiations about the minimum wage in August 2020.

Discussion and conclusion

This chapter provides evidence on the role of social partners in shaping job preservation policies and measures in five CEE countries (Bulgaria, the Czech Republic, Poland, Romania, and Slovakia) in response to the COVID-19 pandemic. We critically explore and comparatively evaluate the policy responses in the background of the evolving role of industrial relations. The examined CEE countries took a relatively similar approach in addressing the COVID-19 pandemic, with governments adopting comprehensive job preservation measures relatively quickly (Table 7.3).

In 2020, the industrial relations developments in the studied CEE countries with respect to their role for shaping labour market and social policies focused on job preservation measures. Based on the punctuated-equilibrium theory, it can be argued that the current pandemic crisis has stimulated rapid changes in employment relations and the character of employment policies, particularly with the massive recourse to short-term work, the process supported by social partners, and with the introduction of teleworking as a novel form of work organisation in CEE countries. However, the role of social partners in the latter change remains unclear.

Based on our findings, the first similarity in terms of policy responses is the focus on short-term working schemes in all the countries covered. In contrast to some previous crises, the financial efforts of the governments have been considerable, and, measured by their financial size relative to GDP, broadly similar to those implemented in older member states. In all five countries, the dominant measure to preserve employment has been also similar, despite the differences in the percentages, sectors covered and so on. In this context, it is important to note that job losses due to COVID-19 have not been substantial in the region, in contrast to what was generally expected at the beginning of the pandemic. The policy choices of the governments seemed to be without much innovation, but rather with a degree of pragmatic imitation. In addition, the policies have been facilitated by

TABLE 7.3 Overview of the job retention measures adopted in CEE

	Bulgaria	*The Czech Republic*	*Poland*	*Romania*	*Slovakia*
Job preservation measures	The scheme '60/40' provides 100% allowance to employees and the contribution of state is 60%.	Programme *Antivirus* wage compensations (60–100%) for obstacles to work on the employee's or on the employer's side or other obstacles to work due to COVID-19. Maximum amounts are specified.	Anti-Crisis Shield wage compensations up to 40% of the national average wage in the previous quarter.	Short-term working scheme with maximum allowance 75% of the national average wage in 2020.	Wage subsidy provisions, covering 80% of the gross wage for employees (in October 2020 changed to 80% of the labour costs)
Social partners' involvement in the formulation of job preservation short-term schemes	Active role	Active role	Relatively limited role	Active role, but selective use of social partners' suggestions	Relatively active role
Scope in 2020	EUR 0.4 billion, about 300,000 employees (about 10% of all employees)	EUR 8.2 billion in compensation to a quarter of employees in the economy	EUR 6.7 billion allocated to job preservation short-term schemes (of EUR 37 billion total spending under the Anti-Crisis Shield)	EUR 1.48 billion	EUR 0.271 billion allocated to two main job retention measures as part of First Aid packages
Anti-crisis measures as a % of GDP	6.8%	14%	13%	4%	7%
Teleworking and other flexible solutions	Individual arrangements. Rare cases of company-level social dialogue	Individual arrangements. Rare cases of company-level social dialogue	Individual arrangements. Rare cases of company-level social dialogue	Individual arrangements. Rare cases of company-level social dialogue	Individual arrangements. Rare cases of company-level social dialogue

Source: Own compilation based on the case studies when not indicated in a footnote.

EU support and the existence of financial levers (e.g., the transfer of ESF funds to anti-COVID-19 measures). In this situation of budgetary generosity, in most countries in the region, social partners were able to eventually engage in a meaningful dialogue and successfully contribute to the shaping of anti-crisis measures, preserving employment, as illustrated by the recent social partner agreements in Bulgaria in June 2020. In Poland, however, despite efforts of social partners at the central level to address challenges posed by the (post)pandemic crisis (expressed in several bipartite resolutions), the government has maintained a unilateral mode of policy-making, and even the potentially fertile ground for re-invigorating tripartism created by the urgent need to regulate remote work has thus far remained unexplored. This seems to confirm that the turn towards some kind of neo-etatism, whose first signs became visible in 2015 (Czarzasty and Mrozowicki, 2018), has continued.

Major policy changes have also taken place in short-time work schemes, especially in Slovakia and the Czech Republic. In these two countries, the COVID-19 pandemic and the economic decline have triggered policy discussions regarding implementation of the German model of *Kurzarbeitsgeld* in the legislation as a long-term policy solution to prevent job losses due to future (potential) crises. Finally, in a paradoxical way, social partners have focused their effort at the national level, where normally tripartite cooperation has a weak impact on policy. It remains to be seen whether this is an exception or a new trend in industrial relations systems in these countries.

While social partners had a voice regarding short-term working schemes, this was not the case for teleworking. This can be evaluated as a missed opportunity because, even though Eurofound (2020b) finds that the CEE region has the lowest proportion of workers who started teleworking because of the COVID-19 pandemic, the extent of telework-able jobs is considerable and some groups of employees are particularly affected, as our analysis shows. While collective bargaining is mainly taking place at the establishment level in CEE, social partners, in the context of the pandemic, were focused on negotiating national level measures that could be visible in society. However, in doing so, they neglected the negotiation of flexible solutions at the sectoral and especially company levels, though there were isolated experiences, as reported in interviews, for example, in the Czech Republic. Furthermore, social partners in CEE countries have limited experience with teleworking and its strengths and weaknesses (e.g., health issues, the costs of teleworking to employees) as well as good practice examples of how to manage teleworking employees (work organisation), in contrast to the old member states. For these reasons, teleworking is not on the agenda and social partners rather focus on wage subsidies as low-hanging fruit.

In conclusion, the COVID-19 pandemic as a major disruptive event (or period) offered a window of opportunity to social partners in CEE. However, they have only made usage of short-term working, changing the usual practice of market-driven restructuring. In this respect, jobs have been preserved thanks to the relatively abundant supply of national and EU funding. However, there are limited indications that this policy change will have effects beyond the pandemic, except for the institutional adoption of short-time working scheme in the Czech Republic and Slovakia.

Acknowledgements

Martin Guzi acknowledges the support from the NPO Systemic Risk Institute (LX22NPO5101) and MUNI/A/1382/2021 project. We thank the Editor, Beata Woźniak-Jechorek, for her support.

Notes

1 National restructuring regimes are defined in the literature as a combination of both 'law-based or informal adjustment mechanisms, and as measures controlled or adopted by a particular group of actors' (Bergström, 2014).
2 For details see Eurofound, 2020 www.eurofound.europa.eu/observatories/emcc/erm/support-instrument/covid-19-income-support-for-workers).
3 https://knsb-bg.org/index.php/2020/03/23/pozicziya-na-knsb-otnosno-neobhodimite-merki-za-preodolyavane-na-negativnite-efekti-ot-zarazata-s-COVID-19-varhu-ikonomikata-i-pazara-na-truda/.
4 www.bia-bg.com/standpoint/view/26668/.
5 www.bia-bg.com/standpoint/view/26866/.
6 https://knsb-bg.org/index.php/2020/04/07/plamen-dimitrov-pred-btv-predlagame-novi-merki-nasocheni-kam-konkretni-grupi-zasegnati-ot-krizata/.
7 https://knsb-bg.org/index.php/2020/04/13/do-kraya-na-mesecza-tristranniyat-savet-sthe-obsadi-nov-paket-ot-merki-za-podkrepa-na-ikonomikata/.
8 www.bia-bg.com/standpoint/view/27197/.
9 www.bia-bg.com/news/view/27221/.
10 www.bia-bg.com/standpoint/view/18517/.
11 www.mpsv.cz/web/cz/antivirus.
12 Statement of the Confederation of Employers 'and Entrepreneurs' Unions of the Czech Republic on the Bill Amending Act No. 435/2004 Coll. On Employment available at: https://ipodpora.odbory.info/dms/soubory/index?file=Stanovisko%20KZPS%2030924_20200902172829.docx.
13 The Minister of Finance is a member of the ANO party, while the Minister of Labour is affiliated with the Czech Social Democratic Party.
14 Statement of OS KOVO, available at: www.oskovo.cz/aktuality/odbory-i-zamestnavatele-chteji-kurzarbeit-od-1-ledna.
15 In 2020, the anti-crisis policy was introduced in a sequential way with a view to following the development in the public health crisis, and took the form of the so-called Anti-Crisis Shield. There were six waves of the Shield (marked as the Anti-Crisis Shield 1.0 to 6.0) by the end of the year.
16 www.kozsr.sk/2020/04/11/rodicia-teraz-dostavaju-menej-ako-ti-ktori-nepracuju-nie-je-to-fer/.
17 Comments of the Confederation of Trade Unions on the Proposal on introducing short work scheme 'Kurzarbeit' in the Slovak legal framework: https://rokovania.gov.sk/RVL/Material/25385/1.
18 www.ruzsr.sk/zamestnavatelia-kurzarbeit-ano-nie-vsak-za-cenu-rastu-odvodoveho-zatazenia.
19 www.ruzsr.sk/ruz-o-pomoci-statu-podnikatelom.
20 www.kozsr.sk/2020/11/26/koz-sr-oznamila-zaciatok-zbierania-podpisov-pod-peticiu-za-vyhlasenie-referenda-na-ochranu-prav-zamestnancov-a-zachovanie-postavenia-odborov-na-slovensku/.

21 www.kozsr.sk/2020/11/06/vlada-zasahuje-do-slobody-zdruzovania-a-autonomie-odborov/.
22 www.kozsr.sk/2020/11/05/koz-sr-informovala-europsku-komisiu-o-porusovani-socialneho-dialogu-na-slovensku/.

References

Atkinson, M. M. (2011). Lindblom's lament: Incrementalism and the persistent pull of status quo. *Policy and Society*, *30*(1), 9–18.

Baumgartner, F. R., & Jones, B. D. (1993). *Agendas and Instability in American Politics*. Chicago: University of Chicago Press.

Bergström, O. (2014). Monitoring learning and innovation in European restructuring. (*IRENE Policy Paper* 14). http://responsible-restructuring.eu/wp-content/uploads/2014/11/IRENE-Policy-paper-no-14-synthesis-report-1411062.pdf

Bergström, O. (2019). Changing restructuring regimes in 11 European countries during and after the financial crisis. *European Journal of Industrial Relations*, *25*(2), 95–111.

Blocul National Sindical. (2020). *Lecţiile crizei pentru piata muncii!* [Lessons from the crisis for the labor market!]. https://bns.ro/info-bns/561-comunicat-de-presa-bns-lectiile-crizei-pentru-piata-muncii

Bohle, D., & Greskovits, B. (2012). *Capitalist diversity on Europe's periphery*. Cornell University Press.

Cartel-Alfa.ro. (2020). *Declaraţia partenerilor sociali din România cu privire la criza economică şi socială cauzată de COVID 19* [Declaration of the social partners in Romania on the economic and social crisis caused by COVID 19]. www.cartel-alfa.ro/ro/comunicate-57/declara%c8%9bia-partenerilor-sociali-din-romania-cu-privire-la-criza-economica-%c8%99i-sociala-cauzata-de-COVID-19–72/

COV-WORK. (2022, January 28). Presentation delivered at the online seminar dedicated to dissemination of the preliminary results of the research project COV-WORK (Socio-economic consciousness, work experiences and coping strategies of Poles in the context of the post-pandemic crisis), Warsaw.

Crowley, S. (2004). Explaining labor weakness in post-communist Europe: Historical legacies and comparative perspective. *East European politics and societies*, *18*(3), 394–429.

Czarzasty, J., Gajewska, K., & Mrozowicki, A. (2014). Institutions and strategies: Trends and obstacles to recruiting workers into trade unions in Poland. *British Journal of Industrial Relations*, *52*(1), 112–135.

Czarzasty, J., & Mrozowicki, A. (2018). Industrial relations in Poland: Historical background, institutional evolution and *research* trends. *Employee Relations*, *40*(4), 674–691.

Delteil, V., & Kirov, V. N. (Eds.). (2016). *Labour and social transformations in Central and Eastern Europe: Europeanization and beyond*. Routledge.

Dingel, J. I., & Neiman, B. (2020). How many jobs can be done at home? *Journal of Public Economics*, *189*, 104235.

Eurofound. (2020a). *Living, working and COVID-19*. COVID-19 series. Publications Office of the European Union. www.eurofound.europa.eu/publications/report/2020/living-working-and-COVID-19

Eurofound. (2020b). *Living, working and COVID-19 first findings – April 2020*. Eurofound. www.eurofound.europa.eu/sites/default/files/ef_publication/field_ef_document/ef20058en.pdf

European Commission. (2020). *Telework in the EU before and after the COVID-19: Where we were, where we head to*. Science for Policy Briefs. https://ec.europa.eu/jrc/sites/jrcsh/files/jrc120945_policy_brief_-_covid_and_telework_final.pdf

Eurostat. (2021, February 20). *Unemployment by sex and age – monthly data (variable une_rt_m)*. Eurostat.

Gardawski, J. (2009). *Dialog społeczny w Polsce: teoria, historia, praktyka* [Social dialogue in Poland: Theory, history, practice]. Ministerstwo Pracy i Polityki Społecznej. Katedra Socjologii Ekonomicznej SGH.

Gazier, B. (2008). Comparing processes across Europe. In B. Gazier, S. Moore, & F. Brüggeman (Eds.), *Restructuring work and employment in Europe* (pp. 11–31). Edward Elgar.

Geary, J. (2015). Economic crisis, austerity and trade union responses: The Irish case in comparative perspective. *European Journal of Industrial Relations*, *22*(2), 1–17.

Guga, S. (2019). *Situatia salariatilor in Romania – studiu annual* [The condition of employees in Romania – annual study]. www.syndex.ro/situatia-salariatilor-din-romania-studiu-anual

GUS. (2020). *Information society in Poland in 2020*. https://stat.gov.pl/download/gfx/portalinformacyjny/pl/defaultaktualnosci/5497/2/10/1/spoleczenstwo_informacyjne_w_polsce_w_2020.pdf

Hayes, M. T. (2001). *The limits of policy change. Incrementalism, worldview, and the rule of law*. Georgetown University Press.

Johnstone, S., Saridakis, G., & Wilkinson, A. (2019). The global financial crisis, work and employment: Ten years on. *Economic and Industrial Relations*, *40*(3), 455–468.

Kahancová, M. (2013). The demise of social partnership or a balanced recovery? The crisis and collective bargaining in Slovakia. *Transfer: European Review of Labour and Research*, *19*(20), 171–183.

Kahanec, M., Martišková, M., & Lichá, M. (2000). *CELSI COVID-19 policy response inquiry (COPReQ) first results*. CELSI Policy Brief 13. CELSI.

Lindblom, C. E. (1959). The science of 'muddling through'. *Public Administration Review*, *19*, 79–88.

Lundgren, M., Squatrito, T., & Tallberg, J. (2017). Stability and change in international policy making: A punctuated equilibrium. *The Review of International Organization*, *13*, 547–572.

Mediafax. (2020a). *Ford România trimite 6.000 de angajaţi în şomaj ethnic* [Ford Romania sends 6.000 employees into technical unemployment]. www.mediafax.ro/economic/ford-romania-trimite-6-000-de-angajati-in-somaj-tehnic-18993990

Mediafax. (2020b). *Dacia, cea mai mare companie din România, opreşte producţia. Angajaţii vor fi în şomaj tehnic* [Dacia, the largest company in Romania halts production. Its employees will be moved onto technical unemployment]. www.mediafax.ro/social/dacia-opreste-productia-din-cauza-coronavirus-angajatii-vor-fi-in-somaj-tehnic-18996728

Müller, T., & Schulten, T. (2020). *Ensuring fair short-time work – a European overview*. ETUI Policy Brief 7. European Trade Union Institute. www.etui.org/sites/default/files/2020-06/COVID-19%2BShort-time%2Bwork%2BM%C3%BCller%2BSchulten%2BPolicy%2BBrief%2B2020.07%281%29.pdf

Müller, T., Vandaele, K., & Waddington, J. (Eds.). (2019). *Collective bargaining in Europe: Towards an endgame*. European Trade Union Institute. www.etui.org/sites/default/files/Collective%20Bargaining%20Vol%20I%20final%20web%20version.pdf

OECD. (2018). *Inclusive entrepreneurship policies: Country assessment notes. Romania 2018*. www.oecd.org/cfe/smes/ROMANIA-IE-Country-Note-2018.pdf

Ost, D. (2000). Illusory corporatism in eastern Europe: Neoliberal tripartism and postcommunist class identities. *Politics & Society*, *28*(4), 503–530.

Ost, D. (2011). 'Illusory corporatism' ten years later. *Warsaw Forum of Economic Sociology, 2*(3), 19–49.

Ost, D., & Crowley, S. (2001a). Conclusion: Making sense of labor weakness in postcommunism. In S. Crowley & D. Ost (Eds.), *Workers after workers' states: Labor and politics in postcommunist eastern Europe* (pp. 219–234). Rowman & Littlefield.

Ost, D., & Crowley, S. (Eds.). (2001b). *Workers after workers' states: Labor and politics in postcommunist eastern Europe*. Rowman & Littlefield Publishers.

Podvršič, A., Becker, J., Piroska, D., Profant, T., & Hodulák, V. (2020). Mitigating the COVID-19 effect emergency policy making in central Europe. (*Working Paper* 2020.07). European Trade Union Institute. www.etui.org/sites/default/files/2020-08/Mitigating%20the%20COVID-19%20effect_2020_web.pdf

Protest organizacji pracodawców i związków zawodowych w sprawie zamachu na niezależność Rady Dialogu Społecznego i autonomię organizacji partnerów społecznych [Protest of employers' organisations and trade unions relating to the assault on independence of the Social Dialogue Council and autonomy of social partners' organisations]. (2020). https://pracodawcyrp.pl/upload/files/2020/05/2020-03-28-protest-rds.pdf

Resolution 87 of the employer and employee sides of the Social Dialogue Council. (2020). www.dialog.gov.pl/gfx/mpips/userfiles/n.krasuska/Uchwaly%20strony%20spoleczznej%20RDS/Uchwala-nr-87.pdf

Resolution 88 of the employer and employee sides of the Social Dialogue Council. (2020). www.dialog.gov.pl/gfx/mpips/userfiles/n.krasuska/Uchwaly%20strony%20spolec znej%20RDS/Uchwala-nr-88.pdf

Resolution 89 of the employer and employee sides of the Social Dialogue Council. (2020). www.dialog.gov.pl/gfx/mpips/userfiles/n.krasuska/Uchwaly%20strony%20spolec znej%20RDS/Uchwala-nr-89.pdf

Resolution 90 of the employer and employee sides of the Social Dialogue Council. (2020). www.dialog.gov.pl/gfx/mpips/userfiles/n.krasuska/Uchwaly%20strony%20spolec znej%20RDS/Uchwala-nr-90.pdf

Resolution 91 of the employer and employee sides of the Social Dialogue Council. (2020). www.dialog.gov.pl/gfx/mpips/userfiles/n.krasuska/Uchwaly%20strony%20spolec znej%20RDS/Uchwala-nr-91.pdf

SmartBill.ro. (2020). *Cerem Guvernului si Parlamentului Romaniei urmatorul set de masuri gandite pentru a ajuta mediul de afaceri sa depaseasca cu bine provocarile aduse de criza COVID19* [We demand the Romanian Government and Parliament for the following set of measures designed to help businesses to overcome the challenges brought by the COVID-19 crisis]. https://petitie.smartbill.ro/?fbclid=IwAR0aIhfs3sxclhqiBVGz20mFCsfS8UXv7ijKfQ-O1XhSPijFPH4GWg6IQJw

Vaughan-Whitehead, D. (2000). Social dialogue in EU enlargement: Acquis and responsibilities. *Transfer: European Review of Labour and Research, 6*(3), 387–398.

Woolfson, C., & Kallaste, E. (2011). 'Illusory corporatism' 'Mark 2' in the Baltic States. *Warsaw Forum of Economic Sociology, 2*(3), 51–72.

PART 2

New Challenges and Policy Needs for the Post-Pandemic Digital Work

Learning from COVID-19 Experiences

8

NAKED AT HOME—HOW REMOTE WORK DURING COVID-19 OPENS DOORS FOR THE OMNIPRESENCE OF EMPLOYERS IN WORKERS' LIVES?

Branka Andjelkovic, Tanja Jakobi, and Maja Kovac

Introduction

The sudden shift to remote[1] and home working[2] has caused much uncertainty about how to strike an appropriate balance between ensuring work is done and protecting the employer, on the one hand, and safeguarding employees' rights and privacy, on the other. The issue of balance became particularly important due to the widespread proliferation of the new surveillance tools aimed at monitoring employee performance in the home or remote setting. In the United States (US) and the European Union (EU) alone, the growth of remote work led to an increase in demand for employee tracking software by 108% in April 2020 compared to 2019 (Ball, 2021). The latest figures suggest that demand has continued to swell (Blum, 2022).

Employee[3] tracking arrangements and new technologies and apps used to collect data mean surveillance of home workers is frequently intrusive and threatens workers' labour rights and privacy. For companies that monitor their employees and collect various personal data, regulating these practices, informing their employees, and ensuring transparency of the process are crucial for permitting dignified work. This is a particularly challenging task given that the evolution of remote worker monitoring has outpaced regulators, which are often late in adopting rules for lawful monitoring and surveillance in new circumstances.

Conceptually, this research seeks to study the practices and ramifications of monitoring remote workers in the context of employees' labour and privacy rights. It explores monitoring and surveillance practices that emerge with remote work and the ways in which they shape the balance between employees' right to privacy and the employers' need to safeguard business interests by employing monitoring tools.

DOI: 10.4324/9781003326779-11

The practice of remote work has lately attracted increased attention of scholars. However, studies dealing with the impact of remote work on the relationship between managers and employees range from the flexibilisation of work to the effect on workers' wellbeing. This exploratory research aims to contribute to the body of research focusing on the controversy between the employers' legitimate interest to run their business effectively and the employees' legitimate concerns for the protection of their privacy within the context of remote work settings in Serbia. As such, this study investigates the Serbian legal framework for remote and home working and the safeguards that apply to employee rights and privacy in these circumstances. The study sheds new light on the topic through the lens of the fundamental privacy and data protection principles of legality, necessity, finality, proportionality, transparency, and data security.

To meet the research objectives, a mixed-method approach was designed that comprised two separate surveys, one of workers and one of employers, who worked remotely during the pandemic. In addition, semi-structured interviews were conducted with legal and personal data protection experts, including representatives of relevant institutions, with the objective of discussing the shifts and developments in policy aimed at enabling dignified work in the context of new technologies and remote work monitoring practices. The research was conducted between July 2021 and February 2022.

The findings of this research aim to better define employee–employer relationships in the context of remote work. Our findings may pave the way to more robust and efficient policies for the stakeholders in the domain of employment relations in the remote work setting in Serbia.

The main findings of the research show that employers exercised their rights beyond lawful and legitimate purposes in all fundamental privacy and data protection domains, namely legality, necessity, finality, proportionality, transparency, and data security. However, this intrusion into the privacy of employees has provoked neither collective action nor individual resistance by Serbian remote workers. They have continued to comply with the new practices primarily due to ignorance of the law. Consequently, new forms of monitoring and surveillance have not affected the levels of employee trust in their employers' practices, which the research found to be rather high.

The chapter is divided into five sections, including this introduction. The next section discusses the existing literature in the field of remote working and new technological forms of surveillance, including the privacy and data protection context. In the section after that, the methodological approach used in the research and the types of data analysed with a view of the main objectives are explained. The following section presents the research findings, while the final section discusses the findings with a view to the conceptual orientation and draws the relevant conclusions.

Literature review

In remote working, employees are completely 'out of sight' of managers and peers, thus enabling only virtual or remote control (Sewell & Taskin, 2015). Consequently, remote work has led to an increased use of surveillance technology to track worker behaviour and performance (Maalsen & Dowling, 2020). These emerging liaisons require a broader framework to balance the legitimate interests of companies on one side with the privacy and labour rights of (remote) workers on the other.

Monitoring and surveillance have become intrinsic to the modern work environment and refer to the use of various methods to gather information about the activities and locations of staff members to improve productivity and protect corporate resources. Surveillance is often considered advanced monitoring, based on the technology and digital tools (Mitrou & Karyda, 2006).

In fact, worker monitoring can be viewed as part and parcel of being employed. Workers expect their performance to be reviewed, objectives to be set, and information about their activities to be collected. By contrast, employers have the right to monitor their staff to ensure that employees comply with the regulations, that resources are used efficiently, and trade secrets are kept confidential. In that sense, monitoring can be seen as a part of good management practice (Mitrou & Karyda, 2006).

The technology used to monitor employees has expanded in recent years to cover a variety of areas, in particular the use of ICT for employee surveillance. This includes workplace video surveillance, software for scanning e-mails, eavesdropping on phone calls, monitoring and recording keystrokes, and for recording web sites visited and remote files accessed.

Graham and Wood (2003) describe the evolution from an analogue or bureaucratic type of surveillance to an increasingly prevalent digital model that has enhanced the efficiency of surveillance and made it ubiquitous. New technologies have allowed supervisors to constantly monitor workers, even when they are not physically present. Modern electronic surveillance options have turned the workplace into a 'panopticon', subjecting it to constant oversight (Manokha, 2020; Frangi et al., 2021)

Under these conditions, the risk of managers, and even co-workers, abusing control and surveillance mechanisms runs high (Curchod et al., 2020). In the debate on digital technologies and their impact on the balance between the employees' privacy rights and the legitimate business concerns, it was observed that the invisibility of remote workers has been associated with a push by managers to increase surveillance powers (Sewell & Taskin, 2015) beyond existing boundaries set in the regular workplace where trust was largely based on visibility and presence (Frangi et al., 2021). Instead, employers opted to rely on the use of often intrusive tools and devices allowing for constant monitoring (Curchod et al., 2020; Nyberg & Sewell, 2014).

A large body of employment relations-related literature predominantly evaluates the relationship between managers and employees in the remote work setting from other perspectives. Some scholars focus on the flexibilisation of work enabled by technology, and the impact on workers' performance (Spreitzer et al., 2017; Kelliher & Anderson, 2010; De Menezes & Kelliher, 2017). Others assess the control and sharing in the virtual environment (Sewell & Taskin, 2015; Nyberg &

Sewell, 2014; Jaakson & Kallaste, 2010). The third group of scholars examines the effect of remote work along several dimensions: work-life balance, job effectiveness, and well-being (Grant et al., 2013; Wright, 2000).

This feature takes a novel perspective by deepening the conversation around the possible derogations and limitations of employees' rights in the remote work from the perspective of the fundamental privacy and data protection principles: legality, necessity, proportionality, finality, transparency, and data security in the work environment (De Hert & Lammerant, 2013).

Privacy, data protection, and work-related relations

In the European context, the right to privacy is considered a fundamental human right.[4] Privacy is freedom from interference or intrusion and includes the right to control information and access to information about an individual (De Hert & Lammerant, 2013). As such, it is also a structural component of the employment relationship (Mitrou & Karyda, 2006). The lack of privacy can have destructive effects on the capacity for free decision-making and employee autonomy.

However, employees' rights to privacy are subject to derogations and limitations, particularly when confronted with the rights and freedoms of employers who are also protected by the law. The issue of how to balance employees' right to privacy while at the same time safeguarding employers' legitimate interests and the need for security steered the debate on what constitutes lawful monitoring, particularly in a remote setting (Samek-Lodovici, 2021; Frangi et al., 2021).

The right to protection of personal data evolved out of the right to privacy and became an autonomous fundamental right in 2000 when the Charter of Fundamental Rights of the European Union was adopted.[5] The EU's 2016 General Data Protection Regulation (GDPR) was another giant step forward.

This data protection framework also applies to work-related relations. In fact, as the extent of surveillance has continued to grow, ethical considerations and key employee rights, such as the right to privacy, have come to the fore of the regulatory discussion (Samek Lodovici, 2021; De Hert & Lammerant, 2013; Mitrou & Karyda, 2006). Employee oversight ought to respect workers' right to privacy, taking into account to what extent this monitoring intrudes into workers' personal lives (Lee & Kleiner, 2003). For workplace monitoring and surveillance to be considered lawful and justified, employers must comply with the following fundamental privacy data protection principles: legality, necessity, proportionality, finality, transparency, and data security (De Hert & Lammerant, 2013). The flexibility of these principles, which are also intertwined to a high extent, allows their application in diverse situations, including remote work and working from home. We briefly introduce these principles here. They will be discussed in more detail in the section 'Empirical Investigation'.

The legality principle assumes that interferences with the protected right have to be based on a legal norm. The citizen should be able to have an indication on which legal rules are applicable and what are the consequences if they are being breached (ibid.). Necessity is a fundamental principle when assessing the restriction of the right to the protection of personal data. The limiting of this fundamental right must be strictly necessary (European Data Protection Supervisor, 2020).

The necessity principle contains the proportionality principle: this criterion restricts authorities in the exercise of their powers by requiring them to strike a balance between the means used and the intended aim. In the context of fundamental rights, proportionality is key for any limitation on these rights (Lasprogata et al., 2004; Electronic Privacy Information Center, 2002).

Transparency is at the heart of personal data protection. Transparency requires authorities to be not only lawful and fair in their data processing activities but to let data subjects know what these processes include and why they are introduced (De Hert & Lammerant, 2013). The transparency principle is commonly accepted as the minimum component of a workplace privacy policy (Mitrou & Karyda, 2006).

The finality principle anticipates that the interference can take place only for the listed legitimate interests. Employers must distinguish between various aspects of the employment relationship and clearly specify the aims for which monitoring is required (ibid.).

The data security principle is a consequence of the finality and necessity principles. This principle defines the way the data are stored and who can access them lawfully.

Methodology

The study employed a mixed-method approach informed by the main aim of the research, seeking to assess how monitoring and surveillance of remote workers by their employers affect their labour rights and privacy.

To address the above objectives, two surveys were conducted, one with workers who had been working from home for at least some time over the previous two years, and one with company managers and executives with experience of these working arrangements that predated the COVID-19 outbreak. Sampling criteria were designed to encompass workers and company managers from existing business sectors in Serbia according to the national statistical classification with the aim of identifying remote worker monitoring practices and different approaches throughout the range of the various business sectors. The qualitative method approach also involved semi-structured interviews with experts and specialists in labour law and personal data protection and other key actors in the research field. This method aimed at probing for more detailed and reflexive responses and so obtaining a richer set of data.

Descriptive statistics was used to present the data. The Chi-square test and T-test were used on demographic data.

Employees survey

The employee survey was conducted online featuring a structured questionnaire facilitated by a Computer Assisted Web Interviewing (CAWI) tool. The survey sample was designed to comprise workers from all business sectors in accordance with the national sector classification in Serbia. Convenience sampling (Etikan et al., 2016) for heterogeneity was applied to enable vast business sectors' variability coupled with low costs of the sampling procedure. A total of 366 respondents from a variety of industries were surveyed in July 2021.

A total of 56% of those surveyed were women, while 44% were men. Slightly more than one-half of the respondents were aged 25–44, while those aged between 18 and 24 years were the least represented in the workers' sample.

Furthermore, the workers surveyed were exceptionally well educated, with 58% being university graduates, while the reminder of the sample held college degrees (13%) and secondary school diplomas (26%).

A breakdown of the sample by industry shows the majority of the respondents were employed in sectors where remote working has been used extensively and that have significant previous experience with these arrangements, such as finance and banking, information and communication, research and development, trade, administrative and support service activities, education, public administration, and the like (see Figure 8.1).

Manager survey

A telephone survey of company managers from all industries in accordance with the national sector classification was conducted with the aim of assessing employers' practices and experiences with remote work monitoring techniques for each selected sector. Thus, sampling procedure for this research method was guided by purposive, heterogeneous principles (Etikan et al., 2016).

FIGURE 8.1 Structure of respondents by activity/business sector (Employees)

Source: Own elaboration.

A total of 113 respondents were surveyed, of which 56% were women and 44% were men. The survey was conducted in August and September 2021.

Most company managers surveyed (57%) were aged between 34 and 54, and a significant share of the executives were university graduates (76%) or had college degrees (12%). As in the employee survey, the majority of respondents came from industries that had had experience with remote working arrangements prior to the pandemic (Figure 8.2). Although the sampling procedure comprehensively targeted all business sectors and related industries, respondent responsiveness was most pronounced in the information and communication sector (28%), followed by the motor vehicle retail sector (17%), and finance and insurance (9%).

It is worth noting that although the two surveys were conducted within the same range of business sectors, this sample selection principle was not applied to individual companies to avoid potential autocorrelation bias. The interdependency of variables at the company level would require different statistical treatment of data while inducing a different research design approach and modification of sample types, from independent to dependent. As a result, a comparative analysis of the results of the two surveys is valid at the level of sectors only.

In addition, both surveys employed structured questionnaires designed to respond to the specific category of respondents, that is, employers or employees. The questionnaires included the following themes: arrangements for working from home; types of data gathered by companies; worker data collection practices, processing, and use; awareness of personal data protection regulations and policies, and right to privacy at work. These themes were assessed through the lens of the fundamental privacy and data protection principles: legality, necessity, finality, proportionality, transparency, and security.

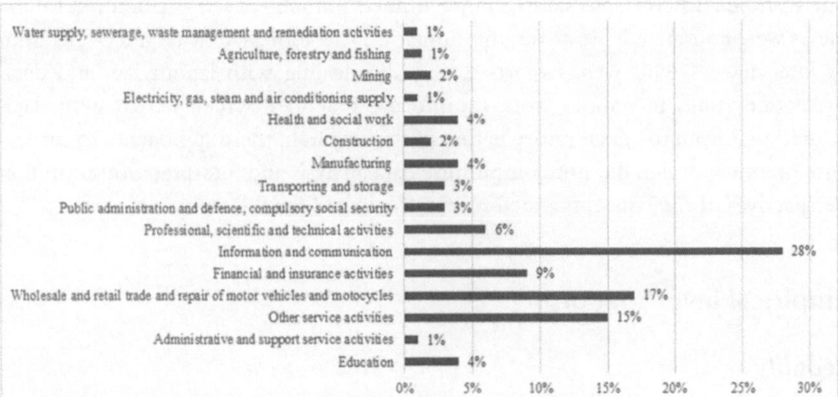

FIGURE 8.2 Structure of respondents by activity/business sector (Employers)

Source: Own elaboration.

Interviews with experts

Semi-structured interviews with experts in labour law and personal data protection, relevant public authorities, independent watchdogs including the Commissioner for Freedom of Information and Personal Data Protection, trade unions, and workers were conducted with the aim of discovering the key nodes of common practices in terms of how employers that use novel technical means to monitor remote work comply with labour law and personal data protection. The selection of research participants was informed by both targeted selection and the snowball method (Amis, 2005). A total of 11 interviews were conducted between October 2021 and February 2022 in Belgrade. Supplemental data were collected through freedom of information requests addressed to the Labour Inspectorate.

This first exploratory research into the surveillance of remote workers that sought to explore asymmetries of power between employers and employees in the context of remote work in Serbia was performed from July 2021 to February 2022. Ethical principles in research data collection and analysis phases were strictly followed with the key aim of protecting respondents' personal data and ensuring data were used responsibly (Townsend & Wallace, 2016).

The methods applied in this research were, thus, designed to collect and analyse quantitative and qualitative data in a triangulated fashion, interpreted through the prism of asymmetric power relations in remote working in Serbia.

Limitations

The survey design strategy involved common business sector classification of the samples in two surveys. However, the surveyed workers and managers came from different companies within the same sector. The main rationale for such an approach was an attempt to minimise the incidence of potential autocorrelation bias. As a result, the data were not analysed comparatively at the company level. Moreover, due to time and cost constraints, only a limited number of semi-structured interviews were conducted. However, this limitation was addressed by targeted selection of interviewees who were experts specifically dealing with labour law and data protection issues in remote work monitoring practices, which led to swift data saturation. Given the exploratory nature of this research, these approaches to survey and interview design did not compromise data analysis and interpretation from the perspectives of the conceptual determinants selected for this study.

Empirical investigation

Legality

In this section, we present the findings showcasing employers-employees relations in remote work settings through the lenses of the legality principle, as one of the fundamental principles of privacy and data protection. It presumes that the protection of employee privacy rights must be based on a legal norm. Accordingly, legitimate monitoring and processing of the derived data must be set in advance, based on a legitimate purpose, and demonstrable to employees beforehand. Therefore, we examine the balance between the employee privacy rights and interests on one side, and legitimate business concerns on the other trough the employment contract or the contract addendum governing remote work and workers' privacy and data protection rights.

Remote work and work from home are governed by the Serbian Labour Law (2005) which also prescribes rules regarding the employee-related data that employers should collect (Andjelkovic and Jakobi, 2022). The basic instrument governing this kind of work is the employment agreement (in cases when employees can work from home as soon as they join a firm) or an addendum to the employment agreement whereby the employees switch from working on company premises to working from home (Labour Law, 2005). The agreement or the addendum must also regulate a number of key issues including the employer's responsibility to provide, maintain, and install the equipment required by the employee; reimbursement the employees are entitled to when using their own equipment; reimbursement of other costs associated with working from home (e.g., broadband costs); employee oversight; working hours, and other aspects.

Accordingly, a firm that does not offer an addendum to the employment agreement with a staff member switching to remote work is committing a misdemeanour that provides for fines, ranging from 6,800 to 17,000 EUR[6] both for the company and its responsible officer. As for the employees, those who believe their rights have been violated may seek protection from the Labour Inspectorate or file a formal complaint with the court.

Personal Data Protection Law – PDPL (2018) governs general rules of personal data processing. The Serbian PDPL provides for penalties in the event of any collection or processing of personal data in contravention of that law, regardless of the person or organisation responsible for the privacy violation, and as such those provisions should apply to all employers handling employee data illegally. Nevertheless, the issue of data processing in the field of labour is governed vaguely and only in the Article 91. The Labour Law and the PDPL were to be harmonised in late 2020 (Andjelkovic and Jakobi, 2022).

According to the results of the research most of the companies (61%) did not offer their staff addenda to employment agreements when shifting to remote work. Only one-quarter of the surveyed managers (26%) claimed to have done so, whilst the remainder (13%) did not answer the question.

Thus, a substantial number of employees worked from home without having signed the required addenda to their employment agreements. This could be considered tantamount to working without a contract at a regular workplace in the traditional office setting.

Yet, the workers showed reluctance to contact the Labour Inspectorate and submit complaints with regards to this practice. As per the insights into the Labour Inspectorate data, the agency received no petitions alleging violations of home workers' rights in the period March 2020–February 2022.[7] The reasons for such a response could be many including the lack of awareness and/or fear of losing one's job. Further research would be needed to provide more insights into the employees' reasoning.

By not signing addenda to their employment agreements, and by being unaware of their right to seek protection from the Labour Inspectorate or hesitant to do so, the employees have exposed themselves to a plethora of risks including those related to illicit surveillance. In this context, the employers abused their powers when shifting the workers to remote work or working from home. The reasons for this practice differ. First, having a regulation that considers failure to sign a contract addendum as misdemeanour in place. The second important point is the lack of alignment between the Labour Law and PDPL. The harmonisation which was due by the end of 2020 has not happened yet. At the same time, as findings show, the workers complied with this practice unquestionably, without even considering submitting petitions alleging violations of their rights. The violation of the legality principle left the workers without proper safeguards in the context of existing policies and labour institutions.

Necessity and proportionality

In this section, we present the findings that shed light on the employers-employees relations in remote work settings through the lenses of the necessity and proportionality principles. These two principles are often assessed together, as proportionality is considered to be an intrinsic part of the necessity dimension.

The necessity principle requires employers to be certain if any form of monitoring is absolutely necessary for a specific purpose before proceeding with such activities. The necessity thus also sets boundaries under which the employers may monitor communications or employee Internet use on the grounds of valid business interests (prevention of illegal or defamatory acts, acts that are contrary to good ethics or which can damage the dignity of another person, etc.) (Belgian National Labour Council, 2002).

For these acts to be considered valid, monitoring should fulfil the principle of proportionality. This principle stipulates that the employers' monitoring policy should be tailored to the type and the degree of risk they face (Mitrou & Karyda, 2006). Therefore, monitoring must be appropriate, relevant, and proportionate to the aims it is pursuing. In this case, the employers are obliged to present the employees carefully written notices on the necessity of the monitoring tools and methods applied, and the purpose of the monitoring. Automatic and continuous e-mail and Internet monitoring of employees is unacceptable under all circumstances (Lasprogata et al., 2004).

According to the Serbian legislation, the companies must have a legal basis for collecting employee data. As a rule, the company's legitimate interest may be considered a valid basis for processing collected data. The Labour Law (2005) stipulates only the data be collected when workers sign the employment agreement regardless of the location where the work is to be done. It is the PDPL that sets principles for personal data processing to be lawful, diligently mirroring the principles of necessity and proportionality.

According to the results of the research (Figure 8.3), the employers listed the following reasons for processing employee data, most of them reflecting the legitimate interest of the employer: collecting data in the public interest (10%), for the research purposes (11%), or statistical purposes (11%). Furthermore, additional grounds for personal information gathering included confidentiality (34%), attendance and performance monitoring (24%), planning and tracking employment policy (19%), protecting intellectual property (17%), preventing abuses of company vehicles and equipment (14%), etc. Some 4% of the companies denied collecting employees' personal data.

Figures 8.4. and 8.5 show types of surveillance common in remote workplaces according to both the employers and employees. The majority of firms monitored employees by requiring oral or written reporting or timesheets. The employers also monitored workers' e-mails, tracked the use of company cars and phones, used performance monitoring apps and video surveillance, with some also following what employees did online or posted on social media. The use of dedicated software for employee surveillance was relatively rare according to both employers and employees (Figure 8.4).

The employees commonly claimed performance monitoring relied on oral and written reporting, e-mail monitoring, mileage tracking for company cars, monitoring of online activity, regular timesheet updating, and video surveillance. Figure 8.5 shows a detailed breakdown of their answers.

With respect to the surveillance of employees, for any surveillance (through apps) to be deemed permissible according to the PDPL, the company needs to assess the existence of a legitimate interest in personal data processing, and in doing so must determine whether the purpose of data processing may be achieved through less intrusive surveillance methods. This assessment of the employer's legitimate interest should be clearly documented. Any surveillance that is not strictly necessary must

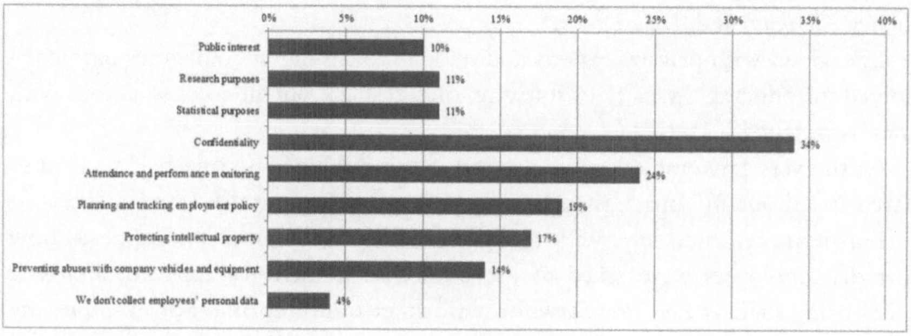

FIGURE 8.3 What are the reasons for processing employee data? (Employers)

Source: Own elaboration.

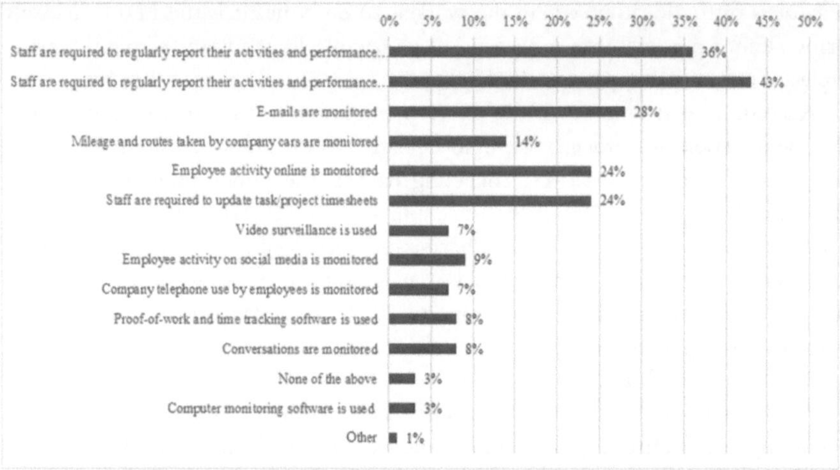

FIGURE 8.4 Reported employee awareness of performance/productivity monitoring: Which of the following applies when you work from home? (Employees)

Source: Own elaboration.

be discontinued if its purpose (here, performance monitoring) may be achieved by less intrusive means of tracking.

This means that the data controller (in this case the employer) is required to carry out an assessment of the impact of the envisaged processing operations on the protection of personal data prior to the data processing. Where a data protection impact assessment indicates that the processing would result in high risk in the absence of measures taken by the controller to mitigate the risk, the data controller shall consult the Commissioner for Freedom of Information and Personal Data Protection prior to processing.

Figures 8.4 and 8.5 show that no more than 3% of managers and 8% of employees surveyed claimed to use the next-generation performance monitoring software such as *Clockify*[8] and *Time Doctor*.[9]

Interviews with privacy experts and trade unions suggest companies have considered introducing a variety of software, only to back out after consultations with lawyers or faced with trade union reactions.

Of the very few employers who reported using these apps, one-half claimed to have carried out an impact assessment, which is necessary as described above.

Furthermore, interviews with the unions and privacy protection experts show that the employees were asked to use otherwise unintrusive apps not aimed at monitoring such as *Zoom* or *Slack* for performance monitoring. For example, the employees were asked to remain logged into *Zoom* and keep their computer cameras on at all times to allow employers to monitor them, or to use *Slack* at very short intervals, which amounted to real-time surveillance.[10]

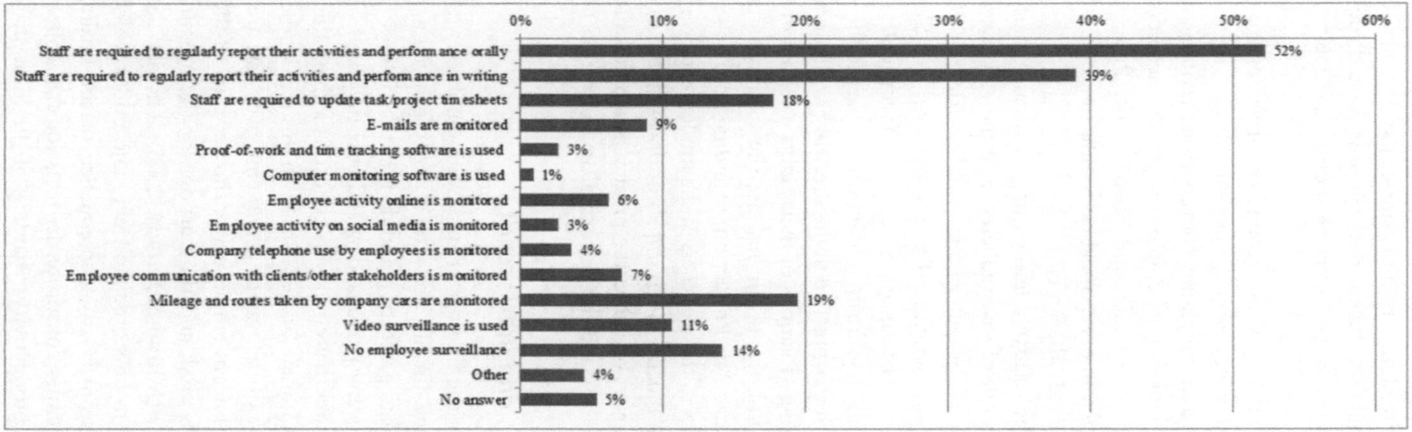

FIGURE 8.5 Which of the following does your company practice when staff work from home? (Employers)

Source: Own elaboration.

Even though the employers seem to have committed violations of the PDPL, the Commissioner for Freedom of Information and Personal Data Protection did not receive any complaints during the reporting period, nor had he found any instances of unlawful use of performance monitoring apps when conducting scheduled oversight.[11]

On one hand, as the findings show, around one-third of the employees were subjected to e-mail monitoring, while video surveillance, tracking of employee activity on social media, and telephone conversation recording were less widespread. This practice is a violation of employees' privacy: according to the Commissioner for Freedom of Information and Personal Data Protection, these types of surveillance are permitted in exceptional cases only and for clearly defined purposes that cannot be achieved otherwise.

On the other hand, the relatively limited use of intrusive performance monitoring apps was not the result of strict adherence of the employers to the law but is rather attributable to poor computer literacy and a variety of deterrents such as legal advice and trade union activism. The use of *Zoom* and *Slack* for monitoring purposes constituted a violation of privacy and a form of data processing that could not be justified by any legitimate interest on the part of the employer.[12] Yet, the workers complied with this practice unquestionably, without even considering submitting petitions alleging violations of their rights. Neither the employees nor the employers consulted institutions (in this case the Commissioner for Freedom of Information and Personal Data Protection) regarding possible violations of their privacy rights which points to the weakness in the implementation and supervision of the relevant legislation. Finally, the examples of unlawful use of certain applications show that the employers breached the privacy of workers in absence of harmonisation of the Labour Law and the Personal Data Protection Law.

Transparency, finality, and data security

In this section, we present the findings of employers-employees relations from the perspective of transparency, finality, and data security principles. Transparency is at the heart of personal data protection and defines the right of the employee to know what happens to his/her personal data and how they are stored. On its side, the finality principle requires that employers collect data about their employees for specified, explicit, and legitimate purposes only. In this regard, the finality principle defines the boundaries of the way in which employee data are processed. The employers are obliged to inform employees of the necessity of the applied monitoring tools, the methods used, and the purpose for the monitoring embodied in the principle of finality (Mitrou & Karyda, 2006). The data security principle defines how the data are to be stored, and who and under which circumstances may access them. Data security is a consequence of the finality and necessity principles. All three principles constitute the basis for data collection and retention, and monitoring of productivity regardless of the location where the work was performed.

However, what may set remote work from regular work settings apart is the ownership of the computer/laptop on which the work is carried out. As shown below, the question of ownership bears important consequences on the right of the employer to access the data stored on the employees' devices.

Pursuant to the PDPL, full transparency is a fundamental right of the employees (otherwise called 'the right to be informed). It requires companies to notify all employees ('data subjects') of any collection or processing of personal data, and the notice must describe the data being processed, the purpose and the basis for such processing, the data retention period, and any transfer of data to a foreign country, and must also communicate the rights of employees in connection with this instance of personal data processing. Further elements of information should include details relevant to the nature and duration of the surveillance, features of technology used and type of information compiled, details of any enforcement procedures outlining the notification of breaches of internal policies, and finally their rights to have access to the data processed about him/her and to correct errors (PDPL, 2018).

The PDPL further provides a detailed description of the purpose (legitimate interest) for which personal data are processed and stored should be prepared through internal corporate policies, and in all its segments fully reflect on the principles of transparency, finality, and data security. Personal data must be stored so that only authorised persons may access them through appropriate systems of access privileges. The PDPL makes it illegal to allow any third party to access employee data, except as permitted by the law or where this is necessary to prove the existence of rights and responsibilities arising from or in connection with employment. Employees may seek damages for any such violation of privacy under the Law of Contracts and Torts.

The research findings suggest that only about half of all employers notified their staff that their personal data were being processed. In other words, 50% of our sample of companies processed employees' personal data illegally.

The companies reported engaging in a variety of activities to notify staff of the collection and processing of their personal data including obtaining employee consent (as mentioned by 32% of the managers interviewed), informing employees about data collection in meetings (27%) or in writing (15%). Only 41% of all the companies had formal policies that governed personal data protection, and only 15% prepared notices that were distributed to all the employees (Figure 8.6). Similar results were obtained through the employee survey: 38% of the workers surveyed were aware of a corporate data protection policy. In addition, only 40% of these knew how to easily find this document.

The Labour Law (2005) stipulates that the employer is obliged to procure, install, and maintain means of work, but it allows employees to also use their own equipment. As said, the ownership of a computer is crucial, since the right to access a device depends on who owns it.

The ability to remotely access computers and data is permitted only where necessary for a legitimate and lawful purpose and if completely transparent and

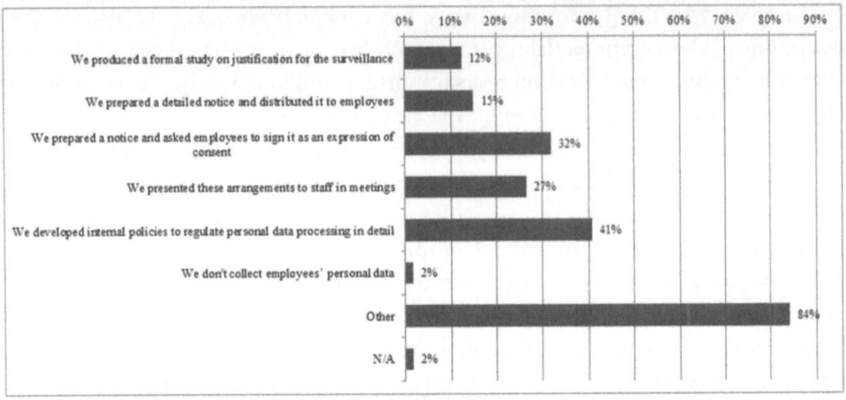

FIGURE 8.6 Which formal procedures did you complete before starting to collect personal data? (Employers)

Source: Own elaboration.

may not be performed without employee permission. The employers have a legitimate interest to access computers and data on the computers provided by the firm for a variety of reasons including the potential loss of control over trade secrets and other confidential information, inability to enforce cybersecurity, substantial risk of a data breach, use of pirated software (in case the firm does not supply licenses for all necessary programmes), and, potentially, undue impact on personal data.

According to the research results, the staff working from home used both company-provided computers and their own devices. Some three-fifths of the workers reported using their own desktop or laptop computers, whilst no more than 27% confirmed their firm had made one available. By contrast, 78% of the managers claimed they had provided devices, whereas 13% admitted the staff was using their own devices. Differences between the two samples go some way towards explaining this discrepancy since the workers and the employers did not necessarily come from the same companies. However, the scale of the gap requires additional investigation into this issue.

With respect to access to the employees' computers in case of remote work, about 30% of workers stated that the employers have remote access to their computers, but they were required to ask for access according to company's policy. In 10% of cases the employers enjoyed remote access to computers of their employees without any limitations. Almost 20% of the respondents are among those who did not know, nor were even sure whether the employer can or cannot access their computer (Figure 8.7).

As the findings further show (Figure 8.8) 18% of the employees were confident that the employers did not monitor their performance and/or productivity, while more than a half were aware that productivity was monitored. Thirty-seven

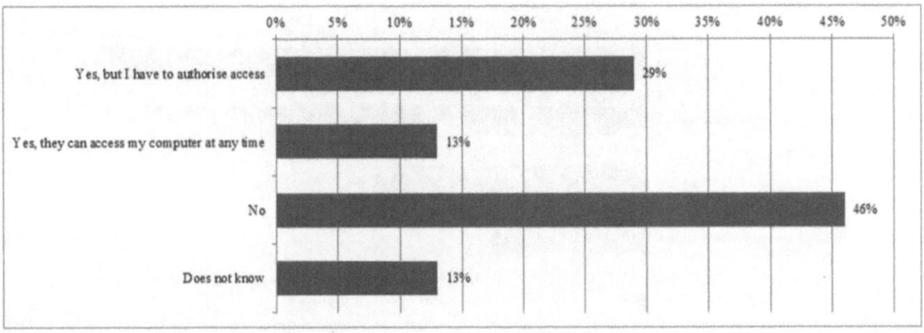

FIGURE 8.7 Can your employer access your computer and data remotely? (Employees)

Source: Own elaboration.

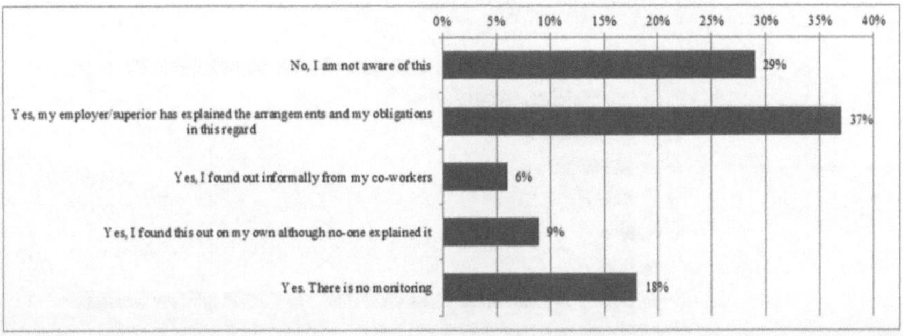

FIGURE 8.8 Reported employee awareness of performance/productivity monitoring? (Employees)

Source: Own elaboration.

percent of those who knew that productivity was monitored, were informed about it formally/by the employer or superior, while the rest either came to the conclusion on their own or were referred by colleagues.

The modality of monitoring workers in remote settings was already showcased earlier (Section Necessity and Proportionality, Figure 8.5).

With regards to data security, most of the surveyed employees (70%) reported their company retained their data in both an electronic and a physical format, while one-third were not aware of where their data were stored. As the below figure shows (Figure 8.9) the greatest percentage of the respondents believed their data could be accessed by the company's human resources (HR) department (61%), line managers (57%), or finance department (31%). Twenty percentage reported their data was available much more widely (to all managers or even all staff).

The manager survey resulted in similar findings (Figure 8.10), with executives reporting employee data could be accessed by the HR department (42%), line managers (16%), and finance department (10%). Worryingly, 46% did not

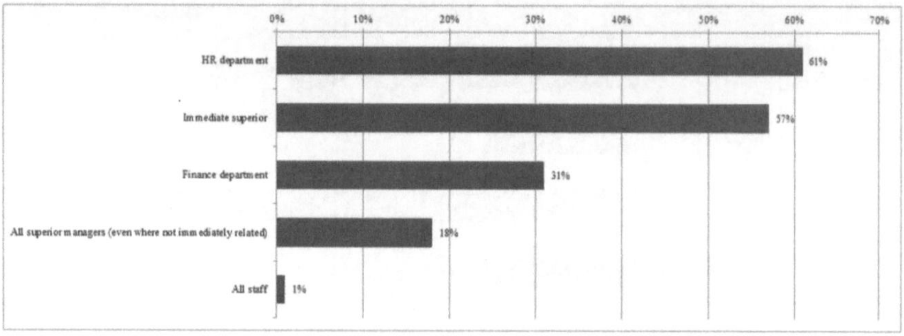

FIGURE 8.9 Who has access to your data? (Employees)

Source: Own elaboration.

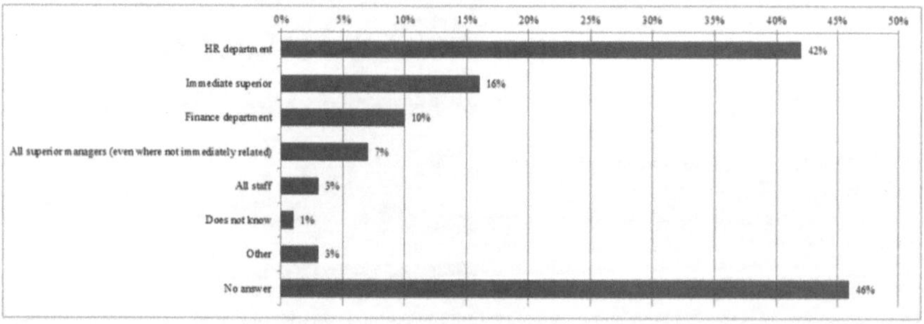

FIGURE 8.10 Who has access to employees' personal data? (Employers)

Source: Own elaboration.

answer the question, whilst a final 10% believed all managers or all staff could access the data.

In the case of performance monitoring-related data storage, as many as 88% of the employees surveyed could not say where performance data were stored, 75% reported receiving no feedback based on performance monitoring, and 43% did not know how often productivity and attendance data were tracked.

Finally, very few employees reported they themselves (7%) or their co-workers (8%) faced situations that could be viewed as infringements of privacy. The type of violation most recognised by the respondents was 'unauthorised access to employee data'. More than 80% of workers polled were 'mostly' or 'completely' certain their firms collected and processed their personal data lawfully, whereas the majority also believed privacy infringements were not particularly widespread in Serbia. By contrast, the managers were less convinced, with 69% of this cohort believing that unlawful data collection was 'relatively' or 'very' common. At the same time, 82% of the executives claimed they had never had reason to suspect they had violated the privacy of their staff. The remaining 18% expressed doubts about whether requiring COVID-19 vaccination, inspecting vaccination certificates, or using facial recognition software to control access to company premises constituted privacy infringements.

The findings suggest that most employers did not meet the PDPL requirements governing data collection, processing, and retention regardless of the location where the work was performed.

On the one hand, the fulfilment of the transparency principle is doubtful: if notified orally, the employees are denied the legally mandated written and accessible notice of data collection, processing, and storage that provides an explanation of their rights. On the other hand, the employers who claimed to have notified their staff in writing may not have done so in full compliance with the PDPL, meaning in an intelligible and easily accessible form, and may not have provided all the information mandated by data protection law. When it comes to consent as the basis for data collection and processing, one has to keep in mind that such consent must be given freely without compulsion, which may be questionable given that employees are legally subordinate to their employers. Consent can also be revoked at any time, making any continued processing based on such consent unlawful.

The absence of internal policies that regulate personal data collection and retention suggests firms are insufficiently aware of the issues involved. Moreover, both employee and manager surveys showed that many employers stored their workers' personal data in a manner that allowed all staff to access them.

Employees rarely reported awareness of being able to access personal data retained by their employers and to demand the deletion of any data not directly related to their work, even though this right is enshrined in the law.

Furthermore, the employees and the executives alike displayed a limited capacity to recognise privacy violations in their companies. This lack of awareness may compromise the employers' ability to appropriately inform staff of their rights. This was also borne out by interviews with experts, who claimed little progress in corporate implementation of the PDPL.

Findings clearly show a lack of awareness of data protection rules among workers, but they seemed to place high trust in their companies not to violate their privacy.

Cleary the ownership of computers, which was not previously researched, requires attention since it has potentially detrimental effects on employee privacy rights. While accessing the data on the company-provided computers is lawful under the above-cited conditions, the ability of employers to collect data from the computers owned and used by employees for collecting and storing both firm and personal data allows the employers to access a variety of data they have no right to. Thus, the vaguely legislated obligation of employers to provide equipment to employees creates space for jeopardising the privacy rights of employees. The only clear-cut solution to this problem would be to use exclusively company-owned computers, whilst staff members' own machines or other devices (such as mobile phones) could be utilised on an ad hoc basis and in exceptional cases, such as to check e-mail and the like, but employers would not be granted access to them.

Conclusions

As demonstrated by the research, the massive shift to remote work during COVID-19 opened the door for increased surveillance of employees often violating their autonomy and their right to stay free from unlawful and unjustified intrusion into their privacy at work. Indeed, employees' rights to privacy were breached with regard to all fundamental privacy and data protection domains, namely: legality, necessity, finality, proportionality, transparency, and data security. Out of the regular workplace and eyes of the employers, workers became only falsely invisible to their managers. The managers used their managerial power to extend control over workers under the pretext of responding to potential employee misbehaviours and misuse in the remote workplace.

With regards to the legality principle, most of the workers were left without addenda to their employment agreements, thus being stripped of their basic privacy and data protection-related rights. This first and most important step was only an introduction to trampling on other principles. In choosing the scope and breadth of surveillance tools used, the employers obeyed neither the necessity nor proportionality principles. While research showed that employers rarely used advanced performance monitoring apps, they did not hesitate to use otherwise non-intrusive tools to monitor employees way above legitimate interests. Lastly, and in consequence, the principles of transparency, finality, and data security were also violated, opening the doors wide to abuse of the employees' data collection and processing. The employers neither ensured policies nor provided notices to the employees regarding the monitoring of their work, and data collection and processing. In most of the cases the employees allowed the stored data of their employees to be widely accessible contrary to the legal provisions set in the PDPL. This resulted in the unlegitimate (unjustifiable) processing of personal data. Therefore, one may conclude that the frontiers of control were pushed in favour of employers in the remote work settings in Serbia.

However, this breach of privacy provoked neither collective action nor individual resistance by the Serbian remote workers. At the same time, our respondents showed rather limited knowledge about their privacy protection and labour rights. This may be an explanation as to why worker expression of agency, either in the form of strike actions or informal expression of dissent, were entirely missing despite a union presence. Workers neither exploited zones of uncertainty to control actors with greater power nor did they vent opposition. It seems that the workers in Serbia were not interested in collective action.

In fact, according to our findings, the remote workers interviewed continued to comply with the new practices imposed by employers primarily due to ignorance of the law. Moreover, they showed a high level of trust in their employers when the question of privacy breaches was raised. Recall that most respondents (80%)

reported completely or mostly trusting their company to use their personal data lawfully while at the same time half of those polled were not aware of whether there was a formal set of rules governing how employees' personal data were used.

In this regard, contrary to the literature that shows that transparency and clarity about data tracking and collection are crucially important for employees (Zielinski, 2020), in Serbia, this is not the case. While elsewhere workers are more likely to accept surveillance, provided they recognise that employers comply with monitoring procedures, the remote workers in Serbia harbour positive attitudes and trust their employers regardless.

It is also essential to accept that the new digital surveillance technologies are still premature and not universally implemented in Serbia. The adoption in the future is dependent on the legal framework and labour laws. The case of Serbia demonstrates that the lack of harmonisation of labour and data protection regulation creates a grey area regarding the privacy of workers both on company premises and whilst working from home. The Labour Law has not yet been brought into line with the data protection law, although the completion of the harmonisation was planned for the end of 2020.[13] To date, the Serbian Labour Law does not devote sufficient attention to protecting workers' personal information, nor does it appropriately define this matter insofar as employees are concerned, including remote workers. In other words, it does not reflect the nature of the subordinate position of employees vis-à-vis employers, meaning that companies are subject to the general penalty provisions of the PDPL only. Because of this, both employees and employers found themselves in an ambiguous position, which employees extensively (mis)used in the remote work setting during the pandemic.

Notes

1 Remote working is defined by the International Labour Organization (2017) as 'the use of information and communications technology such as smartphones, tablets, laptops, and desktop computers, for work that is performed outside the employer's premises', not necessarily from home.
2 Work from home and remote work are used as synonyms in this analysis and generally refer to the work taking place outside the employer's premises. The Serbian Labor Law (Official Gazette of the Republic of Serbia Nos. 24/2005, 61/2005, 54/2009, and 32/2013), recognises work outside the employer's premises, which includes both remote work and work from home (Article 42, paragraph 2).
3 This report uses the terms 'employee' and 'worker' interchangeably.
4 The term was for the first time used in Article 8 of the European Convention for the Protection of Human Rights and Fundamental Freedoms (1953).
5 This Charter contains both the right to privacy in Article 7 and the right to the protection of personal data in Article 8.
6 Violation of other provisions of the law (including breaches of employee rights under Article 42 in connection with agreements allowing staff to work from home) also carries a fine of between 600,000 (c. 5,100 EUR) and 1.5 million dinars (c. 12,700 EUR).
7 Response to a freedom of information request dated 11 February 2022.
8 Clockify is a trust-based time tracker, meaning that individuals are encouraged to be truthful and accountable about the information they put in. Project Timer, The Best

Windows Time Trackers for more productivity in 2020, posted on 6 January 2019, projecttimer.com/best-windows-time-trackers-2020.

9 Time Doctor is one of the most popular employee efficiency trackers that can monitor websites and apps as 'the cure for time-wasting habits'. The developers market their software as a 'productivity' rather than a 'surveillance' tool, but it can be used to track someone without their knowledge.

10 Ibid.

11 Interview with the Commissioner for Freedom of Information and Personal Data Protection, 18 February 2022.

12 Interview with personal data protection expert, 21 January 2022.

13 Interview with the Commissioner for Freedom of Information and Personal Data Protection, 18 February 2022.

References

Amis, J. (2005). Interviewing for case study research. In D. Andrews, D. Mason, & M. Silk (Eds.), *Qualitative methods in sports studies*. Berg.

Andjelkovic, B., & Jakobi, T. (2022). *Svevideće oko: kako je rad na daljinu tokom kovida-19 otvorio vrata za sveprisutnost poslodavaca u životu radnika*. Centar za istraživanje javnih politika. https://www.publicpolicy.rs/publikacije/85a5ece723d2bb1d116f5d5f59028784f05da5f2.pdf

Ball, K. (2021), *Electronic monitoring and surveillance in the workplace*. Publications Office of the European Union. https://publications.jrc.ec.europa.eu/repository/handle/JRC125716

Belgian National Labour Council. (2002). *National collective agreement on the protection of workers' privacy concerning controls on electronic online communications data*. Belgian National Labour Council. https://cnt-nar.be/sites/default/files/documents/CCT-COORD/cct-081.pdf

Blum, S. (2022). *Employee surveillance is exploding with remote work – And could be the new norm* [web log]. www.morningbrew.com/series/the-years-ahead/stories/2022/01/19/employee-surveillance-is-exploding-with-remote-work-and-could-be-the-new-norm

Council of Europe. (1950). *The European convention on human rights*. Directorate of Information.

Curchod, C., Patriotta, G., Cohen, L., & Neysen, N. (2020). Working for an algorithm: Power asymmetries and agency in online work settings. *Administrative Science Quarterly, 65*(3). https://doi.org/10.1177/0001839219867024

Data Protection Working Party. (DPWP). (2002). *Working document on the surveillance of electronic communications in the workplace* 5401/01/Final. https://ec.europa.eu/justice/article-29/documentation/opinion-recommendation/files/2002/wp55_en.pdf

De Hert, P., & Lammerant, H. (2013). *Protection of personal data in work-related relations*. Directorate-General for Internal Policies, European Parliament. www.europarl.europa.eu/RegData/etudes/etudes/join/2013/474440/IPOL-LIBE_ET(2013)474440_EN.pdf

De Menezes, L. M., & Kelliher, C. (2017). Flexible working, individual performance, and employee attitudes: Comparing formal and informal arrangements. *Human Resource Management, 56*(6), 1051–1070. https://doi.org/10.1002/hrm.21822

Electronic Privacy Information Center (EPIC). (2002). *Possible content of a European framework on the protection of workers' personal data*. www.epic.org/privacy/workplace

Etikan, I., Musa, S. A., & Rukayya, S. A. (2016). Comparison of convenience sampling and purposive sampling. *American Journal of Theoretical and Applied Statistics, 5*(1). https://doi.org/10.11648/j.ajtas.20160501.11

Eurofound and the International Labour Office. (2017). *Working anytime, anywhere: The effects on the world of work*. Publications Office of the European Union; International Labour Office.

European Data Protection Supervisor (EDPS). (2020). *Annual report 2020*. https://edps.europa.eu/system/files/2021-04/2021-04-19-annual-report-2020_EN.pdf

Frangi, L., Masi, A. C., Faust, R., & Rohraff, N. (2021). *Digital technologies and workplace relations: Managers, colleagues, trade unions*. https://archipel.uqam.ca/14902/1/Frangi_MasiKSG_main_report.pdf

Graham, S., & Wood, D. (2003). Digitizing surveillance: Categorization, space, inequality. *Critical Social Policy*, *23*(2), 227–248. https://doi.org/10.1177/0261018303023002006

Grant, C. A., Wallace, L. M., & Spurgeon, P. C. (2013). An exploration of the psychological factors affecting remote e-worker's job effectiveness, well-being, and work-life balance. *Employee Relations*, *35*(5), 527–546. https://doi.org/10.1108/ER-08-2012-0059

International Working Group on Data Protection in Telecommunications (IWGDPT). (1996). *Report and recommendations on telecommunications and privacy in labour relationships. (1996)*. International Documents on Data Protection in Telecommunications and Media 1983–2013. Berliner Beauftragter fürDatenschutz und Informationsfreiheit. berlin.de/fileadmin/user_upload/pdf/gremien/BlnBDI_IWGDPT_2013.pdf

Jaakson, K., & Kallaste, E. (2010). Beyond flexibility: Reallocation of responsibilities in the case of telework. *New Technology, Work and Employment*, *25*(3), 196–209. https://doi.org/10.1111/j.1468-005X.2010.00248.x

Kelliher, C., & Anderson, D. (2010). Doing more with less? Flexible working practices and the intensification of work. *Human Relations*, *63*(1), 83–106. https://doi.org/10.1177/0018726709349199

Labour Law, Official Gazette of the Republic of Serbia Nos. 24/2005, 61/2005, 54/2009, 32/2013, 75/2014, 13/2017 – Constitutional Court Ruling, 113/2017, and 95/2018.

Lammerant, H., & de Hert, P. (2016). Predictive profiling and its legal limits: Effectiveness gone forever. In B. van der Sloot, D. Broeders, & E. Schrijvers (Eds.), *Exploring the boundaries of big data* (Vol. 32, pp. 145–173). Amsterdam University Press/WRR.

Lasprogata, G., King, N., & Pillay, S. (2004). Regulation of electronic employee monitoring: Identifying fundamental principles of employee privacy through a comparative study of data privacy legislation in the European Union, United States and Canada. *Stanford Technology Law Review*, 4. https://heinonline.org/HOL/LandingPage?handle=hein.journals/stantlr2004&div=3&id=&page=

Lee, S., & Kleiner, B. H. (2003). Electronic surveillance in the workplace. *Management Research News*, *26*(2/3/4), 72–81. https://doi.org/10.1108/01409170310784014

Levy, P. E., & Williams, J. R. (2004). The social context of performance appraisal: A review and framework for the future. *Journal of Management*, *30*(6). https://doi.org/10.1016/j.jm.2004.06.005

Maalsen, S., & Dowling, R. (2020). Covid-19 and the accelerating smart home. *Big Data & Society*, 7(2). https://doi.org/10.1177/2053951720938073

Manokha, I. (2020). The implications of digital employee monitoring and people analytics for power relations in the workplace. *Surveillance & Society*, *18*(4), 540–554. https://doi.org/10.24908/ss.v18i4.13776

Mitrou, L., & Karyda, M. (2006). Employees' privacy vs. employers' security: Can they be balanced? *Telematics and Informatics*, *23*, 164–178. https://doi.org/10.1016/j.tele.2005.07.003

Nyberg, D., & Sewell, G. (2014). Collaboration, co-operation or collusion? Contrasting employee responses to managerial control in three call centres. *British Journal of Industrial Relations*, *52*(2), 308–332. https://doi.org/10.1111/j.1467-8543.2012.00920.x

Personal Data Protection Law, Official Gazette of the Republic of Serbia No. 87/2018.

Roscigno, V. J., & Hodson, R. (2004). The organizational and social foundations of worker resistance. *American Sociological Review*, *69*(1), 14–39. https://doi.org/10.1177/000312240406900103

Samek Lodovici, M. (2021). *The impact of teleworking and digital work on workers and society*. Policy Department for Economic, Scientific and Quality of Life Policies European Parliament. www.europarl.europa.eu/RegData/etudes/STUD/2021/662904/IPOL_STU(2021)66 2904_EN.pdf

Sewell, G., & Taskin, L. (2015). Out of sight, out of mind in a new world of work? Autonomy, control, and spatiotemporal scaling in telework. *Organization Studies*, *36*(11), 1507–1529. https://doi.org/10.1177/0170840615593587

Spreitzer, G. M., Cameron, L., & Garrett, L. (2017). Alternative work arrangements: Two images of the new world of work. *Annual Review of Organizational Psychology and Organizational Behavior*, *4*(1). https://psycnet.apa.org/doi/10.1146/annurev-orgpsych-032516-113332

Townsend, L., & Wallace, C. (2016). *Social media research: A guide to ethics*. The University of Aberdeen.

Wright, E. O. (2000). Working-class power, capitalist-class interests, and class compromise. *American Journal of Sociology*, *105*(4), 957–1002.

Zielinski, D. (2020). *Monitoring remote workers* [web log]. www.shrm.org/hr-today/news/all-things-work/pages/monitoring-remote-workers.aspx

9

EXPLORING THE RIGHT TO DISCONNECT IN EUROPEAN LABOUR LAW AND IN THE LEGISLATION OF THE MEMBER STATES

Just a Matter of Working Time of Employees?

Olga Chesalina

Introduction

In the last few decades, advanced information and communication technologies (ITC) supported by different mobile work patterns have made it possible to work anytime and anywhere. However, a crucial factor for the substantial change of the way of working and of the management culture was the COVID-19 pandemic-related imposition/recommendation to work from home. The COVID-19 pandemic has drastically prompted working-from-home patterns. Remote work (telework) has a lot of advantages for employees. At the same time, ITC (like smart phones, computers, and other digital devices) contributed to the formation of the 'always on'/'ever-connected' corporate culture.

Continuous availability has resulted in extended working hours, unpaid work beyond regular working time, blurred boundaries between working and rest time and had a detrimental effect on the physical and mental health of workers.

The main reason for regulating the right to disconnect is that legislation and collective agreements on the maximum duration of daily/weekly working time were not sufficient to address the issue of permanent availability of employees via modern digital communication tools.

Lawmakers at the national and EU levels have been seeking to address this challenge, introducing the so-called 'right to disconnect'. Some countries have already taken a legislative approach, while others have preferred a social partnership. On 21 January 2021, a European Parliament Resolution (hereinafter – the Resolution) was adopted with recommendations to the European Commission on the right to disconnect including the Draft Directive (hereinafter – the Draft Directive) on this issue.[1] On 25 March 2021, the Commission responded to the Resolution and outlined its follow-up to the requests of the Resolution. In particular, the Commission invites social partners to find commonly agreed solutions to address the challenges

DOI: 10.4324/9781003326779-12

raised by telework, digitalisation and the right to disconnect. The outcome of these exchanges and research will underpin the Commission's considerations for the need for a possible EU initiative (European Commission, 2021a).

Legislation, practice, and doctrine of the Member States do not use a uniform approach neither to the notion nor to the regulation and scope of application of the right to disconnect. There are no uniform views among scholars on whether the right to disconnect is a right of its own or only part of an already existing right or just a remedy (Timellini, 2020, p. 120), a way to avoid the intrusion of the employer in the private life and rest time of employees.

Research on the right to disconnect is still in its infancy. The right to disconnect has already been the subject of several studies at the European level (Eurofound, 2021; Vargas Llave, 2020; Vargas Llave et al., 2020). So far, only few publications (Timellini, 2020; Waas, 2021) and papers (Kéfer, 2021) have been conducted on the right to disconnect (mostly at the national level) from the legal perspective. The author seeks to fill this research gap. This chapter is dedicated to analysing the legal nature and the regulation of the right to disconnect in the EU member-states and in the EU Draft Directive. With respect to methods, this analysis is based on a systematic legal comparison which takes account of the existing empirical evidence.

This chapter is organised as follows. The section 'The situation at a glance' presents the outcomes of empirical studies on the right to disconnect. Then, section 'The right to disconnect in the legislation of the EU Member States' analyses the regulations concerning the right to disconnect in the EU member states from 2016 up to March 2022. The section 'The right to disconnect in the EU Draft Directive' discusses the character of the right to disconnect, the personal and material scope of this right, the relationship to other labour rights as well as the role of this right in prevention of psychosocial risks. In section 'Enforcement of the right to disconnect', different factors that influence the effective implementation of the right to disconnect are investigated. The conclusion indicates the main findings of the chapter. In this context, the author stresses her opinion concerning the legal nature of the right to disconnect and the preconditions for its effective realisation.

The situation at a glance

Empirical studies at the EU level on the right to disconnect (in the strict sense) are in its infancy. Before the outbreak of COVID-19 a study on the 'Right to disconnect in the 27 EU Member States' was carried out (Vargas Llave et al., 2020). After the beginning of COVID-19 the study 'Right to disconnect: Exploring company practices' was published (Eurofound, 2021).

In empirical studies the issue of the right to disconnect is often connected with research on remote work and work-life balance. The COVID-19 pandemic, which imposed or recommended working from home job patterns due to health reasons, triggered the dissemination of remote work. Before the pandemic only 5% of the employees worked from home, while in the peak of the pandemic, in July 2020 50% of the employees worked remotely (Eurofound, 2021, p. 3). In this context, it should be taken into account that women were more likely to work from home than men (Eurofound, 2021, p. 3).

Working from home has a lot of advantages for employees. At the same time, working from home due to digital communication tools has often resulted in extended working hours, blurring the boundaries between work and private life (Eurofound, 2021, p. 5). Permanent availability makes it more difficult to switch off and contributes to negative psychological health impacts (Eurofound, 2021, p. 5). Especially women with children, who worked only from home during the COVID-19 pandemic, were struggling to balance their work and personal life (Eurofound, 2020, p. 21, 22). Negative effects increase the longer the pandemic and working-from-home lasts. Studies demonstrate that during the COVID-19 pandemic 27% of the respondents who were working from home had worked in their free time to meet work demands (Vargas Llave, 2020). Compared to employees working only at their employer's premises, a higher share of teleworkers worked long hours (between 41 and 60 hours per week). This was true for both 'new' teleworkers and those who had already worked from home before the pandemic (Predotova & Vargas Llave, 2021).

These outcomes also confirm studies that were carried out at the national level (see Predotova & Vargas Llave, 2021). For example, a study from Germany shows that 39% of remote workers are working long hours. Furthermore, more than half of the respondents stated that they can be reached by their employer or customers longer in the home office than at the employer's premises. This is to be explained by the fact that digital communication options increase employer expectations of reaching their employees outside of the contractually agreed working hours for queries or work tasks (Ahlers et al., 2021, p. 17).

So far there is a large gap in empirical evidence concerning the meaning of permanent availability due to digital communication tools concerning other groups of employees, for example, those who combine remote work with work from home or exercise traditional professions that do not presuppose the use of computer or other similar tools.

The right to disconnect in the legislation of the EU Member States

Up to March 2021, seven EU Member States (France, Belgium, Italy, Spain, Slovakia, Greece, and Portugal) had implemented a legislation on the right to disconnect. France was the first to introduce this right in 2016 in the Labour Code (Loi no. 2016–1088 of 8 August 2016) with the goal to establish a balance between private and professional life. According to Article 2242–17 of the Labour Code[2] the conditions for exercising the right to disconnect should be implemented through agreements between employers and trade unions in all companies with at least 50 employees. In the absence of an agreement, after consultation with the social and economic committee, the employer should provide the right to disconnect in a chapter (Timellini, 2020, p. 122). In Italy, Law no. 81/2017 in relation to 'smart' (remote) workers provides a provision that remote working should take place 'within the limits of the maximum duration of daily and weekly working time, as established by law and collective bargaining' (Article 18, para. 1) and that an individual agreement with a smart worker should provide for the worker's disconnection from technological work instruments (Article 19, para. 1) (Vargas Llave et al., 2020, p. 43). In Spain, the right to disconnect for all employees and civil servants was established in Law no. 3/2018 on Data Protection. Article 88 of this Law does not impose an obligation for the social partners to negotiate on this issue but provides for an obligation for all employers to provide and implement an internal policy on the right to disconnect (Vargas Llave et al., 2020, pp. 42–43). In addition, Spain has adapted on 14 July 2021 the not legally binding Charta of Digital Rights[3] which includes the right to disconnect. In Belgium, in accordance with the law on strengthening economic growth and social cohesion, employers with at least 50 employees, have an obligation to consult and negotiate with their health and safety committee about the use of digital communication tools and disconnection from work at regular intervals (Eurofound, 2021, p. 18).

The COVID-19 pandemic has boosted the legislative process on this issue. In Slovakia, the regulation within the meaning of the right to disconnect for each employee working from home was established on 1 March 2021, as a part of the amendments to the Labour Code concerning telework. According to paragraph 52 point 10 of the Labour Code, according to which an employee working from home shall have a right not to use work equipment during his/her continuous daily and weekly rest, unless on-call or overtime work is ordered or agreed with him/her at that time, as well as during his/her leave. An employer shall not punish employees for refusal to perform work during their rest time.[4] In Ireland, on 1 April 2021 the not legally binding Code of Practice on the Right to Disconnect was adopted with the goal to provide practical guidance and best practice to this issue.[5] According to the Code, the right to disconnect is addressed to all employees and includes three main elements: (a) The right of an employee to not routinely perform work outside normal working hours. (b) The right to not be penalised for refusing to attend to work matters outside of normal working hours. (c) The duty to respect another person's right to disconnect (e.g., by not routinely emailing or calling outside normal working hours). On 16 June 2021 in Greece a controversially (Lampropoulos, 2021) labour law reform was implemented, which among other numerous regulations, provided the right for teleworkers to disconnect, meaning the right to completely refrain from performing his/her work or from communicating digitally/answering telephone calls, e-mails, etc. outside working hours and during statutory leave. Any discrimination against the teleworker for having exercised the right to disconnect shall be prohibited. The technical and organisational means that have to ensure the teleworker's disconnection from digital communication tools are mandatory terms of the teleworking contract and shall be agreed upon between the employer and the employees' representatives in the company. In the absence of such agreement, these terms shall be determined by the employer and communicated to all employees.[6] In Portugal, on 1 January 2022 Law no. 83/2021[7] came into force that modifies the teleworking regime and lays down the right to disconnect. The Law stipulates a duty of an employer to refrain from contacting the employee during the rest period, regardless of his/her workplace, except in situations of force majeure. Any less favourable treatment of the employee, in particular in terms of working conditions and career progress, because he/she excises the right to a rest period, constitutes a discriminatory action. A breach of this regulation constitutes a serious administrative offense (Garrigues, 2021).

In Luxembourg, in September 2021 amendments to the Labour Code devoted to the right to disconnect that should regulate technical and training measures on this issue as well as sanctions for the breach of provisions were submitted to the Chamber of Deputies (David, 2021), however until now the draft has not yet been adopted.

One can see, that in the legislation adopted during the COVID-19 pandemic, the addressees of the right to disconnect are teleworkers (not all workers), what can be explained by the substantial increase in working-from-home patterns during the pandemic and the explicit focus of the legislator on this group of workers. In all countries – irrespective whether legislation devoted to the disconnection rights was introduced or not – collective agreements at sectoral and company level are important tools in the determination of the modalities of the right to disconnect (Müller, 2020, p. 45). It seems that the legislative approach encourages and promotes negotiations with social partners on this issue (Eurofound, 2021).

The right to disconnect in the EU Draft Directive

The character of the right to disconnect

Article 3 of the Draft Directive formulates the right to disconnect as a positive, individual subjective right whose addressee is the worker. This right is strengthened by the wording that 'employers 'must' take the necessary measures to provide workers with means to exercise this right'. The Draft Directive refrains from formulating a direct prohibition for the employer to contact the employees, ensuring the strongest protection of this right (Kovács, 2015, pp. 25–26) since the worker, due to his/her subordinated position, can hesitate to exercise this right. Simultaneously, in accordance with the Draft Directive, measures enabling the implementation of the right to disconnect cannot be reduced to a negative obligation of the employer – just to refrain from connecting/contacting a worker. In accordance with Article 4 of the Draft Directive, measures implementing the right to disconnect presuppose positive obligations of the employer. These measures can be realised in the framework of 'hard' or 'soft' approaches. For example, the practical arrangements for switching off digital tools for work purposes resulting in blocking email delivery at specific time is a manifestation of a 'hard' approach. The awareness-raising measures like in-work training belong to a 'soft' approach (Eurofound, 2021, p. 32).

The Draft Directive itself formulates the employees' right, but not a duty (also in relation to co-workers), to disconnect. In contradiction to the Draft Directive, the Resolution stipules that not only the employer should not require workers to be available outside their working time but also co-workers should refrain from contacting their colleagues outside the agreed working hours for work purposes (point 20).

Personal scope of the right to disconnect

1. Article 1 of the Draft Directive defining the personal scope of the Directive refers to 'workers who use digital tools, including ICT, for work purposes' and 'to all sectors, both public and private, and to all workers, independent of their status and their working arrangements'. There are some inconsistences in the wording. It seems that the addressees of the Draft Directive are primarily 'knowledge workers' who use digital communication tools for work purposes irrespective whether they are working at the employer's premises or remotely. During the COVID-19 pandemic, remote work has come to the fore. In the follow-up to the Resolution, the European Commission considers the right to disconnect in its wider context of remote work and will conduct research on the trends, evolution, and implications of remote work beyond the pandemic (European Commission, 2021a). The focus on remote workers can be observed also in the latest national legislation of the Member States. Such restriction seems unjustified. Hybrid forms of work (a combination of work from home and from office) have become even more common than 'exclusively' remote work. In addition, employees working at the premises of the employer are in the majority of cases also available via work mobile phone or email beyond their working time.
2. For the purposes of the Draft Directive, 'disconnect' means not to engage in work-related activities or communications by means of digital tools, directly or indirectly, outside working time (Article 2). Recently, a Digital Compass was launched by the European Commission that articulates the EU's digital targets for 2030 and proposes to develop a framework of digital principles with the goal that the same rights that apply offline can be fully exercised online (European Commission, 2021b). It seems that the Draft Directive addresses first of all the challenges linked to digitalisation and new ways of working ('ever-connected', 'always on', 'constantly on-call', 'infobesity', etc.). Interestingly, the German notion – 'the right to be unavailable' ('Recht auf Nichterreichbarkeit') allows taking a broader approach, not limited to digital communication tools and but also covering more traditional tools like mobile/landline phone and therefore addressed to all employees (e.g., ambulance driver).
3. According to the Draft Directive, the right to disconnect should apply to all workers, independent of their status.[8] This means that the Draft Directive takes a human rights approach. Due to digitalisation, there is an increasing resemblance in terms of work performance by an employee and a self-employed

worker, with the result that many self-employed persons are becoming more dependent (Kurt, 2020, p. 317).

In the European Parliament resolution of 16 September 2021 on 'fair working conditions, rights, and social protection for platform workers – new forms of employment linked to digital development (2019/2186(INI))'[9] in the subchapter related to 'a healthy and safe working environment' it was provided that both on-location and online platform workers should be enabled to exercises the right to disconnect (point 14). In the Draft Directive on improving working conditions in platform work of 9 December 2021, which differentiates between self-employed persons performing platform work and platform workers in an employment relation, this right is not articulated any more, even in relation to platform workers in an employment relationship.

In contradiction to the defined personal scope, the Draft Directive on the right to disconnect imposes the obligation to take the necessary measures to provide workers with the means to exercise their right to disconnect only on employers but not on other actors (e.g., platform providers or principals). From numerous studies and publication is known that many platform workers are not only in an insecure position concerning their employment status but also concerning their working time. Many mobile applications can by means of GPS identify the location of a worker and send task offers even when the worker is offline. For these group of workers, the connection by means of digital tools (in the framework of algorithmic management) can take even more varied forms than in case of remote work.

4. The Resolution emphasises 'that the right to disconnect is of particular importance to vulnerable workers' (section H). At the same time, the proposal does not contain special rules to address the special problems of vulnerable non-standard workers. A similar problem is known in relation to Directive 2003/88/EC of the European Parliament and of the Council of 4 November 2003 concerning certain aspects of the organisation of working time (hereinafter – the Working Time Directive). Vincenzo Ferrante (2019, p. 376) emphasises that up to now, no ruling in relation to the Working Time Directive 'has dealt with the issue of risks to health and safety resulting from having several jobs or other aspects related to working time regulations, particularly problems arising from work-life balance in ordinary or atypical contracts.'

While for standard employees (the right to) limitation of their working time is relevant, for many non-standard, vulnerable workers (on-demand, on-call workers, remote workers, crowd workers) the inclusion of different periods (of their activity, as well as of looking for activity or waiting for it) into working time is at stake. The proposal of the Directive addresses the issue of long (unpaid) working hours rather than the issue of the atomisation (splitting) of working time of non-standard employed workers. For on-call workers and other casual workers whose employment contract does not provide fixed working hours, only the 'actual working time' (time of carrying out his or her activity or duties) is counted as working time. This means that periods (before work starts or standby) are not considered as working time and, at the same time, the worker cannot freely dispose of his/her 'rest time'. Simultaneously, employers can avoid the duty to provide paid rest periods (especially daily breaks). In many countries, the notification period before the commencement of work can be shortened in collective agreements in comparison to the period provided for in the legislation. For example, in the Netherlands a collective agreement can provide the regulation that the zero-hours worker is obliged to accept any work he/she is called upon up to 24 hours before the work starts (Eleveld, 2022, p. 386).[10]

At the same time, the ways of measuring the working time of remote workers and online platform workers in practice are becoming closer. Some employers count as paid working time of remote workers only time during which the computer is switched on. Platform operators in litigations concerning classification of on-demand drivers (e.g., in the United Kingdom) seek to justify a similar view: 'Uber contends that the tribunal should have found that the claimants . . . were only working under workers' contracts during periods when they were actually driving passengers to their destinations' (Judgement of the Supreme Court of the United Kingdom 'Uber BV and others (Appellants) v Aslam and others', point 123). However, the employment tribunal and the Supreme Court did not share this view. The Supreme Court of the United Kingdom in the abovementioned judgement has compared the working time of Uber drivers with the working time of 'on-call' employees who have to be near their place of work. The employment tribunal and the Supreme Court found that a driver was 'working' under such a contract during any period when she/he (a) had the Uber app switched on, (b) was within the territory in which he/she was authorised to use the app, and (c) was ready and willing to accept trips.

Material scope of the right to disconnect

1. Less clear is the material scope of the right to disconnect. The proposal stresses the interrelationship between the use of digital tools and work-life balance, physical and mental health, working conditions and the right to privacy. The proposal of the Directive is founded on the general principles of fair working conditions in accordance with Article. 153 (1)(b) TFEU. The Resolution and the Draft Directive refer to numerous sources of European and international labour law. According to recital 20 of the Resolution, the purpose of this Directive is *to improve working conditions* for all workers by laying down minimum requirements for the right to disconnect. Furthermore, the proposal of the Directive is intended to protect the workers' *health and safety*.
2. The Resolution considers the right to disconnect as a 'fundamental right which is an inseparable part of the new working patterns in the digital era' (letter H). EU law and in particular the Charter of Fundamental Rights of

the European Union (hereinafter – Charter) apply a broad approach to fundamental rights. The Draft Directive refers to Article 31 (2) of the Charter which provides the fundamental right of every worker to working conditions which respect his/her health, safety, and dignity, as well as the right to limitation of maximum working time, to daily and weekly rest periods and to an annual period of paid leave. Thomas Blanke stresses that the right laid down in Article 31 (2) of the Charter has 'more than a general programmatic character. It transforms the general objective of labour law as a whole into a subjective right . . . and elevates this subjective right to the status of a fundamental right' (Blanke, 2006, p. 359). The Draft Directive leaves the question open whether the right to disconnect is a consistent part of the fundamental right laid down in Article 31 (2) of the Charter or if it is a new separate right. Anyway, 'the guarantee of fair and just working conditions in Article 31 (2) of the Charter is open-ended and broad and covers all working conditions, explicitly and not explicitly mentioned in the Charter' (Blanke, 2006, p. 376) that theoretically would allow encompassing the right to disconnect under the umbrella of the right to fair working conditions.

The Resolution (section C) mentions only briefly that the 'always on' culture can have detrimental effects on fair remuneration. The proposal of the Directive does not refer to the ILO Conventions regarding 'fair wage' or the right to fair remuneration as enshrined in Article 4 (2) of the revised European Social Charter or Principle 6 of the European Pillar of Social Rights. One of the purposes of the regulation of working time is the realisation of the right to fair wages in the sense of 'equal pay for equal work'; without the measuring of working time and a limitation of working hours, workers have to work long hours without (adequate) payment. However, the proposal does not attach much importance to this interdependence.

3. Limitations on working time stood, from the very beginning, at the centre of workers' struggle for fair working conditions (Blanke, 2006, p. 359). It is worth mentioning that among the directives and recommendations regulating different labour law aspects, the majority regulate different aspects of working time.

In the digital age, with a growing flexibility in the organisation of working time, questions arise how to legally qualify work that is performed beyond the regular working time (Bjelinski, 2021, p. 215), how to prevent blurring the boundaries between working and rest time and finally, how to address the main (and old) issue of limiting unrecorded and unpaid working time. Different solutions, to address these topical problems concerning the blurring of boundaries between working and rest time, come into question. Some scholars, for example, Alain Supiot and Leszek Mitrus, proposed to introduce the notion of a 'third time' that is neither working time nor rest period (Ferrante, 2019, p. 384) or, in other words, an intermediate category between working and rest time (Mitrus, 2019, p. 395).

According to the proposal of the Directive, the right to disconnect should prevent 'blurring the boundaries between working time and free time' and recall that the time during which a worker is available or reachable for the employer is working time. This shows that the proposal is against the introduction of a third time category, which is also in line with the Court of Justice of the European Union (hereinafter – CJEU) approach to working time and rest time as mutually exclusive notions. According to the case law of the CJEU, all three conditions are required for the qualification of time as working time, namely when a person is (a) working, (b) at the employer's disposal, and (c) carrying out his/her activity or duties. Rest periods are any periods which are not working time (Article 2 of the Working Time Directive).

4. It is questionable – if working time and rest time are mutually exclusive – why we would need 'the right to disconnect', as the employees are free of the obligation to work during their daily rest periods? What is new concerning the right to disconnect? In France, which is a pioneer in the regulation of this phenomenon, in 2002 disconnection was described as 'the right to private life of the twenty-first century' (Timellini, 2019, p. 121). According to one opinion, the right to disconnect already exists because working hours are usually fixed. It means that the employees' availability is limited, and he/she is not obliged to work beyond his/her working time (Klebe, 2017, p. 57). According to another opinion, the right to disconnect has to be differentiated from the work duty of the employee. The right to disconnect means that the employee may prevent the employer from contacting him/her. The 'right to be disconnected' should prevent (protect) the employee from contacts on the side of the employer beyond the working time (Waas, 2022, pp. 1428–1429). In this sense, the disconnection right is closer to a procedural right or a remedy to prevent hyper-connection from the employer's side.

   Sometimes in doctrine (cited: Timellini, 2020, p. 131) as well as in the legislation (in Spain) the right to disconnect is considered as part of digital rights. It is reasonable to consider this right as one of 'digital freedoms' (or 'freedoms from digital technologies'). One can see parallels with the 'remedy' approach. The Draft Directive also mentions (among measures implementing the right to disconnect) another 'digital freedom' – 'switching off work-related monitoring tools' without regulating the digital surveillance in the substantive way.

5. According to the Draft Directive, an important measure implementing the right to disconnect is a provision of the system for measuring working time (Article 4 (b)). On the one side, the same obligation already follows from Article 31 (2) of the Charter in conjunction with Article 3 and 5 and 6 (b) of the Working Time Directive and Article 4 (1) and Article 6 (1) of the Council Directive 89/391/EEC of 12 June 1989 on the introduction of measures to encourage improvements in the safety and health of workers at work. In the case C-55/18, the CJEU held that to ensure the effectiveness of the right to a limitation of the

maximum working time and minimum rest periods the Member States must require employers to set up an objective, reliable and accessible system enabling the duration of time worked each day by each worker to be measured (point 60). On the other side, systems for measuring working time can be considered as an auxiliary tool of 'disconnection' as well as the way of monitoring implementation of the right to disconnect. The consequences of not recording working time can be illustrated by the example of the ICT sector. Employees who do not record their working time tend to work longer: 34.6% report that they regularly work more than 48 hours per week, that they are more likely to do a lot of overtime work and are more likely to be expected to be available outside normal working hours (Schmidt & Skrabs, 2020, p. 125). The introduction of the right to disconnect is nearly in vain, when the legislation allows calculating working time on a yearly basis instead of a weekly basis (e.g., the 'forfeit en jour' regime in France, see Timellini, 2020, p. 123).

6. The implementation of the right to disconnect (in connection with other legislative, practical, and technical measures) addresses different hazards of psychosocial nature. These hazards – in accordance with the new ISO 'Occupational health and safety management – Psychological health and safety at work – Guidelines for managing psychosocial risks' (International Organization for Standardization, 2021) include some aspects of work organisation (lack of control over workload; work overload; unpredictable working hours; continual requirements to complete work at short notice; uncertainty regarding work availability, including work without set hours) as well as some social factors at work (poor communication and relationships between managers, supervisors and workers; work tasks, roles, schedules, or expectations that cause workers to continue working in their own time; conflicting demands of work and home; work that impacts the workers' ability to recover). Interestingly, the ISO document describing factors related to work environment and equipment does not mention factors related to permanent availability (hyper-connection). The Strategic Framework on Health and Safety at Work for 2021–2027 considers the initiative on the right to disconnect as a part of the action plans concerning psychosocial risks. The latter are considered as one of the important challenges in the changing world of work with increased remote-working trends. In this context, the implementation of the right to disconnect takes safety and health approach (by using health and safety regulations and management).

The Resolution underlines the detrimental effect of the ever-greater use of digital tools for work on the physical and mental health of workers as well as safety at work and well-being. Among the measures implementing the right to disconnect, the Draft Directive lists health and safety assessments, including psychosocial risk assessment. Up to now, there are no quantitative data on the impact of the right to disconnect on workers' well-being and mental health (Vargas Llave et al., 2020, p. 52). Monitoring and assessment incidences of stress and burnout can 'provide evidence of the impact of the implementation of the right to disconnect' (Vargas-Llave et al., 2020, p. 57) on work-life balance and mental health.

Enforcement of the right to disconnect

The effectiveness of the right to disconnect depends on many factors. It would increase if it was formulated not only as a right of an employee but also as the positive obligation of the employer accompanied with sanctions for the violation of such obligation. The above-described legislation of the Member States shows that countries with the legislation on this topic (with the exception of Portugal) refrain from laying down a direct prohibition to the employer to contact employees beyond the working time and providing for sanctions for the violation of the right to disconnect. It is very important that the operationalisation of the right to disconnect is detailed in individual and collective agreements.

The empirical evidence shows that even in countries, pioneering the legislative approach on the right to disconnect, limited effectiveness of legal solutions can be observed due to employer reluctance to adopt internal policies. For instance, in Spain in 2019, 60% of the employees have been working under an 'always on' corporate culture (Vargas-Llave et al., 2020, p. 52). In France, only 23% of the companies have adopted a charter and 16% of the companies created rules on the right to disconnect; 67% of French employees do not manage to get out of work during their holidays.[10]

With respect to European labour law, the Member States enjoy a discretion for that purpose; at the same time, they are required to ensure that the effectiveness of these rights is guaranteed in full (CJEU of 14 May 2019 in case C-55/18, point 42). This decision of the CJEU concerning the measuring of working time can serve as an orientation concerning possible problems in the future as regards to the enforcement of the right to disconnect. The core measure for implementing the right to disconnect is to set up an objective, reliable and accessible system ensuring that the duration of time worked each day by each worker can be measured. The CJEU decision has shown gaps in the national legislation of the Member States concerning the recording of working time. For example, in Germany, according to section 16 subsection 2 sentence 1 of the Working Time Law (ArbZG), the employer is obliged to keep record only of working time exceeding its daily duration. In accordance with the CJEU decision, all employers will have to provide a system enabling them to keep record of the working day of each employee for every working day. However, there are still many open questions concerning the implementation of the CJEU decision, and political actors have different opinions on whether section 16 of the Working Time Law has yet to be altered.[11]

The effective enforcement of a right to disconnect depends not only on present legislation and individual/collective agreements on this issue, but also on many other factors. To these factors belong the type of employment relationship (standard open-ended relationship or non-standard, in particular – precarious relationship, e.g., fixed-term employment contract for a short period of time, and on-call work). Due to the coronavirus crisis, many employees have found themselves in insecure job situations that boost unpaid overtime work (from the home office) and prompt the self-exploitation of employees who are ready to work 'voluntarily'. Valerio De Stefano speaks about 'the "implicit threat" mechanism, namely the fear and reluctance to exercise their contractual and labour rights in fear that their temporary contract may not be renewed or prolonged, should they do so' (De Stefano, 2009; De Stefano, 2017, p. 185). For this reason, the realisation of the right to disconnect (and of the right to fair working conditions in general) in relation to non-standard workers should be addressed particularly.

Another important factor is 'the intensity of work'. This criterion has become, over the last few years, a key factor in the evaluation of work quality of employees. Recent studies show that, for example, due to digitalisation the amount of work has increased for 56% of the employees in Germany (Müller, 2020, p. 39). Furthermore, 33% of the employees who are on average working more than two hours longer than their daily contractual working time justify this extension of their working time with the argument that their work cannot be done otherwise (Beermann, 2020, p. 110). The effective realisation of the right to disconnect is not possible by regulating only the quantitative dimension of working time without also addressing the issue of intensity of work. However, the proposal of the Directive leaves this issue open.

Other important factors that influence the exercise of the right to disconnect are the need to work in different time zones; workplace democracy, limitation of working time regimes that are calculated on a yearly basis instead on a weekly basis; transparent measuring of the working time; effectiveness of labour inspections, etc.

Corporate culture is still a decisive factor whether an employee can realise the right to disconnect. The COVID-19 pandemic has shown that corporate culture is not something unchangeable; many countries were forced to move away from the presenteeism culture. The legislation (at the EU and national levels) on the right to disconnect can contribute to a cultural shift also concerning employer expectations in relation to availability of employees beyond their working time.

Conclusion

Remote/mobile work patterns supported by modern communication devices made it possible to work anytime and anywhere. The opposite site of this development is a permanent availability of employees with extended working hours and a lack of separation between working and private life. In the last decade, discussions as well as legislative processes have been started to address this issue in some countries concerning the introduction of the right to disconnect. The COVID-19 pandemic was a decisive factor not only for a significant boom of telework, but it has also triggered legislative initiatives at national levels as well as on the European level with regard to the right to disconnection.

This chapter illustrates that the issue of the right to disconnect is still in development; the EU Member States apply different approaches to this phenomenon.

There are no uniform views on its legal nature and the personal and material scope of its application. Even the wording 'right' is not unambiguous. There are different views whether the right to disconnect is a right of its own or only part of an already existing right (e.g., of the right to fair working conditions) or if it is even just a remedy. The Draft Directive gives answers on some of these questions, while leaving many questions open.

There is also no consensus on the personal scope of the right to disconnect in the legislation of the Member States as well as in the Draft Directive. Remote workers are often seen as the main addressee of this right because of the proliferation of working from home job patterns. The empirical evidence indicates that during the pandemic the number of remote workers drastically increased. There is no doubt that in particular remote workers use digital tools, including ICT, for work purposes and therefore must be protected against permanent availability. The legislation of the Member States (in Slovakia, Greece, and Portugal) adopted during the pandemic, stipulates this right (only) in relation to teleworkers in contrast to the legislation of the Member States (France and Spain) adopted before the outbreak of the pandemic. Even if different groups of workers are differently affected by the 'always on' culture it is not justified to restrict this right (as well as the research on this topic) only to teleworkers. Hybrid forms of work have become even more common than 'exclusively' remote work; platform work offers even more varied/sophisticated digital communication tools than those used by telework.

The right to disconnect has to be differentiated from the regulation of working time and the work duty of the employee. The analysis of legal instruments and opinions of scholars leads the author to the conclusion that the right to disconnect is not a new labour right but rather a remedy to prevent hyper-connection from the employer's side and constant over-accessibility of employees. For this reason, it is justified to consider this right as one of 'digital freedoms' – the freedom to 'switch off work-related monitoring tools.'

The right to disconnect goes beyond the regulation of the maximum duration of working time. Nevertheless, the provision of a system for measuring working time is an important measure to implement this right. Working time regimes that are calculated on a yearly basis (instead of on a weekly basis) represent a serious obstacle for the implementation of this right. Other preconditions for the effective realisation of the right to disconnect are, in particularly, an adequate regulation of the workload, stable employment relationships and a strong corporate culture. Member States with legislation on this topic (with the exception of Portugal) follow 'a soft approach' on the right to disconnect, refraining from laying down a direct prohibition on the employer to contact employees beyond the working time and providing sanctions for the violation of the right to disconnect (what would ensure the strongest protection of this right). In the end, any kind of legislative approach can encourage a cultural shift away from the habit of engaging in work-related electronic communications outside of the working time.

Notes

1 European Parliament resolution of 21 January 2021 with recommendations to the Commission on the right to disconnect (2019/2181(INL)). www.europarl.europa.eu/doceo/document/TA-9-2021-0021_EN.html.
2 Code du travail. www.legifrance.gouv.fr/codes/article_lc/LEGIARTI000039785096/.
3 Carta de Derechos Digitales. https://portal.mineco.gob.es/RecursosArticulo/mineco/ministerio/participacion_publica/audiencia/ficheros/SEDIACartaDerechosDigitales.pdf.
4 Zákonník práce (v znení č 2021–76). www.epi.sk/zz/2001-311.
5 Code of Practice on the Right to Disconnect. www.gov.ie/en/publication/d33e8-code-of-practice-on-the-right-to-disconnect/#.
6 www.taxheaven.gr/news/54932/to-pshfisoen-ergasiako-nomosxedio.
7 Diário da República, 1.a série. https://files.dre.pt/1s/2021/12/23500/0000200009.pdf.
8 The ETUC in their position on the Right to Disconnect takes a human rights approach and stresses that the right to disconnect should be applied to all workers irrespective of their employment status. Adopted at the Executive Committee of 23–23 March 2021. Cf. ETUC Position on the Right to Disconnect. 24.03.2021. www.etuc.org/en/document/etuc-position-right-disconnect.
9 European Parliament resolution of 16 September 2021 on fair working conditions, rights and social protection for platform workers – new forms of employment linked to digital development (2019/2186(INI)). www.europarl.europa.eu/doceo/document/TA-9-2021-0385_EN.html.
10 Respectez le droit à la déconnexion de vos salariés durant leurs congés! www.legisocial.fr/actualites-sociales/4073-salaries-droit-deconnexion-conges.html.
11 European Court of Justice (ECJ) Lays Down Substantial Duties of Employers for the Recording of Working Time Based on the Working Time Directive. https://honert.de/en/european-court-of-justice-ecj-lays-down-substantial-duties-of-employers-for-the-recording-of-working-time-based-on-the-working-time-directive/.

References

Ahlers, E., Mierich, S., & Zucco, A. (2021). *Homeoffice. Was wir aus der Zeit der Pandemie für die zukünftige Gestaltung von Homeoffice lernen können* (Report No. 65). Wirtschafts- und Sozialwissenschaftliches Institut. www.boeckler.de/pdf/p_wsi_report_65_2021.pdf.

Beermann, B. (2020). Menschengerechte Gestaltung der Arbeit – Arbeitsschutz in der digitalisierten Arbeitswelt. In L. Schröder (Ed.), *Gute Arbeit. Arbeitszeit und Digitalisierung – Impulse für eine moderne Arbeitsgestaltung* (pp. 109–118). Bund Verlag.

Bjelinski, R. I. (2021). The impact of digitalisation on individual labour relations: Working time as an outdated concept? In A. Perulli & T. Treu (Eds.), *The future of work: Labour law and labour market regulation in the digital era* (pp. 211–221). Wolters Kluwer.

Blanke, T. (2006). Fair and Just working conditions (Art. 31). In B. Bercusson (Ed.), *European labour law and the EU charter of fundamental rights* (pp. 357–378). Nomos.

David, D. (2021, November 5). Luxembourg is introducing a right for employees to disconnect outside of working hours. *Mondaq*. www.mondaq.com/employee-rights-labour-relations/1128316/a-new-right-to-disconnect-in-luxembourg.

De Stefano, V. (2009). *Smuggling-in flexibility: Temporary work contracts and the "implicit threat" mechanisms. Reflections on a new European path*. Working Document 4. Labour Administration and Inspection Programme LAB/ADMIN, ILO.

De Stefano, V. (2017). Non-standard work and limits on freedom of association: A human-based approach. *Industrial Law Journal, 46*(2), 185–207.

Eleveld, A. (2022). Flexi-insecurity and the regulation of zero-hours work in the Netherlands. *European Labour Law Journal, 13*(3), 375–399.

Eurofound. (2020). *Living, working and COVID-19, COVID-19 series*. Publications Office of the European Union. www.eurofound.europa.eu/publications/report/2020/living-working-and-covid-19.

Eurofound. (2021). *Right to disconnect: Exploring company practices*. Publications Office of the European Union. www.eurofound.europa.eu/sites/default/files/ef_publication/field_ef_document/ef21049en.pdf.

European Commission. (2021a, June 17). *Remote work and the EU legal framework*. Joint UNI Europa/FES Webinar. https://socialdialogue.fes.de/fileadmin/user_upload/Remote_work_and_the_R2D.pdf.

European Commission. (2021b, March 9). *Europe's digital decade: Commission sets the course towards a digitally empowered Europe by 2030*. https://ec.europa.eu/commission/presscorner/detail/en/ip_21_983.

European Parliament. (2022, February). *Legislative train*. www.europarl.europa.eu/legislative-train/api/stages/report/current/theme/a-europe-fit-for-the-digital-age/file/al-legislative-proposal-to-the-commission-on-the-right-to-disconnect.

Federación de Servicios de Comisiones Obreras (CCOO) v Deutsche Bank SAE. CJEU. (2019, May 14). *Case C-55/18. ECLI:EU:C:2019:402*. https://curia.europa.eu/juris/document/document.jsf?docid=214043&mode=req&pageIndex=1&dir=&occ=first&part=1&text=&doclang=EN&cid=3905833.

Ferrante, V. (2019). Between health and salary: The incomplete regulation of working time in European law. *European Labour Law Journal, 10*(4), 370–385. https://doi.org/10.1177%2F2031952519886144.

Gallner, I. (2020). Arbeitszeit- und Urlaubsrecht europäisch gedacht. *Soziales Recht, 50*(2), 45–56.

Garrigues. (2021, December 6). *New rules on the teleworking regime and the right to disconnect*. www.garrigues.com/sites/default/files/documents/portugal_new_rules_on_the_teleworking_regime_and_the_right_to_disconnect.pdf.

International Organization for Standardization. (2021). *ISO 45003:2021 'Occupational health and safety management – Psychological health and safety at work – Guidelines for managing psychosocial risks'*. www.iso.org/obp/ui/#iso:std:iso:45003:ed-1:v1:en.

Kéfer, F. (2021). *The right to disconnect. A response to one of the challenges raised by the digital transition? European and Belgian perspectives* [Paper presentation]. Paper presented at XIII European Regional Congress of the International Society for Labour and Social Security Law, Lisbonne, Portugal. https://hdl.handle.net/2268/259740.

Klebe, T. (2017). Betriebsrat 4.0 – Digital und global? *NZA-Beilage*, 77–84.

Kovács, E. (2015). The legal nature of art. 30 CFREU – A human right, a fundamental right, a right? In M. Vinković (Ed.), *New developments in labour, equality and human rights law* (pp. 11–36). Josip Juraj Strossmayer University of Osijek Faculty of Law/Jean Monnet Chair in EU Labour, Equality and Human Rights Law.

Kurt, S. (2020). *Schutz und Verantwortung in der digitalen und globalen Arbeitswelt*. Nomos.

Lampropoulos, P. (2021, June 19). Greece approves controversial new labor bill. *Jurist*. www.jurist.org/news/2021/06/greece-approves-controversial-new-labor-bill/.

Mitrus, L. (2019). Potential implications of the Matzak judgment (Quality of rest time, right to disconnect). *European Labour Law Journal, 10*(4), 386–397. https://doi.org/10.1177%2F2031952519886149.

Müller, N. (2020). Digitalisierung und psychische Belastungen – Bilanz und Handlungsperspektiven für Gute Arbeit. In L. Schröder (Ed.), *Gute Arbeit. Arbeitszeit und Digitalisierung – Impulse für eine moderne Arbeitsgestaltung* (pp. 34–47). Bund Verlag.

Predotova, K., & Vargas Llave, O. (2021). Workers want to telework but long working hours, isolation and inadequate equipment must be tackled. *Eurofound*. www.eurofound.europa.eu/publications/article/2021/workers-want-to-telework-but-long-working-hours-isolation-and-inadequate-equipment-must-be-tackled.

Schmidt, A., & Skrabs, S. (2020). Arbeitszeit im Spannungsfeld zwischen Digitalisierung und Gesundheitsschutz. In L. Schröder (Ed.), *Gute Arbeit. Arbeitszeit und Digitalisierung – Impulse für eine moderne Arbeitsgestaltung* (pp. 119–140). Bund Verlag.

Timellini, C. (2020). Disconnection: A right in a phase of progressive definition. In J. Wratny & A. Ludera-Ruszel (Eds.), *New forms of employment: Current problems and future challenges* (pp. 119–136). Springer.

Uber BV and others (Appellants) v Aslam and others (Respondents), U. K. S. C. (2021, February 19). www.supremecourt.uk/cases/docs/uksc-2019-0029-judgment.pdf.

Vargas Llave, O. (2020, June 9). COVID-19 unleashed the potential for telework – How are workers coping? *Eurofound*. www.eurofound.europa.eu/publications/blog/covid-19-unleashed-the-potential-for-telework-how-are-workers-coping.

Vargas Llave, O., Weber, T., & Avogaro, M. (2020). Right to disconnect in the 27 EU Member States. *Eurofound*. WPEF20019. www.eurofound.europa.eu/sites/default/files/wpef20019.pdf.

Waas, B. (2021). Das Recht auf Nichterreichbarkeit. In Brose et al. (Eds.), *Grundlagen des Arbeits- und Sozialrechts*, Festschrift für U. Preis zum 65. Geburtstag (pp. 1428–1429). C.H. Beck.

10

UNCONDITIONAL BASIC INCOME AS A POLICY TOOL IN THE POST-COVID TIME

Sven M. Gruner

Introduction

One of the most interesting ideas discussed by both academics and practitioners in the last years is Unconditional Basic Income (UBI). This concept, although not new, gained increased attention in the economic mainstream due to two factors, occurring recently: the accelerating technological change and the COVID-19 pandemic. With reference to this first factor, it is argued that digitalisation and, as postulated by Schwab (2016), the so-called fourth industrial revolution has created opportunities for improving living standards, working conditions, and incomes. In the new digital world, a risk of digital substitution of routinised tasks, however, appears which may culminate in the loss of middle-skilled jobs and subsequent crowding around jobs with non-routinised but low-skilled tasks (e.g., requiring physical dexterity or social skills) and – to lesser extent – around jobs requiring cognitive skills and creativity of human workers (Acemoglu & Autor, 2011; Goos et al., 2014; Vermeulen & Psenner, 2022). In this context, UBI could be treated as a remedy for the growing insecurity of digital labour markets. With reference to the second factor, the UBI could be also seen as a tool for solving problems generated by turmoil in the labour market, being the aftermath of the pandemic (Handelsblatt, 2021). In this context, UBI can also be considered not as the pure solution to poverty from a long-term perspective but as a complementation with other conditional financial support programmes (Ghatak & Maniquet, 2019, p. 926).

Therefore, this chapter aims to discuss the idea of the introduction of the UBI in the post-COVID time. It addresses the question of how UBI can become a tool in reducing the negative aspects of labour market technological changes, which have accelerated during the COVID-19 pandemic. The need for security, as well as economic and social shortcomings, can be treated as preconditions (premises) for the introduction of a basic income. More specifically, the chapter will focus

DOI: 10.4324/9781003326779-13

on UBI in the context of growing flexibility of working relationships, decreasing social security, the need for quick skill adaptation to the new digital environment, remote working development, and work-life balance challenges.

The literature on UBI is majorly related to different variants on UBI realisation in economic structures as well as general political and economic challenges concerning more broadly the use of this tool. Currently, studies on the connection between UBI, labour markets, and the relation to COVID-19 and its impacts on working environments are rarely developed in the literature. In this chapter, these connections should be discovered to gain new insights regarding UBI as a policy tool in the post-COVID time. The chapter reveals findings that COVID-caused elements might be a nutrient medium for UBI. On the one hand, the pandemic exacerbated existing problems and on the other hand – the crisis drew attention to the problems already known but discussed on the border of the mainstream. The COVID time was also an extraordinary period of testing solutions to social problems.

The remainder of this chapter is organised as follows. First, the roots of the UBI concept will be depicted. Then, the next section presents the consequences of the COVID-19 pandemic for the changing working environment. Subsequently, there is a discussion of the potential of the UBI concept as a policy tool for the future of work in post-pandemic time. The last section concludes.

Roots of the unconditional basic income

UBI is a concept and abbreviation that is often mentioned in connection with the more general idea of basic income. Different definitions provide some characteristics that enhance the general understanding of the concept.

For instance, Straubhaar (2018, p. 6) linked the definition of UBI to the Basic Income Earth Network [BIEN] (BIEN, 2020b). Therein, five characteristics are used to describe basic income: (1) periodic payment, (2) payment of money, (3) unconditionality, (4) paid to individuals, and (5) universal payments, without a means test or a link to work. Osterkamp (2016, p. 26) interprets UBI as a state-granted security allowing every citizen a minimum existence income without testing work willingness or ability. Blaschke (2005, p. 1) defines basic income as a state income for individuals which is guaranteed to all people, considering the level of subsistence to prevent poverty and allow people to participate in social life without means testing regarding income, assets, and work obligations. Lewis et al. (2005, p. 587) name the key characteristic of a Basic Income Guarantee [BIG] to understand that the lowest possible income in economies must not necessarily be zero. The German basic income network 'Netzwerk Grundeinkommen' describes basic income as poverty prevention and increasing freedom opportunity (Netzwerk Grundeinkommen, 2020).

Van Parijs & Vanderborght (2019, pp. 8–9, 12), however, address a characteristic that could remain as a condition in UBI. Thus, they address the need for UBI recipients to belong to a defined society, meaning that recipients must be fiscal members of a state. This is more relevant than mere residence or citizenship. A further distinction was made between UBI and minimum income. In this context, UBI is more connected to public assistance. The authors summarise unconditionality by stating that (1) payments are made individually, (2) these payments are characterised by universality, and (3) these payments are made without obligations.

When it comes to concrete features, Standing (2017, pp. 18–19) discovers distinctions between the terms. 'Basic income', in his view, is mostly used to summarise the topic in a simplified way. Distinctions need to be made with the terms 'minimum income' as well as 'minimum wage'. Geographically, Standing considers the term 'Universal Basic Income' as more native to North America and Europe and aimed at equal payment, whereas the term 'Unconditional Basic Income' tends to focus on unconditionality.

Accordingly, basic income terms were analysed regarding the frequency of citation. As a result, 'universal basic income' was the major term in the US media since 2015. 'Guaranteed income' was frequently used as well. In the context of US presidential elections, even the term 'freedom dividend' became relevant regarding the candidate Andrew Yang. In contrast to Standing, they state that the term 'unconditional basic income' can be interpreted as a more European term, which is especially common in Germany (Gonzalez & Bidadanure, 2020, pp. 5–6).

Basic income and its developments illuminate the fact that besides current developments the idea is not an invention of the 21st century. Actually, the origins can be found several centuries ago. In principle, the developments can be explored in connection to the labour market. The historical evolution of UBI shows different milestones, which can be perceived as important evolutional steps until the current stage, discussed in the context of COVID-19. Table 10.1 depicts the major developments to be considered in the context of UBI starting in the 16th century. Referring to the aim of the chapter, the table also provides links to the labour market.

It becomes obvious, when interpreting these views, that constant elements of UBI debates have been technological unemployment, focus on non-economic activities, and reduction of working hours. Just as in the past, today's technological developments (connected with digitalisation and AI) are important drivers and a major unknown regarding the prediction of future working conditions. Keynes' context is comparable to the current UBI environment and potential triggers. Technological unemployment is generally defined as a type of unemployment that arises causally from new technological advances. This can make certain jobs or use of workers redundant (Hashimzade et al., 2017, p. 518). In general, technology can lead to wealth increase, but this does not necessarily mean that it can automatically compensate for the trend of the gap between rich and poor (Brynjolfsson & McAfee, 2019, p. 207). The topic of the digital influence on work was further explored by Frey and Osborne (2013, pp. 37–38; 44). They concluded that 47% of employment in the United States is at high risk of being eliminated or substituted by automation and computer technology during a potential duration of one to two decades. Examples of high-risk jobs are those in the transport and logistics sector, but also administrative jobs.

TABLE 10.1 Historical views on UBI and its links with labour market

Year	*Owner*	*Labour market links*	*Major content*	*References*
1516	Thomas More	Minimum income as a form of security besides employment	Idea of securing livelihood security by minimum income scheme	BIEN (2020a), More (2020, p. 54; pp. 62–77), Blaschke (2015, p. 7)
1797	Thomas Paine	Compensative payment reflects another form of potential existence security	Compensation based on natural law for the loss of natural inheritance	Basic Income Action (2020), Blaschke (2015, pp. 20–22), Paine (2020, p. 78; pp. 83–85)
Approximately 19th century	Joseph Charlier	Guaranteed minimum income to provide for a living apart from labour	Minimum income based on the aim to nationalise land and natural resources	BIEN (2020a), Blaschke (2015, pp. 40–42), Vanderborght & Van Parijs (2005, p. 25), Charlier (2020, p. 141, 151)
Approximately 19th century	Marxian school	Theory of alienation and increasing freedom outside of work	Theory of alienation and links to UBI – Increasing wages not to be interpreted as sustainable improvement	Marx (2017, pp. 50–59, 86)
Approximately 20th century	Keynesian economics	Technological unemployment and a surplus resulting from labour resource saving and redirection of labour	Technological unemployment and links to UBI – Non-economic activities could become more relevant; 15-hour work week might follow from work shifts	Keynes (2020, pp. 246–251)

Source: Own elaboration based on the references mentioned in Table 10.1.

Neoclassical economics delivers another potential consideration.[1] In the neoclassical context, the concept of *homo oeconomicus* is a key element (Söllner, 2012, p. 43). The characteristics of *homo oeconomicus* relate to rational action on markets, considering self-interests, benefit maximisation, complete information, and fixed preferences (Franz, 2004, p. 4). For this reason, the neoclassical view also can be regarded in relation to UBI. In general, the purpose of achieving the optimal outcome based on one's own preferences (Reiß, 2007, p. 420) should meet the advantages of UBI. This would mean, assuming that a *homo oeconomicus* would not choose to work and thereby gain the maximum benefit, UBI could be supportive. Work would not be a necessary condition to receive the full UBI amount. Consequently, a certain amount of money could be achieved with negligible effort.

Apart from theoretical considerations, there have also been some empirical approaches to the issue. Recent empiric UBI developments in practice can be observed by a European initiative initiating a basic income referendum in Switzerland, starting in 2006 (Grundeinkommen, n.d.). In 2016, the referendum ended up being rejected by Swiss voters. One crucial point was the question of realistic finance opportunities for the estimated total amount of approximately CHF 208bn (Bundesamt für Sozialversicherungen [BSV], 2016, p. 2; Bundeskanzlei [BK], 2021; Bundesrat, 2014, p. 6562; ZEIT ONLINE, 2016). This view was confirmed by the Swiss institute 'economiesuisse', which remarks a massive economic disadvantage (economiesuisse, 2012, p. 1). According to De Wispelaere (2016, p. 617) the Swiss initiative and the connected referendum can be interpreted as a 'victory' for increasing basic income attention.

Another European example was the Finnish basic income experiment. Basic income support in Finland received a 69% support rate from those polled in a 2015 survey. The corresponding amount was EUR 1,000 as a median, which was approximately 1.4 times above the minimum Finnish pension amount (Kela, 2016, p. 10). From 2017 until the end of 2018, the experiment was conducted for a group of unemployed people receiving social benefits or subsidies. A monthly payment was provided to the target group without further means testing (Haagh & Rohregger, 2019, p. 45). The randomised controlled trial included a target group of 2,000 unemployed people (Gentilini et al., 2020b, p. 23). The Finnish Social Security Department, provided EUR 560 per month for unemployed citizens between 25 and 58 years. This payment should be a replacement for other existing social benefits with an annual total budget of EUR 20m (Gentilini et al., 2020a, p. 238).

Other empiric developments can be observed in Germany. The initiative 'Mein Grundeinkommen' launched a pilot project in 2020. The objective has been to test basic income and potential effects on an empirical basis (Pilotprojekt Grundeinkommen, 2020).

Historical roots and current developments, theories and empiricism, various terms, and definitions – all of them indicate differences between individual basic income ideas and streams. In the context of a UBI implementation, political and economic influences are relevant, so that new definitions and interpretations beyond the already known ones are also conceivable. The cases of recent developments in Switzerland, Finland, and Germany show the relevance of the topic. These premises were however linked to circumstances (technological changes, the situation in the labour markets, etc.) before a global pandemic. It raises the question of what the interactions of a UBI might look like in a post-pandemic working environment and what premises and triggers for UBI might occur in the light of the COVID-19 pandemic.

The COVID-19 pandemic consequences for the changing working environment

The COVID-19 pandemic revealed several impacts in different areas. It affected not only health-related issues but also economic, political, social, and cultural spheres of human life including working conditions and workplace organisation.

After the COVID-19 pandemic hit the labour market, the unemployment rate increased to 8.8% in April 2020 in OECD countries. Consequently, for 2020, GDP declined by 4.9% in the OECD area, which was the largest fall ever recorded (since 1962). Almost all countries were confronted with falls in GDP in 2020. Among the Major Seven economies, GDP declines ranged from 3.5% in the United States to 9.9% in the United Kingdom (OECD, 2021).

Besides the economic shocks, there was also an important structural change in many sectors. While unemployment raised in the tourism and culture industry, e-commerce has noted significant growth.

The COVID-19 pandemic has also substantially disrupted the workplace and accelerated technological changes. The extensive use of information technologies including cloud computing, video conferencing, collaboration platforms, and broadband Internet ushered development of remote work on a broad scale (Nagel, 2020, pp. 871–872). Next to technological transformations, the new skill transformation of the workforce was needed. Virtual work might require soft skills like adaptability, creativity, or empathy (Bennett & McWhorter, 2021, p. 8). Next to new jobs created by digital technologies, in many other professions, the jobs have become riskier, especially those requiring a physical presence. These changes and tensions between those who can telework and those who cannot enforce economic and social problems (Schilirò, 2021). Consequently, there is growing labour market polarisation between groups and regions with low-skilled, low-wage labour and higher risk of unemployment, and groups and regions with high-skilled, high-wage labour and low risk of unemployment. Moreover, the mass introduction of remote work leads to changing behaviour of employers and employees. A high level of work strain, isolationism, technostress, or fears regarding the disease reveals the threat of mental issues (Giorgi et al., 2020, p. 17) which can impact the

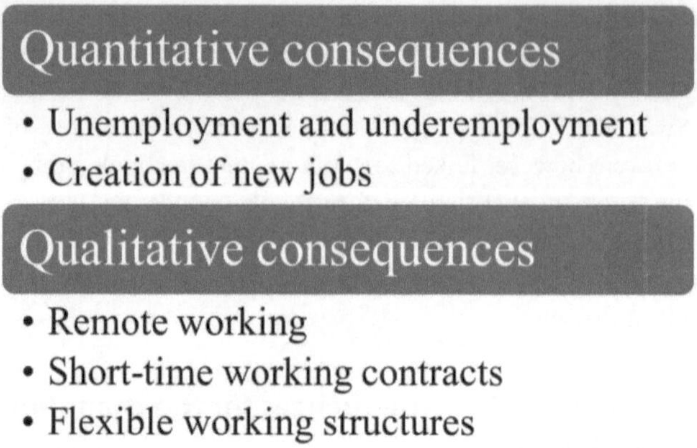

FIGURE 10.1 Pandemic consequences on the working environment

Source: Own elaboration.

productivity and performance of firms and in consequence income and standard of living of employees (Figure 10.1).

UBI as a potential policy tool for insecurity of changing digital labour market

Given the assumption that UBI might be embedded in a post-COVID-19 working environment, certain determinants, and factors favourable should be considered. Several aspects can be derived from the literature and observation of practice (pilot programmes in various countries) to find intersections to a future UBI introduction.

Growing flexibility in working relationships

The new flexibility of labour markets, which appears during the pandemic might be favourable for employers but difficult for workers in precarious jobs (Ståhl & MacEachen, 2021, p. 4). Johnson and Roberto (2020, p. 234) state that a UBI programme can be regarded as a good option for financial relief after COVID-19, especially in the context of precarious employment contracts.

Generally, UBI offers security to people who would generally not be eligible for other social benefits due to their weak employment status. It is estimated that this policy tool would create more independence from the requirements for social welfare measures (Ståhl & MacEachen, 2021, p. 4).

An in-depth discussion of a temporary or permanent introduction of UBI in the response to COVID-19 and related lockdowns was primary related to poverty and inequalities fight (Green et al., 2020, pp. 1–3). Segal et al. (2021, p. 399) point out, however, some issues related to a Canadian UBI introduction. Minimising labour resources through UBI can become problematic. Many small entrepreneurs rely on the availability of low-income or part-time employment contracts. Despite the difficulty regarding the moral issue of such employment contracts, (small) entrepreneurs may face resource scarcity through UBI. UBI could provide more security for some people, but at the same time, it may open doors to new problems, such as decreasing labour market resources.

The pandemic also shed light on the potential of growing flexibility in working relationships. Remote working impacts labour market structures in numerous ways and reveals a new mechanism. It allows people to work from self-selected places anytime. For local-acting employers, it can be interpreted as a new opportunity to access employees even if they are not located in the area of the company or living far from this place. It allows recruiting processes of suitable skilled workers without restrictions regarding the place of living. As a consequence, remote working may cause a decrease of regional development inequalities and an open access to highly skilled workers worldwide. Thus, some forms of exclusion with reference to individual jobs could be eliminated. Simultaneously, the growing global competitiveness might lead to job losses for people with lower qualifications.

Ensuring of social security

Another consequence of COVID-19 has been increasing costs, especially social costs in terms of safeguarding people and businesses. Lockdowns and business restrictions led to some people's social livelihood security being threatened.

Downturns in economic sectors were not equal – their scale and consequences in some of them were significantly higher. In May 2020, the Association of German Chambers of Industry and Commerce [DIHK] reported a sharp drop in revenues in the travel industry, hospitality sector, and in industry (DIHK, 2020, pp. 4–5). Simultaneously, a temporary increase in the resulting unemployment ('corona effect') of up to 638,000 additional unemployed was recorded in Germany (Bundesagentur für Arbeit, 2021, p. 8).

Thus, economic challenges for people caused by COVID have also been present in wealthy nations. However, based on economic strength, there is a better chance of being able to finance a potential UBI. This aspect could play a crucial role in the post-COVID era to support people with livelihood-related issues.

Indeed, measures such as lockdowns cannot be regarded as a permanent solution because of the economic costs, but can only help contain the further spread of the disease in the short term (Susskind & Vines, 2020, pp. S2–S3). Comparable conclusions were investigated in the cost-benefit analysis of Rowthorn and Maciejowski (2020, p. 14). After reaching a potential reduction of spread, it might be a mistake at high costs to keep social distancing measures.

Under such circumstances, UBI would provide more stability, especially for the economic sectors affected by a pandemic. Nevertheless, a general UBI problem is associated with estimating total costs in economic systems. One approach is to multiply expected costs per UBI recipient by the number of inhabitants in a geographical area. Afterward, some costs should be reduced, as tax-based financing would have to be considered a pay-in effect via tax charges and refinancing (Patel & Kariel, 2021, p. 1). In any case, the uncertainty of estimated values in the context of financing entails risks. Especially in times of a pandemic, high costs can become problematic for already fragile economic structures. On top, the financing effect through taxes by employees would also further complicate the financing problem in difficult times.

An important benefit of an UBI implementation in a COVID-19 situation is connected to providing financial security and stability to people and reduction of job dependencies as there will be general security for essential needs like food or housing costs. UBI security enables to reduce of stress for individuals regarding irregular income. Especially in times of a pandemic with temporary economic difficulties, a basic income would result in necessary security in terms of existence (Ståhl & MacEachen, 2021, pp. 4, 6). During the pandemic, Spain aimed to test UBI-comparable alternatives in response to developments in the labour market as well as associated consequences in terms of the poverty (Fischer, 2020, p. 12; Rincon, 2020).

Wealthier nations, like the US or some European countries, might be able to afford implementation of UBI. On the one hand, job losses or major illness can be linked to a financial collapse for people or families (Johnson & Roberto, 2020, pp. 232, 234). On the other hand, states with economic strength would be able to counteract such issues with suitable social support, like UBI for instance. The pandemic crisis revealed the chance for political discussions and made basic income a political option and supporting element in order to help people get through the crisis (Green et al., 2020, p. 11).

Educational needs and skills shifts

Since the onset of the COVID-19 pandemic, people have faced job loss or transition from low-skilled working requirements to workplaces with IT changes and more automated structures. Such developments might go hand in hand with the security of a regular basic income. Then, trainings or educational needs might be realised in a better way (Johnson & Roberto, 2020, p. 234). The increase of online seminars in 2021 can be interpreted as growth in educational interest in pandemic times (Statista, 2021).

UBI may provide the possibility of more training and personal development so that people can discover opportunities for themselves. The pandemic may raise awareness of training, which means that non-work-related income streams can be supportive in initiating desired training.

During the pandemic, it became visible that remote working applicability in particular was accompanied by the fact that these jobs were mostly office-based and required not only digital infrastructure but also skilled workers who could perform tasks autonomously (Eurofound, 2021, p. 11). Thus, the European Economic and Social Committee [EESC] (2021, p. 34) discovered that the importance of countries' ability to work remotely in response to the COVID-19 development depends on the level of digital skills and the related level of digitalisation before the crisis. The study indicated that the digital skills of employees are crucial for the response to COVID-19 measures and that an above-average level of digital skills can increase the security towards technological developments and decisions at the national level.

Green et al. (2020, p. 10) show that a general effect of basic income could be the importance of such a payment on the opportunity for education and training subject to personal interest. Similarly, other activities independent of paid employment may rise in importance, such as volunteering, especially in times of a pandemic.

Remote working development

The pandemic and social distancing measures came together with the thought of teleworking potential. The goal was to prevent further spread of the disease by reduction of social contacts and thus to be able to work from home when possible (Eurofound, 2021, p. 11).

The points made about more remote working in the wake of the pandemic indicate that these developments have the potential for further action in a post-COVID era. In the case of UBI, this could mean that people who plan to continue in paid employment could work remotely more often if their job profile allows it.

In July 2020, approximately 50% of the EU workforce moved work from working spaces other than in physical offices (Eurofound, 2021, p. 1). This shift is to be considered an impact of COVID-19 in the working environment. Before the COVID-19 pandemic began, many employees had not worked remotely on a regular basis. With regard to a GitLab survey from 2020, 56% of the people answered that their remote working duration is less than a year. Due to COVID-19, this development can be interpreted as an indicator resulting from the pandemic situation. Most of the respondents said that remote work is their preference while only a minority indicated that they want to go back to the office (GitLab, n.d., p. 6). In another survey of CFOs and financial leaders, conducted by Gartner, Inc., from 2020 the result was that overall, 74% of companies related to the study plan to implement an intensified remote working structure in post-COVID-19 times instead of an on-site workforce. This might be connected to the recognition of wider possibilities resulting from technological and societal evolutions, that make remote work possible for more positions (Gartner, 2020). According to Eurofound (2020, p. 1), digitalised tasks can be interpreted as less threatened by pandemic developments than low-skilled tasks which are often connected to a lower level of ability to work remotely.

From an economic perspective, a post-COVID-19 increase in remote work will be connected to a decrease in business trips, a reduction of working space requirements (e.g., fewer rent payments if possible), more efficiency due to more concentration and focus as well as a potential decrease of illness absences (EY, 2020). This would mean lower expenses for companies and advantages for employees. Nevertheless, the potential of remote work depends on job activity. Especially business services and financial services might have a huge potential for increased remote work. In the United Kingdom, for instance, the potential is high due to the pronounced service sector. In total, an elaboration from McKinsey came to the conclusion that many advanced economies can have a potential of 28–30% of remote work (Lund et al., 2020).

Changing working environments will shift employees from physical organisational spaces into remote working spaces (Carnevale & Hatak, 2020, p. 183). From a working environment perspective, organisations are in the position to make HR-related topics more virtual, like trainings or recruiting tasks. It becomes more important to simplify the connection between working requirements and family life with regard to managing both social needs (Donthu & Gustafsson, 2020, p. 286). Likewise, the state could take its role in the distribution of wealth in the context of social and political processes and provide UBI as a response to the pandemic and take on a steering role of this concept (Johnson & Roberto, 2020, p. 233).

The context of remote work does not only provide a new home workplace. Rather, it might lead to further issues to be managed by employees from home. In such an environment, UBI could provide securing salaries to allow people to focus more on family and social activities in a new working environment. Thus, more closeness to private life is given. This can also initiate a creative process to encourage personal development in both, business and private life. It can be interpreted as a process that did not allow such freedom under former physical office routines and can be supported by the introduction of UBI.

Work-life balance challenges

The COVID-19 pandemic is also linked to changes in the working environment and employees habits. Where people have to work from home, the issue of balancing work and private life arises. This can create challenges that have a lasting impact on the work environment even in post-pandemic times. Considering this problem with HR-related challenges in pandemic times listed by Carnevale and Hatak (2020, pp. 184–186), the low UBI experience might be combined with also untested changes in the working environment.

With an increase in virtual meetings and working during the pandemic, now it just occurs to what extent these conditions will remain or even expand after the pandemic ends. UBI could be easily confronted with these conditions. Accordingly, the security of UBI could go hand in hand with the need to have more freedom to engage socially and thus counteract mere virtual existence. The change from physical interactions to virtual activities is associated with adaptation errors and negative effects on the well-being of employees, but also productivity losses for companies. In conclusion, this allows the interpretation of challenges in both new experimental fields – UBI and new working environments – that have been intensified by the pandemic.

Besides missing traditional in-person approaches leading to virtual recruitments, a new type of interconnection between work, family, and life occurs. Remote working has to be managed with childcare issues and health-related topics. Former

TABLE 10.2 Areas of COVID-19-related changes to be resolved by UBI application with respect to working condition aspects

Affected areas of change caused by COVID	*Response of UBI regarding COVID-affected changes*
Growing flexibility in working relationships	Uncertainties resulting from limited employment contracts or low-paid jobs persist during the COVID-19 pandemic. UBI addresses this problem with the foundation of livelihood security.
Ensuring social security	Additional social expenditures were caused by the pandemic. Instead of ad-hoc costs, UBI can provide lasting stability that would also have had calculable costs under COVID-19.
Educational needs and skill shifts	UBI can be regarded as a supportive element to assist people to fulfil their educational plans without dependence of an employment.
Remote working development	Changes from the pandemic revealed digital weaknesses regarding remote work. Developments in digital infrastructures can be the fundament for new (remote) working environments supported by UBI payments.
Work-life balance challenges	Increase of digitalised work in combination with UBI can help to intensify social relations and cultural actions. Security of UBI, a less stressful digital working environment and income via UBI will support a positive work-life balance.

Source: Own elaboration based on the references mentioned in the text.

boundaries might shift or be hard to maintain during pandemic times (Carnevale & Hatak, 2020, pp. 184–185; Giurge & Bohns, 2020).

The fast introduction of remote working structures revealed challenges regarding work obligations and private life. In the case of prepared proceedings, the connection between work and life does not mean a loss of productivity. An important factor might be the necessity of managing the well-being of employees (EY, 2020). Moreover, the working culture perspective indicates that working from home could be associated with positive effects. It is possible to increase the satisfaction and commitment of people working remotely from home. Likewise, the mere possibility of working from home already provided positive effects and can strengthen the relationship of trust between employers and employees (WSI, 2020, p. 10). Even if this topic of virtual working and its influences was already researched sometime before the pandemic (Hill et al., 1998, p. 667).

UBI might reveal positive effects on work-life balances. A digital working environment may provide for a less stressful daily routine, without commuting between work and home and the requirement of physical office presence. Consequently, people might become aware of more involvement in social relations and related cultural actions. UBI delivers income security on a regular basis like paid work.

However, it would affect the mindset of people knowing that they can manage work and life without having to commit to paid work but being free to do so. There could also arise the problem of incentives in thinking about free time and aspirations simultaneously.

Regarding the aspects mentioned above, Table 10.2 represents the justification of UBI introduction, regarding the five abovementioned areas in a post-COVID world. They help in understanding the impact which a detailed UBI framework could have, constituting a response to recent changes.

One might argue that COVID-19 justified the necessity of UBI introduction. Yet, further research, political debates, and initiative groups are important instruments to foster movement (and support) for such an introduction. The mere debate and exchange of thoughts and ideas on the issue can already achieve more than hiding from the potential problem areas, such as funding, the group of recipients, or the UBI amount. Therefore, these problems should not be treated as an excuse and as reasons for not reenforcing the discussion on the aforementioned UBI problem areas.

Conclusions

There are various arguments for and against UBI implementation in a post-pandemic environment. Generally, these pros and cons of UBI are connected to the basic idea of UBI: the general security of a regular income and the decoupling of paid work based on employment contracts and secured income in a new digital world.

The goal of this chapter was to discuss the idea of the introduction of the UBI in the post-COVID time in the context of growing flexibility of working relationships, decreasing social security, the need for quick skill adaptation to the digital environment, remote working development, and work-life balance challenges.

The ongoing changes in labour markets that have accelerated due to COVID-19 could be seen as supportive elements for the UBI introduction. In the other words, the COVID-caused elements might be a nutrient medium for UBI. As elaborated, it became apparent that overarching labour market-related macro effects relate to the supply of work and the demanded flexibility for employees leading to additional insecurities for them. Moreover, the macro effect of social spending is connected to short-term decisions regarding labour market changes during the pandemic. From a micro perspective, the working environment, in particular, was characterised by the possibility of personal development opportunities via digital channels during the pandemic. Besides that, the direct daily working environment was shaped by new digital working processes and new interconnections between work and private life challenge to be managed simultaneously during the pandemic.

Still, a general problem of UBI is a small number of trials and experiments. Consequently, further extensive trials, experiments, and empiric research would bring new knowledge to the surface, so that the conclusions derived can enable further planning for successful implementation options of UBI in a post-COVID-19 working environment. This elaboration shows the difficulties to be optimistic about such an implementation. Although there is a long history of the basic income idea, implementation schedules are still in the early stages. The main challenges before implementation are that a precise concept, including UBI amount and financing and the group of recipients, have to be defined. Furthermore, it can be assumed that further experiments and pilot projects will be beneficial to gather new experiences and insights on UBI before considering the actual implementation.

Existing problems became more visible in the course of the pandemic. This period uncovered that, challenges regarding the working environment might further exist or even accelerate. UBI can represent the response to these changes in working environments, regardless of whether these changes will remain or disappear in the post-pandemic era. UBI might be a serious option depending on specific influencing factors in the future to counteract unintended consequences resulting from the pandemic and to contribute to sustainable economies through the intervention of the state. As a result, a more detailed UBI concept could emerge with the opportunity to further research on benefits and problems.

Acknowledgements

The author would like to thank Routledge publishing house, Poznań University of Economics and Business, and in particular dr hab. Beata Woźniak-Jęchorek, Prof. UEP and the author's PhD supervisor dr hab. Paweł Marszałek, Prof. UEP for their steady support in this research conduction.

Note

1 The term 'neoclassical' is used as a leading economic mainstream view influenced by perspectives on debates on capital, growth, and distribution (Reiß, 2007, p. 420).

References

Acemoglu, D., & Autor, D. (2011). *Chapter 12 – skills, tasks and technologies: Implications for employment and earnings* (D. Card & O. Ashenfelter, Eds.; Vol. 4, pp. 1043–1171). Elsevier. https://doi.org/10.1016/S0169-7218(11)02410-5

Basic Income Action. (2020). *What is origin of this idea, the history of basic income?* www.basicincomeaction.org/what_is_origin_of_this_idea_the_history_of_basic_income

Bennett, E. E., & McWhorter, R. R. (2021). Virtual HRD's role in crisis and the post Covid-19 professional lifeworld: Accelerating skills for digital transformation. *Advances in Developing Human Resources, 23*(1), 5–25. https://doi.org/10.1177/1523422320973288

BIEN. (2020a). *A history*. https://basicincome.org/history/

BIEN. (2020b). *About basic income*. https://basicincome.org/about-basic-income/

Blaschke, R. (2005). *Warum ein Grundeinkommen? Zwölf Argumente und eine Ergänzung*. https://www.archiv-grundeinkommen.de/blaschke/warum-ein-grundeinkommen.pdf

Blaschke, R. (2015). *Ein historischer Abriss über Vorschläge und Ideen zum Grundeinkommen*. www.grundeinkommen.de/wp-content/uploads/2016/01/GEschichte.pdf

Brynjolfsson, E., & McAfee, A. (2019). *The second machine age: Wie die nächste digitale Revolution unser aller Leben verändern wird* (2nd ed.). Plassen Verlag.

Bundesagentur für Arbeit. (2021). *Auswirkungen der Corona-Krise auf den Arbeits- und Ausbildungsmarkt.* https://statistik.arbeitsagentur.de/Statistikdaten/Detail/202105/arbeitsmarktberichte/am-kompakt-corona/am-kompakt-corona-d-0-202105-pdf?__blob=publicationFile

Bundesamt für Sozialversicherungen [BSV]. (2016). *Bedingungsloses Grundeinkommen: Kosten und Finanzierung.* https://www.bsv.admin.ch/bsv/de/home/sozialpolitische-themen/soziale-absicherung/revenu-de-base-inconditionnel.html

Bundeskanzlei [BK]. (2021). *Vorlage Nr. 601 Übersicht.* www.bk.admin.ch/ch/d/pore/va/20160605/det601.html

Bundesrat. (2014). *Botschaft zur Volksinitiative «Für ein bedingungsloses Grundeinkommen».* https://www.admin.ch/opc/de/federal-gazette/2014/6551.pdf

Carnevale, J. B., & Hatak, I. (2020, May). Employee adjustment and well-being in the era of COVID-19: Implications for human resource management. *Journal of Business Research, 116*, 183–187. https://doi.org/10.1016/j.jbusres.2020.05.037

Charlier, J. (2020). Lösung des Sozialproblems oder Humanitäre Verfassung. In P. Kovce & B. P. Priddat (Eds.), *Bedingungsloses Grundeinkommen: Grundlagentexte* (2nd ed., pp. 133–156). Suhrkamp Verlag.

De Wispelaere, J. (2016). Basic income in our time: Improving political prospects through policy learning? *Journal of Social Policy, 45*(4), 617–634. https://doi.org/10.1017/S0047279416000039

DIHK. (2020). *Auswirkungen von COVID-19 auf die deutsche Wirtschaft – 3. DIHK-Blitzumfrage Mai 2020.* www.dihk.de/resource/blob/23678/8c0d2a3825d536b5ebc3a71b3caa2cf2/blitzumfrage-corona-nr-3-data.pdf

Donthu, N., & Gustafsson, A. (2020, June). Effects of COVID-19 on business and research. *Journal of Business Research, 117*, 284–289. https://doi.org/10.1016/j.jbusres.2020.06.008

economiesuisse. (2012). Bedingungsloses Grundeinkommen? – Leider nein. *Dossierpolitik, 21*, 1–13. www.economiesuisse.ch/sites/default/files/dossier_pdf/dp21_grundeinkommen_print.pdf

Eurofound. (2020). *COVID-19: Policy responses across Europe.* https://www.eurofound.europa.eu/sites/default/files/ef_publication/field_ef_document/ef20064en.pdf

Eurofound. (2021). *COVID-19: Implications for employment and working life.* https://www.eurofound.europa.eu/sites/default/files/ef_publication/field_ef_document/ef20050en.pdf

European Economic and Social Committee [EESC]. (2021). *COVID-19: Virtual free movement of workers.* www.eesc.europa.eu/sites/default/files/files/qe-05-21-008-en-n.pdf

EY. (2020). *Why remote working will be the new normal, even after COVID-19.* www.ey.com/en_be/covid-19/why-remote-working-will-be-the-new-normal-even-after-covid-19

Fischer, Y. (2020). Basic income, labour automation and migration – An approach from a republican perspective. *Basic Income Studies, 15*(2), 1–35. https://doi.org/10.1515/bis-2020-0027

Franz, S. (2004). Grundlagen des ökonomischen Ansatzes: Das Erklärungskonzept des Homo Oeconomicus. In *International Economics.* www.uni-potsdam.de/fileadmin/projects/prof-fuhrmann-vwl/Publikationen/Grundlagen_des_ökonomischen_Ansatzes_Das_Erklärungskonzept_des_Homo_Oeconomicus.pdf

Frey, C. B., & Osborne, M. A. (2013). The future of employment: How susceptible are jobs to computerisation? *Technological Forecasting and Social Change*, 1–72. www.oxfordmartin.ox.ac.uk/downloads/academic/The_Future_of_Employment.pdf

Gartner. (2020). *Gartner CFO survey reveals 74% intend to shift some employees to remote work permanently*. www.gartner.com/en/newsroom/press-releases/2020-04-03-gartner-cfo-surey-reveals-74-percent-of-organizations-to-shift-some-employees-to-remote-work-permanently2

Gentilini, U., Grosh, M., Rigolini, J., & Yemtsov, R. (2020a). Appendixes. In U. Gentilini, M. Grosh, J. Rigolini, & R. Yemtsov (Eds.), *Exploring universal basic income : A guide to navigating concepts, evidence, and practices* (1st ed., pp. 237–312). The World Bank Group. https://doi.org/10.1596/978-1-4648-1458-7_ov

Gentilini, U., Grosh, M., & Yemtsov, R. (2020b). Chapter 1. The idea of universal basic income. In U. Gentilini, M. Grosh, J. Rigolini, & R. Yemtsov (Eds.), *Exploring universal basic income: A guide to navigating concepts, evidence, and practices* (1st ed., pp. 17–72). The World Bank Group. https://doi.org/10.1596/978-1-4648-1458-7_ov

Ghatak, M., & Maniquet, F. (2019). Universal basic income: Some theoretical aspects. *Annual Review of Economics, 11*, 895–928. https://doi.org/10.1146/annurev-economics-080218-030220

Giorgi, G., Lecca, L. I., Alessio, F., Finstad, G. L., Bondanini, G., Lulli, L. G., Arcangeli, G., & Mucci, N. (2020). COVID-19-related mental health effects in the workplace: A narrative review. *International Journal of Environmental Research and Public Health, 17*(7857), 1–22. https://doi.org/10.3390/ijerph17217857

GitLab. (n.d.). *Out of the office – How the world adapted to working remotely in 2020*. https://about.gitlab.com/resources/downloads/gitlab-out-of-the-office-2021.pdf%0A

Giurge, L. M., & Bohns, V. K. (2020). *3 tips to avoid WFH Burnout*. Harvard Business Review. https://hbr.org/2020/04/3-tips-to-avoid-wfh-burnout

Gonzalez, S. B., & Bidadanure, J. (2020). *Universal basic income: What's in a name?* https://basicincome.stanford.edu/uploads/whats-in-a-name-white-paper__final.pdf

Goos, M., Manning, A., & Salomons, A. (2014). Explaining job polarization: Routine-biased technological change and offshoring. *American Economic Review, 104*(8), 2509–2526. https://doi.org/10.1257/aer.104.8.2509

Green, D., Kesselman, J. R., & Tedds, L. (2020, May). Considerations for basic income as a COVID-19 response. *The School of Public Policy Publications, 13*(11), 1–15. http://dx.doi.org/10.11575/sppp.v13i0.70353

Grundeinkommen. (n.d.). *Über uns*. Retrieved December 28, 2020, from www.grundeinkommen.ch/uber-uns/

Haagh, L., & Rohregger, B. (2019). *Universal basic income policies and their potential for addressing health inequities*. www.euro.who.int/__data/assets/pdf_file/0008/404387/20190606-h1015-ubi-policies-en.pdf?ua=1

Handelsblatt. (2021). *Die Vor- und Nachteile des bedingungslosen Grundeinkommens*. www.handelsblatt.com/finanzen/steuern-recht/steuern/g . . . mmens/25623926.html?ticket=ST-754865-eXvZOOqI7DHSfBw7hywA-ap4

Hashimzade, N., Black, J., & Myles, G. D. (2017). *A dictionary of economics* (5th ed.). Oxford University Press.

Hill, E. J., Miller, B. C., Weiner, S. P., & Colihan, J. (1998). Influences of the virtual office on aspects of work and work/life balance. *Personnel Psychology, 51*(3), 667–673. https://doi.org/10.1111/j.1744-6570.1998.tb00256.x

Johnson, A. F., & Roberto, K. J. (2020). The COVID-19 pandemic: Time for a universal basic income? *Public Administration and Development, 40*(4), 232–235. https://doi.org/10.1002/pad.1891

Kela. (2016). *From idea to experiment – Report on universal basic income experiment in Finland. (Working Papers 106)*. http://hdl.handle.net/10138/167728

Keynes, J. M. (2020). Wirtschaftliche Möglichkeiten für unsere Enkelkinder. In P. Kovce & B. P. Priddat (Eds.), *Bedingungsloses Grundeinkommen: Grundlagentexte* (2nd ed., pp. 246–257). Suhrkamp Verlag.

Lewis, M., Pressman, S., & Widerquist, K. (2005). The basic income guarantee and social economics. *Review of Social Economy, 63*(4), 587–593. https://doi.org/10.1080/00346760500364536

Lund, S., Madgavkar, A., Manyika, J., & Smit, S. (2020). *What's next for remote work: An analysis of 2,000 tasks, 800 jobs, and nine countries*. www.mckinsey.com/featured-insights/future-of-work/whats-next-for-remote-work-an-analysis-of-2000-tasks-800-jobs-and-nine-countries#

Marx, K. (2017). *Ökonomisch-philosophische Manuskripte aus dem Jahre 1844* (4th ed.). Holzinger.

More, T. (2020). Utopia. In P. Kovce & B. P. Priddat (Eds.), *Bedingungsloses Grundeinkommen: Grundlagentexte* (2nd ed., pp. 54–77). Suhrkamp Verlag.

Nagel, L. (2020). The influence of the COVID-19 pandemic on the digital transformation of work. *International Journal of Sociology and Social Policy, 40*(9–10), 861–875. https://doi.org/10.1108/IJSSP-07-2020-0323

Netzwerk Grundeinkommen. (2020). *Die Idee*. https://www.grundeinkommen.de/grundeinkommen/idee

OECD. (2021). *OECD Employment Outlook 2021*. https://doi.org/10.1787/5a700c4b-en

Osterkamp, R. (2016). Fünf Streitfragen um das bedingungslose Grundeinkommen - unaufgeregt betrachtet. *Ifo Schnelldienst, 69*(21), 26–35. https://www.ifo.de/DocDL/sd-2016-21-osterkamp-bedingungsloses-grundeinkommen-2016-11-10.pdf

Paine, T. (2020). Agrarische Gerechtigkeit. In P. M. Kovce & B. P. Priddat (Eds.), *Bedingungsloses Grundeinkommen: Grundlagentexte* (2nd ed., pp. 78–98). Suhrkamp Verlag.

Patel, S. B., & Kariel, J. (2021). Universal basic income and COVID-19 pandemic. *The BMJ, 372*(n193), 1–2. https://doi.org/10.1136/bmj.n193

Pilotprojekt Grundeinkommen. (2020). *Über uns*. www.pilotprojekt-grundeinkommen.de/ueber-uns

Reiß, W. (2007). *Mikroökonomische Theorie: Historisch fundierte Einführung* (6th ed.). Oldenbourg Wissenschaftsverlag.

Rincon, L. (2020). *Living Minimum Income in Spain: Very far from a UBI*. https://basicincome.org/news/2020/06/living-minimum-income-in-spain-very-far-from-a-ubi/%0ABIEN

Rowthorn, R., & Maciejowski, J. (2020, July). A cost-benefit analysis of the COVID-19 disease. *Oxford Review of Economic Policy, 36*, S38–S55. https://doi.org/10.1093/oxrep/graa030

Schilirò, D. (2021). Digital transformation, COVID-19, and the future of work. *International Journal of Business Management and Economic Research (IJBMER), 12*(3), 1945–1952. https://mpra.ub.uni-muenchen.de/108817/

Schwab, K. (2016). Die Vierte Industrielle Revolution. *Handelsblatt*. www.handelsblatt.com/politik/international/davos-2016/davos-2016-die-vierte-industrielle-revolution/12836622.html

Segal, H., Banting, K., & Forget, E. (2021). The need for a federal basic income feature within any coherent post-COVID-19 economic recovery plan. *Facets, 6*(1), 394–402. https://doi.org/10.1139/facets-2021-0015

Söllner, F. (2012). *Die Geschichte des ökonomischen Denkens* (3rd ed.). Springer Verlag.

Ståhl, C., & MacEachen, E. (2021). Universal basic income as a policy response to COVID-19 and precarious employment: Potential impacts on rehabilitation and return-to-work.

Journal of Occupational Rehabilitation, 31(1), 3–6. https://doi.org/10.1007/s10926-020-09923-w

Standing, G. (2017). *Basic income: And how we can make it happen* (1st ed.). Penguin Random House.

Statista. (2021). *Häufiger ausgeübte Freizeitaktivitäten während der Corona-Pandemie 2021*. https://de.statista.com/statistik/daten/studie/1237737/umfrage/haeu ... te-freizeitaktivitaeten-waehrend-der-corona-pandemie/#professional

Straubhaar, T. (2018). Universal basic income – New answers to new questions for the German welfare state in the 21st century. *CESifo Forum, 19*(3), 3–9. http://hdl.handle.net/10419/186080

Susskind, D., & Vines, D. (2020). The economics of the COVID-19 pandemic: An assessment. *Oxford Review of Economic Policy, 36*(S1), S1–S13. https://doi.org/10.1093/oxrep/graa036

Van Parijs, P., & Vanderborght, Y. (2019). *Basic income: A radical proposal for a free society and a sane economy* (1st ed.). Harvard University Press.

Vanderborght, Y., & Van Parijs, P. (2005). *Ein Grundeinkommen für alle? Geschichte und Zukunft eines radikalen Vorschlags* (1st ed.). Campus Verlag.

Vermeulen, B., & Psenner, E. (2022). Exploiting the technology-driven structural shift to creative work in regional catching-up: Toward an institutional framework. *European Planning Studies, 0*(0), 1–26. https://doi.org/10.1080/09654313.2022.2028737

WSI. (2020). *Work-Life Balance im Homeoffice: Was kann der Betrieb tun?* 54. www.wsi.de/de/faust-detail.htm?sync_id=HBS-007598

ZEIT ONLINE. (2016). *Volksabstimmung in der Schweiz: Schweizer lehnen bedingungsloses Grundeinkommenab*.www.zeit.de/politik/ausland/2016-06/schweizer-lehnen-bedingungsloses-grundeinkommen-ab?print

11

THE ASSESSMENT OF THE LABOUR MARKET SITUATION IN THE DIGITAL WORLD – USEFULNESS OF GOOGLE TRENDS DATA

Sławomir Kuźmar and Bartosz Totleben

Introduction

Timely economic data availability is a long-standing challenge both to researchers and policymakers. However, even in highly developed economies lags in releases of main macroeconomic indicators can be counted in months or even years, and the situation is even worse in the case of low-income, developing countries (Narita & Yin, 2018). Facing this problem, a growing body of researchers is looking with excitement at non-traditional data sources, which are available mainly due to the proliferation of large-scale digital data. Satellite imagery data of night-time lights are used to measure the level of economic activity or economic development in countries or sub-regions where data from statistical offices are not available or are of poor quality (Bruederle & Hodler, 2018; Engstrom et al., 2017). Data generated by mobile phones (so-called 'digital prints') are used to assess the level of individual socio-economic characteristics, such as income or wealth (Blumenstock, 2018). The electronic payments data, such as records of debit and credit card transactions are considered to be important indicators of economic activity (Aprigliano et al., 2019; Tkacz, 2013). However, it seems that the biggest interest, as well as research potential, is ascribed to data generated as a by-product of Internet activity, especially those related to Google web searches or queries. Following Choi and Varian (Choi & Varian, 2012), many researchers started to use Google's search volume index to forecast or nowcast socio-economic indicators.

The above-mentioned process of digital data generation accelerated significantly during the COVID-19 pandemic which had led to the dramatic change in the functioning of the labour market at the same time. As a result, the traditional methods of assessment of the current situation on this market are becoming less and less effective. Processes such as the digitalisation of work, the emergence of digital platforms, development of other flexible forms of employment, caused the

DOI: 10.4324/9781003326779-14

rapid increase of informal work agreements. For such, often very short-term contracts, it seems particularly difficult to track the current situation using traditional tools adopted by statistical offices. It appears that Google Trends Data (GTD) may be used as an additional tool in the assessment of a very volatile labour market environment.

Being aware of these important changes on labour market, as well as growing popularity of analyses based on Google web searches data, the aim of our study is to explore the potential of GTD for the assessment of the current labour market situation, paying special attention to the limitation and possible drawbacks of studies based on this data. We hope to contribute to the existing literature by indicating not only the potential of Google search data in economic analysis but also the possible limitations and problematic issues related to the use of such data.

In our study we used data from Google Trends Data service, concentrating mainly on the Google Search Volume Index (GSVI, a publicly available index based on sampled and fractioned part of GTD). To extend our analysis and discover the potential limitations of GTD, we employed OECD data related to the number of individuals using the Internet as well as the age and gender structure of these users.

We employ literature review and quantitative analysis of the Scopus database to show the increasing popularity of articles related to Google Trends after the turn of 2010 and 2011. A large set of empirical research is used to assess the determinants affecting the quality of analyses using GTD. In the process of the assessment of the potential imitations of GTD, a basic statistical analysis was performed.

Our analyses indicate that in the last 10 years a rapid growth of empirical studies based on GTD has been observed in most of the academic scientific fields. Economics belongs to the most popular fields in which these data are used, ranking third after medicine and social sciences in terms of the number of publications in the analysed period. What is more important, the studies related to the assessment of the labour market situation seem to be one of the first economic areas in which Internet search data were used for empirical inquiries and remain still among the most popular. However, surprisingly little attention was paid to the potential limitation and caveats of the used data. To fill that gap, we concentrated on the potential limitations of analyses based on GTD, identifying some external factors that may impact the representatives of search queries and internal conditions directly related to the methodology of data collection and provision adopted by Google Trends. The conducted analysis showed that among general factors that may impact the representatives of search queries and affect the quality of research based on this data special attention to demographic dimensions of Internet users, the differences in search behaviour, and sources used in web searching should be paid. These factors appear to be particularly important for analyses conducted for longer time spans, as the structure and the use of the Internet have changed significantly in recent years. Analysing the internal factors, we pointed out that the results of empirical studies based on GSVI may be impacted by the sensitivity of the time range of downloaded data. It is also possible that the declining value of GSVI may coexist with the growth in the number of searches. Also, unclear categorisation and publishing GSVI based on limited, sampled data are factors which should be especially considered when drawing conclusions based on GTD.

The remainder of this chapter is structured as follows. Section entitled 'Google Trends Data in economics' discusses Google Trends Data and examples of its application in labour market studies. In the next section, we try to identify the potential drawbacks and limitations of analyses based on Google search data. We discuss the obtained results, consider further research avenues, and conclude the analysis in the last section.

Google Trends Data in economics

What are Google Trends and GSVI?

As already mentioned, one of the most popular, as well as potentially useful types of big data, are the data generated as a by-product of Internet activity. One of the biggest sources of these data is data created while using a search engine (mostly Google), alongside the data generated by social network users. Unlike those created in social networks, data sets from Google Trends are available in limited index form via the Google Trends service. Google Trends is a database that shows how often a particular search term (query) is entered into a Google search engine relative to the total search volume across various regions of the world. The Google Trends Data (previously called Google Insight) has been publicly available since 2008 and provided weekly data from January 2004.

Although all the queries submitted to Google are stored, the Google Trends service conducts a random sampling and uses only a fraction of the entire search data to construct and make publicly available an index called the Google Search Volume Index (GSVI). The index measures some fraction of queries that include the search term in question in the chosen geographic region at a particular time relative to the total number of queries at that time. The maximum value of the index is set to 100 (Stephens-Davidowitz & Varian, 2015). Since the meaning and the popularity of a particular search term can differ or evolve over time (e.g., homonyms), it is preferable to work on categories or concepts rather than on specific terms. Google Trends provides users with statistics on sets of terms that are semantically close, called 'categories'. There are 25 main categories with multiple subcategories for each. Bortoli and Combes (2015, p. 47) indicated that the normalisation that Google applies to the series relating to the Google Trends categories is different from that applied to simple queries: The frequency of the category in the first week of 2004 is used as a reference, with the following points in the series being expressed as deviations from this level.

Figure 11.1 presents an example of the GSVI for 'Poland' as a topic, from all over the world ('Worldwide'), without any additional category. Points A and B are calculated as the ratios of searches related to the topic 'Poland' divided by the total searches for all queries from the same location ('Worldwide'), for each period (June 2016 and June 2018). In this case, point A is the maximum of such ratios over

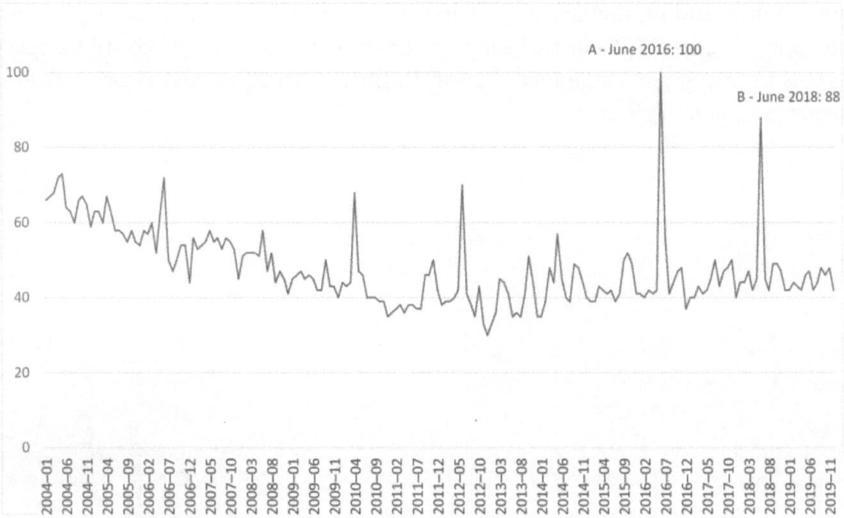

FIGURE 11.1 Example of Google Trends search for 'Poland'

Source: Google Trends Database: https://trends.google.com/trends/.

time, and therefore, the GSVI for June 2016 shows 100 and the SVI for June 2018 shows 88, which is computed as the ratio of B to A multiplied by 100.

Trends of economic literature related to Google Trends

As indicated in the introduction, the pioneering work on the potential of the volume of queries that users enter into Google in a short-term economic prediction was conducted by Choi and Varian (Choi & Varian, 2012). The authors have found that Google query indices were often correlated with various economic indicators and may be helpful for short-term economic prediction. However, they underlined that their main goals were to familiarise readers with Google Trends Data, to illustrate some simple forecasting methods that use this data, and to encourage readers to undertake their own analyses. Even though this work is considered pioneering, it was not the first. It seems the first-published paper to suggest the usefulness of web search data in economic forecasting was published in 2005 (Ettredge et al., 2005).

An explosion of economic papers using Google data was observed after the turn of 2010 and 2011. To illustrate the changes in research related to Google Trends, and the disciplines in which these data are used, we analysed the relevant literature published over the past 15 years (2006–2020). Following the methodology developed by (Jun et al., 2018), we selected the author keywords as variables to analyse the number of papers based on GTD. We concentrated on the Scopus database provided by Elsevier, which contains 18,000 journals published by about 5,000 publishers. Each journal is assigned one or more ASJC codes classified by SCOPUS. This information can thus be considered to provide an objective viewpoint regarding the area and theme of the journal in which the paper was published. Figures 11.2 and 11.3 show the trends in publications related to Google Trends in economic, econometrics, and finance journals, as well as other fields depicted as all disciplines.

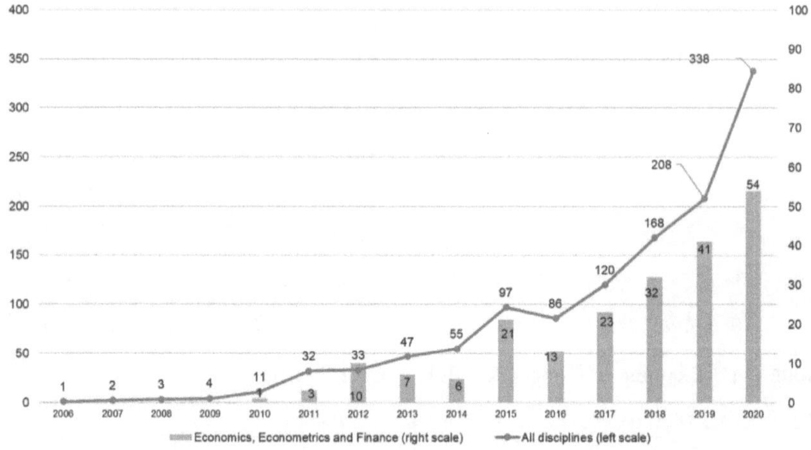

FIGURE 11.2 Publication trends of literature related to Google Trends

Source: Scopus database (www.scopus.com/).

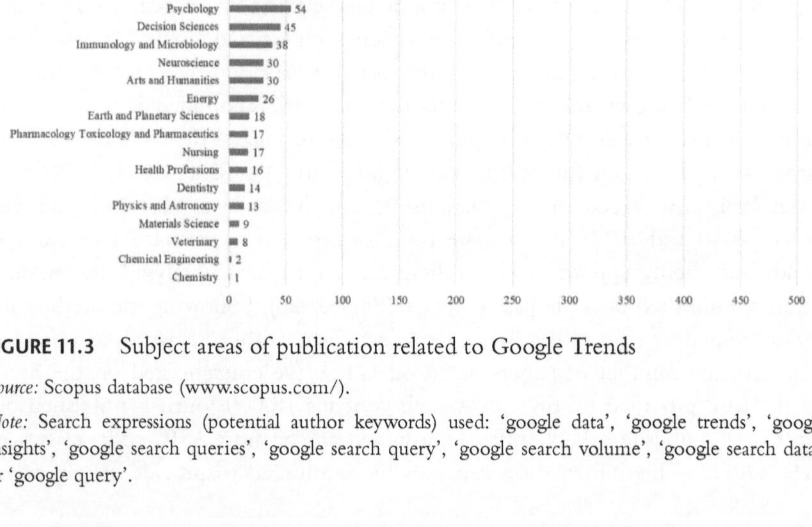

FIGURE 11.3 Subject areas of publication related to Google Trends

Source: Scopus database (www.scopus.com/).

Note: Search expressions (potential author keywords) used: 'google data', 'google trends', 'google insights', 'google search queries', 'google search query', 'google search volume', 'google search data', or 'google query'.

The applied selection of keywords allowed us to distinguish 1205 published articles of which 211 were assigned to the subject area of economics, econometrics, and finance. The presented data indicates that the number of papers related to Google Trends expanded significantly in the analysed period. Beginning with steady growth from 2011 and showing a slight decline in 2016, it has accelerated significantly in the last four years. It is worth emphasising that the share of articles from the subject area of economics stabilised after 2014, amounting to nearly 20%. The subject of economics ranks third after medicine and social sciences in terms of the number of publications in the analysed period.

Assessment of labour market situation using Google Trends Data – examples of empirical studies

The studies related to the assessment of the labour market situation, aimed mainly at the improvement of the availability and quality of unemployment measures, and forecast of this indicator, seems to be one of the first economic areas in which Internet search data were used for empirical inquiries. Most of these studies, incorporate GTD as additional explanatory variables (the variables most often used in traditional models are these related to past economic performance of a particular area, employers' and consumers' expectations, the market sentiment indicators) into models designed to forecast labour market situation.

It seems that the popularity of these analyses stems from the fact that latent labour market sentiment leaves a heavy footprint on Internet search behaviour, particularly from job seekers (Borup & Schütte, 2022). For example in the case of the US population, as a survey made by the Pew Research Centre in 2015 found, that 80% of the US workers use the Internet when searching for a job, and 34% claim that it is the most important resource available to them during the job search process (Smith & Dana, 2015), it can be assumed that currently, these values are much higher.

To the best of our knowledge, the first studies to use Google data to forecast the unemployment rates were (Askitas & Zimmermann, 2009) for Germany and (D'Amuri & Marcucci, 2010) for the USA. In the former study, the authors demonstrated a strong correlation between keyword searches and unemployment rates using monthly German data. In their analysis based on a time-series causality approach using the well-known error-correction model specification, they proved based on the BIC[1] criterium that the Internet activity data is useful to help predict unemployment rates under complex and fast-changing conditions. In their study (D'Amuri & Marcucci, 2009) astutely entitled *Google it! Forecasting the US unemployment rate with a Google job search index* suggested the use of an Internet job-search indicator[2] as the best leading indicator to predict the US unemployment rate. The authors tested the predictive power of Google data using a deep out-of-sample comparison among more than five hundred linear and non-linear forecasting models and concluded that the best models in terms of lowest MSE are always those using the GI as the leading indicator.

In the following years, further studies aimed at the verification of the potential of Google Trends data for the assessment of the labour market situation for other countries have been conducted. To name some examples, McLaren and Shanbhogue (2012) applied the search data to the analysis of the labour and housing markets in the United Kingdom. Fondeur and Karamé (2013) analysed using GTD the youth unemployment in France. Similar studies were conducted for Finland (Tuhkuri, 2016), Visegrad countries (Pavlicek & Kristoufek, 2014), Spain (Vicente et al., 2015), the USA (D'Amuri & Marcucci, 2017), EU countries (Anttonen, 2018), Italy (Naccarato et al., 2018), Romania (Simionescu et al., 2020), or Poland (Drachal, 2020). All these studies highlighted the potential and advantages of the inclusion of GTD in unemployment levels forecasts.

The growing importance of this type of analysis is also evidenced by the fact that experimental analysis of the potential of query terms searched on Google as predictors of the labour market situation are carried out by national and international statistical institutes. For example, an experiment using query terms searched on Google as predictors of unemployment were carried out at Eurostat (Ferreira, 2014). More recently, the team from the Statistics Netherlands institution (Schiavoni et al., 2021), applying the methodology of unemployment estimation used by Statistics Netherlands, extended the model by including auxiliary series of Google Trends data about job-search and economic uncertainty, and claimant counts. Obtained results indicate using these additional data provides reliable unemployment estimates in real-time before LFS data become available. More formally, the stronger predictive power of the models including GTD was corroborated by implementation of likelihood-ratio tests. The authors also pointed out that accuracy of nowcasts is higher (up to 23%–40% depend on characteristics of models) when GTD are used compared to the models without those set of data.

Summing up this review of examples of studies in which GTD data were used for empirical inquiries, it is interesting to point out the main assumptions related to the use of GTD as potentially useful in the assessment of labour market situation. One of the most important assumptions is the one about the close relationship between Internet queries and the real intentions of people using search engines, and their creation of some signals about their actual economic situation, particularly for job seekers. The next assumption concerns the fact that GTD are demographically and spatially representative. It is also important to note that in most empirical studies using GTD, the fact that the Google search algorithm is constantly changing, is not taken into account.

The potential limitations of Google Search Data that may affect the quality of forecasts based on GSVI

External factors impacting the representatives of the indices based on search queries

Given the indicated rapid growth of scientific analysis in economics based on the Google search index, surprisingly little attention has been paid to the potential limitation and caveats of the used data (some of the few exceptions are: (Tkacz, 2013, pp. 18–19; Bortoli, 2015; Jun et al., 2018, pp. 84–85). Taking this fact into consideration in this part of our paper we would like to concentrate on the potential limitations of GSVI, and its hypothetical impact on conducted research and obtained results. In the first part of this section, we will focus on some external factors that may impact the representatives of search queries. These factors include socio-demographic dimensions of Internet users, differences in behaviour and sources used in web searching for information, as well as some linguistic issues causing difficulties in the proper identification of terms (words, queries).

The first area we would like to concentrate on is the impact of demographic dimensions of Internet users, such as age or sex, on search behaviour and in consequence on GSVI in different years and places. For example, Weber and Jaimes (2011) found that young people (born after 1987) were more likely to carry out music and gaming-related searches, while older users (born between 1900 and 1948) were more likely to carry out searches related to finance and travel. Simultaneously, older users tend to be a bit more cautious, submitting more specific queries or using search engines to take them to a specific URL. Additionally, Tkacz (2013) pointed out that search data may be skewed by age structure, as younger people tend to be more active on the Internet than seniors. This could explain, for example, the observed seasonal variations of the downloaded series, as lower search results of economics terms during the summer months may be related to the end of college and university classes. This effect can be additionally strengthened by the fact that the usage of web search engines differs among different age groups. It is worth underlining that (Weber & Jaimes, 2011) in a study based on a large query log of 2.3 million anonymous registered users from a web-scale US search engine data, pointed out that users aged anywhere between 18 and 44 were most likely to be using Google to search the web. Users aged between 45 and 64 were most likely to use Bing (with usage being most common among the 55–64 age group), while for users aged 65+, Yahoo! was the most popular search engine. To analyse the age structure of Internet users (see Figure 11.4), we compared data collected by the OECD (OECD, 2021) on the individuals using the Internet at least once in the period of three months in chosen OECD countries in 2005 and 2019.

Two main findings emerge from the presented data. First, a significant difference in the age structure of Internet users between both for 2005 and 2019 can be observed. In 2019, there are still countries, namely Turkey, Mexico, Greece, Portugal, and Poland, in which less than 50% of people aged 55–74 used the Internet in the period of the last three months. And second, between the analysed years a significant increase in the number of Internet users took place. The most significant increase was observed in countries such as Greece, Ireland, Mexico, and Turkey, in which in 2005, even among the youngest the percentage of individuals using the Internet, was less than 50%; in 2019, it was more than 80%. Nevertheless, having in mind the differences in search behaviour and differences in using web search engines among different age groups, we must consider the fact that the popularity

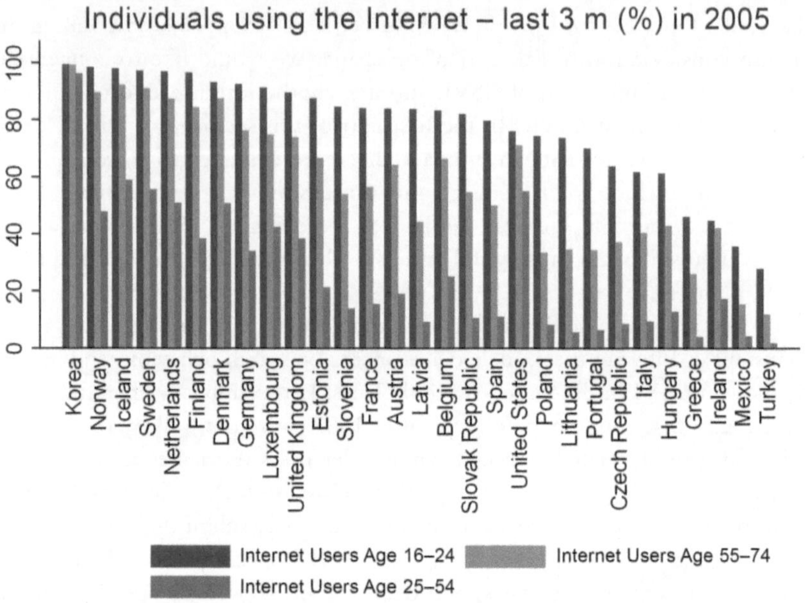

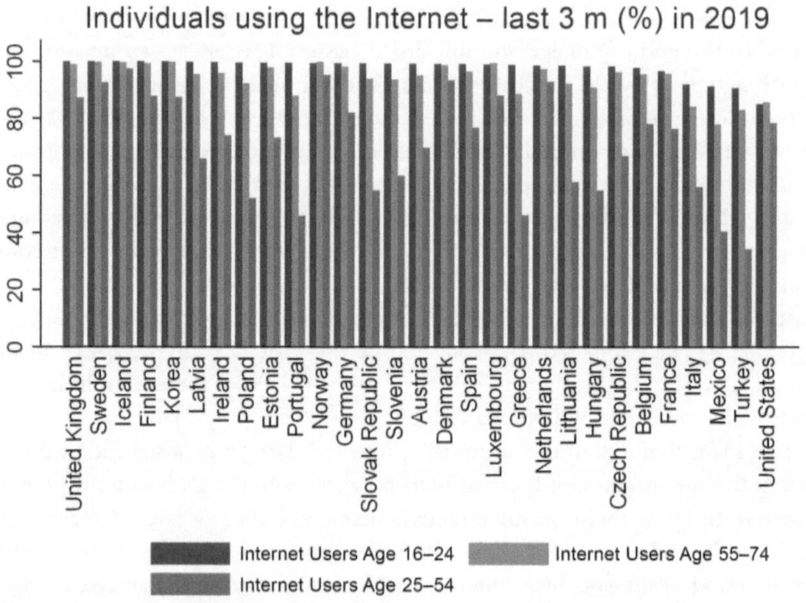

FIGURE 11.4 The age structure of Internet users in chosen OECD countries

Source: Own elaboration based on OECD stats data.

Note: due to a lack of comparable data countries such as Australia, Brazil, Canada, Chile, Colombia, Costa Rica, Israel, Japan, and Switzerland were excluded from the analysis.

of particular queries in different countries may be impacted in some way simply by the age structure of Internet users.

Besides the impact of the age of Internet users on search behaviour, some scholars (Joiner et al., 2005; Lorigo et al., 2006; Weber & Castillo, 2010; Weber & Jaimes, 2011) indicate that gender is another demographic factor that has a measurable influence on search behaviour. In the illustrative example, Weber and Castillo (2010) present the differences between the intention behind the query 'Wagner', pointing out that if the person who made the query is a typical female US web user, has pages about the composer Richard Wagner in mind. However, a male US web user is more likely to be referring to a company called Wagner which produces paint sprayers. Whereas Lorigo et al. (2006) find out that females submitted significantly longer search queries than men, with arithmetic means of 3.8 and 3.4 words, respectively. Even though the relationship between the percentage of women and men using the Internet between the years 2005 and 2019 (see Figure 11.5) had virtually equalised, the issues identified above may affect the popularity of some queries. That may result in statistically significant differences, since the gender distribution of the searchers, cannot be identified.

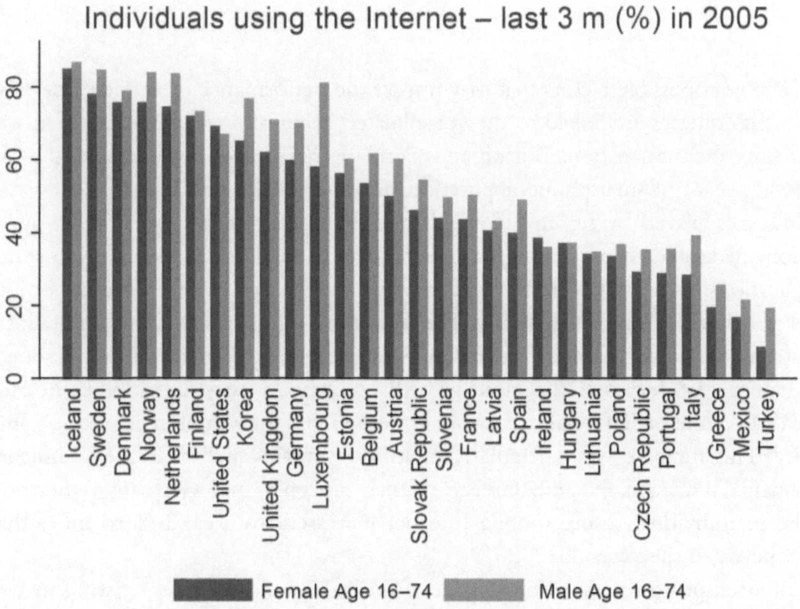

FIGURE 11.5 The sex structure of Internet users in chosen OECD

Source: Own elaboration based on OECD stats data.

Note: due to a lack of comparable data countries such as: Australia, Brazil, Canada, Chile, Colombia, Costa Rica, Israel, Japan, and Switzerland were excluded from the analysis.

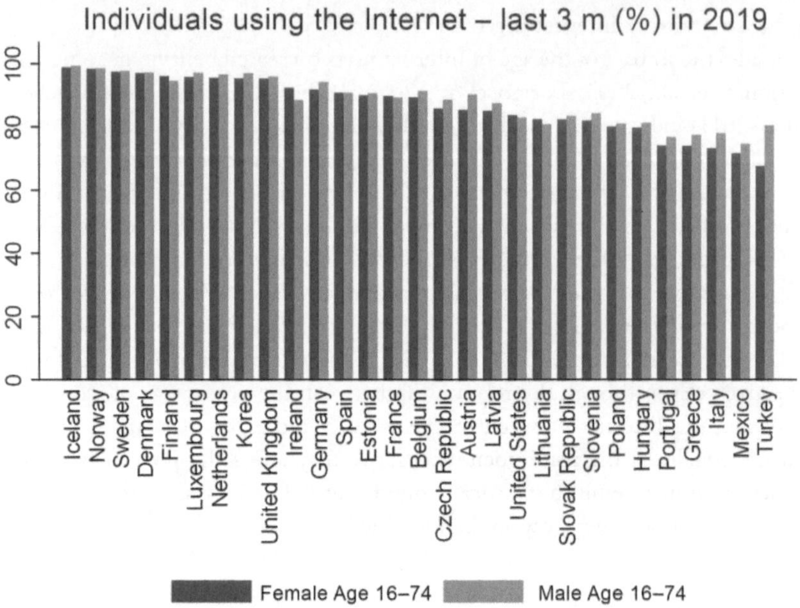

FIGURE 11.5 (Continued)

The next possible factors that may impact the performance of an indicator based on search queries are linked to the consolidated habits and routines existing in web searching for information. Bortoli and Combes (2015) note, for example, that the growing share of smartphone applications in Internet use may lead to a reduction in the role played by search engines if, for example, Internet users favour applications dedicated to purchasing, a similar situation may occur with the Job-search applications. As a result, the ability of trending searches to capture consumer or job-seeker behaviour may be reduced. The increasing significance of this constraint is related to the growing share of smartphones often used as the primary Internet source.

Figure 11.6 indicates the rapid growth of Internet usage in mobility in most OECD countries. This can be attributed to the rapid growth of smartphone popularity. This increase was particularly rapid in countries such as Turkey, Hungary, Lithuania, Portugal, Poland, Greece, Latvia, Slovenia, and Germany, where the share of individuals using mobile Internet increased from ca. 30% to more than 70% between the years 2012–2019.

In attempting to assess the impact of the habits and routines existing in web searching for information, it is also important to point out that the behaviour of web searching for information does not occur in all products or events. In the review of factors affecting online consumer search behaviour Grant et al. (2007) underlined the fact that consumers are unique and their information search behaviours are diversified. However, some basic rules can be observed,

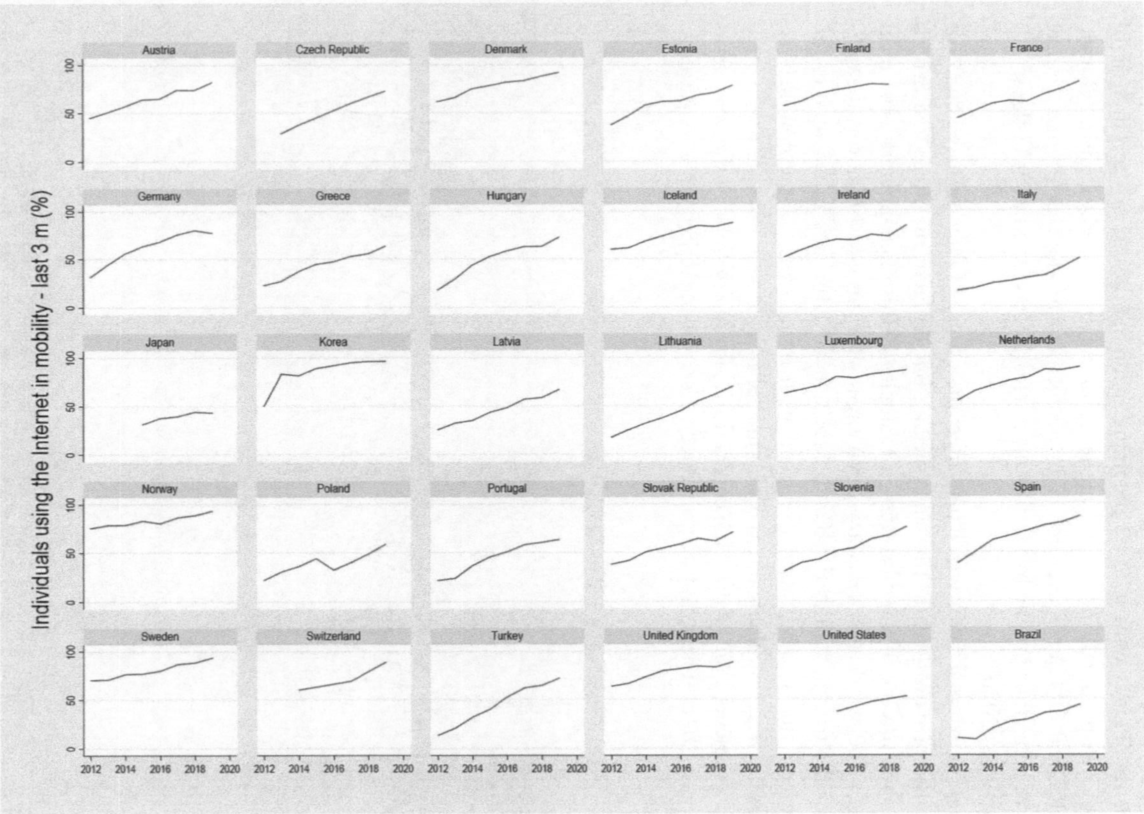

FIGURE 11.6 Individuals using Internet in mobility in chosen OECD countries

Source: Own elaboration based on OECD stats data.

for example researchers have identified risk aversion as the fundamental reason behind information search. Referring to the above, more active searches will be observed when there is a higher perception of risk regarding the product or in cases of high-involvement products or high-priced products. Similarly, we are much more likely to search for information relevant to our health or financial issues. This is why, in cases involving medicine, health or the purchase of high-priced products, there was a higher chance of successfully utilising Google Trends Data. Of course, even for high-involvement products or events, we may observe behaviour in which it is difficult to clearly grasp the intent of the search (Kang et al., 2020).

The last external factor which may affect the quality of forecasts based on GSVI is the use of words having the same spelling but different meanings and origins (homonyms). One of the most known examples of this phenomenon is the term 'Apple'. The raw data provided by search engines for this keyword covers the queries for the fruit as well as the brand. McCarthy (2010) gives an example of the 'depression' query as a potential problem with homonyms. 'Depression' may be used as the term for illness and as economic collapse.

Data presented on Figure 11.7 covers search for query 'Jobs' in the years from 2010 and 2021. The search for all categories is characterised by two patterns:

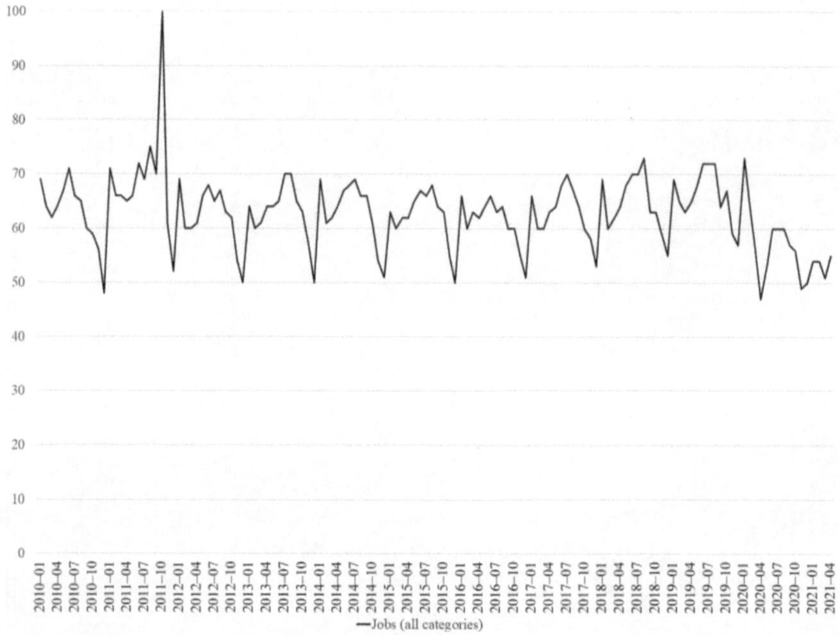

FIGURE 11.7 GSVI for 'jobs' query by categories

Source: Own elaboration based on Google Trends Data.

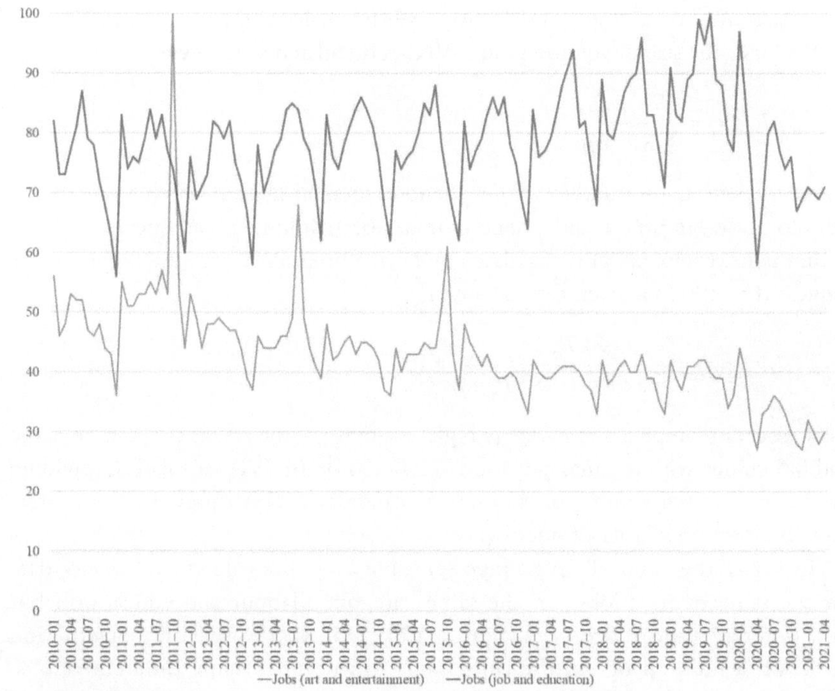

FIGURE 11.7 (Continued)

cyclical changes in each year and one big peak in November 2011 when Steve Jobs passed away. Searching for words which are homonyms without specifying the category distort the results of empirical studies based on it.

However, researchers suggest that this ambiguity issue does not have much impact on the query output due to at least two reasons. First, users can select an appropriate category (for example, Google allows limiting queries of 'Apple' to 'Food & Drinks' or 'Business & Industrial' categories). Second, Roll et al. (2018) describe the potential of machine learning to disentangle homonyms in large text corpora.

Internal conditions directly related to the methodology of data collection and provision adopted by Google Trends

Another group is factors related to the methodology of collecting and sharing data by Google, including: *time range sensitivity, sampling,* and *categorising*. Google Search Volume Index does not provide information about the absolute number of queries. Instead, the value of the index is estimated in the following scale: the maximum number of daily queries in a given time scope is set to 100, and other day values are a fraction of that. Google uses a two-layer normalisation procedure to estimate GSVI. First, the search volume ratio (SVR) is calculated as follows:

$$SVR_{t,l}(q) = \frac{SV_{t,l}(q)}{\sum SV_{t,l}(\breve{q})}$$

where t, l denotes time and location; q denotes total number of searches on query q from location l in time t; and q denotes total search volume on all queries.

In the next step, GSVI is calculated by normalising SVR with the highest value requested to 100 in a given time scope (T_0):

$$GSVI_{t,l}(q) = \frac{SVR_{t,l}(q)}{\max(t \in T_0)SVR_{t,l}(q)} * 100$$

This procedure implies a remarkably high sensitivity of the results to the time range and difficulties with the interpretation. The method of SVR calculation (dividing by the total search volume on all queries) causes that GSVI provides the relative (not absolute) popularity of query q.

To verify the issue of time range sensitivity, we have downloaded raw data for the same query ('jobs') in the same category ('labour and education') but in a different time range (see Figure 11.8). Due to the specific construction of GSVI, a little change in the time range can result in quite different results. Comparing the changes between the same points in time (16 February 2020 and 12 April 2020), we observe a decline in the GSVI of 57.7% (from 82 to 52) in the first case, and 37.0% (from 100 to 63) in the second. This proves that the

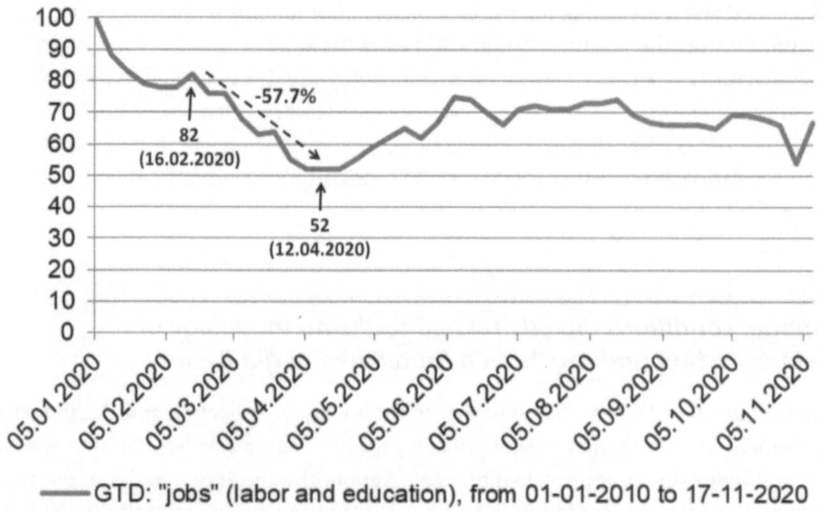

FIGURE 11.8 Google Trends Data for the different time range

Source: Own elaboration based on Google Trends Data.

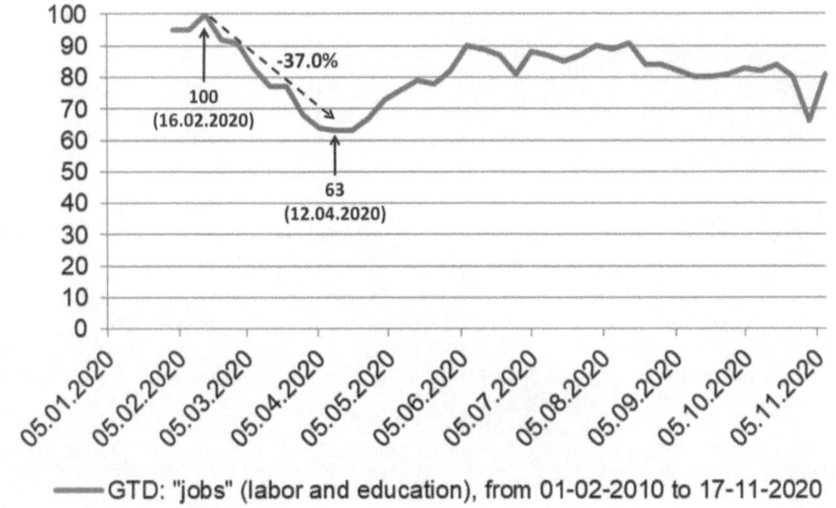

FIGURE 11.8 (Continued)

results of research based on raw data provided by Google are sensitive to the time range. Moreover, Stephens-Davidowitz and Varian (2015) rightly point to another potential limitation: the decreasing (or increasing) value of GSVI in time does not necessarily mean that there are fewer (more) searches of query *q* than there were previously. It only means that there are fewer (more) searches as a fraction of all searches.

Bortoli and Combes (2015) showed another potential limitation on research in which Google Trends Data are used: the value of GSVI depends on the day of data extraction. They proved that the GSVI series are based on sampled data and therefore can differ from one day of the extraction to another. To check the possible impact of sampling data by Google, we have downloaded raw data for three keywords ('unemployment rate', 'crisis', and 'oil price') in the same time scope (1 January 2018 to 30 June 2020). We have extracted GSVI on three different days: 25 April 2021, 14 May 2021, and 28 May 2021.

As we presented in Figure 11.9, the raw data released on various dates are not perfectly the same but still remarkably similar. The value of the Pearson correlation coefficient exceeds 0.99, which means that currently, the sampling and release date does not affect the obtained output. We have no evidence that Bortoli and Combes' hypothesis (2015) of significant differences in raw data depending on the date of extraction is true. Google has probably solved this problem since its study was published.

Another factor that can strengthen results based on GSVI is categorising. The ability to choose a category significantly improves search quality. For example, dividing the search 'job' into two categories ('art and entertainment' and 'job and

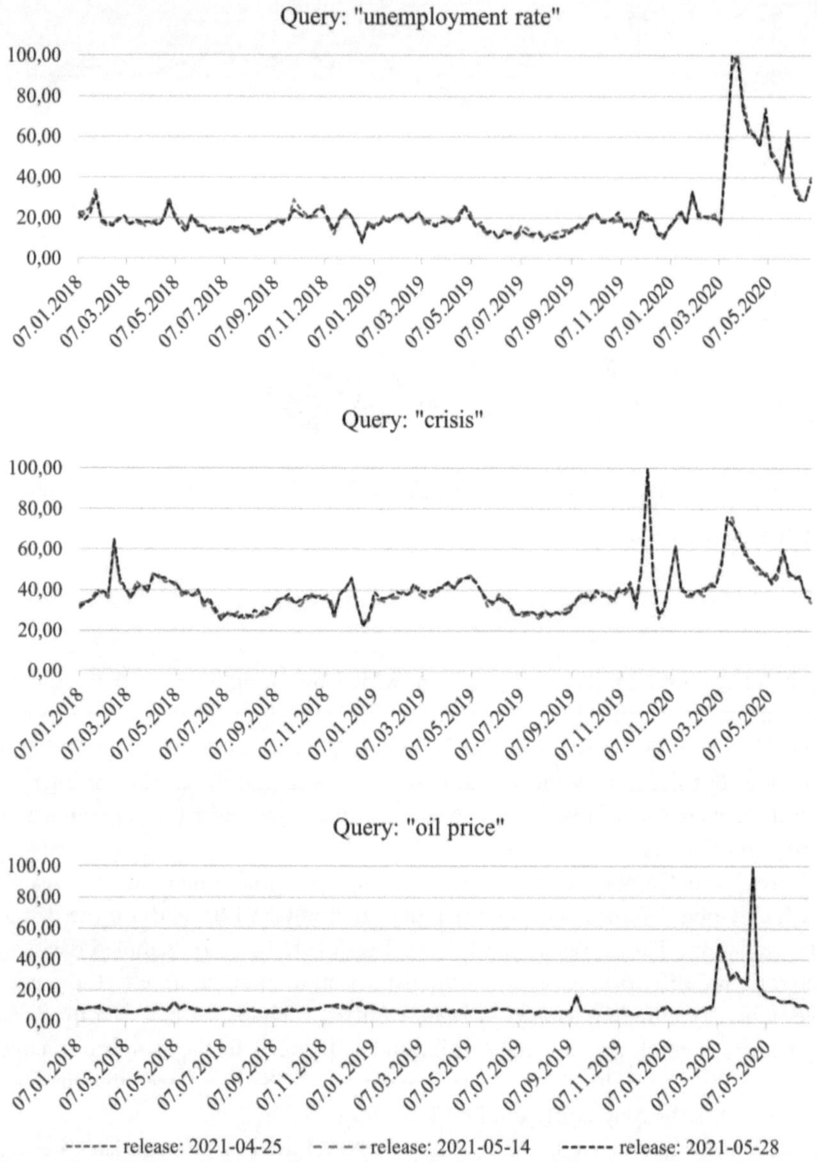

FIGURE 11.9 Impact of the extraction day on GSVI value

Source: Own elaboration based on Google Trends Data.

education', see Figure 11.7) allows for separate searches for Steve Jobs and the labour market. However, it is uncertain how the raw data is categorised, what the frequency of changes within the category is, and whether it is done correctly (Bortoli & Combes, 2015).

Conclusion

This chapter aimed to study the potential of Google Trends Data for economics nowcasting and forecasting. Besides the analysis of the publication trends and the review of some of the empirical examples of studies based on GTD, we tried to identify the possible limitations and problematic issues related to the use of such data.

The analysis of the publication trends of research related to Google Trends based on the data provided by the SCOPUS database indicates that after the turn of 2010 and 2011 the rapid growth of economic papers using Google data was observed. The applied selection of keywords related to Google Trends allowed us to distinguish 1205 published articles of which 211 were assigned to the subject area of economics, econometrics, and finance. The share of articles from the subject area of economics stabilised after 2014, amounts to near 20% of all papers, and ranks third after medicine and social sciences in terms of the number of publications in the analysed period. A deeper analysis of empirical studies in which GTD was used as explanatory variables indicates the enormous diversity of economic areas in which the GTD can be used. The results of most of the empirical papers indicate that using GTD can enhance the prediction performance of conventional models.

Discussing the potential limitations of Internet search data, we focused on some external or general factors that may impact the representatives of search queries, such as the demographic dimensions of Internet users, the differences in behaviour and sources used in web searching. We also concentrated on the factors related to the methodology of collecting and sharing data by Google, including: sampling, time range sensitivity, and categorising.

The analysis of internal factors that may impact the quality of studies based on Internet search data indicated, for example, that search data may be skewed by some demographical factors such as age or sex. For example, there are important differences between the search behaviour of younger and older people. These differences do not just apply to content but also to search engine use. Another important factor that may impact the performance of an indicator based on search queries is linked to the consolidated habits and routines existing in web searching. These habits can be linked with the growing share of smartphone applications in Internet use, and that may lead to a reduction in the role played by search engines or to the fact that more active searches will be observed when there is a higher perception of risk regarding the product or in cases of high-involvement products or high-priced products. The last external factor which may affect the quality of forecasts based on GSVI is the use of words having the same spelling but different meanings and origins, that is, homonyms. So, the analyst needs to remember that searching for homonym words without specifying the category, may distort the results of empirical studies based on it.

Analysing the internal factors, we pointed out that the results of empirical studies based on GSVI can be robust due to the high sensitivity of the time range. It is also possible that the declining value of GSVI may coexist with the growth in the number of searches. Also, unclear categorisation and publishing GSVI based on limited, sampled data are factors that should be especially considered when drawing conclusions based on these data.

Noting the important advantages of Google Trends Data as compared to classical variables used for economic forecasting which results from easy access to near real-time data, we express an opinion that authors and reviewers of studies based on Internet search data should adopt an enthusiastic but critical approach, particularly regarding key assumptions and methodological aspects of their studies. Especially the constant changes of Google search algorithm, high sensitivity to the time range, and some doubts about representativeness are weakening the potential of studies' employing GTD and making the empirical analysis difficult to replicate.

Acknowledgements

The project was financed within the Regional Initiative for Excellence programme of the Minister of Science and Higher Education of Poland, years 2019–2022, grant No. 004/RID/2018/19, financing 3,000,000 PLN.

Notes

1 In statistics, the Bayesian information criterion (BIC) is a criterion for model selection among a finite set of models; models with lower BIC are generally preferred.
2 Basing simple at the incidence of queries using the keyword 'jobs' on total queries performed through Google in the relevant week.

References

Anttonen, J. (2018). Nowcasting the unemployment rate in the EU with seasonal BVAR and Google search data. (*ETLA Working Papers* 62). http://pub.etla.fi/ETLA-Working-Papers-62.pdf

Aprigliano, V., Ardizzi, G., & Monteforte, L. (2019). Using payment system data to forecast economic activity. *International Journal of Central Banking, 15*(4), 55–80.

Askitas, N., & Zimmermann, K. F. (2009). Google econometrics and unemployment forecasting. *Applied Economics Quarterly, 55*(2), 107–120. https://doi.org/10.3790/aeq.55.2.107

Blumenstock, J. E. (2018, May). Estimating economic characteristics with phone data. *AEA Papers and Proceedings, 108*, 72–76. https://doi.org/10.1257/pandp.20181033

Bortoli, C., & Combes, S. (2015, March). *Contribution from Google trends for forecasting the short-term economic outlook in France: Limited avenues* 43. Département des méthodes statistiques.

Borup, D., & Schütte, E. C. M. (2022). In search of a job: Forecasting employment growth using google trends. *Journal of Business and Economic Statistics, 40*(1), 186–200. https://doi.org/10.1080/07350015.2020.1791133

Bruederle, A., & Hodler, R. (2018). Nighttime lights as a proxy for human development at the local level. *PLoS One, 13*(9), 1–22. https://doi.org/10.1371/journal.pone.0202231

Choi, H., & Varian, H. (2012). Predicting the present with Google trends. *Economic Record, 88*(SUPPL.1), 2–9. https://doi.org/10.1111/j.1475-4932.2012.00809.x

D'Amuri, Francesco, & Marcucci, Juri. (2010, April 22). "Google it !" Forecasting the US unemployment rate with a Google job search index. (*FEEM Working Paper No.* 31.2010). Retrieved from SSRN: https://ssrn.com/abstract=1594132 or http://dx.doi.org/10.2139/ssrn.1594132.

D'Amuri, F., & Marcucci, J. (2017). The predictive power of Google searches in forecasting US unemployment. *International Journal of Forecasting, 33*(4), 801–816. https://doi.org/10.1016/j.ijforecast.2017.03.004

Drachal, K. (2020). Forecasting unemployment rate in Poland with dynamic model averaging and internet searches. *Global Business and Economics Review, 23*(4), 368–389. https://doi.org/10.1504/GBER.2020.110684

Engstrom, R., Hersh, J., & Newhouse, D. (2017, December). *Poverty from space: Using high-resolution satellite imagery for estimating economic well-being* 36. http://econ.worldbank.org.

Ettredge, M., Gerdes, J., & Karuga, G. (2005). Using web-based search data to predict macroeconomic statistics. *Communications of the ACM, 48*(11), 87–92. https://doi.org/10.1145/1096000.1096010

Ferreira, P. (2014 April). *Improving prediction of unemployment statistics with Google trends* (pp. 1–6). https://ec.europa.eu/eurostat/cros/system/files/Modelling_unemployment_in_Portugal_with_Google_trends.pdf

Fondeur, Y., & Karamé, F. (2013). Can Google data help predict French youth unemployment? *Economic Modelling, 30*(1), 117–125. https://doi.org/10.1016/j.econmod.2012.07.017

Grant, R., Clarke, R. J., & Kyriazis, E. (2007). A review of factors affecting online consumer search behaviour from an information value perspective. *Journal of Marketing Management, 23*(5–6), 519–533. https://doi.org/10.1362/026725707x212801

Joiner, R., Gavin, J., Duffield, J., Brosnan, M., Crook, C., Durndell, A., Maras, P., Miller, J., Scott, A. J., & Lovatt, P. (2005). Gender, internet identification, and internet anxiety: Correlates of internet use. *Cyberpsychology and Behavior, 8*(4), 371–378. https://doi.org/10.1089/cpb.2005.8.371

Jun, S. P., Yoo, H. S., & Choi, S. (2018). Ten years of research change using Google trends: From the perspective of big data utilizations and applications. *Technological Forecasting and Social Change, 130* (February 2017), 69–87. https://doi.org/10.1016/j.techfore.2017.11.009

Kang, X., Wu, Y., & Ren, F. (2020). Toward action comprehension for searching: Mining actionable intents in query entities. *Journal of the Association for Information Science and Technology, 71*(2), 143–157. https://doi.org/10.1002/asi.24220

Lorigo, L., Pan, B., Hembrooke, H., Joachims, T., Granka, L., & Gay, G. (2006). The influence of task and gender on search and evaluation behavior using Google. *Information Processing and Management, 42*(4), 1123–1131. https://doi.org/10.1016/j.ipm.2005.10.001

McCarthy, M. J. (2010). Internet monitoring of suicide risk in the population. *Journal of Affective Disorders, 122*(3), 277–279. https://doi.org/10.1016/j.jad.2009.08.015

McLaren, N., & Shanbhogue, R. (2012). Using internet search data as economic indicators. *SSRN Electronic Journal, 2010*, 134–140. https://doi.org/10.2139/ssrn.1865276

Naccarato, A., Falorsi, S., Loriga, S., & Pierini, A. (2018). Combining official and Google trends data to forecast the Italian youth unemployment rate. *Technological Forecasting and Social Change, 130* (November 2016), 114–122. https://doi.org/10.1016/j.techfore.2017.11.022

Narita, F., & Yin, R. (2018). In search of information: use of Google trends' data to narrow information gaps for low-income developing countries. (*IMF Working Papers 18/286*). International Monetary Fund.

OECD. (2021). *OECD.Stat database*. Retrieved March 10, 2022, from https://stats.oecd.org/Index.aspx?DataSetCode=ICT_IUSERS.

Pavlicek, J., & Kristoufek, L. (2014). *Can Google searches help nowcast and forecast unemployment rates in the Visegrad group countries?* (pp. 1–11). https://doi.org/10.1371/journal.pone.0127084

Reis, F., Ferreira, P., & Perduca, V. (2014). *The use of web activity evidence to increase the timeliness of official statistics indicators* (pp. 1–35). Retrieved February 7, 2022, from https://ec.europa.eu/eurostat/cros/content/use-web-activity-evidence-increase-timeliness-iaos2014_en

Roll, U., Correia, R. A., & Berger-Tal, O. (2018). Using machine learning to disentangle homonyms in large text corpora. *Conservation Biology*, *32*(3), 716–724. https://doi.org/10.1111/cobi.13044

Schiavoni, C., Palm, F., Smeekes, S., & van den Brakel, J. (2021). A dynamic factor model approach to incorporate Big Data in state space models for official statistics. *Journal of the Royal Statistical Society. Series A: Statistics in Society*, *184*(1), 324–353. https://doi.org/10.1111/rssa.12626

Simionescu, M., Streimikiene, D., & Strielkowski, W. (2020). What does google trends tell us about the impact of brexit on the unemployment rate in the UK? *Sustainability (Switzerland)*, *12*(3), 1–10. https://doi.org/10.3390/su12031011

Smith, A., & Dana, P. (2015). Searching for work in the digital era. *Pew Research Center*, 1–29. www.pewinternet.org/2015/11/19/searching-for-work-in-the-digital-era/

Stephens-Davidowitz, S., & Varian, H. (2015). A hands-on guide to Google data. *Google, Inc.*, 1–25.

Tkacz, G. (2013). Predicting recessions in real-time: Mining Google trends and electronic payments data for clues. *CD Howe Institute Commentary*, 387.

Tuhkuri, J. (2016). Forecasting unemployment with Google searches. (*ETLA Working Papers No 35*). Helsink: The Research Institute of the Finnish Economy (ETLA). http://pub.etla.fi/ETLA-Working-Papers-35.pdf

Vicente, M. R., López-Menéndez, A. J., & Pérez, R. (2015). Forecasting unemployment with internet search data: Does it help to improve predictions when job destruction is skyrocketing? *Technological Forecasting and Social Change*, *92*, 132–139. https://doi.org/10.1016/j.techfore.2014.12.005

Weber, I., & Castillo, C. (2010). *The demographics of web search* [Proceedings]. SIGIR 2010 Proceedings – 33rd Annual International ACM SIGIR Conference on Research and Development in Information Retrieval, April 2014, 523–530. https://doi.org/10.1145/1835449.1835537

Weber, I., & Jaimes, A. (2011). *Who uses web search for what? And how?* [Proceedings]. Proceedings of the 4th ACM International Conference on Web Search and Data Mining, WSDM 2011, 15–24. https://doi.org/10.1145/1935826.1935839

12

INDIVIDUAL WORK PRICING BY NON-FUNGIBLE PERSONAL TOKENS ('NFT GIG TOKENS') – A NEW OPPORTUNITY FOR GIG WORKERS

Kamilla Marchewka-Bartkowiak, Michał Litwiński, and Karolina Nowak

Introduction

The COVID-19 pandemic transformed the way people operate in all fields of their activity – individual, social, economic, cultural, civic, to name the most essential spheres. One of the crucial changes to the rules existing within pre-pandemic societies was the modification of the work environment and principles (Ralph et al., 2020; Masood et al., 2022). The patterns developed within the gig economy, which are based on the idea of flexibility and the use of technological communication platforms, proved to be the most common response to the change (Diab-Bahman & Al-Enzi, 2020).

When it comes to specific problems that were highlighted by the pandemic, the issue of labour pricing occurred to be of concern. The development of online communication tools created new opportunities to provide services and share results of one's work via the Internet. It is worth noting that even before the COVID-19, the issue of work valuation was crucial for some groups, for example, for artists. The token became an important way of work monetisation both for them and the new services providers. More and more one hears about artists converting their artworks (the results of their work) into non-fungible tokens (NFT tokens). But will only celebrities (artists, actors, and influencers) use this tool in the future? This question occurred to be an extremely relevant matter in a (post)pandemic world. It seems that NFT gig tokens are an answer to the challenges occurring on the labour market, related to the popularisation of the employment model in the gig economy and the issue of valuing work offered by gig workers.

The main aim of our research is to find out whether NFT gig tokens can provide an answer to the problem of how to value work in the world of new technologies, in particular – whether NFT gig tokens can be a tool of valuing one's own work that considers both the financial and network dimensions of the individual.

DOI: 10.4324/9781003326779-15

We therefore formulate the thesis that NFT gig tokens has the potential to become a new tool of labour valuation for and by gig workers.

Research on the gig economy has so far been undertaken in relation to the main ideas behind it, such as flexibility or Wikinomics (De Groen et al., 2017; Tapscott & Wiliams, 2006), key features such as openness and horizontality (Florida, 2019) and the risks involved (social security, and cyber security). However, research is lacking on how (means, tools) to value the services, offered by gig workers. This chapter should partially fill this gap. In the gig worker context, personal tokens (PT) can serve as a tool enabling not only a simple market valuation of a labour service but also a network valuation based on the network participants' trust in the token issuer. It is worth noting that the network valuation of work or enterprise is usually performed only in two dimensions – financial (e.g., using the Network-Value-to-Transaction Ratio – NVT) and technological (Marchewka-Bartkowiak et al., 2022). However, we propose a new way of approaching network valuation – based on the axiological dimension. We assume that network valuation is based on trust, which is constructed primarily by a similar axiological vision of the world respected by the issuer and the network participant, that is, the same hierarchy of values, captured as the sense of their actions undertaken in the network (observed on social profiles or purchasing PT). A personal token would therefore not be a tool for valuing the services offered, but rather a means of valuing the issuer's broadly defined personal brand (personality). As such, personal tokens can build the long-term credibility of gig workers in the network as a service provider. Those features of the personal token, referred to by the authors as the 'NFT gig token', are relevant not only for issuers already recognised in social media (celebrity PT) but also for those who are beginning to build their personal brand online (common PT). In the first case, tokens strengthen the celebrity's position by providing a modern and attractive gift for their fans and followers; in the second case, tokens initiate participation and often confirm the credibility of the network participant willing to offer their service. The increased turnover of personal tokens can also be evidence of the market attractiveness of their issuers, also from a financial point of view.

The article is based on empirical data concerning the owners of tokens, which are issued on an intentionally created personal token platform (https://personal-tokens.io/) in the period December 2020–June 2021. The indicated platform is not only a newly explored source of data (to the knowledge of the authors of the study, no research has yet been conducted using it), but also a valuable collection of information dedicated strictly to the subject matter. The study covers 170 personal token issuers, 45 of which were analysed in detail.

We used as methods the quantitative analysis (mainly t-test of significance of correlation coefficients between the included indicators and descriptive statistics of the created indicators) and content analysis in a framework of the cultural approach.

The first contribution of our research includes a classification of the work offered by digital token issuers considered as a part of a gig workers group. We also conduct an original analysis of the relationship between the valuation of 1 labour/service hour using personal tokens by both token owners (labour supply) and the customer network (labour demand). The third contribution of our study is the formulation of the own network valuation proposal, based on the network participants' trust in the PT issuer, by means of identifying the values to which the token issuers referred in their profile description of the work offered.

The remainder of this chapter is organised as follows. We start with a presentation of literature background on NFT, PT, and gig workers. In the subsequent section we focus on research design, namely data and methods. Then we present results of our study. The last section is dedicated to discussion and conclusions.

Literature review

Personal tokens are a kind of digital tokens based on blockchain technology, more widely referred to as distributed ledger technology (DLT). The issue of digital tokens is now considered both in the context of cryptocurrencies (narrow approach) and cryptoassets (broad approach). Taking into account the new blockchain technology regulations proposed at the European Union level in 2020, digital tokens can become the basis for developing technological instruments within the framework of open and decentralised finance. This chapter adopts, as a basis for determining the characteristics of personal tokens, the definition proposed by the European Commission in 2020 as part of the drafts of the new regulations that comprise the Digital Finance Strategy, in particular in the Markets in Crypto-Assets Regulation – MiCA. According to this definition, 'crypto-asset means a digital representation of value or rights which may be transferred and stored electronically, using distributed ledger technology or similar technology' (Proposal for a REGULATION OF THE EUROPEAN PARLIAMENT AND OF THE COUNCIL, COM(2020)593). Thus, considering the general nature of cryptoassets, it can be pointed out that personal tokens (PT) are a type of token otherwise known as digital tokens, which are characterised primarily by the individual ownership of their issuers (both in the celebrity and common person categories) and are mostly intended to provide digital access to a good or service, available on DLT, that are only accepted by the issuers of that token. Technically, personal tokens are non-fungible (NFT), meaning that their feature is personalised (e.g., created according to the ERC-721 standard on the Ethereum blockchain).

NFTs are non-fungible tokens that are present on the cryptocurrency market but are conceptualised differently from cryptocurrencies. The latter are mainly captured as a means of payment, standardised as to its technical characteristics, which can sometimes be used for speculation (Baur et al., 2018), whereas NFTs are digital assets that are unique and heterogeneous in nature. 'The non-fungibility of NFTs is one of the key asset characteristics that is valued' (Dowling, 2021a).

As NFTs are typically purchased using cryptocurrencies as a medium of exchange based on smart contracts (Lisi et al., 2021) and that the leading traders of NFTs are cryptocurrency investors, similarities between the two markets are identified (Dowling, 2021b). Researchers expect some inefficiency in NFT pricing behaviour, similar to early cryptocurrency pricing (Cheah & Fry, 2015; Urquhart,

2016; Dowling, 2021b). As a symbolic date for NFTs to become established in the (not only digital) market as a new form of asset pricing, one can take 11.03.2021, when the London-based Christie's Auction House sold for $69.3m. Beeple NFT, the digital ownership record for Mike Winkelmann's work 'Everydays: The First 5,000 Days' (Crow & Ostroff, 2021) – this was the third highest price achieved by a piece by a living artist.

Personal tokens preserve the properties of NFTs, as they are a digital record of the right to an asset, which is a person, transferred by the issuer to the investor. When raising the category of personal token, one should focus on three main dimensions: (1) who someone is – personality, (2) what someone means online – social personal brand, and (3) what and how someone offers within PT – product, service (Marchewka-Bartkowiak & Nowak, 2020). Those three main dimensions (personality, social prestige, and service specification) are evoked in the context of characterising gig workers, who represent the so-called reputation economy, that is, those who build their position on the market based on their personal brand (Huws, 2014).

Gig workers are conceptualised in the broadest terms as workers who perform and complete short-term on-demand (i.e., gig) work for various employers (Torpey & Hogan, 2016; Best, 2017). A distinguished group are digital workers, consisting of individuals who use technological tools in their work (Colbert et al., 2016), they are also referred to as crowdsourcing workers or eLancers (Schroeder et al., 2021). The work model adopted here implies the idea of Wikinomics, described as a behaviour that combines openness, partnership, sharing, and global action (Tapscott & Wiliams, 2006). Gig workers, representing the reputation economy, are characterised by: design, timeliness (deadline), value estimation, reputation, horizontal labour market ('claims' of the market, of the principal), independence, creativity, ingenuity, innovation, time and space mobility (characteristics of the worker, the contractor) (Degryse, 2016; Donovan et al., 2016; De Groen et al., 2017; Florida, 2019; Dosi et al., 2021). Thus, these are the characteristics that represent the three dimensions of valuation in PT indicated earlier: personality (worker characteristics)-community status-service specification (market claims/expectations).

Research methods

Empirical data for the study were obtained from the personal token platform www.personaltokens.io. in the period December 2020–June 2021. The indicated platform is not only a newly explored source of data (to the knowledge of the authors of the study, no research has yet been conducted using it) but also a valuable collection of information dedicated strictly to the subject matter. The study covers 170 personal token issuers, 45 of which were analysed in detail. Despite the fact that about 500 token issuers are registered on the platform, we decided to analyse only 170 cases as those observations were described in a manner which allowed us to identify the type of services provided and valued by the means of a token.

Moreover, only 45 token issuers specified pricing of their work, enabling us to conduct further analysis as stated in the main text.

Generally, the analysis of types of services offered by personal token issuers was embedded in two classifications. Within the framework of the study, the service descriptions of each of the 170 digital token issuers (personal token issuers who offered services by means of those tokens) were analysed and then classified into a specific group based on the typology characterised in Table 12.1 and Appendix Table 12.6.

It should be foremost said that the development of such a typology is associated with certain challenges: (1) the nature of services is ambiguous (sometimes it is not possible to assign them to a single profession); (2) many services have appeared on the market relatively recently and, in addition, they are performed fully remotely, thus eluding the work typologies recognised in the research community; and (3) the respective literature lacks considerations on classifications of the work offered by digital utility token issuers – typologies of services provided by remote workers were only developed.

Referring to the latter, it is worth noting that the topic most like the area studied by the authors of this chapter is the valuation of work within the gig economy. A classification of that kind of services has been proposed, among others, by Kässi and Lehdonvirta (2018). That typology was adopted by the authors of this paper as the suggested six classes cover the kinds of services offered by digital token issuers relatively well (the classification was presented in appendix, Table 12.6).

Nevertheless, the motivations of utility token issuers seem to be of peculiar nature (especially, because of networking motivation of tokenisation), so their activities in the market of offered services cannot be fully identified with the gig economy. According to the results presented below, some personal token issuers elude the aforementioned typology. The authors of the study therefore developed their own classification of the services offered, based on the motivation for digital token issuers to join the platform on which they can offer their services. These motivations include an interest in new technologies, an interest in financial (or more broadly, economic) issues and a need to be a part of a network. Table 12.1 contains details of the classification.

In the next part of the research, an analysis of the relationship between the valuation of 1 labour/service hour using personal tokens by both token owners (labour supply) and the customer network (labour demand) was conducted. The study used, among other things, financial data relating to the market valuation on a given date (30 June 2021) in the ratio PT:ethereum:dollars.

Lastly, to explore NFT gig tokens as a tool for network valuation of an issuer's personal brand and work, we applied the assumptions of a cultural approach, offering the opportunity to understand how issuers brought meaning to the tokenisation of themselves and their work. We therefore examined the network effect from the axiological perspective – we identified what values issuers referred to when creating and describing their token to make other network participants

TABLE 12.1 Classification of services provided by personal token issuers

Class of services	*Examples of provided services*
Financial/ Economic – E/F	Accounting
	Consulting (financial, investment, real estate, business, and tax advisory)
	Currency exchange
	Human resources
Social (community services) – S	Trainings (incl. online courses)
	Platform CEO/founder
	Advertising/Promotion of ideas
	Language courses
	Consulting (e.g., photography, architecture, and social media)
	Creative writing
	Travelling
	Celebrity (actor, musician, and athlete)
	Community development (YouTuber and blogger)
	Mentoring and coaching
	Fundraising
Technology – T	Web development
	Game development
	Software development
	New technology development
	Software testing
	IT consulting
	Computer graphics
	Video production

Source: Own elaboration.

trust them and become interested in the token, the person, and the service. We conducted our research in a framework provided by the theory of the basic individual values and work values implemented firstly by Shalom H. Schwartz (Ros et al., 1999). We assumed that issuers referred to 10 main axiological areas, such as power, achievement, hedonism, stimulation, self-direction, universalism, benevolence, tradition, conformity, and security (each of these areas has its own associated – Figure 12.1).

The selected 45 personal tokens were analysed in terms of issuer's axiological relation to work. The one was estimated in a five-point Likert scale with the use of content analysis of communication artifacts, that is, information shared in the issuers' personal profiles on the examined platform [justification for the choice of the scale – see Höhne et al., 2021]: 5 – necessary, 4 – desirable, 3 – objectionable, 2 – not desirable, 1 – not necessary. The interpretation of the different communication acts was carried out from a cultural perspective, aimed at identifying

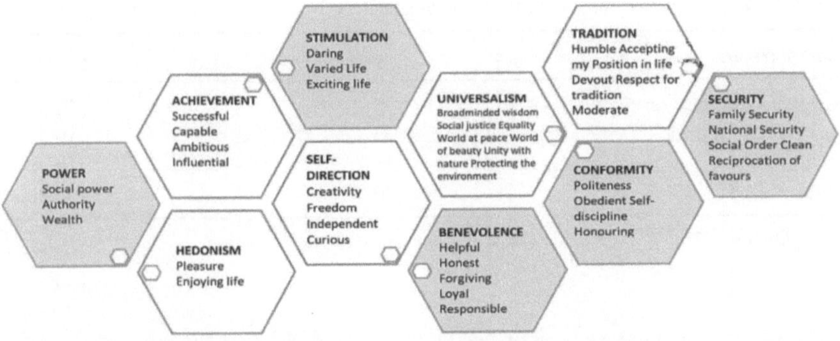

FIGURE 12.1 Types of axiological areas (values) taken into account when evaluating work

Source: Own elaboration based on Ros et al. (1999), p. 52.

the values revealed by the authors (issuers of personal tokens) in the content of the profiles.

Findings

Classification of services offered by PT

The results presented in appendix in Table 12.7 show that about one-third of personal token issuers offer services of professional nature. However, work related to creativity, software development, and clerical tasks are also quite eagerly provided by PT issuers. Interestingly, more than 10% of services offered by workers from the analysed platform elude the classification, which is not surprising when considering the fact that the typology was developed as a part of the research concerning the gig economy. The PT issuers, which were not covered by the classification, focused mainly on developing relations with the community.

Analysis based on the second typology reveals that more than 60% of the analysed 170 PT issuers provide work related to community services (cases, which in the previous classification were captured by professional and creative kinds of services, were partially covered by this type), while the financial and technology classes each account for about 20% of the remaining token owners (Table 12.2). As the classification developed by the authors of the chapter better corresponds to the structure of services offered by PT issuers (specifically, it covers all the types of services), it will be applied in further analysis.

The 45 tokens, which were analysed in detail, roughly resemble the structure in terms of the nature of the services offered (Table 12.3 and appendix, Table 12.8). The largest proportion of personal token issuers provides work having the character of services to the community (almost a half of considered service providers).

TABLE 12.2 Type of services, according to classification by the authors of the chapter

Class of services	*Number of cases*	*Percentage*
Social (community services)	103	60.59
Financial/Economic	33	19.41
Technology	34	20.00
Total	**170**	**100.00**

Source: Own calculations based on data from PT platform.

TABLE 12.3 Share of service types offered by analysed selected 45 token issuers

Class of services	*Number of cases*	*Percentage*
Social (community services)	21	46.67
Financial/economic	8	17.78
Technology	16	35.56
Total	**45**	**100.00**

Source: Own calculations based on data from PT platform.

TABLE 12.4 Basic statistics on the amount of PT per 1 hour of individual work of their owners

	Number of tokens per 1 work hour		
	Mean	*Min*	*Max*
Social (community services)	2,071	1	10,000
Financial/Economic	10,981	151	70,000
Technology	1,922	3	7,500
Total	**3,602**	**1**	**70,000**

Source: Own calculations based on data from PT platform.

However, the technological class accounts for a greater share than in the whole sample of 170 PT issuers.

Personal tokens financial valuation

As can be seen in Figure 12.2 and Table 12.4, 45 owners of utility tokens were quite diversified when it comes to valuation of their work time (from 1 to 70,000 tokens per 1 work hour). The highest average number of personal tokens is observed for the class of financial/economic services (almost 11,000 tokens). The mean for social and technology services is substantially lower and amounts to around 2,000

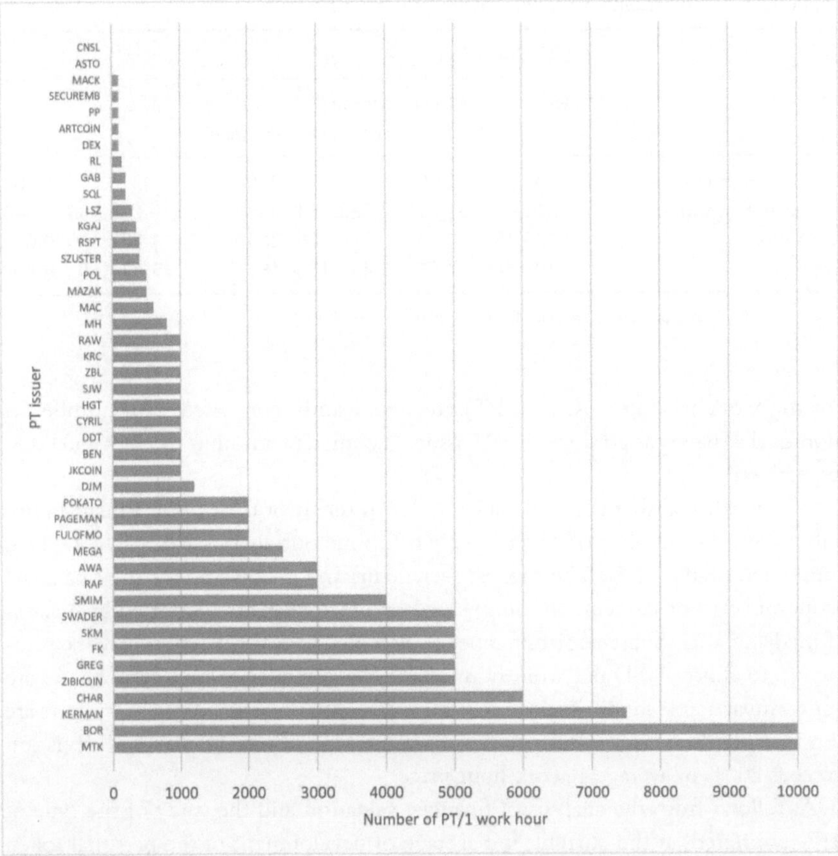

FIGURE 12.2 Market price per 1 hour of individual work of PT owners*

* For a clearer graphical presentation, the figure does not include the case with highest price per token – VIP tokens (70,000 tokens per 1 work hour).

Source: Own calculations based on data from PT platform.

tokens. Similar conclusions could be drawn when analysing the minimum and maximum values.

As further analysis shows, the highest valuation of one hour of labour service offered using personal tokens was not directly related to high customer interest as assessed by the price of respective token (appendix, Table 12.9). Specifically, the correlation coefficient between both number of tokens per 1 work hour and USD price of 1 work hour and token price amounts to −0.05 and 0.01, respectively, and is insignificant at 0.05 level according to t-test. Similarly, labour pricing, measured in USD per 1 work hour, is not significantly correlated with number of tokens per 1 work hour (coefficient at the level of 0.03). Interestingly, neither token price

TABLE 12.5 Work pricing using PT – descriptive statistics

	USD/work hour					
	Mean	*Median*	*Standard deviation*	*Coefficient of variation*	*Max*	*Min*
Social (community services)	36.345	2.054	78.395	216%	310.765	0.009
Financial/Economic	1,312.810	52.617	3,383.654	258%	9,674.685	0.044
Technology	135.154	0.437	356.226	264%	1,251.270	0.000
Total	**298.40**	**0.99**	**1,448.125**	**485%**	**9,674.69**	**0.000**

Source: Own calculations based on data from PT platform.

nor the work pricing (based on PT) are significantly correlated with number of months that have passed since the PT issue – coefficient amounts to −0.2 and 0.08, respectively.

It is worth realising that PT issuers differ in terms of their work valuation not only when the number of tokens per work hour but also unit price in USD is considered (Table 12.5). The highest average pricing is observed for the financial/economic class of services – findings based on mean level are supported by analysis of median value. Substantial difference is also observed for maximum work pricing (up to almost USD per work hour in F/E class) while the minimum values are quite similar across kinds of services. It should be also underlined that PT issuers are considerably diversified within classes. For each type of services standard deviation exceeds 200% of average 1 work hour price.

As follows from the analysis of financial valuation and the study of the type of services offered, at the current, initial stage of development of the personal token market, the financial motivation of the owner, and the class of service offered seem to be secondary criteria for token valuation. The high volatility of pricing, surprisingly low values of the latter and lack of significant relationships between considered categories can support that assumption.

Therefore, we suppose that, in addition to the factors specified above, token owners are driven by an additional motive – obtaining a network effect. This would mean that the main purpose of the token issue is not necessarily to sell services or goods, but to increase the number of users of a given personal token, which may in the long term translate into increased utility of the virtual job offer. In order to confirm the thesis, we carried out the analysis of the axiological background of the decision to use tokens in labour valuation, which was presented in the next section of the chapter.

NFT gig tokens as a network valuation tool of personal brand and offered work – an axiological approach

In the study, we assumed that the issuer creates a specific axiological image of themselves and their work, which is intended not only to attract investors/customers, but at the same time to build the issuer's credibility, enhance trust towards them, and increase their network value as a person.

The research conducted on the linguistic layer of the profiles of issuers who offered work as part of their token reveals that the most vital axiological area referred to by all issuers, regardless of the type of services offered, was achievement (5 – necessary). PTs therefore seem to be considered by each issuer as a means of achieving success and strengthening their impact on the environment. It is also related to building one's own position in the world as a person accomplishing financial success and 'sticking' social prestige to it (power: 5 – necessary, 4 – desirable). The results showing the importance of the 10 axiological areas for all PT issuers and by service type are presented in Figure 12.3.

An analysis of the content and style of the statements included in the profile descriptions and posts of the issuers showed that across all groups there were no significant differences in positioning values such as hedonism (4 –desirable), stimulation (5 – necessary, 4 – desirable), self-direction (5 – necessary, 4 – desirable) high, tradition (2 – not desirable, 1 – not necessary), conformity (2 – not desirable, 1 – not necessary), and security (2-not desirable) low (as unimportant).

That allows us to identify the issuers' worldview as one that is directed more towards the realisation of individual values, associated with social success and individual expression, than towards social values, directed towards the common good and socially supported solutions. It is the individualism and uniqueness of the individual, combined with the 'promise' of success, that is supposed to be a factor that attracts investors. This factor makes the latter trust the issuer and encourages the decision to purchase the token and the service it offers. The network effect appreciated by issuers (in our study understood as axiological valuation) is thus based on an individualistic rather than on a community-based worldview.

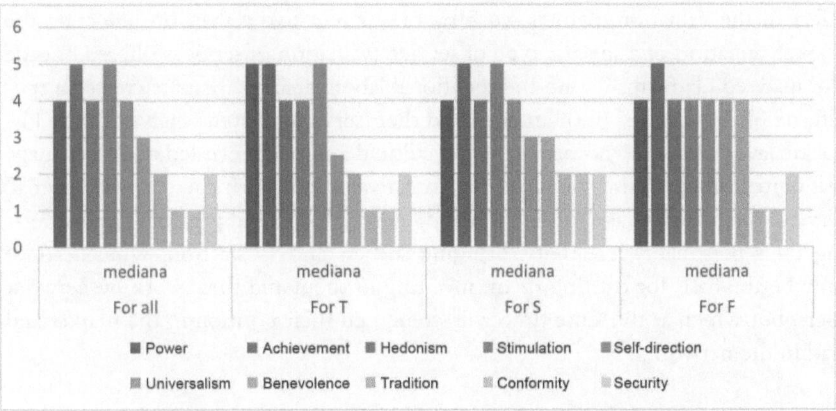

FIGURE 12.3 Relevance of specific axiological areas for all PT issuers and broken down by service type (T-technological, S-social, and F-financial)

Source: Own elaboration based on data from PT platform.

The professional group in which interesting axiological differences arose was the one offering financial services. Issuers representing that group much more often revealed the significance of such axiological areas as universalism (4 – desirable) and benevolence (4 – desirable), so on the one hand – they considered the broad context of changes (social and environmental) occurring in the world in connection with the spread of DLT, and on the other hand, the ability to offer support to others (within or through PT) was crucial for them. Hence, the analysis of those data revealed an atypical approach of that group, as this type of reference to value in the previous labour market model (before the emergence of new online or gig economy work models) was attributed to groups of professions offering services of social nature (Autor & Dorn, 2013). In the study, this occupational group represented a reference to these values only at the 3-objectionable level.

The comparison of market price per 1 hour of individual work of PT owners (number of PT/1 work hour) with the network approach presented by issuers (in our study analysed in terms of respect to certain axiological values; appendix, Figures 12.4 and 12.5) shows that there were five axiological areas to which issuers with the same number of PT per 1 work hour referred regularly: self-direction, universalism, benevolence, conformity, security. It is worth noting that only one of those areas was 'meaningful' for issuers (self-direction) and two gained a little relevance (conformity and security). The respect of issuers from each price group to the other two axiological areas (universalism and benevolence) ranged from being of low importance (2 – not desirable, 3 – objectionable) to being the most vital (5 – necessary). Thus, these results show that issuers tended to represent a similar set of values (individualistic values), any differences appeared only with respect to the two axiological areas associated with community attitudes (universalism and benevolence).

Considering the results of the analyses conducted in this and the previous section of the chapter, it should be argued that issuers focused more on the network effect in the valuation of their work by means of a token than on reflecting the market valuation of a specific type of service (valuation of services offered outside the analysed platform, within the traditional labour market). Issuers created a specific axiological image of themselves and their service; content analysis of the linguistic layer of profiles according to the cultural approach revealed that that image was quite homogenous, grounded in a similar value system. In fact, the issuers of all services built their image (personal brand) as people focused primarily on expressing their personality, creativity, bringing success and satisfaction, which cannot only be the basis for trusting them, investing in them and their work by network users, but which at the same time will strengthen their position in the market and within the network.

Conclusions

A personal token seems to be an appropriate tool for valuation of services offered online. However, the pricing does not necessarily reflect the respective indicators observed at the regular labour market. In fact, the research conducted in the chapter allowed us to draw some important conclusions.

Firstly, the most important group of services offered by token owners are those of a social nature. That result is based on the analysis carried out with the application of the newly developed classification of services provided by issuers of NFT gig tokens.

Secondly, the high volatility of pricing, surprisingly low values of the latter and lack of significant relationships between pricing and certain categories (e.g., time that passed since token issue) are observed. We were unable to identify any regular pattern in the levels of work pricing for the provided services. Thus, the financial motivation of issuers that offer their work applying personal token seem to be a secondary criterion of valuation. Token owners seem to be driven by the additional motive – acquiring a network effect.

Third, the thesis is supported by the results of PT issuers' profiles analysis. In the context of the axiological dimension of the ways issuers value their services, the dominant values represented axiological areas related to the sphere of individual cognitive activity and emotional experience (power, achievement, hedonism, stimulation, and self-direction). The group that presented a slightly different value system from the others was the one offering financial services.

To sum up, at the current stage of development of the personal tokens market, the main motive for the valuation of the offered work is a new factor – the appearance and the development of a network of contacts (customers) in the virtual world, which will enable issuers to achieve a network effect in the long term. This effect can translate into increased financial benefits of PT issuers in the long term by offering their work based on the analysed platform.

Acknowledgements

The chapter was prepared through the project financed within the Regional Excellence Initiative programme of the Minister of Science and Higher Education of Poland, covering the years 2019–2023, grant no. 004/RID/2018/19, financing of 3,000,000 PLN.

References

Autor, D. H., & Dorn, D. (2013). The growth of low-skill service jobs and the polarization of the US labor market. *American Economic Review*, *103*(5), 1553–1597. https://doi.org/10.1257/aer.103.5.1553

Baur, D. G., Hong, K., & Lee, A. D. (2018). Bitcoin: Medium of exchange or speculative assets? *Journal of International Financial Markets, Institutions & Money*, *54*, 177–189. https://doi.org/10.1016/j.intfin.2017.12.004

Best, S. (2017). The U.S. Gig economy: Economic imposition or economic choice? *The Business and Management Review*, *8*(4). https://cberuk.com/cdn/conference_proceedings/conference_93744.pdf

Cheah, E.-T., & Fry, J. (2015). Speculative bubbles in Bitcoin markets? An empirical investigation into the fundamental value of Bitcoin. *Economics Letters*, *130*, 32–36. https://doi.org/10.1016/j.econlet.2015.02.029

Colbert, A., Yee, N., & George, G. (2016). The digital workforce and the work place of the future. *Academy of Management Journal, 59*(3). https://doi.org/10.5465/amj.2016.4003

Crow, K., & Ostroff, C. (2021). Beeple NFT fetches record-breaking $69 million in Christies sale. *Wall Street Journal.* www.wsj.com/articles/beeple-nft-fetches-record-breaking-69-million-in-christies-sale-11615477732?reflink=desktopwebshare_permalink

De Groen, W. P., Lenaerts, K., Bosc, R., & Paquier, F. (2017, August). Impact of digitalisation and the on-demand economy on labour markets and the consequences for employment and industrial relations. Final Study. *CEPS Special Report.* http://aei.pitt.edu/88531/1/EESC_Digitalisation.pdf

Degryse, C. (2016). Digitalisation of the economy and its impact on labour markets. (*Working Paper* 2016.02). ETUI. www.etui.org/Publications2/Working-Papers/Digitalisation-of-the-economy-and-its-impact-on-labour-markets

Diab-Bahman, R., & Al-Enzi, A. (2020). The impact of COVID-19 pandemic on conventional work settings, *International Journal of Sociology and Social Policy, 40*(9/10), 909–927. https://doi.org/10.1108/IJSSP-07-2020-0262

Donovan, S. H., Bradley, D. H., & Shimabukuro. (2016, February 5). *What does the Gig economy mens for workers?* Congressional Research Service. http://bit.ly/29svwkT

Dosi, G., Piva, M., Virgillito, M. E., & Vivarelli, M. (2021). Embodied and disembodied technological change: The sectoral patterns of job-creation and job-destruction. *Research Policy, 50*(4). https://doi.org/10.1016/j.respol.2021.104199

Dowling, M. (2021a). Is non-fungible token pricing driven by cryptocurrencies? *Finance Research Letters,* 102097. https://doi.org/10.1016/j.frl.2021.102097

Dowling, M. (2021b). Fertile LAND: Pricing non-fungible tokens. *Finance Research Letters.* https://doi.org/10.1016/j.frl.2021.102096

Florida, R. (2019). *The rise of the creative class.* Basic Books. ISBN: 978-1541617742

Höhne, K., Krebs, D., & Kühnel, S.-M. (2021). Measurement properties of completely and end labeled unipolar and bipolar scales in Likert-type questions on income (in)equality. *Social Science Research,* 102544. https://doi.org/10.1016/j.ssresearch.2021.102544

Huws, U. (2014). *Labor in the global digital economy. The cybertariat comes of age.* Monthly Review Press. ISBN: 9781583674635

Kässi, O., & Lehdonvirta, V. (2018). Online labour index: Measuring the online gig economy for policy and research. *Technological Forecasting and Social Change, 137,* 241–248. https://doi.org/10.1016/j.techfore.2018.07.056

Lisi, A., De Salve, A., Mori, P., Ricci, L., & Fabrizi, S. (2021). Rewarding reviews with tokens: An Ethereum-based approach. *Future Generation Computer Systems, 120,* 36–54. ISSN 0167–739X. https://doi.org/10.1016/j.future.2021.02.003

Marchewka-Bartkowiak, K., & Nowak, K. (2020). *Get tokenized . . . The specificity of personal tokens in the context of tokenization and axiological categorization* [Proceedings]. Proceedings of the 3rd International Conference on Economics and Social Sciences, Sciendo, 823–831. https://doi.org/10.2478/9788366675162–081

Marchewka-Bartkowiak, K., Nowak, K., & Litwiński, M. (2022). Digital valuation of personality using personal tokens. *Electronic Markets.* https://doi.org/10.1007/s12525-022-00562-y

Masood, Z., Damian, D., & Blincoe, K. (2022). How New Zealand software companies are adapting work settings with changing times. *IEEE Software, 39*(3), 77–84. https://doi.org/10.1109/MS.2021.3129066.

Proposal for a REGULATION OF THE EUROPEAN PARLIAMENT AND OF THE COUNCIL on Markets in Crypto-assets, and amending Directive (EU) 2019/1937 (COM(2020)593.

Ralph, P., Baltes, S., Adisaputri, G., Torkar, R., Kolvalenko, V., Kalinowski, M., Novielli, N., Yoo, S., Devroey, X., Tan, X., Zhou, M., Turhan, B., Hoda, R., Hata, H., Robles, G., Fard, A. M., & Alkadhi, R. (2020). Pandemic programming. *Empirical Software Engineering, 25*, 4927–4961. https://doi.org/10.1007/s10664-020-09875-y

Ros, M., Schwartz, S. H., & Surkiss, S. (1999). Basic individual values, work values, and the meaning of work. *Applied Psychology: An International Review, 48*(I), 49–71, https://doi.org/10.1080/026999499377664

Schroeder, A. N., Bricka, T. M., & Whitaker, J. H. (2021). Work design in a digitized gig economy. *Human Resource Management Review*, 31. https://doi.org/10.1016/j.hrmr.2019.100692

Tapscott, D., & Wiliams, A. (2006). *Wikinomics. How mass collaboration changes everything.* Port-folio, Penguin Group.

Torpey, E., & Hogan, A. (2016). Working in a gig economy. *BLS.gov*. www.bls.gov/careeroutlook/2016/article/what-is-the-gig-economy.htm

Urquhart, A. (2016). The inefficiency of Bitcoin. *Economics Letters, 148*, 80–82. https://doi.org/10.1016/j.econlet.2016.09.019

APPENDIX

All tables can be found under the link: https://zenodo.org/record/6595534#.YzP2k7TP1nJ

TABLE 12.6 Classification of services provided by personal token issuers, according to Kässi and Lehdonvirta (2018)

Class of services	*Examples of provided services*
Professional services - P	Accounting Consulting Financial planning Legal services Human resources Project management
Clerical and data entry - CD	Customer service Data entry Transcription Tech support Web research Virtual assistant
Creative and multimedia - CM	Animation Architechture Audio Logo design Photography Presentations Video production Voide acting

(*Continued*)

Class of services	*Examples of provided services*
Sales and marketing support - SM	Ad posting Lead generation Search engine optimisation Telemarketing
Software development and technology - ST	Data science Game development Mobile development QA and testing Server maintenance Software development Web development Web scraping
Writing and translation - WT	Academic writing Article writing Copywriting Creative writing Technical writing Translation

Source: Kässi and Lehdonvirta (2018).

TABLE 12.7 Type of services, according to classification by Kässi and Lehdonvirta

Class of services	*Number of cases*	*Percentage*
Professional services	63	37.06%
Creative and multimedia	30	17.65%
Software development and technology	27	15.88%
Clerical and data entry	22	12.94%
Sales and marketing support	5	2.94%
Writing and translation	2	1.18%
Other	21	12.35%
Total	**170**	**100%**

Source: Own calculations based on data from PT platform.

TABLE 12.8 Type of services provided by analysed 45 token issuers

Token name	*Class of services*
RAF	Financial/Economic F/E
DJM	Financial/Economic F/E
AWA	Financial/Economic F/E
RL	Financial/Economic F/E
MAZAK	Financial/Economic F/E
FK	Financial/Economic F/E
SKM	Financial/Economic F/E
VIP	Financial/Economic F/E

(*Continued*)

TABLE 12.8 (Continued)

Token name	*Class of services*
BEN	Social (community services) – S
ARTCOIN	Social (community services) – S
ZIBICOIN	Social (community services) – S
LSZ	Social (community services) – S
PAGEMAN	Social (community services) – S
PP	Social (community services) – S
POKATO	Social (community services) – S
DDT	Social (community services) – S
MEGA	Social (community services) – S
CYRIL	Social (community services) – S
SJW	Social (community services) – S
MTK	Social (community services) – S
POL	Social (community services) – S
MAC	Social (community services) – S
MH	Social (community services) – S
KRC	Social (community services) – S
SZUSTER	Social (community services) – S
GAB	Social (community services) – S
BOR	Social (community services) – S
SMIM	Social (community services) – S
CNSL	Social (community services) – S
JKCOIN	Technology – T
DEX	Technology – T
FULOFMO	Technology – T
GREG	Technology – T
CHAR	Technology – T
SECUREMB	Technology – T
HGT	Technology – T
SQL	Technology – T
ZBL	Technology – T
KGAJ	Technology – T
RSPT	Technology – T
RAW	Technology – T
SWADER	Technology – T
KERMAN	Technology – T
ASTO	Technology – T
MACK	Technology – T

Source: Own calculations based on data from PT platform.

TABLE 12.9 Valuation of services and basic information on personal tokens

Token name	*Number of months from PT issue*	*PT price [USD]*	*Number of PT/1 work hour*	*USD/1 work hour*
VIP	34	0.000554	70,000	38.78
MTK	34	0.000044	10,000	0.44

(Continued)

Token name	*Number of months from PT issue*	*PT price [USD]*	*Number of PT/1 work hour*	*USD/1 work hour*
BOR	35	0.009116	10,000	91.16
KERMAN	14	0.105116	7,500	788.37
CHAR	28	0.000466	6000	2.80
ZIBICOIN	32	0.000068	5000	0.34
GREG	34	0.250254	5000	1,251.27
FK	34	1.934937	5000	9,674.69
SKM	28	0.108603	5000	543.02
SWADER	33	0.000088	5000	0.44
SMIM	1	0.000093	4000	0.37
RAF	26	0.000266	3000	0.80
AWA	26	0.022151	3000	66.45
MEGA	27	0.000044	2500	0.11
FULOFMO	34	0.000091	2000	0.18
PAGEMAN	32	0.025276	2000	50.55
POKATO	35	0.020535	2000	41.07
DJM	29	0.147357	1200	176.83
JKCOIN	34	0.028854	1000	28.85
BEN	35	0.025276	1000	25.28
DDT	34	0.02735	1000	27.35
CYRIL	10	0.003351	1000	3.35
HGT	34	0.000066	1000	0.07
SJW	24	0.000532	1000	0.53
ZBL	13	0.000066	1000	0.07
KRC	33	0.005987	1000	5.99
RAW	18	0.000433	1000	0.43
MH	34	0.250254	800	200.20
MAC	32	0.00098	600	0,59
MAZAK	29	0.000088	500	0.04
POL	27	0.000066	500	0.03
SZUSTER	32	0.000022	400	0.01
RSPT	34	0.002279	400	0.91
KGAJ	34	0.250254	350	87.59
LSZ	35	0.009876	300	2.96
SQL	29	0.000621	200	0.12
GAB	25	0.000421	200	0.08
RL	35	0.012451	151	1.88
DEX	35	0.009876	100	0.99
ARTCOIN	34	0.00011	100	0.01
PP	34	0.020535	100	2.05
SECUREMB	34	0.00364	100	0.36
MACK	34	0.000113	100	0.01
ASTO	1	0.000023	3	0.00
CNSL	17	310.7645	1	310.76

* PT prices as on 30th June 2021

Source: Own calculations based on data from PT platform.

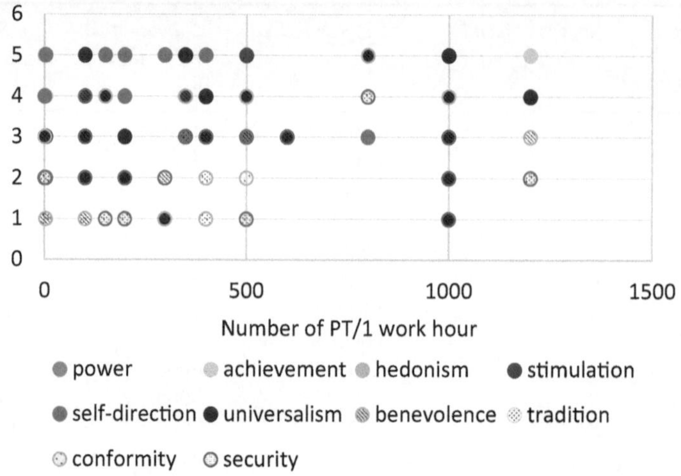

FIGURE 12.4 Market price per 1 hour of individual work of PT owners and network (axiological) valuation (in a range from 1 PT/1 work hour to 1,200 PT/1 work hour)

Source: Own elaboration based on data from PT platform.

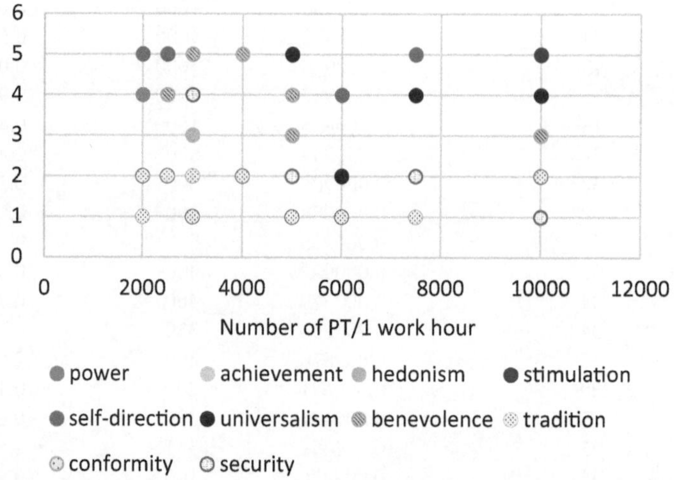

FIGURE 12.5 Market price per 1 hour of individual work of PT owners and network (axiological) valuation (in a range from 2,000 PT/1 work hour to 10,000 PT/1 work hour)*

* For a clearer graphical presentation, the figure does not include the case with highest price per token – VIP tokens (70,000 tokens per 1 work hour).

Source: Own elaboration based on data from PT platform.

INDEX

Note: Page numbers in *italics* indicate a figure and page numbers in **bold** indicate a table on the corresponding page.